PLANNING AND LGBTQ COMMUNITIES

Although the last decade has seen steady progress towards wider acceptance of lesbian, gay, bisexual, transgendered, and queer (LGBTQ) individuals, LGBTQ residential and commercial areas have come under increasing pressure from gentrification and redevelopment initiatives. As a result many of these neighborhoods are losing their special character as safe havens for sexual and gender minorities. Urban planners and municipal officials have sometimes ignored the transformation of these neighborhoods and at other times been complicit in these changes.

Planning and LGBTQ Communities brings together experienced planners, administrators, and researchers in the fields of planning and geography to reflect on the evolution of urban neighborhoods in which LGBTQ populations live, work, and play. The authors examine a variety of LGBTQ residential and commercial areas to highlight policy and planning links to the development of these neighborhoods. Each chapter explores a particular urban context and asks how the field of planning has enabled, facilitated, and/or neglected the specialized and diverse needs of the LGBTQ population.

A central theme of this book is that urban planners need to think "beyond queer space" because LGBTQ populations are more diverse and dispersed than the white gay male populations that created many of the most visible gayborhoods. The authors provide practical guidance for cities and citizens seeking to strengthen neighborhoods that have an explicit LGBTQ focus as well as other areas that are LGBTQ-friendly. They also encourage broader awareness of the needs of this marginalized population and the need to establish more formal linkages between municipal government and a range of LGBTQ groups. *Planning and LGBTQ Communities* also adds useful material for graduate level courses in planning theory, urban and regional theory, planning for multicultural cities, urban geography, and geographies of gender and sexuality.

Petra L. Doan is Professor of Urban and Regional Planning at the Florida State University. She has published numerous articles and chapters on queer planning issues, including several path-breaking articles on transgender experiences of gendered urban spaces. Her edited book *Queerying Planning: Challenging Heteronormative Assumptions and Reframing Planning Practice* was published by Ashgate in 2011.

PLANNING AND LGBTQ COMMUNITIES

The Need for Inclusive Queer Spaces

Edited by Petra L. Doan

Routledge
Taylor & Francis Group

NEW YORK AND LONDON

First published 2015
by Routledge
711 Third Avenue, New York, NY 10017

and by Routledge
2 Park Square, Milton Park, Abingdon, Oxon OX14 4RN

Routledge is an imprint of the Taylor & Francis Group, an informa business

© 2015 Taylor & Francis

Library of Congress Cataloging in Publication Data
Planning and LGBTQ communities : the need for inclusive queer spaces / edited by Petra L. Doan.
pages cm
1. Gay community. 2. Sexual minority community. 3. City planning. I. Doan, Petra L., 1955–
HQ76.25.P58 2015
306.76'6--dc23
2014037759

ISBN: 978-1-138-79815-1 (hbk)
ISBN: 978-1-138-79816-8 (pbk)
ISBN: 978-1-315-75672-1 (ebk)

Typeset in Bembo and Stone Sans
by Saxon Graphics Ltd, Derby

Printed and bound in Great Britain by
TJ International Ltd, Padstow, Cornwall

CONTENTS

FIGURES AND TABLES

Figures

Tables

CONTRIBUTORS

Katrin B. Anacker is Associate Professor at George Mason University in Arlington, Virginia. Her work has been published in the *Journal of Urban Affairs*, the *International Journal of Urban and Regional Research*, *Urban Geography*, *Housing Policy Debate*, *Housing Studies*, and *Housing and Society*. She is the author of *Analyzing Mature Suburbs in Ohio through Property Values* (2009) and the editor of *The New American Suburb: Poverty, Race, and the Economic Crisis* (2015). She is the current book review editor of the *Journal of Planning Education and Research* and the former co-editor of *Housing Policy Debate*. Her work has been supported by the U.S. Department of Housing and Urban Development, the Lincoln Institute of Land Policy, the Urban Land Institute, the Center for Urban and Regional Analysis at The Ohio State University, Lambda Alpha International, and the Horowitz Foundation for Social Policy. She received her Ph.D. in City and Regional Planning from The Ohio State University.

Michael Brown is Professor of Geography at the University of Washington. He received his Ph.D. from the University of British Columbia. His research interests include: governmentality and gay men's health, sexuality, urban public health, electoral geography, poststructural political theory, home hospice care, the closet, the urban politics of AIDS, and suburban exclusionary zoning. He is the author of several books and numerous articles on the subject of sexuality and the city.

John Paul (JP) Catungal is a Killam Honorary and SSHRC Postdoctoral Fellow at the University of British Columbia's Institute for Gender, Race, Sexuality and Social Justice. He received his Ph.D. in 2014 from the University of Toronto's Department of Geography, where he completed a dissertation on the racial politics of social and sexual health service organizations in Toronto, with a focus on the political and spatial practices of ethno-specific AIDS service organizations.

An urban social geographer by training, JP's publications include his work on the urban politics of race, sexualities and sexual health, as well as his collaborative writings with Dr. Deborah Leslie on the governance of creative city policymaking and the social exclusions engendered by such approaches to urban development. JP is also co-editor of the landmark volume *Filipinos in Canada: Disturbing Invisibility*, published in 2012 by the University of Toronto Press.

Petra L. Doan is a professor in the Department of Urban and Regional Planning at Florida State University. She has worked as a development planner and consultant in Africa and the Middle East and has a number of published articles on planning as a tool for empowering marginalized populations in these areas. More recently her work on planning issues for LGBTQ populations has been published in *Environment and Planning A*, *Journal of Planning Education and Research*, and several edited books. In addition her research on transgender perceptions of gendered urban spaces appeared in several articles in *Gender Place and Culture*. Finally, her edited book, *Queerying Planning: Challenging Heteronormative Assumptions and Reframing Planning Practice*, was published by Ashgate in 2011.

Gail Dubrow serves as Associate Dean for Academic Affairs in the College of Design at University of Minnesota, where she holds interdisciplinary appointments as Professor of Architecture, Landscape Architecture, Public Affairs and Planning, and History. She is the author of the prize-winning books *Sento at Sixth and Main*, with Donna Graves, and *Restoring Women's History through Historic Preservation*, coedited with Jennifer Goodman.

Michael Frisch is an Associate Professor in the Department of Architecture, Urban Planning, and Design at the University of Missouri in Kansas City, Missouri. He holds a Ph.D. in Urban Planning from Rutgers University, a Masters of City Planning from Massachusetts Institute of Technology and a B.A. in Economics from Earlham College. His research addresses three major questions: how modern urban planning interacts with the LGBT community, how planning may assist the development of artist communities, and how regional community development and/or environmental initiatives impact neighborhoods. He is the author of the seminal article "Planning as a Heterosexist Project" in the *Journal of Planning Education and Research*.

Kian Goh is a Ph.D. candidate in Urban Studies and Planning at MIT. She researches urban ecological design, spatial politics, and social mobilization in the context of climate change and global urbanization. A licensed architect, she co-founded design practice SUPER-INTERESTING! and previously worked with Weiss/Manfredi and MVRDV. She has taught at the University of Pennsylvania, The New School, and Washington University in St. Louis. Kian served on the board of directors of the Audre Lorde Project, an organizing center for LGBT people of color. She received a Masters of Architecture from Yale University.

Andrew Gorman-Murray is Senior Lecturer in Geography at the University of Western Sydney, Australia. His research interests concern gender, sexuality and space, with key work on LGBT and queer belonging/exclusion in everyday spaces (homes, neighborhoods, suburbs, country towns), exceptional time-spaces (festivals, disasterscapes) and multiple scales (local, urban, national). Andrew has collaborated with Marrickville Council (Sydney, NSW), the Queensland Association of Health Communities, and Gay and Lesbian Health Victoria, to critically assess and redress the gaps in knowledge and provision for LGBT and queer constituents.

Larry Knopp is Professor of Interdisciplinary Arts and Sciences at the University of Washington Tacoma. He has a Ph.D. in Geography from the University of Iowa. He is the author of numerous articles on the spatiality of sexuality, gender and class. His work explores links between various social processes and the construction of place-based gay and queer identities, communities and political movements. It includes numerous collaborations with Michael Brown on the historical-political geography of Seattle's queer communities.

Nathaniel Lewis is currently Assistant Professor in Health Geography at the University of Nottingham in Nottingham, UK. A graduate of the Ph.D. program in Geography at Queen's University in Kingston, Ontario, Canada, he has studied the development of queer spaces and their implications for the health and well-being of lesbian, gay, bisexual, and trans populations. During the past decade, he has both lived in and studied gay neighborhoods in Ottawa, Halifax, and Washington, D.C. His work on relocation decisions among gay men can be found in journals such as *Health & Place* and *The Annals of the Association of American Geographers*. His forthcoming work focuses on immigrant populations and their first encounters with gay neighborhoods and scenes in three different cities in the province of Ontario.

Arianna Martinez is an Assistant Professor of Urban Studies at LaGuardia Community College and a resident of Jackson Heights, Queens. She received a Masters in International Affairs from the New School and her Ph.D. in Urban Planning and Public Policy from Rutgers University. Her first exposure to Jackson Heights was through her father's stories of his immigration and relocation from Colombia to Jackson Heights in the 1970s. She moved back to that neighborhood after graduate school because of its cosmopolitan cross section of queer and immigrant cultures and the presence of numerous gay bars, with names like "Hombres Lounge," that serve a typically Latino Spanish-speaking clientele.

Catherine J. Nash is Professor of Geography at Brock University, Canada. Her research interests are sexuality/queer/feminist/trans geographies, mobilities and digital technologies, and her work encompasses historical geographies of Toronto's gay village, women's bathhouses, trans urban spaces, new LGBT and queer neighborhoods, as well as methodological and pedagogical issues. Catherine worked for over a decade as a development and planning lawyer before moving into academia. Her current work with the LGBT community in Toronto considers changing demographics, community development and spatial organization.

Sarah P. Nusser is Senior Community Development Specialist with the San Francisco Mayor's Office of Housing and Community Development. While completing a Masters in City Planning degree at the Massachusetts Institute of Technology, her research focused on how the design and regulation of city spaces affirm or negate queer identities. This work has been published in the *Journal of Urban Affairs*. As a practitioner, she has been particularly focused on affordable housing development and the potential of the development process to meet a diversity of needs of residents.

Gustav Visser is Professor of Geography, Department of Geography and Environmental Studies at the University of Stellenbosch, South Africa. He graduated from Stellenbosch University and obtained his Ph.D. from the London School of Economics. His research interests relate to identity-based consumption and urban morphological change, as well as practical applications of the tourism system as a Local Economic Development mechanism for developing world countries such as South Africa.

Joan Marshall Wesley is Associate Professor in Urban and Regional Planning at Jackson State University in Jackson, Mississippi. Her research focuses upon social and environmental justice, community engagement/participation and Latino-Black comparative demographics. She has published articles in several outlets, including *Race, Gender and Class Journal*, *American Journal of Science and Engineering* and *Progressive Planning*.

Andrew H. Whittemore has a Ph.D. in Urban Planning from the University of California, Los Angeles. He is Assistant Professor at the Department of City Planning at the University of North Carolina, Chapel Hill and a former resident of Dallas, Texas. His research focuses on urban form and design, planning history and theory, and land use planning and zoning, primarily in the North American context.

Curt Winkle is Associate Professor and Department Head in the Department of Urban Planning and Policy at the University of Illinois in Chicago. He has lived in Chicago for 27 years where his research and teaching focus is on planning healthy cities, including the development of robust urban food systems. He has conducted research on residential services for vulnerable populations and examined the residential and service needs and help-seeking behavior of people with HIV infections. He serves on the Development Committee of the West Loop Community Organization.

ACKNOWLEDGMENTS

I am profoundly grateful to several groups of scholars and planning practitioners whose academic research and professional practice have provided such inspiration to me. The Gays and Lesbians in Planning Division (GALIP) of the American Planning Association (APA) helped to provide a small grant from APA's Division Council for me and a colleague, Harrison Higgins, to begin our work on planning for LGBTQ spaces. Funding for work on queer space issues is a rarity and this tangible support was a big boost as I was beginning this research program. The Sexuality and Space Interest Group of the Association of American Geographers has also consistently provided me with both inspiration and theoretical challenges to dig deeper, think harder, and ultimately to queer my research in delightful new ways. Furthermore, a small core of scholars (Gail Dubrow, Michael Frisch, Ann Forsyth, and Curt Winkle) within the academic planning environment – he Association of Collegiate Schools of Planning (ACSP) – has been meeting regularly to talk about LGBTQ planning issues. This group has now expanded into a vibrant interest group at ACSP, named Inclusion, and this book has emerged in part from discussions held at these meetings.

Finally, I would like to acknowledge my beloved wife, Elizabeth Kamphausen-Doan, who has been my helpmeet in all things, for her untiring support. When my own energy for assembling these chapters was at a low ebb, it was her love and devotion that helped to sustain this project. In addition, her strong editing skills and her passion for clarity have often helped to shape my occasionally unruly prose into more compelling arguments. She is truly my muse!

Petra L. Doan
Tallahassee, FL

1

WHY PLAN FOR THE LGBTQ COMMUNITY?

Petra L. Doan

By the second decade of the 21st century the presence of gays and lesbians in urban areas is widely acknowledged, mostly tolerated, but still rarely considered in public planning processes. Although academic articles on sexuality and urban spaces within the field of geography are quite numerous, in the field of planning lesbian, gay, bisexual, transgender, and queer (LGBTQ) issues are frequently ignored both within the academy and in practice (Forsyth and Cheung 2001). It is difficult to determine whether this resistance is the result of explicit discrimination, a heterosexist bias (Frisch 2002) or simple avoidance by planning officials of politically risky topics. Doan (2011) examines the reluctance of the planning profession to include LGBTQ people as a community of interest and found that within the US planning profession some individuals remained deeply antagonistic towards LGBTQ individuals and felt that planning had no business "pandering" to such people. In addition, Forsyth (2011) illustrates the variety of ways that planning policies shape the lives and recreation possibilities of the LGBTQ community through the creation of LGBTQ enclaves, the provision of LGBTQ social services, the enactment of residential zoning and housing restrictions, and the preservation (or failure to preserve) of LGBTQ cultural areas. With these few exceptions, the planning literature has remained remarkably silent on the question of queer spaces.

Some of the resistance from planning staff may be linked to planners' reluctance to engage with the LGBTQ population because the non-normative nature of this community is stereotypically linked to the topic of sex and the city that many municipalities would rather cleanse or purify (Hubbard 2000 and 2004). For example, in Sydney, Australia there were explicit attempts to regulate LGBTQ establishments using sex-related zoning measures (Prior 2008; Prior and Crofts 2011). Planning regulations in Atlanta are also being used to encourage the redevelopment of LGBTQ areas and exclude "adult businesses," some of which include LGBTQ oriented shops and enterprises (Doan 2014). Forsyth (2011) suggests that popular misconceptions about the relative affluence of white gay men may exacerbate the reluctance of many planners to consider this sub-group in planning processes. However, the LGBTQ population as a whole is much more diverse and less wealthy than popularly imagined (Klawitter and Flatt 1998; Badgett, 2001; Carpenter 2004). Significant portions of the LGBTQ community remain marginalized both socially and economically, and as a result should not be ignored or neglected.

Whatever the cause of the less than stellar planning record vis-à-vis LGBTQ neighborhoods to date, the intention of this book is to provide concrete, relevant and directly-applicable planning and policy perspectives for how planners can improve the lives of LGBTQ individuals, whether they reside in "queer spaces" or not. Given that many gay neighborhoods are struggling and/or declining due to neglect of the specific needs of this multi-faceted population, this book argues that urban planners need to think "beyond queer space"—namely, to move beyond just tolerating LGBTQ individuals, couples, and families by proactively working to address their specific needs for places in which they can live, work and recreate. Building on the findings offered in *Queerying Planning* (Doan 2011) about the need to recognize and protect LGBTQ people, this volume takes the next step by bringing together leading urban planning and geography faculty as well as practitioners to reflect on the kinds of planning interventions required to preserve gay neighborhoods and meet the needs of a wider segment of the LGBTQ population.

While there have been a number of publications within the field of geography to explore theoretical issues of sexuality and space, this book provides a unique *planning* perspective, using place-specific examples in the United States as well as Canada, Australia, and South Africa. Specifically, it considers what kinds of urban and neighborhood development policies have been in place to date as well as the (frequently) negative impacts of these policies for LGBTQ populations. Many of the chapters examine a particular urban context, arguing how planners and policy-makers may have enabled, facilitated and allowed detrimental changes for queer spaces to happen due to neglect of the particular needs of LGBTQ people by planners and policy-makers in terms of affordable housing, accessible social services, safety from discrimination and violence. In addition, several chapters also illustrate the ways that community groups have mobilized to pressure the planning profession to take LGBTQ needs into consideration.

In highlighting the continuing necessity for safe LGBTQ neighborhoods, this book argues that it is necessary to move beyond a narrow fixation with queer space, and consider the actual needs of the various individuals who comprise the "queer" population. The aim of the volume is to provide practical guidance for city planners and officials seeking to strengthen diverse neighborhoods that are not only inclusive of LGBTQ people from the "gayborhoods," but to encourage broader awareness of this marginalized population by policy-makers and planners. To this end, after reviewing historical developments—and the frequent demise of—specific LGBTQ spaces to date, this introduction offers an analysis of their decline before raising important questions needing consideration by planners and policy-makers in planning for the LGBTQ community beyond queer space. Whether they live in "gay space" or in the wider community, the specific concerns of LGBTQ people found in queer neighborhoods (and beyond) must be both acknowledged and addressed.

Changes to LGBTQ Neighborhoods

One of the most visible aspects of the LGBTQ community in urban areas has been the rise of concentrations of gay and lesbian residential and commercial areas that have for the most part been under the radar of planning authorities. Although Podmore (2013) suggests that the gay village has been the "most persistent object of study on sexuality in the city" (p. 3), these studies have been mostly conducted by other social scientists (geographers, sociologists, anthropologists, and historians), not by urban planners. Historical studies of LGBTQ spaces indicate that establishments that welcomed gays and lesbians (bars, restaurants, other public areas) have long existed, but patterns of usage shifted over time in response to various socio-cultural forces linked to overt discrimination and police crackdowns. In the North American context LGBTQ historians (Faderman 1991; Kennedy and Davis 1993; Chauncey 1994; Stryker and Van Buskirk 1996; Stein 2000) have clearly shown that throughout the 20th century gays and lesbians were economically active in many cities, patronizing bars and restaurants, flocking to tourist venues (Newton 1993), as well as appropriating liminal public spaces such as public parks, public toilets, piers, and other areas at the fringes of "proper" society.

The latter half of the 20th century saw a higher level of organization among LGBTQ individuals (D'Emilio 1983). The riots at the Compton Cafeteria in San Francisco (Stryker 2008) and the Stonewall Inn in New York City in the late 1960s sparked a more activist liberation movement which enabled the emergence of distinctly visible clusters of residences and businesses catering to the LGBTQ population. These discrete neighborhoods were immensely attractive to young queer-identified individuals seeking to establish their non-normative identities and create an alternative and fully accepting community. The names used to describe these spaces included: gay village, gayborhood, boys' town, lesbiville, and more recently queer space (Betsky 1997; Ingram et al. 1997; Rothenburg 1995). In some cities such LGBTQ neighborhoods were recognized by municipal authorities,[1] but in many others they have been largely ignored.

These welcoming urban environments provided a space of relative freedom and experimentation for some, but not all, members of the LGBTQ population. A number of critical articles and books have carefully described the problematic and contested nature of these queer spaces (Bell and Valentine 1995; Valentine 2000; Browne et al. 2007). For instance, the typical gay male neighborhood was often quite exclusive and not very hospitable to lesbians and bisexuals (Hemmings 2002), and lesbian neighborhoods did not always welcome transgendered people (Namaste 2000; Doan 2007). In addition, most of these queer spaces were narrowly defined by class and race (Nast 2002; Oswin 2008), leaving out LGBTQ individuals with lower incomes as well as those who identified as people of color (Nero 2005; Manalansan 2005). Walcott (2007) suggests that while gay male spaces do allow a co-mingling of the races, queers of color are often "caught between Eurocentric queer histories and homophobic communities that seek to deny their presence" (Walcott 2007, p. 237). The exclusionary nature of these spaces was especially true for rapidly re-developing residential zones in major metropolitan areas where a steady increase in property values caused higher rents, making it nearly impossible for younger and less affluent LGBTQ individuals to find affordable housing.

In the latter stages of the twentieth and early twenty-first century, many established LGBTQ neighborhoods were subject to considerable gentrification pressures causing significant changes to their LGBTQ nature, leading some to question whether this "de-gaying" would cause the demise of queer space (Ruting 2008; Doan and Higgins 2011). Collins (2004) has suggested that these changes might be part of a more generalizable model for queer spaces. He uses evidence from Soho in London to suggest that gay village development likely follows a regular socio-economic process in which an urban area in decline is selected as a location for one or more pioneer gay clubs. Over time these businesses begin attracting customers who make residential decisions to live in the area, encouraging additional clustering of gay-related businesses. Subsequently, as these businesses become profitable, the area experiences increasing concentrations of other LGBTQ oriented businesses. Finally Collins' model suggests that as LGBTQ residents make aesthetic improvements, property values begin to increase. At the same time the neighborhood's reputation as a tolerant and exciting space makes it more attractive and socially desirable to the wider population. This shift in demand results in the assimilation and integration of the LGBTQ neighborhood into the heterosexual mainstream and a change in its basic queerness.

Others have argued that such linear evolutionary models have limited value. Ruting (2008) argues that when gay districts are in a state of flux such as the de-gaying of the Oxford Street neighborhood in Sydney, Australia, LGBTQ people are not seamlessly integrated with heterosexual couples and families. Rather than integration, such neighborhoods often lose their queer flavor as gay men and other queer residents move elsewhere for a variety of reasons. Reinforcing this point, Gorman-Murray and Waitt (2009) also suggest that gay-friendly neighborhoods are developing outside of the traditional gayborhood in Sydney. While proximity enables more diverse social networks to develop between straight residents and their LGBTQ neighbors, these connections are strongest for those gays who aspire to middle class values.

The Collins hypothesis that the gayness of neighborhoods just happens to fade away is called into question by recent research on planning in Atlanta. Doan and Higgins (2011) argue that the promotion efforts of municipal officials to stimulate redevelopment along Peachtree Street in Atlanta, combined with a studied neglect of the Midtown gayborhood, pushed gay clubs and institutions away from the historic LGBTQ area in Midtown to more peripheral neighborhoods. In a more recent article Doan (2014) argues that coordinated efforts between the city and development interests led to the closure of numerous gay clubs in Midtown, attempts to drive sex workers from the area, and changes to zoning ordinances that shut down adult enterprises. This is not an inevitable process, but one which is triggered by neo-liberal planning interventions to cleanse neighborhoods and make them safe for capital investment.

It is certainly the case that other transformational forces have had significant impacts on LGBTQ neighborhoods, most notably the AIDS epidemic. One recent epidemiological study of the effects of HIV/AIDS (Rosenfeld et al. 2012) argues that the massive number of HIV/AIDS deaths among urban gay males of the baby-boom generation in North America had a powerful effect in the largest metropolitan areas where thriving gay neighborhoods had developed in the 1970s. An earlier study (Rosser et al. 2008) also explored this question by asking a sample of gay informants from 17 cities and 14 countries how the epidemic had influenced gay communities. The responses from nearly all the respondents indicated that their communities were undergoing "structural decline," and that gay neighborhoods were disappearing as gay men assimilated into the suburbs. In addition, the number of gay bars/clubs was also declining, possibly due to increased use of the internet or simply the aging of the gay male population in many cities.

Recent evidence confirms the proposition that the LGBTQ population is widely dispersed, reinforcing previous studies that have found LGBTQ people living in both rural and urban areas (cf. Kramer 1995; Forsyth 1997; Valentine 1997; Kirkey and Forsyth 2001; Cody and Welch 1997, McCarthy 2000; Anacker 2011). Data on same-sex partner households from the 2000 Census suggests that every county in the United States has at least one same-sex partner household and most have higher numbers (Gates and Ost 2004). Although same-sex couples are still more concentrated in large metropolitan areas (Black et al. 2000; Smith and Gates 2001), Gavin Brown (2012) contends that many LGBTQ people do not live in the largest cities that are often studied by social scientists, suggesting the need for more nuanced analysis of a broad range of LGBTQ habitation experiences and patterns. Anacker (2011) argues that suburbs are being increasingly queered as LGBTQ people move out of traditional central city or inner ring suburban settings to more affordable suburban environments. Accordingly, it is critical to incorporate research from a variety of large and small urban and suburban areas about the experiences of LGBTQ people in these spaces, including whether their needs are being met.

It is also necessary to expand the horizons of what is considered queer space since these spaces are more mobile and transitory than much of the traditional research on gay villages would suggest. The queer community comes together to party, to protest, or otherwise expropriate public spaces on a temporary basis through the use of parades, festivals, and what Manalansan (2005) has called "demarcated moments." The most visible examples of these transient spaces are the Gay Pride parades that are now big business in many large metropolitan areas and are usually centered in and around the LGBTQ neighborhoods (Forsyth 2011).

Other manifestations of such temporary spaces outside the gayborhood include gay days at Disney World in Orlando, Florida (Chapman 2011) and the regular influx of gays and lesbians to Pensacola Beach in Florida over Memorial Day (Philipp 1999). Other more radical uses of space include the camps used by radical faeries (Morgensen 2008) and the temporary spatialization of radically queer eruptions (Brown 2007) that demonstrate the process through which spaces can be queered while LGBTQ people inhabit them.

More recent scholarship notes that younger LGBTQ people appear absent from many existing gayborhoods. In New York as the West Village was becoming increasingly gentrified, LGBTQ youth of color organized to protest against being excluded by the redevelopment of Pier 40 which had been a frequent venue for young queer people to gather and create community (Goh 2011). This kind of gentrification causes younger LGBTQ people to be completely priced out of existing gayborhoods. However, Nash (2012) argues that there is also a generational divide such that some younger LGBTQ people in Toronto who identify as "post-mo" (post-modern homosexual) are less interested in the more traditional spaces of Toronto's gay village, preferring hipper neighborhoods such as Parkdale or Leslieville. Gudelunas (2012) suggests that the use of technology to meet other LGBTQ individuals may also contribute to changing recreation patterns among more technologically sophisticated young people. Whether these changing use patterns are due to more empowered youth creating their own spaces or to actions taken by assimilationist village residents that make queer youth feel uncomfortable, as younger LGBTQ people continue to locate outside traditional LGBTQ neighborhoods, the queerness of those spaces will fade away.

At this point it is premature to elaborate a single model for gay village development and its possible decline and dispersal. The experiences of the past 40 years are much too short a time period to develop sophisticated models of change, and facts on the ground are still in a state of flux. If the gay village model has been fueled by the increasing tolerance for LGBTQ populations in metropolitan areas over the past four decades, it is risky to assume that the assimilation of gay villages into gentrified urban spaces for metrosexuals bodes well for the LGBTQ community as a whole. Podmore (2013) cautions against viewing recent increases in tolerance and acceptance of LGBTQ individuals as part of a linear trend. While support for same-sex marriage does seem to be growing especially among younger people, LGBTQ historians such as D'Emilio (2006) question whether the current fixation with marriage is really helping the LGBTQ community to move forward, or is increasing the possibility of hostile responses from social and political conservatives.

The backlash may already be occurring. The brutal murder of Mark Carson on May 18, 2013 in Greenwich Village in New York City by a man alleged to have yelled anti-gay epithets is one recent example of a continuing trend of anti-gay violence.[2] Although Comstock (1991) found that anti-LGBTQ violence was higher in gayborhoods than elsewhere, dense concentrations of queer folk does allow swifter organizing in response to hate violence. For example, in New York City during May and June of 2013 a weekly meeting was organized to protest the wave of violence and pressure the city to take action. Urban planners must recognize that tolerance on the part of some does not provide protection from the intolerance of the few. Urban designs should consider the particular needs for safety of the LGBTQ population.

All of these trends indicate that there is a continuing urgency to plan for the ways in which LGBTQ people use spaces both within and beyond traditional gay neighborhoods. Michael Brown (2013) has argued that in spite of the problematic nature of queer spaces for some theorists, there are a number of outstanding research issues about gay villages that should be addressed. Planning for these spaces must recognize that changes in overt discrimination and perceptions of wider tolerance do not alter the need for safe and accepting urban spaces for the entire LGBTQ spectrum. In short, planning academics and practitioners ought to examine more explicitly how existing policies have enabled LGBTQ neighborhoods to develop or have contributed to their demise.

Problems Related to Changing LGBTQ Neighborhoods: Pressing Questions for Planners

Given the significant changes to existing LGBTQ neighborhoods that challenge planners who wish to preserve and strengthen diversity within their cities, there are several key problem areas and critical questions that are addressed in this volume. The first critical issue for planners and policy-makers is whether existing gay villages should be preserved or simply allowed to transform into more widely acceptable bohemian heterotopias. Over the last decade or so even the iconic gayborhoods have experienced considerable pressure due to gentrification (Ghaziani 2010; Doan and Higgins 2011; Doderer 2011). One of the reasons for the change in gay villages is the displacement of less wealthy people from existing gayborhoods because of increasing demand for in-town neighborhoods from "super-financiers" (Lees 2000). In addition many suburban heterosexual couples seeking more hip, inner ring communities also desire housing with shorter commutes and more walkable design features. Should planning effort be expended in preserving enclaves of high income individuals, no matter what their sexual orientation? Or should time and resources be spent to ensure that gay villages remain distinctive, safe and affordable?

A second and related area of critical concern is the issue of displacement that complicates the question of whether to protect the affordability of the gay neighborhoods. As described above, higher property values may trigger a kind of cascading gentrification when younger and less wealthy LGBTQ individuals and couples are priced out of traditional gay villages, causing them to seek more affordable housing elsewhere and use their "sweat equity" to create the next generation of queer space. These new queer spaces often emerge in vulnerable neighborhoods inhabited by people of color and can result in displacement of long-time residents. For example, the Kirkwood neighborhood in Atlanta was the site of an ongoing struggle between young LGBTQ-identified residents seeking lower cost housing alternatives and African-American families who had inhabited this area for a number of years (Doan and Higgins 2011; Doan Forthcoming). Does ignoring the dissolution of a well-established gay neighborhood mean that several new ones will crop up elsewhere with related displacement effects on less well-organized communities of minorities and immigrants? Or can planners work to diversify these minority communities without encouraging displacement?

An additional challenge for planners related to changing gayborhoods is the provision of specialized social services to the LGBTQ community. Dense concentrations of LGBTQ residents in existing queer spaces often attract the location of social service agencies working with this population. While not all these agencies provide what Andrucki and Elder (2007) have called "emancipatory space," such organizations function as a critical element in the web of community connectedness that characterizes queer space. However, as rents in gentrifying queer neighborhoods become increasingly expensive, many of these specialized service agencies for the LGBTQ community may also be displaced. Alternatively, their ongoing location in gentrified areas with fewer LGBTQ residents may make it more difficult to fulfill their missions. Another consideration raised by Doderer (2011) is that cities still must find ways to provide safe environments in which non-normative genders and sexualities can explore their identities and organize to create social and activist communities. How can planners support agencies to ensure full access to a range of social services by the most highly marginalized LGBTQ members if there is no central location from which to serve them? How can planners justify the higher costs and degree of difficulty in serving LGBTQ populations if they are widely dispersed throughout an urban area?

Yet another area of critical concern is the issue of the most vulnerable LGBTQ populations. Racial and ethnic minorities whose gender or sexuality is non-normative face a complex web of intersecting discriminations. One scholar has suggested that in order to understand queerness in the African-American community more fully, it is essential to use "an intersectional analysis that recognizes how numerous systems of oppression interact to regulate and police the lives of most people" (Cohen 2005, p. 25). This can present challenges to planners trying to reach out to marginalized communities. For instance in Atlanta the divide between LGBTQ minorities and the more dominant LGBTQ white population is so extreme that there are two separate Pride celebrations, Black Pride held over Labor Day weekend and Atlanta Pride held a month or so later.

Urban planners and policy-makers also need to increase their awareness of the needs of other marginalized LGBTQ populations: youth, people living with AIDS, and the transgender population. LGBTQ young people who may have been kicked out of their family homes due to their sexual orientation or gender identity are an especially vulnerable community of interest, often arriving in large metropolitan areas with minimal resources and few skills with which to make a living (Reck 2009). LGBTQ youth programs such as LYRIC (Lavender Youth Resources and Information Center) in the heart of the Castro District of San Francisco provide one model for serving this population in a dense urban area.

Another population requiring special attention is the segment of the LGBTQ community living with HIV/AIDS. As the HIV positive population lives longer due to the use of antiretrovirals, access to additional health services may also be needed. Many large cities have organized special services like Philadelphia's Manna "meals on wheels" program that delivers food to individuals suffering from cancer and HIV related illness. How can planners ensure that LGBTQ youth and people living with HIV/AIDS continue to be served if the LGBTQ population becomes even more dispersed?

Lastly, while only a small segment of the overall LGBTQ community, the transgender population is one of the most vulnerable (Namaste 2000; Doan 2007 and 2010; Grant et al. 2011). Because many transgendered women remain visibly gender non-conforming, they experience high levels of employment discrimination. For those who have lost their jobs, sex work may be the most lucrative means of making a living available, resulting in a higher risk of contracting HIV/AIDS (Weinberg et al. 1999; Clements-Nolle et al. 2001). Although education programs can be tailored to this population like those offered by the 519 Community Center in the heart of Toronto's gay village, as LGBTQ people are dispersed throughout the wider urban area, these kinds of programs may no longer be viable. In addition, gentrification adds to the tension between trans sex workers working at the margin of the gayborhood and the more affluent individuals engaged in "cleaning up" LGBTQ spaces as evidenced in Washington, DC (Edelman 2011), Atlanta (Nouraee 2008) and Toronto (Baute 2008). How can cities provide services to these highly marginalized populations if they have been scattered throughout the wider metropolitan area? Does municipal neglect of this population amount to a new form of transphobia in which these populations are forced from the urban center to suburban areas that are even less able or willing to care for them?

Description of the Book

In spite of the challenging issues presented by most existing queer spaces, these environments have fired the imagination of many LGBTQ people as concrete demonstrations that through community organizing, collective endeavor, and sweat-equity gentrification, urban spaces can be "queered" and safe zones created for non-normative individuals. However, given recent demographic trends in these areas, their "safe" nature as LGBTQ places is at risk and requires planning intervention. This volume builds on the work of a previous volume, *Queerying Planning: Challenging Heteronormative Assumptions and Reframing Planning Practice* (Doan 2011) that urged planners to recognize the situation of LGBTQ people in cities, but extends the argument in several key areas. The bulk of the work that remains to be done on the "project" of ensuring the safety of marginalized LGBTQ populations within urban areas involves broadening the scope of planning for sexual and gender minorities by expanding on traditional queer space. Accordingly this book is divided into several sections. The first section of the book goes beyond the most common examples of queer space (the Village in New York, the Castro in San Francisco, the Gay Village in Manchester, and Soho in London) by examining less well-studied queer neighborhoods that are primarily gay male spaces. These initial chapters explore different ways of conceptualizing traditional gay neighborhoods, highlighting the role that planning has taken in hindering or facilitating this process.

The second section examines the ways in which LGBTQ populations outside traditional gay villages organize themselves and make demands for better and safer urban environments. Because much of the academic literature on queer urban spaces has concentrated on the exploration of white male neighborhoods, the second section explicitly considers the ways that cities and planners can improve the experiences of the wider LGBTQ community by including people of color, recent immigrants, and lesbian women. More specifically, the chapters in this section consider how LGBTQ spaces have evolved outside of the traditional gay neighborhood.

The third section of the book examines the concept of intersectionality and considers how it can be usefully applied in planning for the needs of LGBTQ people. It is very important for planning officials and practitioners to be aware that in marginalized populations like the LGBTQ community, there are many intersecting forms of discrimination at work. This term *intersectionality* has been used by scholars to refer to the web of discriminations that exclude LGBTQ people from urban spaces by virtue of their race or class (Valentine 2007), as well as ability, age, and gender identity (M. Brown 2012). This intersectionality often limits the ability of these citizens to access urban services and can at times make them invisible to planning officials. The chapters in this section elaborate the ways that failure to address intersectionality can influence planning impacts. The authors highlight the often neglected, but significant presence of LGBTQ African-Americans, queer immigrants, and women who identify as queer and "post-mo" (Nash 2012).

In the final section of the book the chapters address the interplay between health and social activism within the municipal arena. The authors argue that planners who understand and are able to forge strong links with local activists and service providers are better equipped to strengthen the LGBTQ community. They describe the vital role played by activists both inside and outside the state in forging a strong set of relationships to ensure that vital community services are delivered to the LGBTQ population. Each of the chapters argues that planners must be ready to identify and develop a strong working relationship with non-traditional planning partners to ensure that the most urgent needs of this marginalized community are met.

In summary, this collection raises critical issues for planners about the nature and future prospects of LGBTQ neighborhoods, as well as the broader issues of how to ensure that queer spaces are maintained. The academics and planning practitioners who have contributed to this volume draw on their collective wisdom and years of experience to focus on a range of important questions that are highly relevant for urban policy-makers regarding the LGBTQ population living in cities, including: affordable housing, access to vital social services, urban safety, and the need for community organizing. While change is inevitable in the context of urban development, not all progress needs to exclude marginalized populations. The intent of this volume is to provide new insights and policy perspectives on how to enable cities to evolve beyond traditional understandings of queer spaces in ways that are more inclusive of a broader diversity of LGBTQ populations.

Notes

1   Places with municipal support include: the City of San Francisco's Harvey Milk transportation plaza and rainbow flags on street lights in the Castro (Stryker and Van Buskirk 1996), the rainbow pylons along North Halsted Street in Boystown in Chicago (Reed 2003), the Gay Village designation of Church and Wellesley in Toronto, Canada (Nash 2005 and 2006), as well as a similar designation of Canal Street in Manchester, England (Quilley 1997; Binnie and Skeggs 2006).
2   The New York City Anti-Violence Project reports that there were 11 violent anti-LGBTQ hate crimes during May 2013 alone (Anti-Violence Project 2013).

References

Anacker, K. 2011. Queering the suburbs: Analyzing property values in male and female same-sex suburbs in the United States, pp. 107–125 in P. Doan (ed.) *Queerying Planning: Challenging Heteronormative Assumptions and Reframing Planning Practice*. Farnham, UK: Ashgate.

Andrucki, M.J. and Elder, G.S. 2007. Locating the state in queer space: GLBT non-profit organizations in Vermont, USA *Social and Cultural Geography* 8, 1: 89–104.

Anti-Violence Project. 2013. Community Alert: May 31, 2013. New York, NY. Accessed at www.avp.org/storage/documents/2013.5.31_ca_avp_kevinkiaddi.pdf

Badgett, M.V.L. 2001. *Money, Myths and Change: The Economic Lives of Lesbians and Gay Men*. Chicago, IL: University of Chicago Press.

Baute, N. 2008. Take a walk on someone else's wild side, *The Toronto Star* September 06, 2008. Accessed May 15, 2013 at www.thestar.com/news/2008/09/06/take_a_walk_on_someone_elses_wild_side.html

Bell, D. and Valentine, G. (eds.) 2005. *Mapping Desire: Geographies of Sexuality*. London: Routledge.

Betsky, A. 1997. *Queer Space: Architecture and Same Sex Desire*. New York, NY: William Morrow & Co.

Binnie, J. and Skeggs, B. 2006. Cosmopolitan knowledge and the production and consumption of sexualized space, pp. 246–253 in J. Binnie et al. *Cosmopolitan Urbanism*. London: Routledge.

Black, D., Gates, G., Sanders, S. and Taylor, L. 2000. Demographics of the gay and lesbian population in the United States: Evidence from available systematic data sources. *Demography*, 37: 139–154.

Brown, G. 2007. Mutinous eruptions: Autonomous spaces of radical queer activism. *Environment and Planning A*, 39: 2685–2698.

Brown, G. 2012. Homonormativity: A metropolitan concept that denigrates ordinary gay lives, *Journal of Homosexuality* 59, 7: 1065–1072.

Brown, M. 2012. Gender and Sexuality I: Intersectional Anxieties. *Progress in Human Geography*, 36, 4: 541–550.

Brown, M. 2013. Gender and sexuality II: There goes the gayborhood? *Progress in Human Geography*. Published online April 29, 2013. DOI: 10.1177/0309132513484215.

Browne, K, Lim, J. and Brown, G. (eds.) 2007. *Geographies of Sexuality: Theory, Practices, and Politics*. Aldershot, UK: Ashgate.

Carpenter, C. 2004. New evidence on gay and lesbian household incomes. *Contemporary Economic Policy*, 22, 1: 78–94.

Chapman, T. 2011. Queering the Political-Economy: Anti-discrimination Law and the Urban Regime in Orlando, Florida, pp. 145–155 in P. Doan (ed.) *Queerying Planning: Challenging Heteronormative Assumptions and Reframing Planning Practice*. Farnham, UK: Ashgate.

Chauncey, G. 1994. *Gay New York: Gender Urban Culture and the Making of the Gay Male World*. New York, NY: Basic Books.

Clements-Nolle, K., Marx, R., Guzman, R. and Katz, M. 2001. HIV prevalence, risk behaviors, health care use, and mental health status of transgender persons: Implications for public health intervention. *American Journal of Public Health*, *91*, 6: 915–921.

Cody, P. and Welch, P. 1997. Rural gay men in northern New England: Life experiences and coping styles, *Journal of Homosexuality* 33, 1: 51–67.

Cohen, C.J. 2005. Punks, bulldaggers, and welfare queens: The radical potential of queer politics, pp. 22–51 in E.P. Johnson and M.G. Henderson (eds.) *Black Queer Studies: A Critical Anthology*. Durham, NC: Duke University Press.

Comstock, Gary David. 1991. *Violence against Lesbians and Gay Men*. New York, NY: Columbia University Press.

Collins, A. 2004. Sexual dissidence, enterprise and assimilation: bedfellows in urban regeneration. *Urban Studies* 41, 9: 1789–1806.

D'Emilio, J. 1983. *Sexual Politics, Sexual Communities: The Making of a Homosexual Minority in the United States 1940–1970*. Second Edition. Chicago, IL: University of Chicago Press.

D'Emilio, J. 2006. The Marriage Fight Is Setting Us Back. *Gay & Lesbian Review Worldwide*, (Nov.–Dec.): 10–11.

Doan, P. 2007. Queers in the American city: Transgendered perceptions of urban spaces. *Gender, Place, and Culture*, 14, 57–74.

Doan, P. 2010. The tyranny of gendered spaces: Reflections from beyond the gender dichotomy, *Gender, Place, and Culture*, 17, 5: 635–654.

Doan, P. (ed.) 2011. *Queerying Planning: Challenging Heteronormative Assumptions and Reframing Planning Practice*, Farnham, UK: Ashgate.

Doan, P. 2014. Regulating adult business to make spaces safe for heterosexual families in Atlanta, in P. Maginn and C. Steinmetz (eds.) *(Sub)Urban Sexscapes: Geographies and Regulation of the Sex Industry*. London: Routledge.

Doan, P. Forthcoming. Planning for sexual and gender minorities, Chapter 6 in M. Burayidi (ed.) *Planning Cosmopolitan Cities: Concepts, Trends, and Strategies*. Toronto, Canada: University of Toronto Press.

Doan, P. and Higgins, H. 2011. The demise of queer space? Resurgent gentrification and LGBT neighborhoods. *Journal of Planning Education and Research*, 31, 6–25.

Doderer, Y.P. 2011. LGBTQs in the city, queering urban space, *International Journal of Urban and Regional Research*, 35, 2: 431–436.

Edelman, E.A. 2011. This area has been declared a "prostitution free zone": Discursive formations of space, the state, and trans "sex worker" bodies, *Journal of Homosexuality*, 58, 6–7: 848–864.

Faderman, L. 1991. *Odd Girls and Twilight Lovers: A History of Lesbian Life in Twentieth-Century America*. New York, NY: Penguin Books.

Forsyth, A. 1997. 'Out' in the Valley, *International Journal of Urban and Regional Research*, 21, 1: 36–61.

Forsyth, A. 2011. Queerying planning practice: Understanding the non-conformist populations, pp. 21–51 in P. Doan (ed.) *Queerying Planning: Challenging Heteronormative Assumptions and Reframing Planning Practice*. Farnham, UK: Ashgate.

Forsyth, A and Cheung, G. 2001. Queers and planning. *Progressive Planning Magazine*. March/April 2001. www.plannersnetwork.org/2001/03/queers-and-planning

Frisch, M. 2002. Planning as a heterosexist project. *Journal of Planning Education and Research* 21: 254–266.

Gates, G.J. and Ost, J. 2004. *The Gay & Lesbian Atlas*. Washington, DC: Urban Institute Press.

Ghaziani, A. 2010. There goes the gayborhood? *Contexts*, Vol. 9, No. 4: 64–66.

Goh, K. 2011. From and toward a queer urbanism, *Progressive Planning Magazine*, Spring 2011. Accessed May 15, 2013 at www.plannersnetwork.org/2011/04/from-and-toward-a-queer-urbanism

Gorman-Murray, A. and Waitt, G. 2009. Queer-friendly neighbourhoods: Interrogating social cohesion across sexual difference in two Australian neighbourhoods, *Environment and Planning A*, 41: 2855–2873.

Grant, J. M., Mottet, L.A., Tanis, J., Harrison, J., Herman, J.L. and Keisling, M. 2011. *Injustice at Every Turn: A Report of the National Transgender Discrimination Survey*. Washington: National Center for Transgender Equality and National Gay and Lesbian Task Force.

Gudelunas, D. 2012. There's an app for that: The Uses and Gratifications of Online Social Networks for Gay Men, *Sexuality & Culture*, 16: 347–365.

Hemmings, C. 2002. *Bisexual Spaces: A Geography of Sexuality and Gender*. London: Routledge.

Hubbard, P. 2000. "Desire/disgust: Mapping the moral contours of heterosexuality," *Progress in Human Geography,* 24: 191–217.

Hubbard, P. 2004. Cleansing the metropolis: Sex work and the policy of zero tolerance. *Urban Studies*, 41, 9: 1687–1702.

Ingram, G.B., Bouthillette, A. and Ritter, Y. 1997. (eds.) *Queers in Space: Communities, Public Places, and Sites of Resistance*. Seattle, WA: Bay Press.

Kennedy, E.L. and Davis, M.D. 1993. *Boots of Leather, Slippers of Gold: the History of a Lesbian Community*. New York, NY: Penguin Books.

Kirkey, K. and Forsyth, A. 2001. Men in the Valley: Gay male life on the suburban-rural fringe. *Journal of Rural Studies*, 17: 421–441.

Klawitter, M. and Flatt, V. 1998. The effects of state and local antidiscrimination policies on earnings for gays and lesbians. *Journal of Policy Analysis and Management*, 17, 4: 658–686.

Kramer, J. 1995. Bachelor framers and spinsters: Gay and lesbian identities and communities in rural North Dakota, in D. Bell and G. Valentine (eds.) *Mapping Desire: Geographies of Sexualities*, London: Routledge.

Lees, L. 2000. A reappraisal of gentrification—towards a geography of gentrification. *Progress in Human Geography*. 24 (3): 389–408.

McCarthy, L. 2000. Poppies in a wheat field: Exploring the lives of rural lesbians. *Journal of Homosexuality*, 39: 75–94.

Manalansan, M.F. 2005. Race, violence, and neoliberal spatial politics in the global city, *Social Text*, 23, 3–4: 141–155.

Morgensen, S.L. 2008. Arrival at home: Radical faerie configurations of sexuality and place, *GLQ* 15, 1: 67–96.

Namaste, V. 2000. *Invisible Lives: The Erasure of Transsexual and Transgendered People*. Chicago, IL: University of Chicago Press.

Nash, C.J. 2005. Contesting identity: Politics of gays and lesbians in Toronto in the 1970s. *Gender, Place and Culture* 12 (1), 113–134.

Nash, C.J. 2006. Toronto's gay village (1969–1982): plotting the politics of gay identity. *The Canadian Geographer* 50 (1), 1–16.

Nash, C.J. 2012. The age of the 'post-mo'? Toronto's gay village and a new generation. *Geoforum*, http://dx.doi.org/10.1016/j.geoforum.2012.11.023

Nast, H. 2002. Queer patriarchies, queer racisms, international, *Antipode*, 34(5): 874–909.

Nero, C. 2005. Why are gay ghettos white? in E.P. Johnson and M. Henderson (eds.), *Black Queer Studies: A Critical Anthology*. Durham, NC: Duke University Press.

Newton, E. 1993. *Cherry Grove Fire Island: Sixty years in America's first gay and lesbian town.* Boston, MA: Beacon Press.

Nouraee, A. 2008. One man's battle against Midtown prostitutes and their johns, *Creative Loafing*, January 16, 2008. Accessed March 28, 2013. http://clatl.com/atlanta/one-mans-battle-against-midtown-prostitutes-and-their-johns/Content?oid=1271636

Oswin, N. 2008. Critical geographies and the uses of sexuality: deconstructing queer space. *Progress in Human Geography*, 32, 1: 89–103.

Philipp, S. 1999. Gay and lesbian tourists at a southern USA beach event. *Journal of Homosexuality*, 37, 3: 69–86.

Podmore, J. 2013. Critical commentary: Sexualities landscapes beyond homonormativity. *Geoforum*, 49: 263–267 http://dx.doi.org/10.1016/j.geoforum.2013.03.014

Prior, J. 2008. Planning for sex in the city: Urban governance, planning and the placement of sex industry premises in Inner Sydney, *Australian Geographer*, 39:3, 339–352.

Prior, J. and Crofts, P. 2011. Queerying urban governance: The emergence of sex industry premises into the planned city, pp. 185–208 in P. Doan (ed.) *Queerying Planning: Challenging Heteronormative Assumptions and Reframing Planning Practice*. Farnham, UK: Ashgate.

Quilley, S. 1997. Constructing Manchester's new urban village, in G. Ingram et al. (eds.) *Queers in Space: Communities, Public Places, and Sites of Resistance*. Seattle, WA: Bay Press.

Reck, J. 2009. Homeless and transgender youth of color in San Francisco: "No one likes street kids"— Even in the Castro. *Journal of LGBT Youth*. 6: 223–242.

Reed, C. 2003. We're from Oz: Making ethnic and sexual identity in Chicago. *Environment and Planning D: Society and Space*, 21: 425–440.

Rosenfeld, D., Bartlam, B. and Smith, R.D. 2012. Out of the closet and into the trenches: Gay male baby boomers, aging and HIV/AIDS. *The Gerontologist*, 52, 2: 255–264.

Rosser, B.R., West, W. and Weinmeyer, R. 2008. Are gay communities dying or just in transition? Results from an international consultation examining possible structural change in gay communities. *AIDS Care: Psychological and Socio-medical Aspects of HIV/AIDS*, 20, 5: 588–595.

Rothenburg, T. 1995. And she told two friends: Lesbians creating urban social space, pp. 165–181 in D. Bell and G. Valentine (eds.) *Mapping Desire: Geographies of Sexuality*. London: Routledge.

Ruting, B. 2008. Economic transformations of gay urban spaces: Revisiting Collins' evolutionary gay district model, *Australian Geographer*, 39, 3: 259–269.

Smith, D.M. and Gates, G. 2001. Same-sex unmarried partner households. *Urban Institute Papers*, August 22. Washington, DC: The Urban Institute.

Stein, M. 2000. *City of Sisterly and Brotherly Love: Lesbian and Gay Philadelphia, 1945–1972.* Chicago, IL: University of Chicago Press.

Stryker, S. 2008. *Transgender History*. Berkeley, CA: Seal Press.

Stryker, S. and J. Van Buskirk. 1996. *Gay by the Bay: A History of Queer Culture in the San Francisco Bay Area*. San Francisco, CA: Chronicle Books.

Valentine, G. 1997. Making space: lesbian separatist communities in the United States, pp. 105–117 in P. Cloke and J. Little (eds.) *Contested Countryside Cultures: Otherness, Marginalization and Rurality*. London: Routledge.

Valentine, G. (ed.) 2000. *From Nowhere to Everywhere: Lesbian Geographies.* New York: Harrington Park Press.

Valentine, G. 2007. Theorizing and researching intersectionality: A challenge for feminist geography. *The Professional Geographer.* 59, 1: 10–21.

Walcott, R. 2007. Homopoetics: Queer space and the black queer diaspora, pp. 233–245 in K. McKittrick and C. Woods (eds.) *Black Geographies and the Politics of Place.* Boston, MA: South End Press.

Weinberg, M.S., Shaver, F. and Williams, C. 1999. Gendered sex work in the San Francisco Tenderloin. *Archives of Sexual Behavior,* 28: 503–520.

PART I

Planning and LGBTQ Populations in Traditional Gay Neighborhoods

INTRODUCTION TO PART I

Petra L. Doan

While many planners are familiar with the most common examples of queer space (Greenwich Village in New York, the Castro in San Francisco, Soho in London, and the Gay Village in Manchester), most LGBTQ people do not live in these iconic places. While later sections in this book consider planning issues for dispersed LGBTQ populations living in suburbs as well as outside major metropolitan areas, it is useful to examine neighborhoods in less well-known cities and draw lessons from the evolution of these other gay spaces.

Each chapter in this section pays special attention to the role that planning has taken in hindering or facilitating the evolution of these predominantly gay neighborhoods. One recurrent theme is the central role played by gay commercial establishments and what might be termed the gay-oriented real estate sector. These businesses are an important element in the development of gay neighborhoods, providing jobs, paying taxes, and also creating spaces that are clearly marketed to attract the business of gay men who might not feel welcome elsewhere in the city. In Chapter 2 Curt Winkle considers the experience of gay commercial districts in the city of Chicago over the past 90 years, using historical maps of gay bars and clubs to illustrate the shifting locus of gay business activity. He also discusses the role of planned municipal investments intended to support Chicago's Boystown neighborhood that have helped to establish a highly visible gayborhood, but have not fully stabilized gay residential patterns because of the fluidity of LGBTQ residents. In Chapter 3 Andrew Whittemore describes the link between gay male home ownership and political empowerment in the case of Dallas, Texas, arguing that the "Dallas Way" uses real estate as a method of gaining social and political power in the urban context. Finally, in Chapter 4 Nathaniel Lewis analyzes the evolution of the gay male neighborhood in Washington, DC which has moved north and east from its original hub around Dupont Circle. He suggests that this evolutionary process reflects the fractures and fissures of postmodern spaces, thereby presenting challenges to planning practitioners seeking to support queer spaces. Another common theme in all of these chapters is the struggle to maintain a visible gay or queer identity in these neighborhoods in the face of a steady increase in land rents as a result of gentrification. Some gentrification in Dallas, for instance, is geared to the upscale gay population, but other redevelopment efforts are simply trying to capitalize on the increasing attractiveness of in-town living. These changes create tension in formerly marginal neighborhoods that gay men have worked hard to stabilize; some men wish to maintain the gay identity of the place, and others simply want to capitalize on their investments and move on.

2

GAY COMMERCIAL DISTRICTS IN CHICAGO AND THE ROLE OF PLANNING[1]

Curt Winkle

Introduction

Planners play important roles in shaping places, whether intentionally or unintentionally. Places with gay men are often identified as gayborhoods, enclaves or commercial districts, and have become the subject of renewed interest in academic planning and geography literatures (Doan and Higgins, 2011; Brown, 2013; Lewis, 2013; Podmore, 2013; Ruting, 2008). I argue that static conceptions of gay places in space can both be inaccurate and hamper effective planning.

This paper traces the historically shifting gay spaces in Chicago, briefly identifies some of the elements of planning and governance that may have been at work in each period, and reflects on the ways in which dynamic conceptions may improve the effectiveness of planning in addressing the issues of lesbian, gay, bisexual, transgender and queer (LGBTQ) people.

The Role of Planning in Shaping Gay Places

Planners often fail to directly address the needs of LGBTQ people. Forsyth (2001) and Doan (2011) argue that planners need to know more about nonconformist lesbian and gay populations. Planning documents and processes rarely directly engage or address gay populations, which is all the more poignant since planning documents frequently address ethnic populations (Forsyth, 2001). Doan and Higgins (2011) further confirm the relative invisibility of LGBTQ issues in planning, finding that planning documents for Atlanta gay communities, including Midtown, do not mention the lesbian and gay populations. Collins (2004) finds that development of a Soho gay village in London is not addressed in any direct way by the Westminster City Council planning or in local economic development documentation, while the adjacent London Chinatown is addressed. However, he does note that the Westminster Council and police attempt to constrain the sex and porn industry through planning.

The reasons for this lack of direct attention by planners may be that, as Doan (2011: 7) notes, "the planning agenda is in large part shaped by those in power, and does not readily expand to include other minority groups without sustained pressure from specific interest groups." Forsyth (2001: 341) states that planning tends to take an assimilationist approach, perhaps because, "It is also the main approach of planning itself as a social movement or an approach to social change; even those in the progressive tradition often work inside government, in quasigovernment organizations, or create parallel institutions that interact with governments, to achieve social reform or social transformation." Gorman-Murray (2011: 143) examines the problems and opportunities of multiscalar governance in meeting the needs of LGBTQ populations and finds that, in Australia, the multiscalar framework of planning has both limited the inclusion of some LGBTQ people in planning and created opportunities for other LGBTQ people to engage at other levels of government.

Even without explicitly addressing LGBTQ issues, planning can impact LGBTQ people. Frisch (2002) identifies planning as a heterosexist project that reinforces the development of a heteronormative city, showing that planning and, particularly, zoning works to repress LGBTQ communities. Doan and Higgins found that "planners' use of zoning in the Midtown area in Atlanta was designed to make the area appealing not only to big business but to heterosexuals and their families," thus facilitating resurgent gentrification and "a clear attempt to recloset the LGBTQ population that provided much of the energy and investment for the initial regeneration of many neighborhoods"(2011: 14).

There are some notable and recent cases where planners have taken an active role in creating or shaping gay places such as Chicago's Boystown (North Halsted Street) streetscape in 1997 (Forsyth, 2011). There is also the tourist-oriented gay village in Manchester, England (Binnie and Skeggs, 2004; Hughes, 2003) and the later creation of Ottawa's Le/The Village in 2011 (Lewis, 2013). While these initiatives may create or strengthen gay places, they may also create a Disneyfied version of gay space that serves economic development while excluding some LGBTQ people.

Planning has an impact on gay places and people, but in most cases could play a stronger positive role that may be shaped by the ways in which gay places are conceived by planners.

Gay Enclaves and Commercial Districts

Much of the literature on gay enclaves and commercial districts seeks to describe them and explain their development. As shown below, the literature often focuses on single locations within a city rather than evolving spatial patterns and places across the city or region.

Gay enclaves have been identified as a way to develop identity, create safety and develop political power (Castells and Murphy, 1982; Lauria and Knopp, 1985).

Nevertheless, while political organizing was seen as important in San Francisco (Castells and Murphy, 1982), Nash (2006) argues that Toronto's gay village formed despite opposition in the 1970s by gay political leadership that argued for an assimilationist approach and that it was wrong to ghettoize gay populations.

One of the primary functions of the gay district is to serve as a ghetto, accommodating those people or functions that are excluded from other parts of the city. But lesbian and gay individuals may be able to hide their status to some degree, which would allow the choice of some LGBTQ people to live in parts of the city where LGBTQ people may not be accepted if identified. There is evidence that gay industry is excluded from parts of the city. Prior and Crofts (2011) examine the emergence of sex industry permits that allowed gay bathhouses. They examined the shifting role that planning plays in regulating order within cities, arguing that gay bathhouses are associated with disorder. There was a "rapid shift in rhetoric away from gay bathhouses as offending against moral and legal order, to offending against planning order" (2011: 207).

Some explanations for gay enclaves focus on economic arguments. Collins (2004) presents a four-stage model of the evolution of gay spaces. He argues that, in the first stage, historical accidents result in the initial concentration and that this provides a seed for a process of agglomeration. He cites Black et al.'s (2002) argument that gay men seek out areas with high amenities, that are gay friendly and that have low market values. In a second stage, there is a clustering of gay male recreational activities with renovation of gay bars, followed by a third stage of expansion and diversification where there is more gay density and visibility. With the addition of more gay bars and services, the area becomes an urban gay village that is recognized by the mainstream and generates tourism. Finally, there is a stage of integration where more heterosexual customers, businesses and residents are attracted to the area resulting in the outflow and perhaps suburbanization of gays. Note that this progressive model examines a single place over time, but does not incorporate movement of gay enclaves over time.

Ruting (2008) revisits the Collins model in relation to the declining gay orientation of the Oxford Street district in Sydney, Australia. He finds that economic theories, particularly the idea of declining demand, can help explain the de-gaying of the area, something not specifically considered in Collins' model. Ruting notes that the exclusion of non-stylish people from Oxford Street might have helped to encourage development of alternative gay enclaves. In addition, he suggests the Internet may have reduced the need for gay people to visit the Oxford Street area, although local planning documents portray the area as economically stagnant. Therefore lack of demand and the exclusion of some LGBTQ people might lead to the decline of a gay area and the development of other gay areas.

Sibalis (2004) examines the development of the Marais in Paris as a gay ghetto and shows that particularly desirable conditions of the space such as low rents, proximity and good transportation were well suited to gay people at a time when gay community was developing. He concludes that, "each and every gay ghetto has to be studied not only in terms of broad social and economic trends, but also within the context of a particular cultural, social and political environment" (2004: 1755).

Most of the literature above suggests that the creation of an enclave or commercial district can occur with little intervention by planning or other governance mechanisms. This is consistent with planning literature that shows that planning documents rarely directly address LGBTQ issues (Forsyth, 2001; Doan and Higgins, 2011; Collins, 2004). Other literature examines gay commercial districts that have been given official identity and sanction by governance structures.

Bell and Binnie (2004) examine an entrepreneurial model of homonormativity in which neoliberalism results in governance structures that create visible gay villages. They propose that sexual citizenship can be accepted as part of urban entrepreneurialism and that governance structures then use the perceived authenticity of gay enclaves for commodification and economic development. Florida's (2004) "creative class" is part of the discourse that allows for commodification of gay space. This homonormativity produces a "global repertoire of themed gay villages, as cities throughout the world weave commodified gay space into their promotional campaigns" (2004: 1807). This does not necessarily explain the initial concentration or enclave. Neo-liberal governance structures, including nongovernmental organizational partnerships, promote gay space to be visibly gay at the national and sometimes at the international level in order to enhance economic development.

Lewis (2013) identifies the case where Ottawa's Le/The Village was designated as a gay village by municipal government in 2011, even though there was little gay identity to the area before. Governance structures in a mid-sized city created a legibly gay commercial district without involvement of LGBTQ people or organizations. Despite what might be read as local government creating a gay commercial district for the sake of economic development, he points out that this village is not normalizing, over-commercialized, exclusionary or passé. He argues that decline of gay villages is not a forgone conclusion, but rather depends on characteristics of cities and those who experience them. He also points out that this case challenges the 'village evolution' model.

Tourism-oriented literature examines the gaying effect of events. Markwell (2002) demonstrates how Mardi Gras has become a major tourism event in Sydney, Australia that challenges heteronormative ideas about use of public space and major cultural icons such as the Opera House. Chapman (2011: 154) argues that, "The bottom line on the cultural commodification of such large scale spectacles is, of course, the need to accommodate the queer tourist for purposes of capital accumulation."

A number of authors have pointed out that gay enclaves can become exclusionary of some gay people. Ruting (2008) speculated that exclusion of uncool people in Sydney's Oxford Street district might have led to the creation of other gay districts. Doan and Higgins (2011) found that resurgent gentrification in Midtown Atlanta excluded gays with low incomes. Lewis (2013: 8) argued that, in the creation of a gay village in Ottawa, "The lack of centrally provided or subsidized services that might be afforded in a gay village has also tended to result in 'privilege by default' to those with the greatest financial means." Myrdahl (2011: 160) examines creative class concepts and gays, arguing that "It follows that in order to be 'consumable,' difference must be perceived as legitimate and it must be recognizable."

Most studies of gay enclaves and commercial spaces, with the exception of Ruting (2008), address a single space, perhaps over time, rather than a dynamic system of spaces over time. Indeed Brown (2013: 6) reviews the literature on gay concentrations and calls for more historical-geographical analysis to, "help us remember the processual nature of urban morphology." While studies have looked at the role of planning in shaping gay spaces, the question of when and why planning explicitly addresses gay communities, particularly in a spatially and temporally dynamic system, has not been fully addressed. A better understanding of the dynamics of gay concentrations within a city may help planning to better address the needs of LGBTQ people.

Method

This study seeks to trace the dynamics of gay spaces over time, examine variations in the role of planning and governance across the system, and reflect on their implications for planning for LGBTQ people. A case study method is employed to trace the movement of gay commercial institutions within the City of Chicago by decade between the 1920s and 2010s. The study identifies tight clusters of institutions that might be described as gay commercial districts in each decade. Limited and preliminary evidence of the role of planning and other forms of governance that might have shaped the space during each decade is examined. From this, implications for planning practice regarding LGBTQ people are drawn.

The City of Chicago is an ideal location for this historical case study in that it is a large city with a population of about three million people, and has multiple community areas and neighborhoods available to become gay commercial districts. It currently has two gay neighborhoods, Boystown and Andersonville, both near Lake Michigan on Chicago's north side with Andersonville newer than Boystown (Ghaziani, 2014). Unlike so many other cities where planning documents are silent on LGBTQ issues, the City of Chicago's planning documents for the 1997 streetscaping project on North Halstead Street in an area otherwise known as Boystown explicitly address gay issues, providing some variation in the role of planning for LGBTQ people across districts and time.

The question of whether or not it is appropriate to trace gay spaces over such a long period of time may be raised. Ghaziani (2014) describes current 'gayborhoods' as characterized by the presence of gay symbols, ritual gay events, a concentration of gay residents, as well as a clustering of gay-owned or gay-friendly institutions including businesses, nonprofit organizations and community centers. Gay neighborhoods that might fit this description are seen as having emerged after World War II, but there were clearly spaces where gay people concentrated or met each other in earlier historical periods (D'Emilio and Freedman, 2012; Chauncy,

1994). Gay neighborhoods developed increased concentration and visibility in the 1970s and 1980s, and may be currently waning and decentralizing in what may be described as a post-gay period (Ghaziani, 2014). These shifting designations and changing roles for gay spaces are methodologically challenging.

In the face of fluctuating gay culture and identity, Ghaziani (2014) identifies two approaches to measuring gay culture: anchor institutions such as bars and community centers; and commemorations that mark places as having had gay culture. He develops these two approaches though interviews with people in Chicago's two gay neighborhoods, Boystown and Andersonville. Since not all once gay places have commemorations in place, I have selected the presence of clusters of gay institutions to measure the presence of gay commercial districts by decade.

Accordingly, this chapter plots the location of gay commercial districts by mapping the location of gay bars and clubs using two main data sources. The first is a directory of gay-related business *Damron Men's Travel Guide*, which has been in existence in one form or another since the 1960s. I selected only gay bars and clubs in the guide for inclusion, excluding restaurants that may be gay-owned, gay nonprofit organizations and cultural centers. The definitions and level of inclusion of non-bar/club institutions varies over the publication of the *Damron Guide*, so limiting analysis to bars and clubs creates more consistency in the data. The location of gay bars and clubs from 1910 to 1950 comes from the second source, a book on Chicago gay history, *Chicago Whispers: A History of LGBTQ Chicago before Stonewall* (2012) by de la Croix. The author conducted interviews with numerous LGBTQ individuals about their experiences and identified the names and addresses for many of Chicago's historic LGBTQ bars, clubs, and tearooms. Many of these institutions had both gay and straight clientele. The addresses of the gay bars and clubs from these two sources were geocoded and mapped.

Data on bar and club locations were mapped by decade, but the method for determining the decades during which establishments were operated differs between the decades before and after 1960. Data for the 1910s to the 1950s comes from de la Croix, which organizes the presentation of stories and other references to bars and clubs roughly by decade. Bars and clubs are coded for the decade in which a de la Croix chapter mentions them. Since de la Croix does not usually indicate the date when the establishment opened or closed, it is possible that some establishments mapped for one decade actually predate the decade for which they are coded, or continued to exist into subsequent decades. Post-1960 institutions for each decade were found in the *Damron Guide* for at least one of the following years: either the 1965 or 1968–9 *Damron Guide* for the 1960s; either the 1974 or 1979 guide for the 1970s; either the 1984 or 1989 guide for the 1980s; the 1999 guide for the 1990s; 2009 for the 2000s; or the 2013 guide for the 2010s. The number of institutions after the 1990s may be slightly under estimated compared to the decades 1960s, 1970s and 1980s since only one guide-year was used for later decades. This analysis examines location of clusters, not the total number of bars, so the bias should be minimal.

Bars and clubs are included whether they predominantly served gay men, lesbians or transgendered patrons, but the overwhelming majority of bars and clubs included served gay men. The data are far less robust in identifying institutions that serve women or transgender people.

Clusters of gay bars and clubs are identified as gay commercial districts, and named based on the two sources. While most of the district names are fairly specific to a single, usually walkable place, the term Bronzeville/Southside is loosely used here to describe a wider area of Chicago's south side.

To examine the role of governance and planning documents, I look at gay histories of Chicago particularly de la Croix (2012), planning documents, newspaper accounts and documents from governance institutions such as Chambers of Commerce, but it is very far from a comprehensive history of commercial districts and the role of planning over this 100-year period.

Overview of Gay Commercial Districts, 1920–2010

Given the literature on gay neighborhoods and commercial districts summarized above, we might expect that Chicago would have one or two gay commercial districts that are relatively static. Figure 2.1 shows all gay bars and clubs identified between 1920 and 2010. Taken over time, Chicago gay bars and clubs hardly cluster in a small enclave but rather show a widespread distribution along a 10-mile-long band along Lake Michigan, extending north from the 'Loop' or downtown area. Exceptions include a scattering of establishments in a pie-shaped wedge inland from the north lakeshore. This band and pie-shaped wedge have populations that are predominantly white. There is a cluster of bars and clubs on the predominantly black south side loosely clustered along the lake, and a scattering of bars and clubs in inland communities. The suburbs are beyond the scope of this map and analysis, but have also been home to scattered bars and clubs, though not in clusters large enough to be called commercial districts.

The movement of gay bars and clubs followed a relatively dynamic progression of gay commercial spaces between the 1910s and the early 2010s. In the 1910s and 1920s gay space was located just north of the Loop in an area that was then called Towertown. In the 1920s and 1930s, there were clubs in the south side Bronzeville community (see Figure 2.2). Over the next decades bars and clubs moved to the Near North area around the intersection of Dearborn and Division Streets where the number of establishments grew considerably. In the 1970s, bars proliferated in the mid-north neighborhood of Lakeview in an area that was to become known as Boystown, and in a loose cluster on the south side near the lake around the Hyde Park community (see Figure 2.3). By the 1980s, an Andersonville cluster developed as bars in the Near North area became substantially reduced in number and Boystown continued to be a dominant gay commercial area. By the 2000s and into the early 2010s a gay commercial district had developed in the Andersonville neighborhood, reaching toward the northern border of the city (see Figure 2.4). Boystown continues to have a large number of gay bars and clubs, but

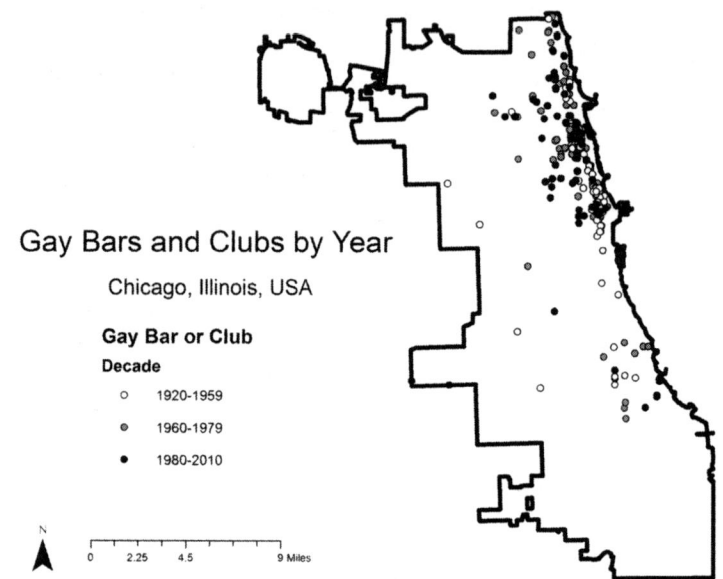

FIGURE 2.1   Overview of the location of gay bars and clubs by year, 1920–2010, Chicago, Illinois

Source: Compiled by author. Pre 1960 establishments from *Chicago Whispers* and *Damron Address Book* (aka *Damron Guide*).

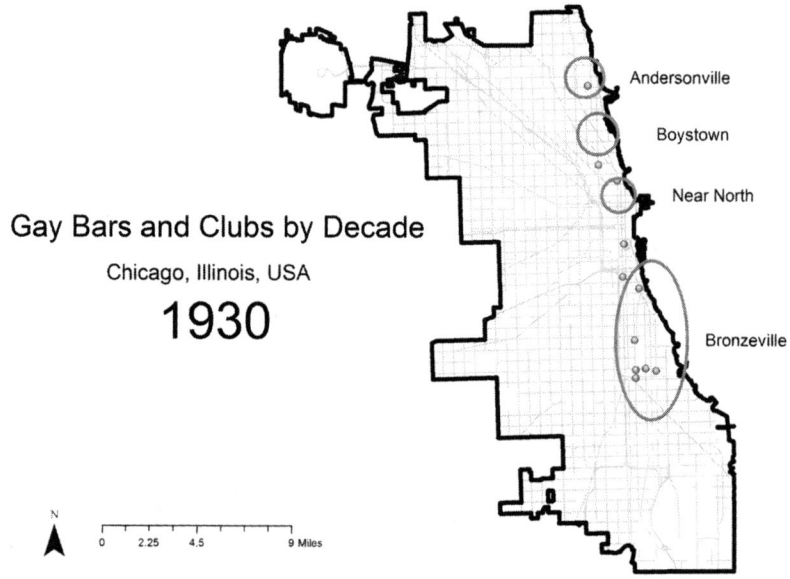

FIGURE 2.2   Gay bars and clubs, 1930s, Chicago, Illinois

Source: Compiled by author. Pre 1960 establishments from *Chicago Whispers* and *Damron Address Book* (aka *Damron Guide*).

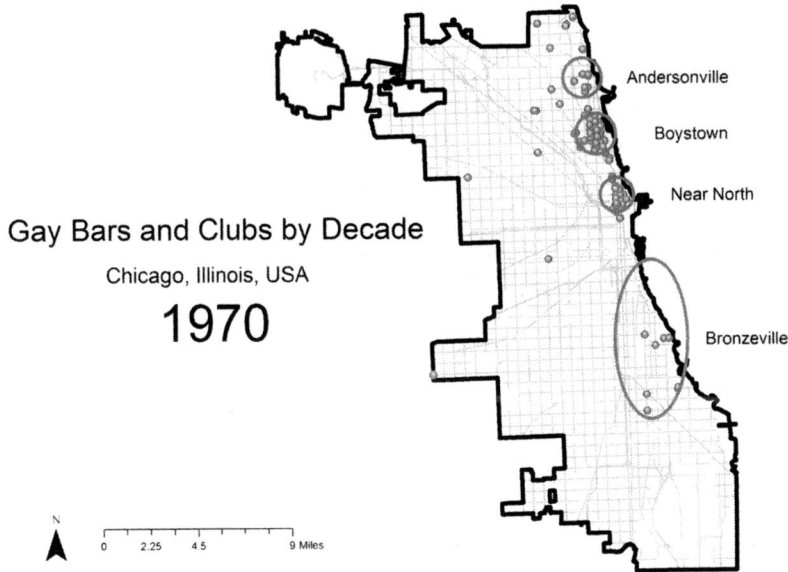

FIGURE 2.3   Gay bars and clubs, 1970s, Chicago, Illinois

Source: Compiled by author. Pre 1960 establishments from *Chicago Whispers* and *Damron Address Book* (aka *Damron Guide*).

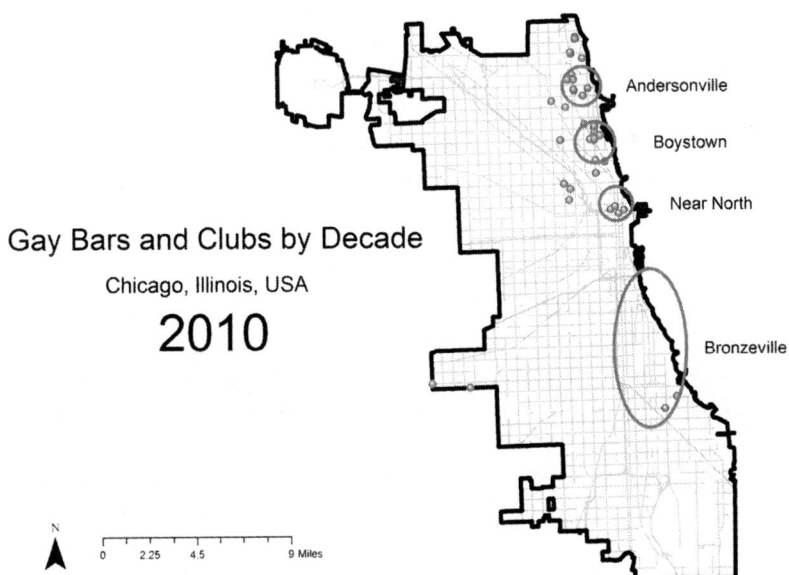

FIGURE 2.4   Gay bars and clubs, 2010s, Chicago, Illinois

Source: Compiled by author. Pre 1960 establishments from *Chicago Whispers* and *Damron Address Book* (aka *Damron Guide*).

they are more tightly focused along North Halstead Street than they were in the 1980s (see Figures 2.5 and 2.6).

Based on this overall pattern, we should not think of the gay commercial district as a single location that may develop and decline over time, but rather as part of a larger system, or even a progression of districts supplemented with scattered commercial establishments outside of those districts. In many ways, the Chicago pattern looks like the 'invasion and succession' of an ethnic group as observed by the sociologists of the Chicago School in the 1930s.

A full understanding of the dynamics of these gay spaces would require detailed historical analysis of each period, which is beyond the scope of this study. Instead, I offer a quick overview of each of Chicago's gay commercial districts over time, and make a scan of planning or other governance mechanisms that may have helped shape it.

Towertown

The Towertown of the 1910s and 1920s was a bohemian area referred to as The Village north of the Loop and named after the old Chicago Water Tower that was once used to regulate pressure in Chicago's water system. It was home to homosexual men and women (Mumford, 1997) and had clubs that accommodated them (de la Croix, 2012). Bughouse Square (otherwise known as Washington Square) was a celebrated free-speech forum located in Towertown. The area included a number of counterculture tearooms that became the focus of gay activity including: the Dil Pickle Club, a nonprofit institution that promoted arts, science and literature including a lecture by Magnus Hirschfield "In Defense of Homosexuality"; The Wind Blew Inn, a sex-oriented establishment run by a homosexual; and the Green Mask, run by a lesbian couple (de la Croix, 2012). In 1924 Henry Gerber established a very early homosexual rights organization called The Society for Human Rights in Old Town, but moved into Towertown in 1925.

Low cost property made homosexual behavior and homosexual commerce possible in Towertown, but Progressive Era social reform brought police activity to crack down on 'vice,' including raids of homosexual venues. Towertown became less of a gay cluster after the Green Mask was raided, but "The North Loop League turned it into a must-see tourist spot for visitors to the upcoming 1933 Century of Progress Exposition" marketed as a Latin Quarter (de la Croix, 2012). As gay presence declined, the image of the neighborhood was commodified as a spectacle that promoted the city for the Century of Progress fair. Henry Gerber, homosexual rights activist, was arrested for indecent behavior and Baugher (2001) suggests that although, "he [Gerber] was able to operate in relative obscurity in Old Town, he was far more visible closer to Chicago's Loop," in Towertown which may have led to his arrest.

Bronzeville

By the 1930s there were bathhouses and commercial establishments with female impersonators in the Towertown area (de la Croix, 2012), but Mumford (1997) observes that the vice reforms of the 1910s and their relaxation in the 1920s resulted in the movement of vice into black communities creating what he calls "Interzones" where black and white, homosexual and straight people mixed. Indeed Chicago's entertainment-oriented Bronzeville of the 1930s had a 'pansy craze' with female impersonators and balls similar to the ball scene in Harlem, New York City.

Near North

The Near North area of Chicago, particularly the intersection of Dearborn and Division Streets, became the dominant gay nightclub area from the mid-1940s until the mid-1960s and was nicknamed "Queerborn and Perversion" (de la Croix, 2012). Density increased from the 1940s to the 1970s and then decreased to just a few establishments in the 1990s. Piano bars, hotel bars, drag impression and a few lesbian bars were popular (de la Croix, 2012).

Governance shaping the area in the 1950s through the early 1970s was dominated by a combination of organized crime and police raids. Although Illinois had decriminalized sodomy by consenting adults in 1961, de la Croix describes a process by which organized crime and the police worked together to regulate bars and clubs catering to LGBTQ people:

> [It was] common knowledge the mob had a stake in Chicago's gay bars, and that police were shaking them down...This is how it worked: After a bar was targeted for shakedown, police visited several times in one evening, brandishing shotguns, checking the liquor license, and lining the customers up against a wall to check IDs. Later the owner was invited to join the "vice club" with a promise that harassment would end and police would "slant" reports of any trouble on the premises. Each bar paid upward of a hundred dollars a month, the money shared between vice cops, Captain Brasasch, and others at police headquarters. (de la Croix, 2012)

It is not clear at this point whether or not there was a conscious effort in City government to concentrate gay commercial activity in the area of Division and Dearborn, but it is a distinct possibility.

At the same time, urban planners shaped the Near North in ways that, probably incidentally, helped create opportunities for a thriving gay commercial area. The City of Chicago developed a comprehensive plan that was driven by a growth coalition seeking to concentrate the central business district in the Loop, controlling growth by bounding it with residential land uses to the north and south. Unlike many cities of the time that relied heavily on urban renewal to clear slums in the 1950s, 1960s and 1970s, Chicago planned a combination of urban renewal and community conservation (Hunt and DeVries, 2013). This plan and its related initiatives preserved much of the physical structure in the Near North, allowing rundown areas to serve as locations for gay bars and clubs. At the same time, urban renewal brought the development of Carl Sandburg Village, a mega-block residential project in the 1960s between Division Street and North Avenue between Clark and LaSalle Streets. This project displaced a Puerto Rican community creating plentiful moderately priced modern housing on the Near North that could provide housing for gay people and others who may have preferred to live in the Near North.

Boystown

In the 1970s, gay bars and clubs became more numerous and progressed north, particularly along Clark Street and Halsted Street. By the 1980s, (Figure 2.5) many of the gay bars were scattered around North Halsted Street in the Lakeview community that was to become known as Boystown. By the late 1980s, some bars had large windows opening to the street. By the 2000s (Figure 2.6) and into the early 2010s, most Boystown bars and clubs came to be located directly on North Halsted Street. Boystown closely fits the description of a gay neighborhood given by Ghaziani (2014) having gay symbols, events, residents and institutions. Among the many institutions is The Center on Halstead, a LGBTQ community center. In the 2010s, the Boystown commercial district remains busy despite perceptions that gay people are moving to other parts of the city (Ghaziani, 2014).

FIGURE 2.5   Boystown/North Halsted Street gay bars/clubs in the 1980s, Chicago, Illinois

Source: Compiled by author. Pre 1960 establishments from *Chicago Whispers* and *Damron Address Book* (aka *Damron Guide*).

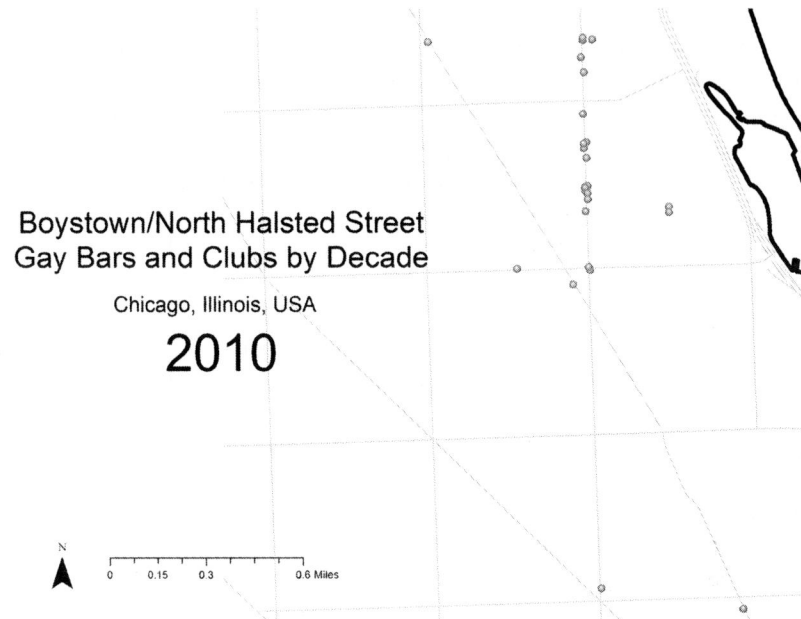

FIGURE 2.6   Boystown/North Halsted Street gay bars/clubs in the 2000s, Chicago, Illinois

Source: Compiled by author. Pre 1960 establishments from *Chicago Whispers* and *Damron Address Book* (aka *Damron Guide*).

The City of Chicago passed a non-discrimination ordinance in 1988 that, together with the earlier decriminalization of sodomy, set the stage for a reduced role for organized crime and for more prominently visible gay bars. In the 1970s and 1980s, many bars opened north of the Near North district in Lincoln Park and Lakeview. Why did bars in the Lincoln Park and Lakeview areas go from being fairly widely dispersed to being located mainly on North Halsted Street itself? It is likely that planning played an important role.

In 1997, planners created a streetscaping project on North Halsted Street that would mark it as gay including, "midblock commercial district identity columns with pride theme" (Chicago Department of Transportation, 1997). The project was initiated by the Mayor's office rather than by the community, very much in line with several other streetscaping projects in ethnic neighborhoods including a gateway to a largely Puerto Rican neighborhood that took the form of a Puerto Rican flag and a Chinese-themed gateway to Chinatown (Reed, 2003). The design specified that, "the columns rise from the street and climb to a graceful peak, and will contain colored rings which pay tribute to the gay and lesbian community and to the rainbow of diversity that has historically been the great strength of the Lakeview community" (Chicago Department of Transportation, 1997). The streetscaping plan was modified in response to community concerns that the plan would mark not just Halsted Street as gay, but also the intersecting neighborhood streets such as Roscoe and Buckingham (Chicago Department of Transportation, 1997; Reed, 2003). In a compromise, the pylons were reduced in number and planters with side-street names were added to the corners, marking borders between gay space and neighborhood residential space. Later, in 2012, the pylons were supplemented with memorials to LGBTQ figures by the nonprofit organization Legacy Project.

Andersonville

Soon after the North Halsted Street project was installed, it was clear that gay bars were becoming more numerous in the Andersonville area of Edgewater, particularly along Clark Street. Unlike Boystown, the Andersonville community does not have public or nonprofit infrastructure that marks it as gay. It is attractively streetscaped, but signifiers emphasize the Swedish character of the community's history. This is noteworthy because there is no particular Swedish ethnic enclave, although there are Swedish-oriented commercial establishments. Some commercial establishments do display gay flags.

In what way have planning and other forms of governance shaped the Andersonville gay commercial district? The government-installed streetscaping does not mark the area as gay. Nor does the Chamber of Commerce mark the area as gay, although its website does note that the area is diverse, including gay people along with people who have other identities. Anecdotally, housing prices became quite high in Boystown and LGBTQ people who were priced out moved north into Andersonville. Gay bars and clubs may have followed LGBTQ residents to Andersonville, or residents may have followed gay bars and clubs. This is worth further investigation. It is interesting to note that the northerly progression of gay bars and clubs largely skipped over the low-income Uptown neighborhood just to the north of Boystown and to the south of Andersonville. The Alderman for the Uptown area publicly sought to limit gentrification in the area during the 1990s, which may have made his district less attractive to gay pioneers who sought to build capital through housing, and perhaps explain why the area did not develop a large gay commercial district.

Summary

From this analysis it is clear that Chicago gay commercial districts have moved northward over the course of the 20th century. Analysis of a single space at one point in time, or even a single space over time, would have failed to capture the story of Chicago's gay commercial districts. Governance structures associated with each area were different, moving from the Progressive Era vice police in the 1910s and 1920s, to organized crime in collaboration with policing in the 1940s though the 1960s, and to decriminalization and antidiscrimination protections in the 1970s and 1980s. In the 1990s, the creation of a City-initiated streetscape marked

Boystown as a gay commercial space in a way that was consistent with the tourism-orientation of Chicago planning at the time. By the 2000s there was further development of a commercial district in Andersonville, north of the now reified Boystown. Unlike Boystown, Andersonville did not have a formal government sanction as a gay space.

There are a number of limitations to this overview of gay commercial spaces over time. First, there is much room for more detailed historical analysis of the changes in gay commercial districts in each period and of the role of planning in each period. Second, this work is based on analysis of a single large city in the United States. Third, it is unlikely that all gay bars and clubs were captured for the analysis. Fourth, the study has not captured adequately distinctions among commercial establishments and districts for subgroups within the LGBTQ community. Fifth, electronic spaces such as Grinder or Manhunt may have played a role in shaping recent gay commercial space that is not considered here.

Implications for Planning

This study has a number of implications for the practice of planning for LGBTQ communities.

1. *Plan for movement of gay space.* Gay commercial districts should not be planned as single places, but should be understood within the context of an historical system of gay commercial districts. The development of Andersonville may have served those who were priced out of the Boystown area. Planners might consciously shape future districts to serve LGBTQ groups that are least well served by existing gay commercial districts.

2. *Commemorate gay spaces.* As gay commercial establishments become less prevalent in districts such as the Near North or Bronzeville, it may be useful to include markers of gay histories for current and future generations. Some have questioned the utility of gay-oriented streetscaping in Boystown when gay populations may be moving out of the area, but these markers help gay Chicagoans and tourists alike find this gay commercial district, which might otherwise be open to the initiated only. It is yet to be seen whether the gay-oriented streetscaping will maintain the districts' gay identity.

3. *Plan for LGBTQ communities even when economic development is not at stake.* In all the iterations of Chicago's gay commercial space we saw evidence of direct planning intervention in LGBTQ issues in only one case—Boystown. Bell and Binnie's (2004) entrepreneurial neoliberalism concepts do an excellent job of explaining the strong role of planning in marking Boystown as gay during a period when Chicago prepared to compete in a global market where creative class development policies had begun to circulate. Given willingness to plan for queer space in Boystown, one might have expected planners to do the same for Andersonville, but they did not. Andersonville is marked as a diverse district, but not a gay district. Perhaps Boystown had already fulfilled the

economic-developed-related need for Chicago to have an image of diversity. It is possible that Andersonville's image as *diverse* rather than *gay* allows the district to meet the needs of a range of nonconforming LGBTQ groups, but there is no evidence that this was the intent.

4. *Understand both planning's limitations and potential in shaping gay commercial districts.* Non-planning governance mechanisms such as the police and mobs played central roles in shaping early gay commercial districts. The decriminalization of sodomy and the non-discrimination ordinance, both beyond the traditional scope of planning, allowed gay commercial districts to expand and move out of the Near North in the 1970s and 1980s. But planning has played a role in shaping gay commercial spaces, both inadvertently and purposively. Neighborhood conservation and urban renewal policies may have helped shape the Near North gay commercial district, even though it was unlikely that this was the intent. Gay streetscaping in Boystown may have intentionally helped focus gay bars and clubs directly onto North Halsted Street and correspondingly mark areas surrounding North Halsted Street as less gay. Even with the lack of LGBTQ-specific planning, Andersonville developed as a gay commercial district serving those priced out of Boystown.

Planning's role in serving LGBTQ people can and should be further developed though conscious attention to the dynamics of gay commercial districts.

Note

1 Thank you to research assistant Jim Brown for assistance with data entry and geocoding, to Nina Savar for assistance with geographical information systems and to Damron Publishing for access to early versions of the Damron Guide.

References

Baugher, S. (2001). *Hidden History of Old Town*. Charleston, SC: History Press.

Bell, D., & Binnie, J. (2004). Authenticating queer space: Citizenship, urbanism and governance. *Urban Studies, 41*(9), 1807–1820.

Binnie, J., & Skeggs, B. (2004). Cosmopolitan knowledge and the production and consumption of sexualized space: Manchester's gay village. *The Sociological Review, 52*(1), 39–61.

Black, D., Gates, G., Sanders, S., and Taylor, L. (2002). Why do gay men live in San Francisco? *Journal of Urban Economics, 51*(1), 54–76.

Brown, M. (2013). Gender and sexuality II: There goes the gayborhood? *Progress in Human Geography.* Published online April 29, 2013. DOI: 10.1177/0309132513484215.

Castells, M., & Murphy, K. (1982). Cultural identity and urban structure: The spatial organization of San Francisco's gay community. *Urban policy under capitalism*, 237–259.

Chapman, T. (2011). Queering the political-economy: Anti-discrimination law and the urban regime in Orlando, Florida, in P. Doan (ed.) *Queerying planning: Challenging heteronormative assumptions and reframing planning practice*. Farnham, UK: Ashgate. 145–155.

Chauncey, G. (1994). *Gay New York: Gender, urban culture, and the making of the gay male world, 1890–1940*. New York: Basic Books.

Chicago Department of Transportation, City of Chicago (1997). North Halsted Streetscape: Project Description and Concept Design. November 11.

Collins, A. (2004). Sexual dissidence, enterprise and assimilation: Bedfellows in urban regeneration. *Urban Studies*, *41*(9), 1789–1806.

de la Croix, S. (2012). Chicago whispers: A history of LGBTQ Chicago before Stonewall. Madison, WI: The University of Wisconsin Press.

D'Emilio, J., & Freedman, E.B. (2012). *Intimate matters: A history of sexuality in America*. Chicago, IL: University of Chicago Press.

Doan, P. (2011). Why question planning assumptions about queer space? *Queerying planning: Challenging heteronormative assumptions and reframing planning practice*, Farnham, UK: Ashgate. 1–27.

Doan, P., & Higgins, H. (2011). The demise of queer space? Resurgent gentrification and the assimilation of LGBTQ neighborhoods. *Journal of Planning Education and Research*, *31*(1), 6–25.

Florida, R. (2004). The rise of the creative class and how it's transforming work, leisure, community and everyday life (Paperback edn.). New York: Basic Books.

Forsyth, A. (2001). Nonconformist populations and planning sexuality and space: Nonconformist populations and planning practice. *Journal of Planning Literature*, *15*(3), 339–358.

Forsyth, A. (2011). Queering planning practice: Understanding non-conformist populations, in P. Doan (ed.) *Queerying planning: Challenging heteronormative assumptions and reframing planning practice*. Farnham, UK: Ashgate. 21–51.

Frisch, M. (2002). Planning as a heterosexist project. *Journal of Planning Education and Research*, *21*(3), 254–266.

Ghaziani, A. (2014). Measuring urban sexual cultures. *Theory and Society*, 1–23.

Gorman-Murray, A. (2011). Queering Planning in Australia: The Problems and Possibilities of Multiscalar Governance for LGBTQ Sexual Minorities. In P. Doan (ed.) *Queerying planning: Challenging heteronormative assumptions and reframing planning practice*, 129–143.

Hughes, H. L. (2003). Marketing gay tourism in Manchester: New market for urban tourism or destruction of 'gay space'? *Journal of Vacation Marketing*, *9*(2), 152–163.

Hunt, B., & DeVries, J. (2013) *Planning Chicago*. Chicago, IL: American Planning Association Planners Press.

Lauria, M., & Knopp, L. (1985). Toward an analysis of the role of gay communities in the urban renaissance. *Urban Geography*, *6*(2), 152–169.

Lewis, N.M. (2013). Ottawa's Le/The Village: Creating a 'gaybourhood' amidst the death of the village. *Geoforum*, 49: 233–242.

Markwell, K. (2002). Mardi Gras tourism and the construction of Sydney as an international gay and lesbian city. *GLQ: a journal of lesbian and gay studies*, *8*(1), 81–99.

Mumford, K.J. (1997). *Interzones: Black/white sex districts in Chicago and New York in the early twentieth century*. New York: Columbia University Press.

Myrdahl, T. (2011). Queering creative cities, in P. Doan (ed.) *Queerying planning: Challenging heteronormative assumptions and reframing planning practice*. Farnham, UK: Ashgate. 157–166.

Nash, C. J. (2006). Toronto's gay village (1969–1982): Plotting the politics of gay identity. *The Canadian Geographer/Le Géographe canadien*, *50*(1), 1–16.

Podmore, J. (2013). Critical commentary: Sexualities landscapes beyond homonormativity. *Geoforum,* 49: 263–257.

Prior, J., & Crofts, P. (2011) Queering urban governance: The emergence of sex industry premises into the planned city, in P. Doan (ed.) *Queerying planning: Challenging heteronormative assumptions and reframing planning practice.* Farnham, UK: Ashgate. 184–208.

Reed, C. (2003). We're from Oz: Marking ethnic and sexual identity in Chicago. *Environment and Planning D, 21*(4), 425–440.

Ruting, B. (2008). Economic Transformations of Gay Urban Spaces: Revisiting Collins' evolutionary gay district model. *Australian Geographer, 39*(3), 259–269.

Sibalis, M. (2004). Urban space and homosexuality: the example of the Marais, Paris "Gay Ghetto". *Urban Studies, 41*(9), 1739–1758.

3

THE DALLAS WAY

Property, Politics, and Assimilation

Andrew H. Whittemore

Introduction

At the opening of a 2000 television documentary made by Dallas' KERA, "Finding Our Voice," an interviewee jests that in Dallas the chant for LGBT equality should be longer than the national standard: "We're here, we're queer, we work, we pay our taxes, we keep our yards up" (KERA 2000). According to historian Michael Bronski, American LGBT people, along with other minorities, have continually sought acceptance by downplaying differences and saying we are "just like you" (Bronski 2011, 241). Bronski argues that this assimilationist strand of LGBT politics is apparent in high-profile struggles such as that for participation in the very traditional institution of marriage (Bronski 2011, 242). However the effort to be "just like" is not only waged on such a visible front. This chapter discusses the assimilationist practices of property enhancement and related neighborhood activism by LGBT Dallasites, and the repercussions of this activity for LGBT neighborhoods and rights.

Of course property enhancement and neighborhood politics are not in themselves LGBT activism, but in Dallas, where the LGBT community has historically been non-confrontational, they may have been a dominant mechanism of assimilation. That this mechanism has been overwhelmingly of an assimilationist, as opposed to a liberationist orientation, is obvious: that property enhancement and neighborhood activism has any association with LGBT politics is only based on the coincidence that their perpetrators are openly LGBT. The channeling of LGBT advancement through such conventional activities is a point of pride among major historical figures in the city's LGBT community, who call their path to assimilation "The Dallas Way," a "struggle" plainly "unlike the ones on the east and west coasts."[1] Even then, the LGBT movement in Dallas was not without its liberationists, running for Council on gay rights platforms or confronting the assimilationist mainstream in zoning feuds over gay clubs.

While the LGBT community of Dallas is currently in the midst of a history building project (www.thedallasway.org), the historical record of LGBT Dallas is best maintained in the archives of the city's LGBT paper, the *Dallas Voice*. This chapter is for the most part based on the review of this publication. Aside from the *Voice* the findings of this chapter are also dependent on interviews with prominent local LGBT political figures and activists of the past four decades, some previously recorded interviews conducted by others, and other media sources.

"The Dallas Way" may have been tailored to the city's situation in the Bible Belt, but given that Dallas is not the only city where such non-confrontational processes as property enhancement and neighborhood activism by LGBT households have taken place, there is probably a bit of "The Dallas Way" everywhere. The collusion of LGBT assimilation with such conventional practices does have its disadvantages. Insofar as LGBT assimilation is pioneered by those privileged enough to acquire and enhance property, this form of assimilation can leave the needs of those less fortunate, whether non-males, minorities or youths, of secondary concern, and indeed ignore a continuing, general desire for camaraderie within the LGBT community (Pew Research 2013).

The Materialist Dimension of LGBT Assimilation

Thirty years ago Manual Castells discussed property enhancement by gay male households as the infiltration of conventional market processes into spaces otherwise appreciated by LGBT communities for their use value (Castells 1983, 166–167). As a result he feared that gay communities would forget the social value of their spaces, cash in on their market value and self-destruct before they could achieve the larger task of wider cultural transformation (Castells 1983, 168).

However, missing from Castells' interpretation was the role of property enhancement and other forms of participation in market accumulation by LGBT people in the acceptance of a LGBT community. LGBT enhancement of exchange value represents participation with the mainstream in capital accumulation, a venture that American consciousness holds in high esteem. In spite of the flight of heterosexual families from the Castro, for example, property values increased in the area by five times in the 1970s (Godfrey 1988, 121), which I would argue sets the stage for assimilation in a society highly preoccupied with accumulation. In the act of property revitalization, gay homeowners forged a "cross-cultural alliance" with their heterosexual counterparts based on mutual class interests (Knopp 1990, 337).

The market itself may not create or diminish rights, but the process of being out and having a market impact may do just that in a liberal democracy where law favors those with economic privilege, whoever they may be (Chasin 2000). Lisa Penaloza observed that "Marketing to gays and lesbians serves to legitimize them in the U.S. as individuals *and* as members of a subculture" (italics added, Penaloza 1996, 33).

In this way gay communities may be quite unlike the ethnic enclaves to which Stephen Murray (1979) and others since have compared them: whereas traditional ethnic enclaves have been sites of social and political empowerment in spite of their isolation from market investment, gay enclaves have been sites of social and political empowerment in part via their participation in the wider market. Lawrence Knopp has noted: "more so than most other minority groups in the city (e.g., blacks, native Americans, Hispanics), gay community activists' use-value objectives do not necessarily conflict with other's interest in exchange values" (1990, 338).

Where does this leave LGBT households not privileged enough to participate in property ownership and enhancement? Knopp concluded: "The perpetuation of male economic privilege within the context of the gay community's influence on a land market is … a testament to the resilience of male social dominance" (Knopp 1990, 349). Lesbians too, it is worth noting, have been gentrifiers, if "marginally" (Rothenberg 1995). But undoubtedly this has been an endeavor dominated by gay economically privileged white men.

Furthermore, the role of LGBT households in the property market, important to assimilation as it is, may only be transient. Neighborhoods refurbished by LGBT sweat equity gain appeal to a second generation of mostly heterosexual gentrifying urban professionals capable of paying higher rents (Doan and Higgins 2011). Planning is often a partner in this process of heterosexual gentrification, facilitating corporate investment in redevelopment and remaining silent on LGBT contributions to these areas at the same time redevelopment leverages them (Collins 2004; Doan and Higgins 2011).

Significantly, many LGBT households express a preference for living in traditional, visibly gay neighborhoods (Ghaziani 2010), and Doan and Higgins (2011) suggest this longing may be strongest among the young and poor. Doan and Higgins questioned if long-term, mostly white LGBT property owners of traditional gay neighborhoods had chosen "to ignore certain aspects of the gay liberation political agenda in exchange for economic integration," echoing Castells' (1983, 168) concern of thirty years prior.

A Visible Community and a Stymied Movement

Big business and growth machine politics form the famous backdrop for North Texas' fantastic pace of urbanization. One dimension of rapid growth is great diversity fueled by domestic and international immigration. LGBT people in Dallas have gone from relatively recent invisibility to composing the largest metropolitan LGBT population in the South after Washington (Gates 2006, 7). Prior to the 1960s there were known bars and cruising spots in various central Dallas neighborhoods,[2] but by the 1970s gay life in the city became focused on Oak Lawn and in particular the Cedar Springs Road "strip" north of Turtle Creek Boulevard, where several bars and gay-owned businesses were concentrated (see Figure 3.1).[3]

The area was multi-ethnic, featured many cheap subdivided mansions and apartment houses, an entertainment district, and the wholesale trade centers along

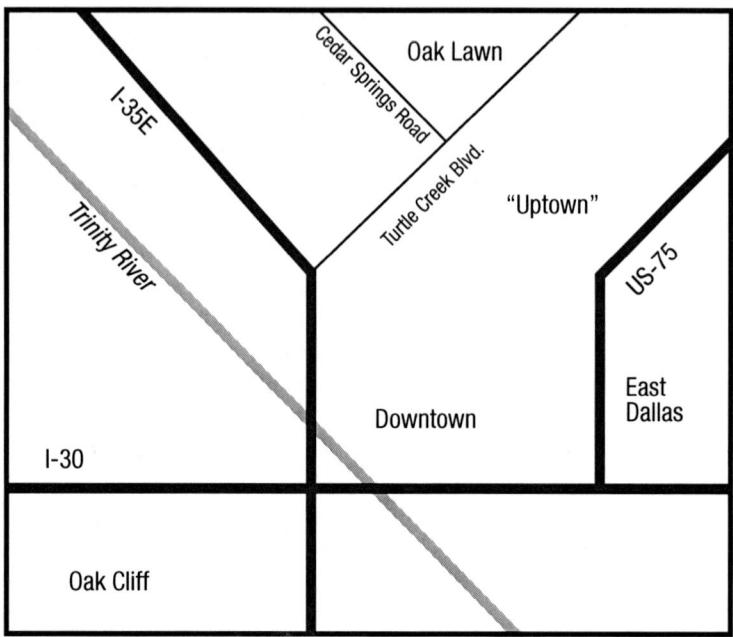

FIGURE 3.1 Map of central Dallas

a stretch of I-35E north of downtown that brought retail professionals to Dallas from around the country. Rental discrimination against gays was flagrant here early on, manifested in "No Queers" signs in the 1970s, and evident into at least the mid-1980s.[4] Even here, gay residents did not feel particularly safe into the 1990s,[5] and law enforcement was compromised by the hesitancy of closeted men and women to report being victims of crime in the city's gay neighborhood.[6] Non-LGBT businesses were also very slow to adapt to the neighborhood's identity: the local chain grocery store refused to sell the *Dallas Voice* well into the 1980s.[7]

The political history of LGBT Dallas begins in 1964, with the meeting of a "Circle of Friends."[8] One outgrowth of this group was the 1970 founding of a Dallas congregation of the Metropolitan Community Church, a California-based church with a primary mission to gay people (Mims 2006, 4). Membership grew to over a hundred in the 1970s, to over 500 by 1985[9] and over 1,200 by 1994, by which point it was billing itself as the world's largest gay congregation.[10] The organizational spirit begun with the Circle of Friends produced a pride parade in 1972, and activists founded the Dallas Gay Political Caucus (DGPC) in 1977.

A debate existed among activists and within the wider community as to whether or not challenging issues such as employment discrimination and violence against gays was worth the controversy.[11] Despite, or perhaps due to, ongoing rejection by mainstream society in the form of discrimination and violence, only worsened by the onset of the AIDS epidemic, Dallas gays and lesbians remained dedicated to fitting in as much as possible. The conservative tone of Texas politics was also undoubtedly a factor: according to activist Louise Young, the notion of achieving equality "The Dallas Way" originated in the late 1970s when DGPC president Steve Wilkins urged fellow activists to wear pin-striped suits, wing-tipped shoes and carry briefcases (Young 2012, personal interview with author).

Young and her fellow activists focused on the election of openly gay, Democratic, precinct chairs to establish a presence of gay people in the Texas Democratic Party. The most significant goal related to this strategy was the overturn, by act of the legislature, of the state sodomy law,[12] a consistent basis for discrimination against and harassment of gay people in the state. Already by 1980 LGBT activists had "fortified" Oak Lawn's precinct chairs, all of whom were now Democratic and most of whom were openly gay, through the mobilization of the LGBT vote (Young 2012, personal interview with author).

Bill Nelson, "through and through a gay activist" in Young's view (2012, personal interview), was in 1985 the second openly LGBT candidate to run for City Council (the first was MCC reverend James Harris in 1978[13]). A nondiscrimination ordinance was central to his platform. Nelson was the first with any significant support outside of the LGBT community because he was also a neighborhood activist. He was the president of the Vickery Place Neighborhood Association in an area a mile to the northeast of Oak Lawn, and he gained the endorsement of the Dallas Homeowners' League. The Homeowners' League was likely the first citywide civic organization to ally itself with the LGBT community, not only supporting Nelson in 1985 but two years later criticizing City Council's actions to deny gay nominees to city boards.[14] Although Nelson was very vocal about homeowner issues, he openly criticized those gays in politics who "would rather stress their concern for economic or neighborhood issues" when it came to their priorities.[15] This may have been his error as far as being elected was concerned. Although Nelson lost, the Oak Lawn community gained an ally in Councilwoman Lori Palmer, who fought redistricting schemes for the area she argued would "dilute" the gay voice in City Hall.[16]

The origin of mainstream support for the LGBT community in the Homeowners' League was telling of the extent to which LGBT households had already permeated the property market and homeowner activism in and around Oak Lawn, despite the difficulty that unmarried LGBT couples experienced in establishing co-ownership of property. Aid to the community in homebuying was slow to come: the *Voice* began publishing financial advice for homebuyers beginning in 1987,[17] and gay and lesbian realtors began to develop businesses oriented to the needs of their own community in the first half of the 1990s.[18]

Evidence of LGBT households' geographic distribution was evident in the advertisements published in the *Voice* for rental and for-sale properties. Renters gravitated to Oak Lawn, and buyers gravitated to the nearby streetcar suburbs of East Dallas and Oak Cliff. Advertisements for rental properties were often sexualized, and those concerning for-sale properties, mostly in Oak Cliff, began appearing in the *Voice* in 1988, and stressed architectural details such as hardwood floors and stained glass windows,[19] or simply that Oak Cliff was "the trend."[20] LGBT households valued Oak Cliff along with some East Dallas neighborhoods because it offered architecturally unique single-family homes in proximity to downtown and Oak Lawn, at lower prices than could be found in Oak Lawn's few small single-family enclaves. Oak Cliff also had some appeal as a quiet alternative to Oak Lawn, a place where stereotypes of LGBT households as party and sex-focused "went away."[21]

For-sale homes in other areas of Dallas or the suburbs were not advertised in the *Voice* until 1992. Some of these advertisements had a jocular quality to them, using the cliché "We're Everywhere!" in promoting living beyond the established territories.[22] Oak Lawn had limited homeownership opportunities outside of small single-family enclaves, but in the condominium and townhome construction boom of the 1990s[23] this quickly changed.[24]

Now the property interests of Oak Lawn homeowners began to come into conflict with the use value of the neighborhood embedded within its status as an LGBT entertainment district. A 1991 zoning feud pitted LGBT Oak Lawn homeowners and their City Hall allies against less networked LGBT entertainment venues and their patrons. The conflict represented a short-term assertion of liberationist politics in the face of an assimilationist trend propelled by the presence of LGBT homeowners in wider civic discourse. The influence of Oak Lawn homeowners was enshrined in 1982's Oak Lawn Special Purpose District, which assured that new development in the neighborhood offered ample landscaping, upper-story setbacks, and off-street parking. City Hall created a neighborhood association, the Oak Lawn Committee, to steward the district, and it has historically had gay leadership.

The Oak Lawn Committee has remained especially vigilant about maintaining an adequate supply of off-street parking for new residences and businesses, which placed them in conflict with bars and their patrons. In 1991 Council proposed legislation allowing the city to revoke bars' and clubs' permits in the district if they could not demonstrate their ability to accommodate guest parking every two years, even as new venues increased the burden on shared parking areas. Bar owners accused City Council's gay rights advocate, Lori Palmer, and the Oak Lawn Committee of anti-gay bias.[25] Bar owners gathered 10,000 signatures from patrons, and organized an Oak Lawn Concerned Citizens Coalition (OLCCC) voicing concern over "serious lack of communication between established citizens' groups … and the majority of the residents and business owners in Oak Lawn."[26] In the end, legislators agreed to accept club-owners' "best efforts" as warranting a permit.[27]

The OLCCC argued it represented majority interests in the LGBT community, which were not those, in its feeling, of the homeowner-dominated Oak Lawn Committee. Taking the focus away from parking, the OLCCC organized a neighborhood crime watch in 1992 as a means of taking control of community safety from a City Hall it viewed as oblivious to the issue.[28] At the time, violent crime in Oak Lawn's gay entertainment district was higher than in the city's other nightlife areas.[29] Within a few months of the OLCCC's organization, police established a "zero tolerance" policy toward crimes targeting gay men in Oak Lawn parks.[30] Having had success in its efforts to stem crime and preserve Oak Lawn's night life, the OLCCC faded from the scene. Although the Oak Lawn Committee has remained vigilant in demanding parking for new residential developments in the area, often in excess of requirements, the bars and their weekend traffic have become an accepted feature of Oak Lawn life.

The Dallas Way

It was ultimately homeowner politics, not liberationist politics, that would bring basic protections to Dallas' LGBT population. In 1991 a judge increased minority access to City Council by ordering the number of single-member districts to expand from eight to fourteen (Cloud 2007). Leaders of neighborhood and business associations of all ethnicities and orientations suddenly found themselves to be bigger fish in smaller ponds. It was a watershed moment for LGBT advancement (Luna 2012, personal interview with author).

In 1993, openly gay Craig McDaniel won Council District 14, a district covering half of Oak Lawn and many adjacent neighborhoods, on his record of service to his neighborhood association, and the City via his appointment on various planning boards and commissions. The *Voice* barely mentioned his campaign in the run-up to the election, instead focusing on an ultimately unsuccessful Oak Cliff candidate endorsed by gay political groups.[31] McDaniel stated to the author: "I didn't get involved in city politics because I was gay ... my focus was on things like neighborhood development and improving city services." But, he added that "Just by being there and being known as openly gay and being accessible to my colleagues on the Council, it removed a lot of the unknown." McDaniel argues it was his and others' conventional interactions with heterosexuals—as neighbors, colleagues, and representatives—that advanced the cause of LGBT people in Dallas.[32] He summarized: "I understand that in some cities it could be seen as something less than bold, but that's not the way we ever achieved our clout" (McDaniel 2012, personal interview with author). Councilman Chris Luna, closeted upon his first election in 1991 but out before his 1995 re-election, similarly explained to the author that in Dallas the basis of the LGBT movement was "a homeowners association, a neighborhood crime watch, a business association" (Luna 2012, personal interview with author).

With Luna's coming out Dallas had two openly gay Councilmen. With this presence in Council, the City in 1995 passed an ordinance forbidding employment discrimination against city employees[33] after decades of firings and denied applications, especially on the police force. By 1996 there were around thirty LGBT individuals serving in appointed positions, composing 10% of total appointees.[34] The victories of McDaniel and Luna paved the way for candidates more explicitly concerned with LGBT issues: in 1997 John Loza succeeded Luna in the District 2 seat saying he wished to sustain an "unprecedented sense of access to city government" for gay Dallasites.[35] A gay constable was appointed to head the

Oak Lawn precinct in 2001.[36] Ed Oakley, founder of the defunct OLCCC, joined a re-elected Loza in 2001.[37] With this weight on City Council the City passed a citywide nondiscrimination ordinance that went into effect in October of 2002.[38] Ten of fifteen Councilmembers walked in the 2003 pride parade.[39] Voters elected out lesbian Lupe Valdez as Dallas County Sheriff in 2004 and she has retained that office since. In 2004 Dallas introduced benefits for domestic partners of city employees.[40]

These accomplishments mirrored a wider trend in the civic life of the city involving the rise of LGBT people to prominent positions in the arts especially.[41] By 2001 organizations including Preservation Dallas, Friends of Fair Park, the Sixth Floor Museum, the Shakespeare Festival of Dallas, and the Texas International Theatrical Arts Society all had LGBT leadership.[42] The *Dallas Morning News* covered the local LGBT community's celebration of National Coming Out Day for the first time in 2002, a first for any major news publication in Texas.[43] The openly gay president of the Oak Lawn Committee ascended to the City Plan Commission in 2001, where he remained until 2009.[44]

Even when LGBT candidates were not in elections, the role of LGBT voters had clearly been established. LGBT-supported Laura Miller, an Oak Cliff councilwoman, stated "North Oak Cliff is strong and valuable and fabulous for one reason—the gay community found a beautiful neighborhood and came in and fixed this neighborhood up."[45] Miller was elected mayor in 2002, an event celebrated by the *Voice* as demonstrative of LGBT "muscle."[46] In 2009, a year in which there were no LGBT people on City Council after fourteen consecutive years of there being at least one,[47] Oakley said it spoke volumes that he considered LGBT people to still be spoken for.[48]

While at the same time the proportion of LGBT-led households in established enclaves like North Oak Cliff rose to a third or a half in local realtors' estimates,[49] many LGBT households were feeling less drawn to traditional residential clusters. By the early 2000s, largely due to the work of a lesbian realtor, Lory Masters, Northwest Dallas featured a growing number of LGBT homeowners. Steering an ethnic minority in such a fashion may be a questionable if not illegal practice, but this simply reflected that LGBT households in their spread from traditional enclaves continued to prefer each other's presence. Northwest Dallas was however different from traditional enclaves because, unlike Oak Lawn, East Dallas, or Oak Cliff, it consisted largely of 1960s tract development, and has never hosted the commercial or entertainment institutions that underpin traditional gayborhoods. LGBT households at the time were beginning to describe mainstream businesses as places they felt comfortable, leaving the bookstores and bars catering to them behind.[50] Indeed national chains were also making inroads on the Cedar Springs strip.[51] While a concentration of LGBT households has developed in Northwest Dallas, honorably dubbed "Loryland," it is not composed of households seeking safety or liberation, as much as the conventional security of suburban life, or "inner city flight" as another realtor called it.[52]

Beyond Dallas, LGBT households and businesses were leading the renewal of suburban Carrollton's downtown in the 2000s.[53] LGBT people formed "part of the general population flow"[54] into suburban Collin County, twenty miles north of downtown, where they founded a Gay and Lesbian Alliance in 2003. Rather than being concentrated, Collin County LGBT households seemed "scattered all over the place."[55] According to the *Advocate*, out of the one-hundred largest cities in the United States, Collin County's largest city Plano moved from ninety-eighth to sixteenth place in the number of same-sex households per thousand households between 2000 and 2006 (Graham 2008). Plano realtors responded to the *Advocate* piece by posting advertisements in the *Voice* citing the article and proclaiming "Move to Plano!"[56]

Reflecting the diaspora, LGBT business owners, previously only prominent in some local Oak Lawn organizations, founded a regional Chamber of Commerce in 2005.[57] The Gay and Lesbian Fund for Dallas meanwhile described the targets of its donations to be "scattered out all over the Metroplex."[58] If homebuyers feel a level of comfort in the suburbs or less LGBT-dominated urban neighborhoods, it follows that renters feel comfortable there too. Dallas activist Phil Johnson spoke of all LGBT households when he said they are less cohesive because they "don't need to be." (Flick 2007)[59]

Elsewhere, however, LGBT households formed new enclaves. In Fort Worth, LGBT enclaves were developing by the early 2000s in disinvested areas on the south and east sides.[60] LGBT enclaves were also developing in tandem with heterosexual gentrification, for instance in the "M Streets" neighborhood of East Dallas.[61] Oak Lawn's zip code held the highest number of same-sex households of any in Texas in 2000, but this number composed only 7% of the metropolitan total number of same-sex households.[62]

The trend toward homeownership, at least among the *Voice* readership, has been fast and indicates the extent to which at least a disproportionately male, white, educated segment of the LGBT population has moved toward reflecting the economic characteristics of their straight counterparts. A 1996 *Voice* survey found homeownership at 42%—among a population that was 83% male, 88% white, and among which 56% had completed college.[63] The contemporary readership profile indicates that 66% of readers own their primary residence (*Dallas Voice* Readership at a Glance 2012[64]). Whether non-white LGBT households had a significant role in these trends is unclear. LGBT Latinos, though prominent in politics as evidenced by the successes of Luna, Loza, and Valdez, have faced more difficult circumstances. A 2005 survey estimated 2,500 same-sex Latino couples to be living in the metropolitan area, who on average were living on $25,000 less than white LGBT couples, and were three times more likely to be raising a child.[65] Insofar as the gay rights movement in Dallas has been couched in an affinity between white middle-class heterosexual property activists and their counterparts, the "Dallas Way" may be a movement of limited potential.

There Goes the Gayborhood?

The work of activists, LGBT businesses and households in improving the physical environment of Oak Lawn and other neighborhoods not only translated into political gains, but the appeal of these spaces to a wider variety of users. In the 2000s fears of heterosexual gentrification arose in Oak Lawn.[66] Heterosexuals were willing to move into new developments in Oak Lawn, especially south of the Cedar Springs strip toward downtown. They did not however believe themselves to be moving to Oak Lawn: realtors, local businesses and developers pursued the purposeful disassociation of the southern portion of Oak Lawn in the 2000s, branding that portion of the neighborhood as "Uptown" in the 2000s. In the opinion of Oak Lawn Committee treasurer Mike Milliken those interested in this transformation "don't know the history of the area and they don't want to know it."[67]

LGBT persons of all backgrounds now faced the prospect that their traditional enclaves would no longer be available. By the late 1990s, long-time gay business owners found themselves being displaced by rising rents around the Cedar Springs strip,[68] and national chain stores began tearing down and redeveloping previously gay-owned commercial properties.[69] After the strip's gay bookstore and leather shop closed in 2007, the Cedar Springs Merchants Association voiced its plans to pursue a vaguely alternative, more widely accessible "eclecticism" on the strip.[70]

Long-time residents welcomed some changes: the Cedar Springs area dropped from third to seventh on the city's list of high-crime areas in the 2000s.[71] Some were resigned to a more mainstream future for Oak Lawn. One long-time resident explained: "People have a right to make their communities look the way they want. …people who are buying in now—it's theirs."[72]

That Oak Lawn has been changing is undoubted, but it may not be becoming "straighter" as much as continuing on a decades-long path toward gentrification by upper-income LGBT and heterosexual households alike,[73] losing cultural diversity and therein perhaps the appearance of queerness. It will remain the case that "gays are an affinity group,"[74] as one *Voice* journalist noted. LGBT people will therefore continue to demand some number of institutions, businesses, and even residences that may mutually benefit from proximity to one another, as recent Pew research has shown (2013). While some cities, Chicago and Philadelphia among them,[75] may have seen merit in public expenditure on gayborhood branding, in Dallas such improvements have remained in private hands, and with eclectic results. While the Cedar Springs Merchant Association has pursued conventional improvements including street trees and improved lighting,[76] the Oak Lawn Committee and the local Legacy of Love endowment supporting those living with HIV/AIDS pursued the construction of a monumental pillar at the neighborhood's principal intersection, at the base of which is emblazoned "Oak Lawn: A Legacy of Love" (see Figure 3.2). When a Subway franchise moved on the Cedar Springs strip, it was "gayed up"[77] by the owner with granite countertops and black vessel top-mounted bowl sinks in the restrooms.

FIGURE 3.2   Oak Lawn's Legacy of Love monument, dedicated 2006

In 2010, Oak Lawn's zip code, according to preliminary analysis of 2010 census data by on-line real estate site Trulia, remained the "gayest" neighborhood in Texas (and eighth in the country), in terms of the proportion of households composed of two men.[78] As two gay bars closed in 2009, prompting announcements that such institutions were set to "die off," two others opened.[79]

The city's LGBT center, the Dallas Resource Center, is currently in the process of building a larger facility in Oak Lawn and diversifying its mission to have a greater focus on youth and family programs in addition to maintaining its traditional focus on health.[80]

Oak Lawn is seeing significant redevelopment as Dallas recovers from the recession of the late 2000s. Developers are razing older two-story apartment buildings and replacing them with four to five story apartment buildings, cashing in on the appeal of urban living for young singles and childless couples, both LGBT and straight. The homeowner dominated Oak Lawn Committee, which stewards development in the area, has been content to support changes to zoning that allow developers to reap profits in light of increasing land values.[81] The maintenance of existing affordable housing, or the creation of new affordable housing stock has so far not been a priority of the current crop of Oak Lawn community activists. As property owners they stand to benefit from increased market investment, and the city's planners, following the Dallas Comprehensive Plan's general recommendation for more housing (Dallas 2006, II-1-14), support upzoning in the area without attention to the type of new housing being built.[82]

One national developer, the Crosland Group, has seen an opportunity in the area's gay identity, and in 2008 constructed a multi-use full-block development along the Cedar Springs strip, the Ilume, to be explicitly marketed to gay men. For example, the *Voice*-rewarded title of "Gayest apartment complex 2012" is one that the Ilume's management "wears proudly" according to its website.[83] Crosland summarized its case for such an unconventional corporate product saying that the pride parade, aside from the Cotton Bowl and the state fair, was where the most people in Dallas could be found at one time.[84] In 2009 Crosland gave one of the ground-floor retail spaces to the regional GLBT Chamber "as part of an overall commitment to the district."[85] In 2012 Crosland began construction on a second rental property of 559 units, also located on Cedar Springs, the second of sixteen slated for gayborhoods around the country.[86] Such developments, while they may conserve the gay orientation of the Cedar Springs strip, are in the minority of area development. New developments, gay-oriented or not, all capture high rents and replace older, more affordable housing stock attractive to lower-income LGBT people, those perhaps feeling the greatest need for a cohesive LGBT neighborhood (Doan and Higgins 2011).

Conclusion

There have been immense changes in the conditions of LGBT people in Dallas over the last forty years. An evaluation of the historical evidence does not demonstrate that conditions changed because LGBT politicians appealed to LGBT-related issues, as has been the case in many cities. Rather, it is likely that a particular subset of the LGBT population composed mostly of white, gay male middle-class homeowners, gained visibility as effective promoters of neighborhood revitalization in a city challenged by inner city decline.

For McDaniel, Luna and others, the ends have justified their "less than bold" means. The large role of a privileged subset of the LGBT population has also benefited many LGBT people outside that subset insofar as protection from discrimination and other rights are concerned. As many out LGBT Dallasites purchase homes and become politically active outside of Oak Lawn, Oak Cliff and East Dallas, an evolution for the wider region may be in store. Oak Lawn meanwhile continues to offer diverse opportunities for LGBT Dallasites in terms of entertainment, health, youth and family services. The city however remains intent on redevelopment, and oblivious to the value of existing or new affordable housing in its changing inner neighborhoods. One could picture current trends continuing to an extreme in which Oak Lawn becomes a commercial and institutional downtown for an entirely dispersed LGBT population. That scenario likely presents challenges to the necessary cohesion of LGBT youth and the provision of services. This potential problem represents the principal shortcoming of "The Dallas Way" and represents an important new task for local activists and politicians sensitive to LGBT concerns, and this may involve more openly addressing how LGBT people stand out from the general population, a discussion with which LGBT Dallasites have historically been uncomfortable.

Interviews

Chris Luna
Craig McDaniel
Mike Milliken
Louise Young, PhD

Notes

1 Activist Don Baker quoted in Vercher, Dennis "KERA debuts gay documentary" *Dallas Voice* 23 June 2000, p. 1.
2 Webb, David "Gay historian recollects past for benefit of youth" *Dallas Voice* 23 June 2006, pp. 6, 8; Webb, David "Repeating history" *Dallas Voice* 30 June 2006, pp. 6, 10; Webb, David "Oak Lawn's transformation dates way back" *Dallas Voice* 9 February 2007, p. 6; Johnson, Phil "The best of times, the worst of times" *Dallas Voice* 23 November 2007, pp. 30–31.
3 Jones, Arnold Wayne "Bronx, Cheers!" *Dallas Voice* 1 April 2011, p. 24; Webb, David "Gay historian recollects past for benefit of youth" in *Dallas Voice* 23 June 2006, pp. 6, 8.
4 Craig, Ron "Oak Lawn Christian Realtor Discriminates Against Gays" *Dallas Voice*, 10 May 1985, pp. 1, 23.
5 "Dallas gays at high risk of violence, survey shows" *Dallas Voice* 8 June 1990, p. 3.
6 Ritz, Don "Dallas Police Sergeant Urges Gay Community to Report Crimes" *Dallas Voice* 1 March 1985, p. 1; Lerro, Mark. "Violent crime up in Oak Lawn; gays often a target" *Dallas Voice*, 1 August 1986, p. 6.
7 Vercher, Dennis. "Tom Thumb prohibits distribution of 'Voice'" in *Dallas Voice* 20 June 1986, pp. 8, 10.
8 Wright, John "Dallas Gay and Lesbian Alliance celebrates 30 years of activism" *Dallas Voice* 15 June 2007, pp. 12–14.

9 Ritz, Don "MCC Opens Activity Center Doors" *Dallas Voice* 19 July 1985, p. 6.

10 Vercher, Dennis "World's largest gay congregation celebrates 25th anniversary" *Dallas Voice* 30 June 1995, p. 1.

11 "What Do Gays Want?" letter to the editor, *Dallas Voice* 26 July 1985, p. 4.

12 Statute 2106 was only overturned by the US Supreme Court in 2003 in *Lawrence v. Texas* (539 US 558).

13 Wright, John "Coming out of Dallas' political closet" *Dallas Voice* 22 May 2009 pp. 75–77, 80–81.

14 Vercher, Dennis "Council Vote against gay man criticized" *Dallas Voice* 8 May 1987, p. 16.

15 Piazza, Carl "Meet District Two Council Candidate Bill Nelson" *Dallas Voice* 22 March 1985, pp. 1, 22.

16 "Council kills redistricting" *Dallas Voice* 21 November 1986, p. 3.

17 Ritz, Don "Trials and tribulations of homebuying" *Dallas Voice* 3 July 1987, p. 12.

18 Susan Melnick was among the first gay realtors to establish a significant presence, see advertisement "Affordable North Oak Cliff" *Dallas Voice* 19 June 1992, p. 15, and advertisement "Buying or Selling a home?" *Dallas Voice* 18 September 1992, p. 11; Lori Masters was another gay realtor who marketed significantly to gay households, early on, see advertisement "A home buyer's workshop for our community" *Dallas Voice* 12 March 1993, p. 18.

19 Justiss and Justiss advertisement in *Dallas Voice* 17 June 1988, p. 11; in "Stage Models of Gentrification" (1990, p. 628) Robert Kerstein found the dominant motivation among variably profiled gentrifiers in purchasing homes to be "architectural or historical character" of the homes.

20 Justiss and Justiss advertisement, *Dallas Voice* 16 September 1988, p. 13.

21 Nash, Tammye "Cliff-dwellers tout friendly neighborhoods" *Dallas Voice* 20 October 1995, pp. 1, 26.

22 See advertisements by Peter Fitzgibbons in *Dallas Voice* 17 July 1992 p. 9, 14 August 1992 p. 24, 21 August 1992 p. 21, and 25 September 1992 p. 11.

23 David, Bradley "Home sweet townhome" *Dallas Voice* 4 June 1999, p. 58.

24 "Realtors see rebirth of interest in inner-city neighborhoods" *Dallas Voice* 21 January 1994, p. 7; Vercher, Dennis "Uptown Realtors opens for business in area" *Dallas Voice* 28 May 1993, p. 3.

25 Vercher, Dennis "Proposals threaten gay clubs" in *Dallas Voice* 11 October 1991, p. 1.

26 "OLCCC holds forum on Oak Lawn" in *Dallas Voice* 8 November 1991, p. 3.

27 Vercher, Dennis "Council OKs Controversial Zoning Plan" in *Dallas Voice* 1 November 1991, p. 1.

28 Ritz, Don "Patrols planned in neighborhood" *Dallas Voice* 3 January 1992 p. 3; "OLCCC patrols beefed up" *Dallas Voice* 21 August 1992, p. 3.

29 Nash, Tammye "Nightclub districts show high crime rates" in *Dallas Voice* 1 October 1993, p. 7.

30 Nash, Tammye "Police set 'zero tolerance' zone" in *Dallas Voice* 28 August 1992, p. 1.

31 Vercher, Dennis "Hutchison stressed Oak Cliff development" *Dallas Voice* 9 April 1993, p. 7.

32 Also see Wright, John "Coming out of Dallas' political closet" *Dallas Voice* 22 May 2009, pp. 75–77, 80–81.

33 Barlow, Gary "Dallas anti-bias ordinance?" *Dallas Voice* 8 December 2000, pp. 1, 14.

34 Nash, Tammye "Council Members tout appointments of gays, lesbians" *Dallas Voice* 19 January 1996, pp. 7, 9.

35 Nash, Tammye "Retiring Dallas councilmen say most goals met" *Dallas Voice* 13 June 1997, p. 6.

36 Webb, David "Gay constable takes over Oak Lawn precinct" *Dallas Voice* 21 December 2001, p. 8.

37 Barlow, Gary "Two gay men take City Council oath" *Dallas Voice* 15 June 2001, p. 1.

38 Webb, David "First complaint filed under bias ordinance" *Dallas Voice* 18 October 2002, p. 6.

39 Webb, David "These times they are a-changing" *Dallas Voice* 26 September 2003, p. 1.

40 Wright, John "5 years later, benefits policy remains unchallenged" *Dallas Voice* 2 October 2009, pp. 10–11.

41 McCoy, John "Vincent takes helm at Arts District Friends" *Dallas Voice* 4 August 1995, p. 7.

42 Hobson, Julian P. "They did it brilliantly" *Dallas Voice* 9 November 2001, pp. 1, 10; Hobson, Julian P. "Block by block" *Dallas Voice* 9 November 2001, p. 11.

43 Webb, David "*News'* gay ad insert a 1st in Texas" *Dallas Voice* 18 October 2002, p. 6.

44 Wright, John "Emmons stepping down from Dallas City Plan Commission" *Dallas Voice* 2 October 2009, p. 9.

45 Barlow, Gary "Commission finalizes city remap plan" *Dallas Voice* 24 August 2001, pp. 1, 9–10.

46 Webb, David "Gays, lesbians flex political muscle, become force in city" *Dallas Voice* 8 January 2004, pp. 1, 12.

47 Waugh, Anna "Dallas could gain gay councilmember" *Dallas Voice* 3 August 2012, pp. 12–13.

48 Wright, John "Coming out of Dallas' political closet" *Dallas Voice* 22 May 2009, pp. 75–77, 80–81.

49 Webb, David "State of Mind" *Dallas Voice* 21 December 2001, pp. 24–27.

50 Vercher, Dennis "Landmark shop marks 20 years" *Dallas Voice* 21 December 2001, pp. 27–29.

51 Geralds, Angela "Business owners worry about incursion of national chain" *Dallas Voice* 20 June 2003, pp. 30–31.

52 Webb, David "Northwest Dallas an Enclave for Gays" *Dallas Voice* 19 October 2001, pp. 26, 28.

53 Taffet, David "Getting ahead of the LGBT boom in Carrollton" *Dallas Voice* 23 October 2009, pp. 25–26.

54 Roger Weddell quoted. in Webb, David "Collin gays turn out in force for new group's meeting" *Dallas Voice* February 28, 2003, pp. 6, 12; also see Webb, David "Activism, and activists, moving to the suburbs" *Dallas Voice* 30 January 2004, p. 8. and advertisement by Bob McCranie, realtor "Gay people north of the LBJ? Who knew?" *Dallas Voice* 17 September 2004, p. 30.

55 Webb, David "Stonewall Democrats establish new chapter in Collin County" *Dallas Voice* 21 October 2005, p. 8.

56 Advertisement for Kimberly Davis Group, *Dallas Voice* 22 August 2008, p. 26.

57 Nash, Tammye "GLBT Chamber is open for business" *Dallas Voice* 28 January 2005.

58 Nash, Tammye "GLFD marking 10th anniversary of giving" *Dallas Voice* 5 November 2010, pp. 4, 20–21.

59 Flick, David "Chapter closes on epicenter for gay activism in Dallas" *Dallas Morning News* 1 December 2007, A1.

60 Webb, David "Growing Tarrant-Dallas connection" *Dallas Voice* 18 January 2002, p. 25.

61 Wayne, Arnold "The rainbow tour" *Dallas Voice* 30 April 2004, pp. 38, 40.

62 Russell, Howard Lewis "That bulge in your zip" in *Dallas Voice* 10 November 2006, p. 6.

63 Vercher, Dennis "1996 Dallas Voice marketing survey confirms upscale readership profile" *Dallas Voice* 19 April 1996.

64 Document produced by the newspaper for advertisers.

65 Nash, Tammye "Report profiles gay, lesbian Latin couples" *Dallas Voice* 4 November 2005, pp. 1, 18.

66 Kusner, Daniel A. "There goes the gayborhood" *Dallas Voice* 27 January 2006, p. 39; see also Lopez, Rich "There goes the neighborhood" *Defining Homes* 4 March 2011, pp. 20–21, and Cliff Pearson's letter in "Viewpoints" *Dallas Voice* 31 August 2012, p. 18.

67 Webb, David "Oak Lawns boundaries disappearing" *Dallas Voice* 7 December 2007, pp. 6, 14.

68 Vercher, Dennis "Retail properties being readied in Oak Lawn gay business district" *Dallas Voice* 21 January 2000, p. 27.

69 Nash, Tammye "Controversial oil giant plans store" *Dallas Voice* 18 February 2000, p. 1; Geralds, Angela "Business owners worry about incursion of national chain" *Dallas Voice* 20 June 2003, pp. 30–31.

70 Nash, Tammye "Cedar Springs group wants to reclaim strip" *Dallas Voice* 30 November 1997, pp. 1, 18.

71 See Wright, John "Cedar Springs/Wycliff area drops to 4th on DPD's list of worst crime spots" *Dallas Voice* 23 October 2009, p. 4 and Wright, John "Oak Lawn crime stats drop" *Dallas Voice* 16 July 2010, p. 4.

72 Webb, David "Memorable Oak Lawn house faces demolition" *Dallas Voice GLBT Real Estate Magazine* 14 July 2006, pp. 1, 12–13.

73 See Webb, David "Oak Lawn's transformation dates way back" *Dallas Voice* 9 February 2007, p. 6.

74 Varnell, Paul "Business in 'gayborhoods' will have to adapt to survive" *Dallas Voice* 18 January 2008, p. 29.

75 Varnell, Paul "Business in 'gayborhoods' will have to adapt to survive" *Dallas Voice* 18 January 2008, p. 29.

76 Nash, Tammye "Fundraiser for Cedar Springs improvements brings in $16,000" *Dallas Voice* 27 March 2009, p. 1.

77 Taffet, David "Restaurant, bar fill Cedar Springs vacancies" in *Dallas Voice* 26 March 2010, p. 14.

78 Shimm, Suzy "America's gayest ZIP codes, in two tables" *Washington Post* 15 June 2012, www.washingtonpost.com/blogs/ezra-klein/post/americas-gayest-neighborhoods-in-two-charts/2012/06/15/gJQAv4pVfV_blog.html, accessed December 2013.

79 Wright, John "2 Dallas bars close; 2 new ones open" *Dallas Voice* 19 June 2009, pp. 1, 32.

80 Waugh, Anna "Resource Center rebrands for 30th" *Dallas Voice* 6 September 2013, www.dallasvoice.com/resource-center-rebrands-30th-10156407.html, accessed December 2013.

81 Brown, Steve "Business booms in Oak Lawn" *Dallas Morning News* 24 August 2012, D01; Brown, Steve "Oak Lawn Project Under Way" *Dallas Morning News* 28 July 2008, 1D.

82 Dallas Zoning Case Z067-274, see City Plan Commission report to mayor and City council 26 September 2007.

83 http://ilume.com/2013/09/2608, accessed December 2013.

84 Taffet, David "Ilume-inating design" *Defining Homes* 10 October 2008, pp. 10–11.

85 Nash, Tammye "Crosland group gives GLBT Chamber office space at Ilume" *Dallas Voice* 19 June 2009, pp. 6, 14.

86 Taffet, David "Developer breaks ground on Ilume Park" *Dallas Voice* 24 August 2012, pp. 13, 16.

References

Bronski, Michael. 2011. *A Queer History of the United States*. Boston, MA: Beacon Press.

Castells, Manuel. 1983. *The City and the Grassroots*. Berkeley, CA: University of California Press.

Chasin, Alexandra. 2000. *Selling Out: the Gay and Lesbian Movement Goes to Market*. New York: Palgrave.

Cloud, John. 2007. "The Lavender Heart of Dallas" *Time* May 17 www.time.com/time/magazine/article/0,9171,1622593,00.html

Collins, A. 2004. "Sexual Dissidence, Enterprise and Assimilation: Bedfellows in Urban Regeneration" *Urban Studies* 41, 9: 1789–1806.

Dallas, City of (2006) *forwardDallas! Comprehensive Plan* http://dallascityhall.com/forwardDallas/index.html, accessed March 2014.

Doan, Petra L. and Harrison Higgins (2011). "The Demise of Queer Space? Resurgent Gentrification and the Assimilation of LGBT Neighborhoods" *Journal of Planning Education and Research* 31: 6–25.

Gates, Gary J. 2006. "Same-Sex Couples and the Gay, Lesbian and Bisexual Population: New Estimates from the American Community Survey" Los Angeles, CA: UCLA Williams Institute. http://williamsinstitute.law.ucla.edu/wp-content/uploads/Gates-Same-Sex-Couples-GLB-Pop-ACS-Oct-2006.pdf

Ghaziani, Amin. 2010. "There Goes the Neighborhood" *Contexts* 9: 64–66.

Godfrey, Brian J. 1988. *Neighborhoods in Transition: the Making of SF's Ethnic and Nonconformist Communities.* Berkeley, CA: University of California Press.

Graham, Adam H. 2008. "Where the Gays Are" *Advocate.* Issue 1005, 34–39.

KERA. 2000. *Finding Our Voice: the Dallas Gay and Lesbian Community.* Television documentary.

Kerstein, Robert. 1990. "Stage Models of Gentrification" *Urban Affairs Quarterly* 25: 4, 620–639.

Knopp, Lawrence. 1990. "Some Theoretical Implications of Gay Involvement in an Urban Land Market" *Political Geography Quarterly* 9: 4, 337–352.

Mims, Michael. 2006. "Interview with Richard Vincent" University of North Texas Oral History Collection Number 1615.

Murray, Stephen. 1979. "The Institutional Elaboration of Quasi-Ethnic Community" *International Review of Modern Sociology* 9: 165–177.

Penaloza, Lisa. 1996. "We're Here, We're Queer, and We're Going Shopping! A Critical Perspective on the Accommodation of Gays and Lesbians in the U.S. Marketplace" in *Gays, Lesbians and Consumer Behavior: Theory, Practice and Research Issues in Marketing,* Daniel L. Wardlow, ed. New York: Harworth. 9–38.

Pew Research, 2013. "A survey of LGBT Americans" www.pewsocialtrends.org/2013/06/13/a-survey-of-lgbt-americans, accessed April 2014.

Rothenberg, Tamar. 1995. "And She Told Two Friends: Lesbians Creating Urban Social Space" in *Mapping Desire: Geographies of Sexualities,* David Bell and Gill Valentine, eds. London: Routledge. 165–181.

4

FRACTURES AND FISSURES IN 'POST-MO' WASHINGTON, D.C.

The Limits of Gayborhood Transition and Diffusion

Nathaniel M. Lewis

Introduction

Amidst an established body of research on the creation of urban queer spaces, scholars have recently turned their attention to the transition, diffusion, and even dissolution of those spaces (Brown 2014). The discussion is often animated by a certain common-sense evolutionary logic that the factors giving rise to gay and queer spaces (e.g., gay villages) in the 1980s and 1990s, such as the need for safety, political power, and even economic gain in an exclusive and discriminatory milieu (Lauria and Knopp 1985; Knopp 1992; Collins 2004; Nash 2006), are no longer as present. The centripetal forces under which visible (and sometimes overtly branded) gay and queer spaces coalesced have been replaced by centrifugal forces such as changing tastes in nightlife and consumption (Ruting 2008; Reynolds 2009; Andersson 2009), a desire for social mixing and suburban living (Gorman-Murray and Waitt 2009; Tongson 2011), or a more direct disavowal of gay villages as passé and incongruent with modern-day queer or 'post-mo' identities (Nash 2013). Alongside these demand-side explanations based on preferences of the queer 'community,' others have suggested that gay and queer villages and venues have also been developed from the top-down in ways that promote mainstream (i.e., heterosexual) consumption rather than gay community development (Binnie and Skeggs 2004), exclude gay and queer identities that fall outside of white, middle-class, 'homonormative' mainstream (Nast 2002; Bassi 2006), or promote ill-health due to an ostensible emphasis on drugs, alcohol, and casual sex (Valentine and Skelton 2003; Egan et al. 2011; Buttram and Kurtz 2013).

Sexuality and space researchers often highlight gentrification as a process that mediates both the commercialization and the 'decline' of gay villages. In models of gay village evolution (Collins 2004), property and business development initiated by gay and lesbian actors in the 1970s and 1980s (Lauria and Knopp 1985; Knopp

1992) ultimately precipitates a rent gap (Smith 1987) in which gay neighborhoods become desirable for further redevelopment by the mainstream population and upwardly mobile segments of the gay community. A few scholars, however, have countered that the decline of visibly gay neighborhoods is not merely a by-product of capital accumulation. Doan and Higgins (2011), for example, have suggested that municipal governments may *purposely* 'de-gay' neighborhoods (e.g., by denying permits for gay festivals) to make them more attractive to property developers in the first place. Lewis' case study of Ottawa, Canada (2013) suggests that gay villages are not necessarily designated or branded for purposes of capital accumulation, particularly in smaller cities without large tourist markets or established histories of gay community development. Although such designations may now be more top-down (e.g., from municipal governments) than bottom-up, they re-assert the importance of traditional gay villages as signifiers of safety, acceptance, political inclusion and relevant services such as gay-specific health care (Forest 1995; Myslik 1996; Brown 2014).

Given the variety of processes to which gay village formation and evolution is attributed, it is perhaps unsurprising that the 'death of the village' also has many different spatial expressions. In the most pessimistic portrayals, gay villages such as Davie Street (Vancouver) and Darlinghurst (Sydney) are proclaimed 'declining' or 'dead' due to the pricing out of queer residents and businesses, with the former moving to cheaper, out-of-center locations and the latter replaced by mainstream businesses (Miller 2005; Ruting 2008; Reynolds 2009). Other portrayals assert a more definitive *shift* of the village. In cities such as Chicago, the shift from the heavily commercialized Boystown gay village northward to more residential Andersonville (see Winkle, Chapter 2 in this volume) aligns with the shift to homonormative (e.g., coupled, domestic, and conservative) lifestyles following the advent of greater social acceptance for sexual difference in most U.S. cities (Duggan 2002).

In other cities, however, the shifts have been toward neighborhoods that may offer cheaper rent and alternative nightlife and social opportunities. Here, new queer spaces have both moved *beyond* the familiar bar-and-bath house configurations of traditional gay villages while going *back* to the types of peripheral areas where gay villages were first generated. In Toronto, the westward shift from the Church-Wellesley village to Queen West has been seen as representative of a younger post-mo generation that prefers sexually mixed social environments and 'edgier' venues that are not necessarily full-time gay bars (Nash 2013; Nash and Gorman-Murray 2014, also Nash and Gorman-Murray, Chapter 11 in this volume). Meanwhile, London's shift from Soho to Shoreditch has been connected to an emergent desire for the aesthetic of urban decay and the feeling of 'authenticity' this lends to queer space (Andersson 2009). Yet other work suggests that urban queer space has not died or shifted as much as it diffuses into a multiplicity of 'queer-friendly' neighborhoods, suburbs, or even regional cities and towns (Gorman-Murray and Waitt 2009). At the same time, it has been argued that these less visible spaces are often accessible only to upwardly mobile populations who are 'in the know' (Lewis 2013; Nash and Gorman-Murray 2014).

These interventions tend to paint the decline of traditional gay and queer spaces as a reflection of changing social milieux that allow queer people to delve into previously uncharted spaces or to thrive in a multiplicity of urban and suburban settings (but see Lewis 2013). They also suggest that 'new' queer spaces and neighborhoods are more inclusive, 'queerer' alternatives to over-commercialized gay villages where venues cater mostly to a white, gay (and increasingly heterosexual) middle class (Ruting 2008; Andersson 2009; Nash 2013). Yet most of these studies have taken place in metropolitan 'world cities' that have both the tourism to support heavily commercialized gay villages, as well as the population and capital needed to create perpetual regeneration and expansion into peripheral neighborhoods. Relatedly, few interventions have examined the fractures and fissures resulting from recent reconfiguration of urban queer spaces in historically homophobic or segregated regions (e.g., the American South), or the planning measures that might be taken to stem these social and structural gaps.

The following exploratory case study of Washington, D.C., U.S.A., seeks to examine the social and spatial after-effects of three trends in the reconfiguration of queer space: (1) the decline of Dupont Circle as a visibly gay/queer space, (2) the broader (albeit partial and invisible) diffusion of queer residents and businesses into a variety of neighborhoods, and (3) the purposeful de-gaying of more peripheral gay commercial areas used by diverse segments of the population. The findings suggest that these changes – owing in part to Washington, D.C.'s cultural makeup and history of socio-spatial segregation – have had somewhat different effects than those observed in cities such as Toronto, London, and Sydney. Using the narratives of 24 gay-identified men living in the Washington, D.C. metro area, this chapter highlights several trends: the inaccessibility of 'new' queer spaces to young and less monied gay men, the replacement of inclusive queer spaces with ones geared to the white middle class, and the reinforcement of racial segregation in the queer community. While the interviews were originally part of a larger project (2009–2010) on migration decision-making among gay men, their narratives also offer firsthand observations of the spatial reconfiguration of queer Washington, D.C. in the 1990s and 2000s, and the social fractures and fissures accompanying it.

The Washington, D.C. Context

During the past several decades, Washington, D.C. has mirrored its larger U.S. counterparts as an urban beacon for gay and queer inclusion. The growth of the government sector in the 1950s and 1960s offered work environments that were less overtly homophobic than those of more industrial southern and Midwestern cities such as Baltimore, Cincinnati, Pittsburgh, and Atlanta. Meanwhile, the emergence of D.C. as a headquarters for the gay liberation movement's Mattachine Society, led to widespread (albeit clandestine) socializing and political organizing in the homes and bars around P Street, a desire to claim urban space, and ultimately the establishment of a more visible gay community in the Dupont Circle neighborhood in the 1980s and 1990s (Rimmerman 2002; Dean 2003; Johnson 2004). Since then, however, the queer space in D.C. has evolved somewhat differently than in larger metropolitan counterparts. Interviewees pointed to three resultant characteristics of D.C. 'culture' that have moderated the evolution of queer space in the city: socio-spatial segregation, transient and careerist work cultures, and conservatism in the queer community.

Long characterized by a stark division between the higher-income, white neighborhoods in western Northwest D.C., and the lower-income, African American neighborhoods in most of the other areas, Washington, D.C. has also become a far more complicated demographic patchwork since 2000. The ongoing expansion of the government sector and corollary industries (e.g., biomedicine, consulting), growing interest in living within the city center (Florida 2005), and drastic increases in international immigration (Price et al. 2005; Benton-Short et al. 2005) have prompted the geographic expansion, diffusion and diversification of 'middle-class' neighborhoods, both among the queer population (McChesney 2005) and more generally (Leap 2009). The economic and demographic transitions are often framed as positive contributions to urban social sustainability and queer inclusion. Ruble (2005), for example, suggested that the changes have created a type of 'diversity capital' that diffuses long-standing tensions between black and white populations in D.C. Gary (35, white) agreed with this theory:

> As D.C.'s evolving, I don't think it's simply becoming more hip, its own layers are beginning to blend together better, that whatever inhibitions that people have had about blending, and a lot that could also come from people coming in from out of town, who don't have the same inhibitions as the people who've lived here, they don't have the same prejudices.

Others, however, have argued that while D.C.'s socio-spatial divisions have become more complex, they are no less entrenched. Both individually led gentrification and municipally led strategies such as business improvement districts (BIDs) have tended to redevelop and reconfigure growing numbers of neighborhoods for a white, professional middle class (including queer people), while keeping African American families and new immigrants at the margins (Schaller and Modan 2005, Lewis 2010). BIDs, which are government-designated areas where businesses pay a property surtax for enhanced beautification and design services, have been leveraged in every quadrant of D.C. during the past two decades. In D.C., many of the newest BIDs have used their funds for mixed-use luxury condominium development and additional security services from off-duty police officers, creating islands of wealth and protection in close proximity to low-income neighborhoods (Lewis 2010).

Many interviewees observed that the accelerating spatial fragmentation of D.C. was spurred on by the transient nature of the labor market. According to George (39, white), Washington, D.C. is "basically a place that rich people from America come—generally supported by their parents—to go to law school or to like become a government tool. It's kind of being like trapped in junior high forever..." Brian (27, white) described this population as spatially separated from the city-at-large in Northwest-quadrant neighborhoods such as Dupont Circle, Georgetown, and Adams Morgan. "I live in the bubble, I live in the little Northwest corridor where all the young professionals come and live before they go transition off to whatever's next." Interviewees also noted the individualism and an aspirational culture among those working in politics and related sectors. Joseph (38, white) added:

> It's definitely a lot more status-driven here and ... everybody asks ... first question they ask you is what you do, which I don't exactly think that's that pretentious, I think that's kind of, you know, it's a big part of what you do, I think it's a big part of who you are.

Others observed that the key social spaces of Dupont Circle were professionalized networking environments rather than inclusive community spaces. Max (31, white) said, "Like you see there are places that only [Capitol] Hill staffers go here ... I think the gay bars here, or at least sort of the mainstream gay bars serve a similar networking function, to sort out bars that cater to specific industries."

Some interviewees, mirroring historical studies of gay D.C. (Rimmerman 2002; Dean 2003; Johnson 2004) and other capital cities (Lewis 2012), suggested that working for the federal government still prevented gay men and lesbians from living their lives openly enough to create a demand for visible gay space. Comments such as, "there are a lot of high-profile jobs," "you have to maintain yourself," and "I thought they would refuse me a security clearance because I was gay," reflected a certain resignation about the limited potential for more vibrant queer futures in Washington, D.C. The potentially individualistic, conservative motivations of some queer residents seem to reflect back onto both the political orientation of the queer community and the structure of gay commercial space. According to Max (31, white):

> D.C. is a political town, and the gay community here is a political entity as much as it is a social entity ... I think you're seeing that taken to a pretty large extreme here ... this group concentrating together, glomming together for, uh, like a, to sort of like, I don't know, secure political power, essentially.

Yet Max and others were careful to articulate that the politics of queer residents were more *national* in scale than the community oriented "municipal socialism" (e.g., voting bloc formation) that Knopp (1992) describes in his study of gay gentrification in New Orleans. Political activity, many interviewees said, was mostly in the form of 'black tie activism' exemplified by federal advocacy organizations such as the D.C.-based Human Rights Campaign (HRC). "I just think [HRC people are] excruciating!" said Tim (27, white):

> I mean ... I don't think they do enough in promoting causes ... like they just seem to be going to parties all the time and they're raising money for AIDS

research. Great, but what about like sex, you know, education, sexual health, what about the gay elderly, what about gay teens who are getting harassed in high schools, that kind of thing?

Wesley (34, white) added:

> [The radical] brand of activism is not really welcome in Washington, at least not by the people who are the Washington establishment, it must be very uncomfortable ... [HRC] alienates D.C. activism from the rest of the country ... they don't really do anything, they throw fundraisers and have a nice building.

Taken together, these three elements of D.C.'s socio-historical environment provide a unique backdrop for the evolution of queer space in the city. The conservatism and fear associated with living in a 'government town' seems to have resulted in both a relatively short heyday for concentrated spatial visibility for the queer population in Dupont Circle (see also Podmore 2013), and a hesitancy toward re-creating that type of public space in any meaningful way. Moreover, the individualism and professionalization of the transient, government-related workforce, combined with the prioritization of a *national* gay rights agenda, implies both a potential lack of interest in the development of a *local* queer community and the onset of a depoliticized homonormativity. At the same time, these factors have not impeded either the rapid (albeit fragmented and invisible) spread of *de facto* queer space through individually led gentrification processes or the elimination of other commercial queer spaces through municipal redevelopment. In an environment of pronounced socio-spatial segregation, these dual processes seem to have created further fractures and fissures in both the queer and broader communities.

The Decline of Dupont

Dupont Circle carries the status of queer 'homeland' (e.g., Weston 1995; Fortier 2001) in a similar vein to neighborhoods like the Castro (San Francisco) or Greenwich Village (New York). Marked by a strip of gay bars, restaurants, and a sex shop along Seventeenth Street, 'Dupont' became a *de facto* gay village following the initial establishment of gay bars and businesses in the mid-1980s. Following Collins' (2004) gay village evolution model, gay men and lesbians—who had long worked on Capitol Hill but had only a few social venues clustered on P Street closer to the wealthy neighborhoods Georgetown and Kalorama—saw an opportunity to create a village in the cheaper, more peripheral areas of Connecticut Avenue and Seventeenth Street. Connecticut Avenue served as the organizational and intellectual hub, marked by the offices of the *Washington Blade* newsweekly and the Lambda Rising bookstore, while Seventeenth Street, a few blocks to the east, was the commercial center featuring still-existing landmark bars such as JR's and Cobalt (now 30°). Myslik's (1996) study of Dupont characterized the neighborhood as a beacon of safety and a disruption of heteronormative power in an otherwise conservative city.

Today, however, Dupont is marked by the mostly 'mainstream' shops, restaurants and businesses associated with the later stages of Collins' (2004) gay village evolution model. Adam (34, white), connected the decline of Dupont with the shift in inclusion discussed elsewhere as having "something to do with just acceptance generally of gays.... people used to clump in those areas for comfort, I think ... because they knew other people were around that would accept them. Now, I just don't think that that's as necessary." Another interviewee, Max (31, white) described the decline as a short-term loss but an overall social good:

> You've seen a lot of the old, sort of, um, like centers of gay culture here dissolve. I mean, Lambda Rising closed. *The Blade* closed. Those were two, I think, huge, like, I mean, sort of psychic artifacts ... in the minds of the gay media here. Some of that ... I think, is probably due to a generational shift as much as it is just shifts in D.C., because ... things have changed so much, people don't feel as strong a need to like, uh, live in a sort of ghetto or, or only pay attention to specialized businesses ... I mean, it insulated, you know, a lot of people from a lot of really bad things, so ... all of those things vanishing can also be a sign of progress of things getting better.

Others connected Dupont's decline with its transition into a safe, established neighborhood that had become a desirable neighborhood for the upper class (see also Collins 2004; Miller 2005; Ruting 2008). Two interviewees felt that cost was the major barrier to new gay and lesbian residents choosing to live in Dupont. "I don't know, D.C.'s different, it's changed a lot in the last ... well since I moved here D.C. [queer space] isn't as centric as it was five or six years ago," Nick (26, white) said, "... ideally, I think most people would probably want to live in Dupont, but it's just not affordable." Doug (26, white) observed that the disjuncture between Dupont's gay homeland status and relatively mainstream appearance was particularly confusing for queer newcomers:

> There was this sort of gay mecca here for a long time and then, you know, it became a sanctuary, I think for a lot of gay people ... they come from the Midwest, and they come here to live their lives ... and not being viewed as total freaks has certainly helped shape that [gay-friendly] image.... [But when he actually moved there in the early 2000s] I guess it wasn't as gay as I thought it was, especially going to Dupont Circle ... 'cause you hear about the stories and ... Dupont Circle just seemed like a normal part of the town to me ... there weren't like rainbow flags everywhere ... it wasn't like you see on television ... San Francisco, guys walking down the street in leather chaps ... it wasn't like that at all ... I mean even when you walk through Dupont, I mean there are a couple of sex shops ... that are a little 'flagrant'

about it—I put that in quotes—but I don't … think there's that sense of like in your face.

Dupont's decline therefore seems driven by two mutually reinforcing tends. The neighborhood improvements and influx of middle-class heterosexual residents that led to the closure of many gay businesses in the early 2000s might also keep new, younger queer residents from moving into the area and patronizing existing queer businesses or starting new ones.

Residential and Commercial Transition and Diffusion

Amidst the decline of Dupont as the flagship gayborhood, several additional areas have been framed as queer spaces in Washington, D.C. Unlike Sydney, Toronto, or London, which are dominated by discourses of gayborhood 'replacement' (i.e., replacing Darlinghurst with Newtown, Church-Wellesley with Queen West, and Soho with Shoreditch), D.C.'s 'new' gayborhood is more multi-nodal. In yearly polls (2010–2014) by online blog Borderstan asking "where is the gay neighborhood?", east-of-Dupont (i.e., Logan Circle) has typically earned a plurality of votes but has been closely followed by Columbia Heights, U Street, Shaw, and finally, Dupont itself. The rise of Logan Circle as a gayborhood is attributable to its emergence as the next neighborhood after Dupont to experience a significant albeit short-lived rent gap, which led gay residents who could not afford Dupont to buy up property in the 1990s and early 2000s. Yet Logan was quickly replaced by Shaw (to the east) and Columbia Heights (to the north) as the neighborhoods offering the highest returns on property investments. Nick (26, white) described the gayborhood as "spreading" in an eastward semi-circle from Dupont: "most of the gays probably live in the Logan/Dupont sort of area … but now it's spreading out to like Columbia Heights and Shaw." Some saw gentrification among gay men as a logical pursuit of capital accumulation, especially in a city dominated by mid-range government jobs rather than jobs in business or finance. "You're not gonna make a lot of money in D.C. in a lot of other ways, so people want to make money on gentrification" (Ian, 31, Hispanic). Adam (34, white) felt that the movement continues to expand eastward into neighborhoods like Shaw where there was greater opportunity for gain:

> As I've been here I've noticed that people have moved out from [Dupont Circle, Logan Circle, and Columbia Heights] more … some of that has to do with property values, you know, it's just all in those areas property's so expensive that it's easier if you want to buy a house and make an investment to go out further into those other areas.

Other interviewees had more conflicted perspectives on the diffusion of the gayborhood. Jeffrey (42, Asian) explained that while the decline of the gay population in Dupont could be taken as evidence of more protection and freedom, it also hindered his continued sense of belonging to a community and the potential for collective action on issues such as adoption and (at the time of interviews) repeal of the military's Don't Ask Don't Tell Policy:

> I think it's disparate at this moment in time; it ebbs and flows. You know, like as you see … like when I first moved here [in 1989]. I felt much more part of a gay community because of Dupont, and then Dupont transitioned and got gentrified and then Logan got gentrified and then everybody wanted to go to Logan but then didn't, and now they're up in Columbia Heights, but not quite. So I think that there's a whole dispersement [sic] which in an interesting way might have to do with the new sense of freedom that like, does the gay community ultimately have to cloister or be in a ghetto once their rights are more protected? But I think now would be a time to push as a community a little bit harder.

The birth of another gayborhood, however, was seen as an impossibility to most of the interviewees, given the rapid spatial shifting of gentrification and the ongoing tendency for local neighborhood associations (e.g., Logan Circle Community Association) to veto the development of new businesses (e.g., Shulman 2004; Najafi 2008). Joseph (38, white) explained that replacing Dupont Circle's Seventeenth Street with a new gayborhood on Logan Circle's Fourteenth Street had been a passing fancy in the media that never materialized:

> If you watch like Fourteenth Street, how it's coming up [in the early 2000s], it was kind of like, there's a couple of things there … And then 7 years later … it's come a long way but it kind of hasn't … I think there's a lot of red tape … I mean even the little things like people trying to open up a bar, and the neighborhood association being able to veto it … you're not allowed the bar to be established or even expand, you know?

While the failure of Fourteenth Street as a 'gayborhood' might be due to fickle NIMBY-ism, other gay business districts in the city have also been exposed to more heavy-handed redevelopment.

The De-Gaying of Peripheral Commercial Spaces

The same forces preventing the birth of new gayborhoods (e.g., maintenance of neutral, middle-class spaces through zoning regulations and veto power) have also worked to eliminate existing queer spaces in peripheral neighborhoods. As observed by Doan and Higgins (2011) in nearby Atlanta, some queer spaces are not just quietly 'mainstreamed' (as in Dupont) but rather actively 'de-gayed' for mainstream consumption. In 2005, several gay venues on O Street in Southeast D.C.—many of which were patronized by queers of color—were forced to close under D.C.'s eminent domain provision to make room for the Nationals Park baseball stadium and associated businesses supported by the Capitol Riverfront Business

Improvement District (O'Bryan 2005; Najafi 2008; Leap 2009; Lewis 2010). Several miles from Dupont Circle, this mostly-defunct commercial zone near the industrial Navy Yard area—what Brian (27, white) called "a little gayborhood in Southeast D.C."—supported dance clubs (Nation), an African American gay bar (the still-existing Bachelors Mill), and strip clubs (Ziegfeld's, Wet) that also served as workspaces and social spaces for gay and trans sex workers. Much like residential gentrification, these commercial transitions have tended to displace the most marginalized segments of the queer population. Shane (27, African American) described a mixed effect on the segregation of the queer community:

> I think it's because gay businesses have shut down, because of the baseball stadium, that whole section closed down … Chaos on Seventeenth Street closed down, which a lot of people of color went to … so I think because of those closing off businesses, you know, we're forced to mingle a little bit more.

While Shane in some ways reinforces Ruble's (2005) diversity capital thesis, he ultimately suggests that the scene remains segregated, if not by bars then by floors of bars:

> I think because the places shut down … Cobalt to me is a perfect example, like I remember the first time I went, everyone was all white. But now, it's like, wow, there were, there was one night we were joking, like oh my god, we think there are more people of color here than there are white people … then you go to places like Mova, formerly known as Halo, and you have bottom floor, all black people, and then white people or whoever's left over, upstairs … The same thing at the Fireplace, there are a number of white people who are downstairs … but when you go upstairs … there are almost like no white people.

Many of the venues emerging in out-of-center areas (e.g., Southeast D.C.), however, are not necessarily community spaces or visibly queer spaces, but rather 'gay-friendly' places that seem to cater to a (mostly white) patron base of recent gentrifiers. Adam (34, white) explained:

> It used to be that gays would go to gay bars and straights would go to straight bars. But I've noticed in the last few years, there are very mixed bars … one of the ones I've gone to is called Wisdom, down in Southeast … It's kind of an area that's up and coming now … it's a martini bar, basically, but it's—any night of the week, if you go there, you'll get a whole mix of gay and straight people … even with the gay bars … nowadays … any night of the week, I've seen, you know, 25, 50% of the people are straight … and just during the day … a lot of straight couples in there watching, you know, sports and all that, so … um … I think the bars are more neighborhood-based now than anything.

Although Adam's narrative paints a positive—or at least neutral—picture of social mixing in newly re-developed neighborhoods and venues, it elides the accessibility of these spaces for the broader queer population. For local queers of color, these spaces might not provide the same camaraderie and social support of a traditionally African American bar, might still be perceived as white spaces, or foster a mixing of sexual identity groups that might not be comfortable for men who have experienced homophobia or are not out in their own communities.

Social Implications

The decline of Dupont, the creation of new, quasi-gay spaces, and the de-gaying of peripheral queer commercial spaces have distinct, individually felt impacts on segments of the gay population, such as younger men and men of color. Collectively, these three transitions also have larger implications for the cohesion, sustainability, and futurity of the queer and broader communities in D.C. First, a diffuse, less visible queer geography may compromise the safety of the queer population and the availability of social support for newcomers to the community. As some of the previous narratives indicate, the landscape of D.C. is still highly variegated in terms of both overall crime and social acceptance for queer people specifically. Since many nominally 'queered' neighborhoods are still very much in socioeconomic transition, the patterning, visibility, and reliability of 'safe space' is less obvious than might be presumed. George (39, white) described D.C. as more openly hostile to homosexuality than New York City, where he had moved from. George indicated that he had heard:

> You know, 'fuck you faggot' … just like on the street, all the time, I've heard more shit like that, more than I've ever heard anywhere in my life—cumulatively—it's, it's a very different vibe and not what I'm used to, not what I want to be used to.

Shane (27, African American) explained that his own experiences with hate crime had actually increased during the past year, particularly in transitional areas, despite political advancements such as the advent of gay marriage in D.C.:

> There have been plenty of times when I walked down U Street, like holding hands with my boyfriend and/or friends … almost, 100% of the times I walk down the street holding hands with another guy, someone says something. So, I mean, politically, we're all good … for the most part, but that doesn't immunize us to … harassment and violence … I don't know how much like there was because I was targeted because, again, my gender expression or if it was, um, just random. I don't know. But I mean three times in three months … Here, one was Seventeenth and P, one had been by Logan Circle, the other was … near my house, near right next to my house … back over by Shaw area.

Max (31, white) attributed the uptick in anti-gay hate crimes to the very processes of gentrification to which queer space is often thought to diffuse. "That's probably the gentrification backlash ... there's always been these spikes. Nellie's [gay sports bar], which is at Ninth and U, just got robbed at gunpoint two weeks ago. You know, you're pushing into underprivileged neighborhoods ..."

The overall landscape of safe space for queer people has also become more complicated in post-mo D.C. With no clear 'gay neighborhood' in which to congregate and most out-of-center queer diffusion being residential, younger queer people have few visible points of 'first contact' for support services or potential friends, mentors, and romantic relationships. In this new milieu, organizations like Supporting and Mentoring Youth Advocates and Leaders (SMYAL) in Southeast D.C. have taken over this role, albeit during carefully circumscribed meeting and drop-in times. Speaking about African American youth, Shane explained that safe community spaces such as SMYAL were important as a place to 'escape' to within their own neighborhoods or to find 'refuge' if they lived outside of the District (e.g., in Prince George's County, Maryland):

> I do also know that young people get a lot of harassment in the communities, and a lot of young people come from low-income areas ... I think, if you're from the city, if you're from lower-income communities, the city's a place you escape ... and if you come, if you're outside of that, the city's a place you go to for refuge. And so it depends on who you are, the city and its sense of safety and comfort, I think, may change based on where you come from. (Shane, 27, African American)

Several participants had also suggested that the only opportunities for affirming one's gay identity or connecting with queer compatriots were at 21-and-over bars or during Capital Pride. Philip (43, African American) said, "I don't know that it's unique to D.C. but one of the things that ... I don't care for all that much lately is I feel like ... there's not that much to do other than going to bars." Doug (26, white) said, "The only times you see [overt displays of sexual identity] are at the Gay Pride Parade ... where people feel more free to express themselves, and that's one time where it's encouraged and expected, I think, in this city." But for John (33, white) Pride was just an extension of the limited bar scene that represented the only visibly queer space:

> Because there's such a heavy emphasis on the bars—which I avoid actually, I don't go to the bars—you do kind of feel outside. [Going to Pride] it's like ... just the bar crowd out in the streets. My one fear is like; well I feel like I don't fit into the community as a whole, so that's why I've only gone a couple of times.

Adam (34, white) compared D.C. to Dayton, Ohio, where—despite less critical mass and financial resources—the gay community had seemed to have a greater sense of unity across neighborhoods and generations:

It tended to be more structured, I think because there were people, but I think they were more focused on small community and building a community of people. Um, the gay pride events were just kind of a joke, I think. But they were fun, you know, they were small but they were, you know, and so you kind of knew everybody.

In the absence of a concentrated, well-connected gay community, many interviewees felt that home ownership within a gay-friendly neighborhood or suburb was the only way to establish a sustainable connection to a gay community. Philip (43, African American) felt:

There wasn't a huge advantage to living in the city because ... I never found the gay ghetto to be all that big and depending on what you were looking for it's not like New York ... Um, (partner's name) and I, when we first moved in together a couple of years ago, we lived on Capitol Hill. And then I ... have to admit that I told him that when we bought a house we were not buying it in the District ... the District government, it just seemed to me like wasting money and ... there was such a huge difference moving to the suburbs.

Exodus to the D.C. suburbs, however, was not necessarily a common-sense solution for gay men in search of sustainable links to community—queer or otherwise. Brian (27, white) explained that residential neighborhoods in Maryland and Virginia would not be sensible for single gay men or even partnered men who are not adopting children (or, in Virginia, legally forbidden from adopting children):

And then there are people a decade later, who are getting married and having families ... and once people have families, they worry about the school system and, uh, there's a lot more incentive to live outside of the district ... so I think that a lot of gays stay central and don't have that sort of next step to move back to the 'burbs.

The resulting perpetuation and expansion of 'gaytrification' (Podmore 2013) in central D.C., however, is not without its own tensions. In addition to the potential linkages with anti-gay hate crimes in mixed areas, gaytrification also challenges rights to space in historically black areas. Gary (35, white) explained, "We're on the edge of gay gentrification right now, where we're living in Shaw, and the biggest pushback has probably been ... gentrifiers fighting with the churches because they were parking, like double parking, the Sunday parking issue." As with other forms of gentrification, new residents are calling for the enforcement of parking regulations that were overlooked when such neighborhoods were almost completely black and Christian.

Finally, the narratives show that the simultaneous deterioration and expansion of queer space seems to have maintained or even amplified understandings of the 'gay community' as a white, middle-class entity. This division may be partially due to the grafting of an educated, white liberal elite population onto a historically black city in order to maintain a federal government work force. Nominally part of the American South, D.C. also experienced the mandatory segregation of schools and public facilities in the 1950s and 1960s. The black-white division was evident in how men of color described their own experiences and conceived of 'black D.C.' George (39, African American) said, "It's funny ... I never felt any form of discrimination until I moved to D.C., coming from the south. Like catching a cab is extremely hard for me here, even when I'm in a suit." At the same time, white interviewees described the 'black community' as monolithically poor, Christian, and homophobic:

> There's got to be at least a few African American gay boys living down in Southeast who don't have the same experience of D.C. that I do by any stretch of the imagination I would say ... their life is probably much more like my life back in [town in rural Colorado]. (Nick, 26, white)

> I'm assuming that if I were a poor African American and I was gay in D.C. ... I would, I would encounter somewhat more resistance ... certainly what you've seen in the press for people protesting the gay marriage law in D.C. was primarily African American pastors ... and I think [African Americans] probably tend to be more religious in general. (Martin, 46, white)

> We've definitely kind of all heard about how there's ... a lack of ability for ... black men, I think, to be out and some of the communities here ... they tend to be very, um, church-driven in some of the ... poorer areas of town. (Adam, 34, white)

The persistent characterizations of black and white communities as opposing forces in D.C. infiltrated queer space, discursively and materially excluding men of color from the gay community while circumscribing the new, 'post-Dupont' queer spaces as white and middle class by default. Most suggested that white and non-white segments of the community remained separate, with the latter rendered mostly invisible. Nick (26, white) explained:

> But like in Columbus [Ohio], there was a higher African American maybe almost integration with like the gay community it seemed ... I feel like I knew more, I at least had friends, more friends that happened to be black in Columbus than here.

Two more interviewees felt that most gay bar spaces, unless otherwise identified, registered as white and middle class. Barry (Asian, 42) described his first experience of queer space in D.C. as feeling out of place:

> I remember the first bar I went to ... my first impression was that, oh my god it's so white ... and I felt like I'm so out of place, you know. My demographic of understanding of D.C. is, it's a black city ... and don't see that many black people ... you know, not in the gym, not in basically, you know, different areas.

Philip (43, African American), referencing the same bar, claimed that the division had actually amplified with the closure of more racially mixed spaces along Seventeenth Street and in Navy Yard:

> I think [racial division] is reflected in the gay community here. Um, this is not a particularly integrated community ... just walk into [Seventeenth Street bar]. I mean this city is, you know, 55% African American, um, and, you know, 5 or 10% Latino. You would assume that most of the—at least half of the people in the bar or a third of the people in the bar would be people of color and that's just not true and there's a reason for that ... it's gotten marginally worse and I don't see that getting better anytime soon.

Adam (34, white) felt that this was symptomatic not just of the bars in Dupont and Logan, but also of the venues in newly gentrified areas. "There's definitely a racial component to even upscale venues, I guess.... I think it's segregated but not in like a ... not, not in a conscious way."

Philip (43, African American), however, felt that gay men of color did not necessarily feel welcome either in the remaining Dupont and Logan bars or those in newly gentrified areas; they tended to gravitate to the one historically black bar with a black clientele:

> For example, Bachelors' Mills, I understand that it's a lot busier than it ever has been—and that's the black bar. It is truly an African American bar, and it's where African American men go to meet African American men, um, and that's who's there ... It's busier than it has been, and that has to be— because depending on who you are and what your comfort level is—you might not want to walk into [Seventeenth Street bar] and you certainly might not want to walk into there by yourself.

George (39, African American) agreed that segregation of queer space had become further entrenched, but with decreasing allocations of space for queer men of color:

> There's white gays and there are black gays and they don't—outside of a few of us—we don't interact. I mean, you have ... Bachelor's Mill and the Fireplace, which are the black bars, um, and you have all the others, which are the white bars. It's weird how ... I can go easily between both, um, a lot of blacks don't go to [Dupont bar] JR's or [newly gentrified bars] Town or

Nellie's ... and there's a regular Capital Pride and there's black pride, and I tell my white friends why there is a black pride. Because 15 years ago, as a black man, if you walked into JR's, you wouldn't get served.

Even in post-mo D.C., however, the diffusion of queer space does not seem to have opened possibilities for hybrid, 'queerer' or more racially inclusive spaces. In fact, many interviewees asserted that the dominant conception of D.C.'s gay community remains white, middle-class, and migrant or transient. Gary (35, white) says:

> I mean it seems sort of insulting when people say, you know, all the gay guys are from somewhere else ... because there is this [black gay] culture and they just haven't mixed very much in the past ... and there's still an odd segregation ... but there's also a Latino mix coming into it now too that had not even been part of the conversation 10 years ago.

Max (31, white) suggested that despite this diversity, white professionals have tended to articulate what and where queer space is:

> What most people mean when they say the gay community is very white, and in a lot of ways, uh, strangely conservative in terms of like, um, like, how restrictive, uh, the, the sort of rules of that culture are. But certainly if you go looking, you can find ... other like sort of communities.

Nick (26, white), crystallized some of the tensions in the understandings of queer space in D.C., expressing dismay at the circumscription of the community by white, middle-class actors:

> Like the whole HRC kind of gay crowd, like they tend to go out more and go out to these places ... it's changed a little bit obviously in the last couple of years—but that used to be the biggest criticism of HRC was that it was all catered to like the upper-middle-class white man and I guess a lot of, sort of, like the, the D.C. crowd is that. They're college educated, and you know, they have ... they're upper-middle-class, they have good jobs, and they rent or they own a condo, and they have designer stuff, and they go out all the time. That's D.C. in a nutshell.

Planning Implications

Despite the recent blurring (or at least a complicated redrawing) of lines between black, white, rich and poor, the discursive conception of the gay community in D.C.—from both within it and outside it—seems now more entrenched than ever as white, professional, upwardly mobile, and middle class. Moreover, the mainstreaming of Dupont, expansive and successive gaytrification, and the more purposeful removal of other peripheral queer areas seems to have replaced more visible and inclusive queer spaces with diffuse spaces that read as white and middle-class. Amidst the flattening of queer public space, these changes also seem to position individually led gentrification as the new imperative for attachment to the gay community. These changes might be particularly isolating for gay men of color who have few spaces where they feel a sense of belonging and ownership, and for newly out or recently moved younger gay men who are unable to detect where, exactly, safe spaces in D.C. might be located.

One approach to planning for queer space in D.C. would be to re-emphasize Dupont Circle as a historical center, highlighting both the D.C. and national gay liberation movements. The development of a historical visitors' center showcasing D.C.'s 'lavender landmarks' coupled with a community center, would be one way to re-establish Dupont and Logan—still highly trafficked, central neighborhoods and the site of relevant services such as the Whitman-Walker sexual health clinic—as visible queer spaces. Emphasizing historical rather than commercial ties to the queer community might also offer an opportunity for the more visible signage and branding (e.g., as 'America's gay village') adopted in areas like Boystown in Chicago and Le/The Village in Ottawa (Reed 2003; Lewis 2013). Such developments could attract new businesses that—even while continuing to draw a mixed crowd—might offer services beyond bars and clubs.

Second, the D.C. Metropolitan Police Force should consider taking more comprehensive stock of the types and patterns of crimes, including anti-LGBT hate crimes, in newly gentrifying areas. One option would be to create a pamphlet or handbook that addresses safety issues for LGBT people in D.C. The document would not only involve safety precautions, but also points of cultural sensitivity and tips for being a good neighbor in socially diverse neighborhoods. The municipal government might also consider funding a more critical multi-year study of the social pitfalls and challenges of gentrification, especially amidst the development of public-private actors (e.g., BIDs) that tacitly approve and encourage rapid gentrification (Lewis 2010). In addition, the police force could consider deploying additional officers, especially those within the Gay and Lesbian Liaison Unit (GLLU), to areas with reported spikes in LGBT hate crime. Incidentally, the city's GLLU officers have recently been redeployed to street patrol in the Sixth and Seventh Police Districts in Southeast D.C., which have high levels of overall crime but not necessarily hate crime (Chibbaro 2014). Their training, which allows them to remain on constant call to respond to hate crimes *throughout* the city, could also be utilized in a permanent patrol post in the areas with the highest LGBT hate crimes.

Third, municipally sponsored youth programming in marginal areas of the city must include a sexual diversity education component, particularly one that makes newly out or questioning youth aware of the available resources in the city (e.g., health care, counseling). Given that these resources are still disproportionately concentrated in Dupont and Logan, it may be even more ideal to provide funding to established branches of SMYAL or even the more recently created (2012)

Leading Youth Forward Everyday (LYFE) Program in outlying, historically black and minority areas of the city, such as Anacostia, Stadium-Armory, and Deanwood. Although the development of such programs in the 2000s was an important step toward establishing both social supports for individual youth and the perceived inclusivity of the gay community overall, their visibility is now even more important within a city where queer populations, venues, and practices (e.g., property development) read as white.

Collectively, the findings suggest that the transition, diffusion, or reconfiguration of the 'gayborhood' does not always open significant possibilities for a more transgressive, radical, or inclusive queer futurity (Bassi 2006; Nash 2013). Instead, depending on the urban contexts in which these processes occur, they might also retrench divisions in the queer populations and further cordon off the most privileged segments from those with fewer opportunities. The findings here therefore reinforce Natalie Oswin's (2005) argument that daily processes of work, consumption and mobility—no matter how 'queer' the actors carrying them out might be—always have the possibility to reinforce extant inequalities in capitalist societies. The practice of planning has thus become more important than ever to not just defend the interests and safety of 'minority' groups but to connect the most vulnerable populations with the spaces and resources they need to flourish.

References

Andersson, J. 2009. East End localism and urban decay: Shoreditch's re-emerging gay scene. *The London Journal* 34(1): 55–71.

Bassi, C, 2006. Riding the dialectical waves of gay political economy: a story from Birmingham's commercial gay scene. *Antipode* 38: 213–235.

Benton-Short, L., Price, M., and Friedman, S. 2005. Globalization from below: The ranking of global immigrant cities. *International Journal of Urban and Regional Research* 29(4): 945–959.

Binnie, J., and Skeggs, B. (2004). Cosmopolitan knowledge and the production and consumption of sexualized space: Manchester's gay village. *The Sociological Review*, 52(1), 39–61.

Buttram, M., and Kurtz, S. 2013. Risk and protective factors associated with gay neighborhood residence. *American Journal of Men's Health* 7: 110–118.

Brown, M. 2014. Gender and sexuality II: There goes the gayborhood? *Progress in Human Geography* 38(3): 457–465.

Chibbaro, L. 2014. Police gay liaison unit transferred to patrol duty. *The Washington Blade*, February 12. www.washingtonblade.com/2014/02/12/police-gay-liaison-unit-transferred-patrol-duty

Collins, A. 2004. Sexual dissidence, enterprise and assimilation: bedfellows in urban regeneration. *Urban Studies* 41(9): 1789–1806.

Dean, R. 2003. *Imperial brotherhood: gender and the making of Cold War foreign policy*. Boston, MA: University of Massachusetts Press.

Doan, P., and Higgins, H. 2011. The demise of queer space? Resurgent gentrification and the assimilation of LGBT neighborhoods. *Journal of Planning Education and Research* 31(1): 6–25.

Duggan, L. 2002. The new homonormativity: the sexual politics of neoliberalism. In R. Castronovo and D. Nelson (eds.), *Materializing democracy: towards a revitalized cultural politics*. Durham, NC: Duke University Press, 175–194.

Egan, J., Frye, V., Kurtz, S., Latkin, C., Chen, M., Tobin, K., Yang, C., and Koblin, B. 2011. Migration, neighborhoods, and networks: approaches to understanding how urban environmental conditions affect syndemic adverse health outcomes among gay, bisexual, and other men who have sex with men. *AIDS and Behavior* 15: S35–S50.

Florida, R. 2005. *Cities and the Creative Class*. New York: Routledge.

Forest, B. 1995. West Hollywood as Symbol: the significance of place in the construction of a gay identity. *Environment and Planning D: Society and Space* 13(2): 133–157.

Fortier, A.-M. 2001. Coming home: queer migration and multiple evocations of home. *European Journal of Cultural Studies* 4: 405–424.

Gorman-Murray, A., and Waitt, G. 2009. Queer-friendly neighborhoods: interrogating social cohesion across sexual difference in two Australian neighborhoods. *Environment and Planning A* 41(12): 2855–2873.

Johnson, D.K. 2004. *The Lavender Scare: The Cold War Persecution of Gays and Lesbians in the Federal Government*. Chicago, IL: University of Chicago Press.

Knopp, L. 1992. Sexuality and the spatial dynamics of capitalism. *Environment and Planning D: Society and Space* 10: 651–659.

Lauria, M., and Knopp, L. 1985. Toward an analysis of the role of gay communities in the urban renaissance. *Urban Geography* 6(2): 152–169.

Leap, W., 2009. Professional baseball, urban restructuring and (changing) gay geographies in Washington, DC. In *Out in Public: Reinventing Lesbian/Gay Anthropology in a Globalizing World*. New York: Blackwell, 202–222.

Lewis, N.M. 2010. Grappling with Governance: The Emergence of Business Improvement Districts in a National Capital. *Urban Affairs Review* 46 (2): 180–217.

Lewis, N.M. 2012. Gay in a 'Government Town': the settlement and regulation of gay-identified men in Ottawa, Canada. *Gender, Place and Culture* 19(3): 291–312.

Lewis, N.M. 2013. Ottawa's Le/The Village: Creating a Gayborhood amidst the 'Death of the Village'. *Geoforum* 49: 233–242.

McChesney, C. 2005. Cultural Displacement: Is the GLBT Community Gentrifying African-American Neighborhoods in Washington, D.C.? *The Modern American* Spring.

Miller, V. 2005. Intertextuality, the referential illusion and the production of a gay ghetto. *Social & Cultural Geography* 6(1): 61–79.

Myslik, W. 1996. Renegotiating the social/sexual identities of places: gay communities as safe havens or sites of resistance. In Duncan, N. (ed.), *Bodyspace: Destabilizing Geographies of Gender and Sexuality*. London, UK: Routledge, 156–169.

Najafi, Y. 2008. The return of Ziegfeld's. *Metro Weekly*, April 9. www.metroweekly.com/ 2008/04/the-return-of-ziegfelds

Nash, C. 2006. Toronto's gay village (1969–1982): Plotting the politics of gay identity. *The Canadian Geographer* 50: 1–16.

Nash, C. 2013. The age of the 'post-mo'? Toronto's gay village and a new generation. *Geoforum* 49: 243–252.

Nash, C., and Gorman-Murray, A. 2014 LGBT neighborhoods and 'new mobilities': towards understanding transformations in sexual and gendered urban landscapes. *International Journal of Urban and Regional Research* 38(3): 756–772.

Nast, H. 2002. Queer patriarchies, queer racisms, international. *Antipode*, 34(5): 874–909.

O'Bryan, W. 2005. Bob Siegel responds to D.C. land grab. *Metro Weekly*, October 25. www.metroweekly.com/2005/10/bob-siegel-responds-to-dc-land

Oswin, N. 2005. Towards radical geographies of complicit queer futures. *ACME: An International E-Journal for Critical Geographies* 3(2): 79–86.

Podmore, J. 2013. Lesbians as village 'queers': the transformation of Montreal's lesbian nightlife in the 1990s. *ACME: An International E-Journal for Critical Geographies* 12(2): 220–249.

Price, M., Cheung, I., Friedman, S., and Singer, A. 2005. The world settles in: Washington, D.C. as an immigrant gateway. *Urban Geography* 26(1): 61–75.

Reed, C. 2003. We're from Oz: marking ethnic and sexual identity in Chicago. *Environment and Planning D: Society and Space* 21(4): 425–440.

Reynolds, R. 2009. Endangered territory, endangered identity: Oxford Street and the dissipation of gay life. *Journal of Australian Studies* 33(1): 79–92.

Rimmerman, C.A. 2002. *From Identity to Politics: Lesbian and Gay Movements in the United States*. Philadelphia, PA: Temple University Press.

Ruble, B.A. 2005. Creating diversity capital: Transnational migrants in Montreal, Washington, and Kyiv. Washington, DC: Woodrow Wilson Center Press.

Ruting, B. 2008. Economic transformations of gay urban spaces: revisiting Collins' evolutionary gay district model. *Australian Geographer* 39(3): 259–269.

Schaller, S., and Modan, G. 2005. Contesting public space and citizenship: implications for neighborhood business improvement districts. *Journal of Planning Education and Research* 24(4): 394–407.

Shulman, R. 2004. Mark Lee: fighting for DC's nightlife. *Metro Weekly*, January 7. www.metroweekly.com/2004/01/mark-lee

Smith, N. 1987. Gentrification and the rent gap. *Annals of the Association of American Geographers* 77(3): 462–465.

Tongson, K. 2011. *Relocations: Queer Suburban Imaginaries*. New York: New York University Press.

Valentine, G., and Skelton, T. 2003. Finding oneself, losing oneself: the lesbian and gay 'scene' as a paradoxical space. *International Journal of Urban and Regional Research* 27, 4: 849–866.

Weston, K. 1995. Get thee to a big city: sexual imaginary and the great gay migration. *GLQ: A Journal of Lesbian and Gay Studies* 2: 253–277.

PART II

Planning and LGBTQ Populations Outside the Gay Village

INTRODUCTION TO PART II

Petra L. Doan

The second part of this book expands the focus away from traditional gay villages, by examining the ways that LGBTQ populations outside the traditional gayborhood organize themselves and make demands for better and safer urban environments. Because much of the academic literature on queer urban spaces has concentrated on the evolution of white gay male neighborhoods, the second part of this volume provides alternative perspectives about the usefulness of the gay village as an organizing framework. The chapters in this section examine the ways that the LGBTQ community has used urban spaces in the Global South (in particular in South Africa), as well as in smaller communities in the United States that never developed traditional gay neighborhoods.

Each of the chapters asks questions about the meaning of queer space and how it might be located in urban areas. In Chapter 5 Gustav Visser suggests that the gay village as the archetype of queer space does not fit the South African context. His work challenges many of the basic premises of queer space developed in the West that are largely irrelevant to gay populations located in diverse settings outside the United States and Britain, arguing that at a global scale, the current understanding of the relationship between gay identities and space does not explain much of the lived reality of the global LGBTQ population.

Other chapters examine LGBTQ commercial and residential patterns in smaller urban areas that are less well studied. For example in Chapter 6 Sarah Nusser and Katrin Anacker consider how pervasive heterosexism shapes the way that queer-identified people experience commercial spaces in Cambridge, Massachusetts. This chapter uses a framework derived from Kevin Lynch's approach to urban design, analyzing the specific design characteristics of urban spaces that are both overtly queer and other places that are "queering" which the authors describe as diverse and welcoming, but not explicitly queer. In Chapter 7 Petra Doan examines an LGBTQ-friendly residential area in a small city in Florida, exploring what it means to be queer friendly. She illustrates the ways that homophobia still constrains LGBTQ residential choices in the deep south, arguing that planning support is needed for the kinds of progressive neighborhoods that provide a quiet welcome for the LGBTQ community.

5

THINKING BEYOND EXCLUSIONARY GAY MALE SPATIAL FRAMES IN THE DEVELOPING WORLD

Gustav Visser

Introduction

Sexual and gender minorities have struggled for fundamental inclusion in the social, political and economic life of their communities for centuries (Binnie, 2004; Casey, 2004; Hubbard, 2012; Johnston and Longhurst, 2010). A number of political and theoretical strategies have been deployed to challenge and resist the underpinnings of accepted theorization about gender, sexuality, embodiment, and attendant social relations (Browne et al., 2007a; Heaphy, 2011; Waitt and Markwell, 2006). Over the past decade there has been considerable growth in the different feminist and queer thinking of homonormativity opening up a range of divisions, as well as new alliances between and amongst both theorists and activists (Richardson, 2005; Rushbrook, 2002; Waitt and Markwell, 2006). Potentially, these gendered and sexual politics are engaged in the formation of new so-called equality landscapes, whilst often being critical of the legislative equalities that are seen as normalizing once queer lives through institutions such as marriage, the adoption of children, and the introduction of partner pension schemes and medical insurance (Ahmed, 2006; Hekma, 2004). However, although much debate has been generated about the fluidities and anti-normativities of these new conceptualizations, the assertion has in many ways remained that certain spaces that were once political and filled with radical opportunities are no longer queer, edgy, or different enough, having been absorbed into neoliberal urbanity (Hekma, 2004, Ghaziani, 2008; Zanghellini, 2009). Such spaces include traditional gay villages and other supposedly normalized sites (Casey, 2007; Chasin, 2000).

There has been increased interest in changes within LGBTQ neighborhoods and/or precincts in different cities and regions across the world, particularly, but perhaps not only, in the West. This includes concerns from some LGBTQ constituencies about the decline – or de-gaying – of some queer neighborhoods

(Casey, 2004; Hekma, 2004), coupled with commentary about the emergence of newer places, sometimes espoused as mixed, gay-friendly, or post-gay (Ghaziani, 2011; Gorman-Murray, 2006) – but how centrally should these debates stand in places beyond the developed Western world?

This chapter draws inspiration from suggestions that the "old gay [male] ghetto debates" are in some ways parochial, both spatially and theoretically (Hubbard, 2012) and the dominance of such concerns in queer spatial sciences that are so pervasive in Western gay space theorization must be challenged (Johnston and Longhurst, 2008; Tucker, 2009). This chapter focuses attention on Western spatial planning theorizations of "what gay is," a seeming preoccupation with the link between gay male sexualities, and specific forms of physical spaces such as gay ghettos and neighborhoods. The contention is that gay spaces in the form of consolidated physical or symbolic spaces are not a necessary outcome of lived gay identities. Two key points are made in this investigation. Drawing on the South African example, it is illustrated that (1) differently constructed gay identities are differently spatialized relative to context, and (2) that Western experiences in relation to the construction and associated decline of gay space is not universal. In addition, a general call is made for a more positive argument in researching the relationship between gay sexuality and space. The type of argument should not be one that shows that gay ghettos and neighborhoods are being displaced and are declining in necessarily negative terms, but rather that they are being replaced by new kinds of spaces, which are assuming their clearest forms beyond the West, and could be pointing towards greater inclusion and acceptance of gay minorities.

This argument is developed through three sections of discussion and analysis. First, a review of Western discourse focused on the relationship between gay male identities and physical and symbolic spaces is outlined. In the following section, the central concern that arises is that gay identities cannot be kept stable in non-Western contexts, such as South Africa, to facilitate the theorization of a relationship between space and sexualized identity/identities. It is argued that relative to experiences elsewhere, the current Western discourse requires extensive empirical testing, as the current theorizations of gay sexualities relative to space-formation are regional Western sexuality/space reflections or narratives and not (as presently implied) ready for large scale theorization. Current Western theory is not only insufficient to explain gay spatial realities in the Western/Northern context itself, but it totally ignores (and is irrelevant to) the majority gay population located in different and diverse settings elsewhere. The South African experience serves as an example of this contention.

Thinking beyond the Current Debates on "Being Gay" and its Spatial Manifestations

There has been increasing debate surrounding essentialized notions of what being gay might mean (Luongo, 2007; Tamale, 2011; Tucker, 2009). Investigators such as Tucker (2009), along with others (Habib, 2009; Howell, 2007; Quirogo, 2000;

Reid-Pharr, 2002; Ross, 2005; Wallace, 2002), contend that the representations of gay/straight, "in the closet"/"out of the closet" are being questioned through their application to contexts, communities, and societies that do not place such prominence on proclaiming a particular "authentic" sexual identity located around a particular Western or European gay/straight binary. The contention is that different individuals will relate to heterosexual society(ies)/communities/families in different ways and therefore may choose to reveal their sexuality/identity but do so in ways that might not lead to unilateral ideals of sexual liberation associated with the Western notion of "the closet" and "coming out" (Tucker, 2009). Investigators working outside the Western milieu have avoided and questioned deploying Western sexuality descriptors such as gay/straight/bisexual as a way of exploring sexual identities. This work is focused on the uniqueness of particular forms of sexual identity in different racialized locations, or on the way these identities are later affected by and in turn affect Western influences (Rink, 2008; Jackson, 2001; Oswin, 2005; Sonnekus, 2010). The investigations have aimed to historicize the experiences of gay men in places such as sub-Saharan Africa, in part explaining why other types of societies' or communities' understanding of sexual identity may be so different to those mostly studied in key sites in the West (Elder, 2003; Epprecht, 2004, 2010; Moodie, 2001; Murray and Roscoe, 1998; Tucker, 2009). Others have, for example, explored effeminate gender identities and their relationships to forms of non-heteronormativity (Herdt, 1994). Some of this scholarship has also therefore ended up calling into question whether it is even possible to call some of these groups "homosexual" (Ratele, 2011).

While these debates are ongoing, broader gay studies investigations, for the most part, have failed to meaningfully include empirical evidence from outside the Western context as to what gay might mean for space creation and attendant social relations (Tamale, 2007). For example, the complexity of sexualities in Africa as explored in Sylvia Tamale's (2011) recent collection of essays problematizes the stability of sexual identity as a whole – not least, homosexual identities. Indeed, most of this work emphasizes the fluidity of sexual identity and spaces in which it is or might be expressed. One of the key arguments in her collection is that Western researchers still view sexuality within the narrow spectrum of the sex act (see review by Hubbard, 2012), and seldom investigate the extraneous factors that impact and shape our multivarious sexualities (Tamale, 2011: 11). She goes on to argue that scholars from the African context caution against oversimplifying and essentializing the practice and discourses of sexualities in Africa, "urging us to read their multiple and contextual meanings" (Tamale, 2011: 11). Sexuality has to be referred to in the plural as it points to the diverse forms of orientation, identity, and status. Tamale (2011: 11) argues that her collection of essays is "a political call to conceptualize sexuality outside the normative social orders and frameworks that view it through the binary oppositions and simplistic labels". The suggestion is that thinking in terms of multiple sexualities is crucial to disperse the essentialism embedded in so much of current (Western) sexuality research.

The collection of essays edited by Luongo (2007) echoes Tamale's concerns. It is demonstrated that counter to prevailing views of the invisibility of an Arab gay world, there is one which is fluid both in terms of what being gay might mean, and the spaces in which such an "identity" is expressed. For example, it is demonstrated that some public spaces are both homosexual and straight. The realm of gay sexual activity is not as visible as in the West, like in for example New York, Los Angeles, or San Francisco, and much of it is a negotiation of private spaces. In addition, what could appear to Western observers as gay gestures (like two men holding hands or kissing) is interpreted differently – and does not necessarily indicate homosexuality. Similarly, Waitt and Markwell (2006) have pointed towards similar issues in South East Asia. What these studies illustrate is the complexity of naming the Western gay identity in the African, Middle Eastern and North African contexts – and yet, the act of naming stands central to being able to theorize the relationship between sexuality and consolidated physical (and arguably symbolic) space, whether in the process of forming (gaying) or imploding (de-gaying/homonormalizing) gay spaces.

So what does it mean to be "gay" in a country like South Africa? As suggested above, this is a matter that has seen significant debate in the academic press not only internationally but within South Africa (Oswin, 2005; Sonnekus, 2010; Tucker, 2009; Visser, 2003a, 2003b). However, it has not, in my view, been fully appreciated how complex it is to apply these identity markers in the context of the Global South, let alone influence various theoretical claims made around the relationship(s) between sexuality and space seen in Western discourses. While investigating gay cohorts in urban South Africa, for example, it has been relatively straightforward to identify and interview white gay male survey participants (for example, Rink, 2008; Tucker, 2009; van Zyl and Steyn, 2005; Visser, 2008a). However, colonialism and apartheid imposed different racial categories along with diverse understandings of gender performativity and where those performances are allowed to take place. Research into "other" race groups' sexuality – in terms of gayness – is more complicated because the identity marker "gay" does not necessarily hold a clear or stable meaning over space and through time (Ampofo and Boateng, 2011; Ratele, 2011).

Indeed, this gestures to a broader issue of the role of positionality, identity and political-temporal contingency in the production of South African research and those that are being "investigated" (Hoogendoorn and Visser, 2012; Visser, 2001). Gune and Manual's (2005) "Doing research on sexuality in Africa: ethical dilemmas and the positioning of the researcher," along with Tamale (2011) provides direct and substantial insight as well as critique into the complexities of sexuality research in the African context. In a review of Morgan and Wieringa's (2005) *Tommy Boys, Lesbians and Ancestral Wives*, Tamale (2008) notes that:

> [I]t must be pointed out that a book on African lesbians that is steered by allegedly altruistic impulses from researchers in the North … imports several problems of perspective, positioning and conceptualization beyond the

specific topic under analysis ... the approach adopted ... only helps to fuel the misconceptions and myths surrounding [sexuality] ... it becomes clear that the project was not 'owned' by the African participants who engaged it. The whole top-down approach is starkly bound up in what can only be described as manifest p/maternalism that smacks of racism and imperialist politics. (Tamale, 2008: 137)

My broader point is that researching different sexualities in South Africa presents a range of challenges.

Investigating white gay men might be relatively easy (for many reasons which include class, race and "Westernized" conceptions of queer identity), however, the same cannot be suggested for many other South Africans (who might be described as gay from a Western perspective), not because there are no black men that seek out same-sex emotional and/or physical intimacy, but because the marker "gay" simply does not stick, and they do not agree with such "naming." The question then is that if the gay identity as a descriptor cannot be kept relatively stable, how does one insist upon gay space formation or a relationship between a gay sexuality and space?

Moving onto the matter of queer identity in space is thus the challenge of identifying and naming the "subject/object" of analysis. The issue of moving or imploding "gay ghettos" implies a relationship between sexuality and space – that there is some sort of ghetto/neighborhood, which potentially occurs in any given densely populated urban space (Castells, 1983; Gorman-Murray, 2009). The question is whether there is a necessary spatial basis for gay sexuality in South Africa, as suggested by both current and pioneering scholars of this contention such as Bell and Valentine (1995), Castells (1983) or Knopp (1992), Browne et al. (2007b), as well as Gorman-Murray (2006). In the South African context, such a scale of analysis would not provide much evidence to support such a claim. A rather "classic" contention in academic literature is that "gay space" (and "gay neighborhoods" in particular) represent so-called fields of care in which gay or lesbian individuals cultivate and reaffirm identities, and develop emotional attachments based on repeated experiences within bounded spatial limits (Johnston and Longhurst, 2010). Empirically, this theoretical claim does not stand in South Africa. Perhaps networks of people form the basis of "fields of care", as clearly demonstrated in the work of Oswin (2005) and Tucker (2009) but, as shown below, it certainly does not necessitate fixed physical or symbolic space.

In South Africa, there is limited evidence of the "sexuality begets specific space" scenario across race and class boundaries (Visser, 2008a, 2008b). The historical record demonstrates that some white gay cohorts did demonstrate such behavior in city spaces in some neighborhoods in both Cape Town and Johannesburg. In Gevisser and Cameron's (1993) collection of essays it is shown that during the 1970s and 1980s there were concentrations of gay leisure venues in Hillbrow and later in Mellville (Johannesburg) during the late 1990s. As such, there was some sort of understanding that these were neighborhoods in which there resided more openly gay people, along with some gay leisure venues. However, this did not result in consolidated spatial units as seen in the Western interpretation of gay ghettos or neighborhoods (cf. Castells, 1983). Similar claims can be made for other South African cities with the CBD, Green Point and Sea Point areas of Cape Town hosting a number of gay venues over the years (Visser, 2003a, 2008a, 2008b). Lately, the De Waterkant area of Green Point has attracted some research attention (Visser, 2003a, 2003b; Rink, 2008). For white gay men, however, sexuality was generally "lived through" networks of people, not in fixed neighborhood sized spaces (Gevisser and Cameron, 1993; Visser, 2008a).

In terms of other racial categories, a similar point is made in the collection of essays edited by van Zyl and Steyn (2005). The work of Leap (2005) on Cape Town also shows how black, colored, and white gay men interpreted different neighborhoods as the location of "gay" places, but certainly not whole neighborhoods. These areas are dispersed across the city and racialized and classed, however, with no real neighborhood focus. Historically, black South Africans had no claim to urban space until the late 1980s, which makes the notion of a gay neighborhood in the past problematic and place-specific. In a black, gay male context, these spaces were far more complicated. For example, Elder (2003) as well as Murray and Roscoe (1998) described spaces such as mine hostels in which man-on-man emotional and sexual relationships were expressed and tolerated, but seldom (if ever) moved outside those spaces – and they certainly never moved into formal gay neighborhoods or ghettos. Nor did the relevant participants identify themselves as gay. A gay ghetto (whether white, black, or racially mixed) never developed in South Africa.

On a smaller scale of analysis, it has to be acknowledged that over the decades, some white gay men created gay leisure places for themselves (Gevisser and Cameron, 1993; Tucker, 2009; Visser, 2003a, 2003b, 2008a, 2008b, 2010). Reasons for this included acceptance, community and sexual opportunity (Gevisser and Cameron, 1993; Tucker, 2009; Visser, 2003a, 2003b, 2008a, 2008b, 2010). Although these spaces were usually white and middle class, in Cape Town, for example, there were instances of bars and clubs that were mainly geared towards the Malay/colored gay community (Gevisser and Cameron, 1993; Tucker, 2009). Towards the end of the twentieth century, and with a progressive constitution, it appeared as if an opportunity might have opened for the creation of a gay neighborhood in Cape Town (Rink, 2008; Visser, 2003a, 2003b). Although there was and is a concentration of gay leisure activities in Cape Town's De Waterkant, a ghetto (or neighborhood) has not developed and I would argue, along with Rink (2008), is highly unlikely to do so in the future – there being no need for the exclusion of gay men is complicated and their apparent inclusion is more forthcoming than Northern theory might suggest (Oswin, 2005; Rink, 2008; Tucker, 2009; Visser, 2008a). Indeed, it is an important consideration. However, as Tucker (2009) and Visser (2008a) have demonstrated, race/class identities are probably at the root of this "acceptance" in the South African context. A key observation is that the "ghetto" in all its forms has been premised on the idea of fear, exclusion and seeking identity, but the point is that the creation of a neighborhood or ghetto is not a necessary outcome of these marginalizations or sought inclusions of homosexuals. On the contrary, for most white gay men the gaying of limited straight space would, for the most part, more accurately describe their leisure and residential spatial realities (Visser, 2008a, 2008b, 2010).

This leads to the underlying notion in theorizing the sexuality/space nexus that gay men are necessarily not accepted in a range of communities (cf. Brown-Saracino, 2011). Acceptance is a problematic concept to start with. The academic and empirical record reflects the horrors of not being accepted as being gay across the globe (see the collection of essays by Morgan and Wieringa, 2005, as well as Tamale, 2011). Nevertheless, there is a need to resist the "anti-gay" meta-narrative in academic or general media discourses surrounding gay "acceptance." The current literature seems to be fixated on the rejection of queer lives in heterosexual life-worlds (cf. Brown-Saracino, 2011; Browne et al., 2007b). In South Africa, Canada, the Netherlands, Belgium and Spain, acceptance from a legislative point of view has to be acknowledged. In South Africa, from a legislative/constitutional point of view, one's sexuality is a non-issue (Tucker, 2009). Socially, however, the same is not true (Human Rights Watch, 2011; Posel, 2011). For example, acceptance of black lesbians in South African society is limited at best – in fact, a string of corrective rape cases proves the opposite (Morgan and Wieringa, 2005). However, extending this claim more broadly is problematic (Lahiri, 2011). There are, in fact, many contradictions of acceptance to be found (Visser, 2008a, 2008b). Race, class, and gay sexuality might be seen as a nexus that could predict "acceptance" – for example, turning attention, particularly to the white middle class urban youth. Leisure spaces of all kinds can serve as spaces of identity development, consolidation and sexual exploration (Tucker, 2009; Visser, 2008a, 2008b, 2010). Yet, as Tamale (2011) suggests, here is a locational and/or class and race (or gender) issue, for this claim can best be made relative to specific locations: mainly large cities, white areas and relatively expensive places. However, even in small South African cities (in fact in small towns in the rural expanses of central South Africa) the issue of race and class in many cases overrides the importance of sexual orientation (Ingle, 2010). Although the general community might not approve of gay lifestyles, gay men are generally accepted because they are not poor and "at least they are white" – read "one of us". For white gay men, all manner of homophobia can be negotiated, merely because in a racialized and classed society such as South Africa, being "white" and broadly of the same "class" – the "us" – overrides sexuality as a major marker of difference (Leap, 2005; Rink, 2008; Visser, 2008a). By the same token, being black, poor and gay will certainly find little acceptance in white leisure space, although it will in some black township spaces (Human Rights Watch, 2011; Visser, 2008b). Locational context and variability is thus important and acceptance/exclusion is not monolithic but locally negotiated through race and class identities.

In addition, we might add that exclusion/inclusion/acceptance is also "the individual in community" contingent. For example, there are ample cases of black gay men who are accepted in their communities as gay (Rink, 2008; Tucker, 2009). In fact, a case study in Bloemfontein indicates that many black gay men seek leisure in "straight" township leisure spaces (Visser, 2008a, 2008b). Tucker (2009) has also found that the negative social consequences of being gay in some black townships can be overcome, not because of heteronormative performativity, but owing to the individual's unique negotiation of his spatial context. In many of these cases, the performativity of the individual's sexuality stands central. Being a black or colored gay man is/can be performed in a markedly different manner from many gay white men – totally effeminate or alternatively homonormalized perhaps but context-specific (culturally, economically, historically, socially, and locationally) nevertheless (Tucker, 2009). For example, acceptance of a truly effeminate black gay man in a larger community context that is in many ways deeply homophobic, is possible (Tucker, 2009).

It is my contention that this points to a glaring gap in current assertions not only concerning sexuality and acceptance generally but their manifestation in the South African context specifically. There is clearly a connection in this claim to issues of performativity, but some people are plainly able to negotiate their immediate heterosexual world "better," not because they are homonormalized in their sexual performativity, but because of who they are as individuals. Gay studies need to be more sensitive to such variance.

Finally, the issue of relocating/de-gaying gay villages/neighborhoods in South Africa requires attention. I would first argue that, empirically, the notion of a gay neighborhood or village is not appropriate in most South African contexts. In different cities, there are different narratives. Cape Town's De Waterkant has certainly seen some animated academic and general media debates (Rink, 2008; Tucker, 2009; Visser, 2003a, 2003b). While the area is gay coded (both within the gay "community" and outside by the "heterosexual community"), it hardly qualifies as a gay village or neighborhood as compared to areas in cities such as Amsterdam, New York or San Francisco (Rink, 2008; Tucker, 2009; Visser, 2003a, 2003b). Recent evidence also suggests that other large metropolitan regions such as Durban, Johannesburg or Pretoria have neighborhoods that might be populated more densely by leisure services that cater to gay leisure needs, but there has certainly not been any consolidation of gay space, leisure or otherwise. The point is: there is no gay ghetto to move to or from in South African cities or towns. In addition, the growing role of virtual spaces of gay interaction such as Gaydar, Grindr and a range of other social networks might undermine not only the development of consolidated gay space but even gay bars and clubs. In this respect, however, there is certainly scope for directed empirical research, as currently this point is supported by investigations in which virtual meeting spaces are only mentioned by survey participants in passing (cf. Visser, 2008a). Additionally, a range of issues linked to who the main participants in these networks are, and in what way class or education might impact on such claims (Visser, 2008a) needs to be explored. However, on the whole, this realizes the challenge of how to think about the movement between and across the continua of real/virtual spaces, public/private spaces and physical/virtual relations.

The second contention relates to how people deal with visibility in terms of sexuality. The theoretical position has been that gay people use alternative spaces, or transform existing spaces to resist heteronormativity – to resist what society dictates as acceptable behavior: body language, sexuality, and activity (Colomina and Bloomer, 1992; Hubbard, 2012). Social bonds develop among sexual dissidents in these resistive spaces, and these spaces can in turn produce and strengthen these bonds. Such claims are of course made with reference to gay pride marches, drag shows, "coming out days," etc. in specific cities: Sydney, Provincetown, New York, and London, or countries such as the US, UK and Australia (Knopp, 1998, 2007). Yet, that is simply not the case everywhere. On the contrary, if repression was the genesis and means by which gay space or neighborhoods would develop, then Africa, the Middle East, and South America should be teaming with gay villages, gay ghettos, gay marches, and the like. However, this could be a matter of gay men in these regions just being terrified – they simply cannot take any action owing to current legislative frameworks. The point is: making the claim that exclusion and oppression is (as theory suggests) an adequate set of conditions to lead to consolidated queer spaces developing does not hold.

In addition, legislative protection is certainly no guarantee for the development of gay neighborhoods or villages either. South Africa has extraordinarily progressive legislation that technically makes discrimination on sexuality grounds illegal. Indeed, so too do a number of northern European countries. Seen from this angle, one might argue that the extension of the "social bonds" position would be that gay men would seek out the development of consolidated queer spaces. The empirical fact, however, is that, as a rule, they do not. Many assumptions in gay/lesbian debates concerning the relationship between sexuality and space require empirical testing. Even at the most basic scale of visibility (in terms of leisure), this verification is required to prove key current theoretical positions.

Theorizing Beyond Dedicated Gay Male Space

Perhaps one of the great issues holding back the theorization of gay male space is a preoccupation with the West and its activist past of the 1970s and 1980s, which have formed the focus of key authors in the gay space debates. Exclusion/inclusion/acceptance/rejection and a necessary link to physical or symbolic spaces still form the backbone of these debates (Oswin, 2008). The theoretical base of this discourse has been derived from a small number of Anglo-American scholars describing a limited geographical reality. There is a lack of empirical evidence from outside the Western core with the outcome that these theoretical debates are simply a form of localized (particularly American and British) introspection. In the process, the theory is not only insufficient to explain gay spatial realities in the Western/Northern context itself, but totally ignores and is irrelevant to the majority gay population located in different and diverse settings elsewhere. The point is that at a global scale, the current theoretical positions on the relationship between gay identities and space do not explain much of the global gay lived reality – and this investigation is only one example of this contention.

This chapter has mainly been concerned with the empirical realities of South African scholarship, yet is illustrative of general debates into the sexualities/space nexus vis-à-vis a broadly framed Western investigation. It gestures to further issues we should consider in the Global South relative to the North. Gay debates from a Northern perspective are correct in asserting that heteronormativity is still the key social guide in sexualized relations. However, not only is what constitutes heteronormativity a moving target over time, it is extremely diverse across space. These are points that the scholarly community focusing on gay men in space is either struggling with or overlooking. It has to be acknowledged that not only is heterosexual society changing in terms of what it means to be heterosexual, but presenting essentialized images of "the heterosexual" world vis-à-vis its negotiation of "non-heterosexuals" (another moving target) is too narrow. The overarching point is that answers to such suggestions are to be found in a vastly expanded empirical project that is inclusive of various spatial realities.

Parallel to this there is the issue of new spaces in which "community" is found and developed (Johnston and Longhurst, 2008). Virtual spaces in the form of chatrooms, websites, Facebook or Gaydar lead to spaces for meeting, developing and reaffirming gay identities of various kinds. An issue that requires insight is in what way these virtual spaces are impacting a range of physical spaces. Heterosexual leisure spaces are and can be used as spaces in which men meet men for negotiating sex or companionship, enabled by such technologies. Spaces with gay inscriptions, either physical or symbolic, are not necessarily required. We might find a particular physical space being the meeting place simultaneously of a straight couple hooking-up via virtual meeting spaces, sitting at a table next to two gay men who have done the same. The question is: how does one describe and theorize spaces that hold myriad inscriptions to both heterosexuals and homosexuals?

Given the insistence on greater inclusion, this point might appear to undermine the general tenor of this paper. It might be argued that such technologies would only be applicable to the developed North and that a young African gay male in a remote rural landscape does not have such opportunities. However, the developing South is now well served in terms of cell phones and linked web technology to access virtual gay communities from which interaction can be arranged. Gay men would in turn negotiate their historical, cultural, and social location-specific contexts for their interaction. Not to follow a teleological line of reasoning, but this might well result in gay space development never taking off, with no ghetto ever developing, and gay bars and clubs left to de-gay.

In the end, gay ghettos and their demise, owing to de-gaying, or homonormalization and heteronormativity infiltrating gay or lesbian lives as currently communicated in Western discourse only serve to show how many gay lives are excluded and just how parochial the current gay debates are. The underlying idea of this investigation is that the perspective could change to one in which it is shown how new kinds of spaces are being created, and pointing towards something more inclusive and accepting of gay men.

References

Ahmed, S. 2006. Orientations: Towards a queer phenomenology, *GLQ*, 12, 543–574.

Altman, D. 1997. Global gaze/global gays, *GLQ*, 3, 417–436.

Ampofo, A., & Boateng, J. 2011. Multiple meanings of manhood among boys in Ghana. In S. Tamale (Ed.) *African Sexualities*. Cape Town, South Africa: Pambazuka, 420–436.

Bell, D., & Valentine, G. 1995. *Mapping Desire: Geographies of Sexualities*. London, UK: Routledge.

Binnie, J. 2004. *The Globalization of Sexuality*. London: Sage.

Browne, K., Lim, J., & Brown, G. 2007a. *Geography of Sexualities: Theory, Practices and Politics*. Aldershot, UK: Ashgate.

Browne, K., Lim, J., & Brown, G. (Eds). 2007b. "It's something you just have to ignore": understanding and addressing contemporary lesbian, gay, bisexual and trans safety beyond hate crime paradigms, *Journal of Social Policy*, 40(4), 739–756.

Brown-Saracino, J. 2011. From the lesbian ghetto to ambient community: The perceived costs and benefits of integration for community. *Social Problems*, 58(3), 361–388.

Casey, M. 2004. De-dyking queer space(s): heterosexual female visibility in gay and lesbian spaces. *Sexualities*, 7(4), 446–461.

Casey, M. 2007. The queer unwanted and their undesirable otherness. In K. Browne, J. Lim & G. Brown (Eds), *Geography of Sexualities: Theory, Practices, and Politics*, Aldershot, UK: Ashgate, 125–135.

Castells, M. 1983. *The City and the Grassroots*. Berkley, CA: University of California Press.

Chasin, A. 2000. *Selling Out: The Gay and Lesbian Movement Goes to the Market*. Basingstoke, UK: Palgrave.

Colomina, B., & Bloomer, J. 1992. *Sexuality and Space*. New York: Princeton Architectural Press.

Elder, G. 2003. Malevolent geographies: Sex race and the apartheid legacy. Ohio University Press, Athens.

Epprecht, M. 2004. *Hungochani: The History of Dissident Sexuality in Southern Africa*. London: Ithaca.

Epprecht, M. 2010. The making of "African" sexuality: early sources, current debates. *History Compass*, 8(8), 768–779.

Gevisser, M., & Cameron, E. 1993. *Defiant Desire: Gay and Lesbian Lives in South Africa*. Johannesburg: Raven.

Ghaziani, A. 2008. *The Dividends of Dissent: How Conflict and Culture Work in Lesbian and Gay Marches on Washington*. Chicago, IL: University of Chicago Press.

Ghaziani, A. 2011. Post-Gay Collective Identity Construction. *Social Problems*, 58(1), 99–125.

Gorman-Murray, A. 2006. Homeboys: use of home by gay Australian men. *Social and Cultural Geography*, 7(1), 53–69.

Gorman-Murray, A. 2009. Queer-friendly neighborhoods: interrogating social cohesion across difference in two Australian neighborhoods. *Environment and Planning A*, 41, 2855–2873.

Gune, E., & Manual, S. 2005. Doing research on sexuality in Africa: ethical dilemmas and the positioning of the researcher. Available at http://dspace.cigilibrary.org/jspui/bitstream/123456789/31871/1/bulletin-jun-2007.pdf?1

Habib, S. (Ed.). 2009. *Islam and Homosexuality*. New York: Praeger.

Heaphy, B. 2011. Gay identities and the culture of class. *Sexualities*, 14(1), 42–62.

Hekma, G. 2004. Queer: the Dutch case, *GLQ*, 10, 276–280.

Herdt, G. (Ed.). 1994. *Third Sex, Third Gender*. New York: Zone.

Hoogendoorn, G., & Visser, G. 2012. Stumbling over researcher positionality and political-temporal contingency in South African second homes tourism research. *Critical Arts*. (in press).

Howell, P. 2007. Foucault, sexuality, geography. In J.W. Crampton & S. Elden (Eds), *Space, Knowledge, Power: Foucault and Geography*. Aldershot, UK: Ashgate.

Hubbard, P. 2012. *Cities and Sexuality*. Oxford, UK: Routledge.

Human Rights Watch. 2011. "We'll show you you're a woman": *Violence and Discrimination against Black Lesbians and Transgender Men in South Africa*. Human Rights Watch, Johannesburg.

Ingle, M. 2010. A 'creative class' in South Africa's arid Karoo region. *Urban Forum*, 21(4), 405–423.

Jackson, P. 2001. Pre-gay, post-queer: Thai perspectives on the proliferating gender/sex diversity in Asia. *Journal of Homosexuality*, 40(3/4), 1–25.

Johnston, L., & Longhurst, R. 2008. Queer(ing) geographies 'down under': some notes on sexuality and space in Australasia. *Australian Geographer* 39 (3), 247–257.

Johnston, L., & Longhurst, R. 2010. *Space, Place and Sex*. Lanham, MD: Rowman and Littlefield.

Knopp, L. 1992. Sexuality and the spatial dynamics of capitalism. *Environment and Planning D: Society and Space* 10, 651–669.

Knopp, L. 1998. Sexuality and urban space: gay male identities, communities and cultures in the U.S., U.K. and Australia. In R. Fincher & J. Jacobs (Eds) *Cities of Difference*. New York: Guilford.

Knopp, L. 2007. From lesbian to gay to queer geographies: past, prospects and possibilities. In G. Brown & J. Lim (Eds) *Geographies of Sexualities: Theory Practices Politics*. Chichester, UK: Ashgate.

Lahiri, M. 2011. Crimes and corrections: Bride burners, corrective rapists, and other black misogynists. *Feminist Africa*, 15, 121–134.

Leap, W. 2005. Finding the Centre: Claiming gay space in Cape Town, South Africa. In M. van Zyl & M. Steyn (Eds.) *Performing Queer: Shaping Sexualities 1992–2004*. Cape Town, South Africa: Kwela Press, pp. 235–266.

Luongo, M. 2007. *Gay Travels in the Muslim World*. Binghampton, NY: Harrington Park Press.

Lynch, F. 1987. Non-ghetto gays: a sociological study of suburban homosexuals. *Journal of Homosexuality*, 11, 83–95.

Moodie, T. 2001. South African mine migration and the vicissitudes of male desire. In R. Morrell (Ed.), *Changing Men in South Africa*. Pietermaritzburg: University of Natal Press.

Morgan, R., & Wieringa, S. 2005. *Tommy Boys, Lesbian Men and Ancestral Wives: Female Same-Sex Practices in Africa*. Johannesburg, South Africa: Jacana.

Murray, S., & Roscoe, W. 1998. *Boy-Wives and Female Husbands: Studies of African Homosexualities*. Basingstoke, UK: Macmillan.

Oswin, N. 2005. Researching 'gay Cape Town', finding value-added queerness. *Social and Cultural Geography*, 6(4), 567–586.

Oswin, N. 2008. Critical geographies and the uses of sexuality. *Progress in Human Geography* 32 (1), 89–103.

Posel, D. 2011. Getting the nation talking about sex: reflections on the politics of sexuality and nation-building in post-apartheid South Africa. In S. Tamale (Ed.) *African Sexualities.* Cape Town, South Africa: Pambazuka, 130–144.

Quirogo, J. 2000. *Tropics of Desire: Interventions from Queer Latin America.* New York: New York University Press.

Ratele, K. 2011. Male sexualities and masculinities. In S. Tamale (Ed.), *African Sexualities.* Cape Town, South Africa: Pambazuka, 399–419.

Reid-Pharr, R. 2002. Extending queer theory to race and ethnicity. *The Chronicle of Higher Education,* 48/49 (August), B7.

Richardson, D. 2005. Desiring sameness? The rise of a neoliberal politics of normalisation. *Antipode,* 37, 515–535.

Rink, B. 2008. Community as utopia: Reflections on De Waterkant, *Urban Forum,* 19(2), 201–217.

Ross, M. 2005. Typing, doing and being: Sexuality and the internet. *Journal of Sex Research,* 42, 342–352.

Rushbrook, D. 2002. Cities, queer space, and the cosmopolitan tourist. *GLQ,* 8(1–2), 183–206.

Sonnekus, T. 2010. Invisible queers: investigating the 'other' other in gay visual cultures, MA-thesis, University of Pretoria, Pretoria.

Tamale, S. 2003. Out of the closet: unveiling sexuality discourses in Uganda. *Feminist Africa,* 2, 42–49.

Tamale, S. 2007. *Homosexuality: Perspectives from Uganda.* Sexual Minorities Uganda (SMUG). Kampala.

Tamale, S. (Ed.) 2011. *African Sexualities: A Reader.* Cape Town, South Africa: Pambazuka Press.

Tucker, A. 2009. *Queer Visibilities: Space, Identity and Interaction in Cape Town.* Oxford, UK: Wiley-Blackwell.

van Zyl, M., & Steyn, M. (Eds.) 2005. *Performing Queer: Shaping Sexualities 1994–2004.* Roggebaai, South Africa: Kwela Books.

Visser, G. 2001. On the politics of time and place in a transforming South African research environment: new challenges for research students. *South African Geographical Journal* 83(3), 233–239.

Visser, G. 2003a. Gay men, leisure space and South African cities: the case of Cape Town. *Geoforum,* 34, 123–137.

Visser, G. 2003b. Gay men, tourism and urban space: reflections on Africa's 'gay capital'. *Tourism Geographies,* 5(2), 168–189.

Visser, G. 2008a. The homonormalization of white heterosexual leisure spaces in Bloemfontein, South Africa, *Geoforum,* 39(3), 1347–1361.

Visser, G. 2008b. Exploratory notes on the geography of black gay leisure spaces in Bloemfontein, South Africa, *Urban Forum,* 19(4), 413–423.

Visser, G. 2010. Leisurely lesbians in a small city in South Africa, *Urban Forum,* 21(2), 171–185.

Waitt, G., & Markwell, K. 2006. *Gay Tourism: Culture and Context,* New York: THHP.

Wallace, M. 2002. *Constructing the Black Masculine: Identity and Ideality in African American Men's Literature and Culture.* Durham, NC: Duke University Press.

Zanghellini, A. 2009. Queer, Anti-Normativity, Counter-Normativity and Abjection. *Griffith Law Review,* 18(1), 1–16.

6

THE PERVASIVENESS OF HETERO-SEXISM AND THE EXPERIENCES OF QUEERS IN EVERYDAY SPACE

The Case of Cambridge, Massachusetts

Sarah P. Nusser and Katrin B. Anacker

Introduction

"[S]paces can [...] take on quite disparate meanings for different people and for diverse social situations" (Edelman, 1995, p. 74). The geography of queers[1] concentrates on the usage of space over time and the formation, development, and consolidation of identity (Bell, 1991). Space and identity are important for queers as most public space is heterosexualized, and queer expressions are often contested by the heterosexual public (Bell, 1991; Duncan, 1996; Frisch, 2002; Knopp, 1992; Myslik, 1996; Nusser & Anacker, 2013; Pritchard et al., 1998, 2002; Valentine, 1993, 1996).

The phenomenon of queer spatial concentrations with mixed, i.e., residential and entertainment, uses has been documented for decades. In the 1950s, queer entertainment areas were located on the edges of cities and in abandoned areas of downtowns. In the 1980s, some queer residential areas were established, and since the 1990s, many queer neighborhoods with mixed uses have sprung up in large cities, such as San Francisco (Black et al., 2002; Boyd, 2003; Castells, 1983; Lyod & Rowntree, 1978; Weightman, 1981; Winters, 1979), New York (Rothenberg, 1995; Winters, 1979), New Orleans (Knopp, 1990, 1997; Moss, 1997), Paris (Winchester and White, 1988), Montreal (Podmore, 2001, 2006), and smaller cities (Forsyth, 1997a, 1997b; Kidder, 1999), but also in select suburbs in select metropolitan areas (Anacker, 2011; Hodge, 1995; Lynch 1987, 1992). Over the past few years a subset of queer spatial concentrations have been documented, for example, the phenomena gay ghetto; gay village; gay district; gay mecca; gay neighborhood; and the "gayborhood," which primarily caters to gays and to a lesser degree to lesbians, bisexuals, and transgendered individuals (Bell & Binnie, 2004; Brown, 2013; Browne & Bakshi, 2011; Chisholm, 2005; Christensen, 2006; Collins, 2004; Fetner, 2008; Knopp, 1997; Kuhr, 2004; Levine, 1979; Lewis,

2013; Miller, 2005; Nash, 2006; Pritchard et al., 2002; Reed, 2003; Reuter, 2008; Ruting, 2008; Sibalis, 2004; Visser, 2003; Waitt & Markwell, 2006). Somewhat recently, queer-friendly neighborhoods, "where same-sex-attracted residents, businesses, and institutions are welcomed in a dominantly heterosexual milieu, and intergroup interaction fosters dialogue" have been analyzed (Browne & Bakshi, 2011; Gorman-Murray & Waitt, 2009, p. 2870). While some have argued that gay neighborhoods have degayed, declined, or demised (Browne & Bakshi, 2011; Doan & Higgins, 2011; Pritchard et al., 2002), others have argued for their continuing relevance and attention (Brown, 2013; Lewis, 2013).

Cambridge, Massachusetts, has never had queer or gay neighborhoods, although it has historically been considered a safe and accepting place for queer people. This chapter explores how queer people experience residential and entertainment space in Cambridge, MA, one of the most progressive cities in its region. Queer people who participated in in-depth interviews were asked about the spaces they feel the most and least comfortable being queer. These spaces were then analyzed for common characteristics within a Lynchian framework, including fit, control, and access. Ultimately, this chapter seeks to understand how relationships between the planning, design, and management of spaces create hostile or inclusive environments for queer people.

Theoretical Background

This contribution is theoretically based on Lynch (1984), who developed a general normative theory of city form that systematically states general relationships between the form of a place and its value assumptions. Lynch created a set of performance characteristics, such as vitality, sense, fit, access, and control. These characteristics can be measured through a number of spatial analytics and are sufficiently flexible to capture the fact that different city forms have different values and motives. For this contribution, we reduced the framework to fit, access, and control, the three characteristics we found most relevant for our study.

Fit evaluates the relationship between the activities people (want to) conduct in spaces and the physical characteristics of spaces. It assumes the possibility of difference between a place's actual spatial and temporal patterns and the desired behaviors of that place's user. This is especially important for queers whose desired behaviors might include the ability to express identity in a non-normative way, to exhibit displays of affection, to interact with people like themselves, or to be highly visible or discreet about sexual identity in public. Lynch utilizes two indicators strongly associated with fit, i.e., comfort and satisfaction, to which physical elements of space may contribute or detract from. To evaluate fit, we explore spatial volume, degree of enclosure, the formality or informality of decoration, and the connotations of various building materials in this contribution.

Access generally refers to the degree of choice offered among accessible resources, including human, material, activities, or information. However, we apply this performance characteristic to analyze how spaces signal welcome and to whom, focusing on queers. According to Lynch, access is central for an understanding of the social system and for analyzing the psychological impact of the city. In this contribution, we look at the connection of each analyzed space to its public realm, the number of transition spaces between a site and the street, and the permeability of its borders.

Control is the performance dimension that addresses the regulation of space and behavior through city codes, private legal contracts, private management of space, and the perpetuation or disruption of norms symbolized in space. Control includes not only ownership rights but the right to be present in, behave freely in, appropriate, or modify a space. Differentiating between the right to be present and the right to behave freely in the public domain is especially important when it comes to the level of control queer people have in a city. To analyze control we consider the management policies employed by business owners or the public sector, the level of one-way visibility in an indoor space, signs and symbols, and the options for activities and movement in space in our contribution.

In sum, our analyzed spaces in Cambridge exhibit varying degrees of fit, access, and control. We will discuss these dimensions in greater detail below, applying the three-pronged framework to the districts and commercial spaces identified in local interviews.

Data and Methods

The fieldwork for this study took place in February 2010 in Cambridge, Massachusetts. We conducted 13 interviews, hoping to follow up with a survey with a larger sample size. Cambridge was chosen because of its progressive politics and its history of queer activism. For example, Cambridge City Hall processed the nation's first gay marriage applications at 12:01 a.m. on May 17, 2004, after Massachusetts had previously become the first state in the United States to make gay marriage legal. Despite the increase in queer rights in Cambridge over time, there has been a decrease in the number of queer spaces since the 1990s. The remaining queer and queering spaces were the focus of our study.

Figure 6.1 below illustrates Cambridge's local history of enacting queer-friendly legislation, culminating in the formation of Cambridge's GLBT Commission. We began our fieldwork in Cambridge, speaking to the co-chairs of the GLBT Commission, which was created by the City Council and codified in the Municipal Code in 2005. We believe that such a commission is unique in the United States. Its expressed purpose is to:

> [A]dvocate for a culture of respect and to monitor progress toward equality for all persons with regard to sexual orientation and gender identity. We are committed to promoting and monitoring policies and practices that have a positive effect on the health, welfare, and safety of all persons who live, visit, or work in the City of Cambridge with respect to sexual orientation and gender identity. (City of Cambridge, GLBT Commission, n.d., n.p.)

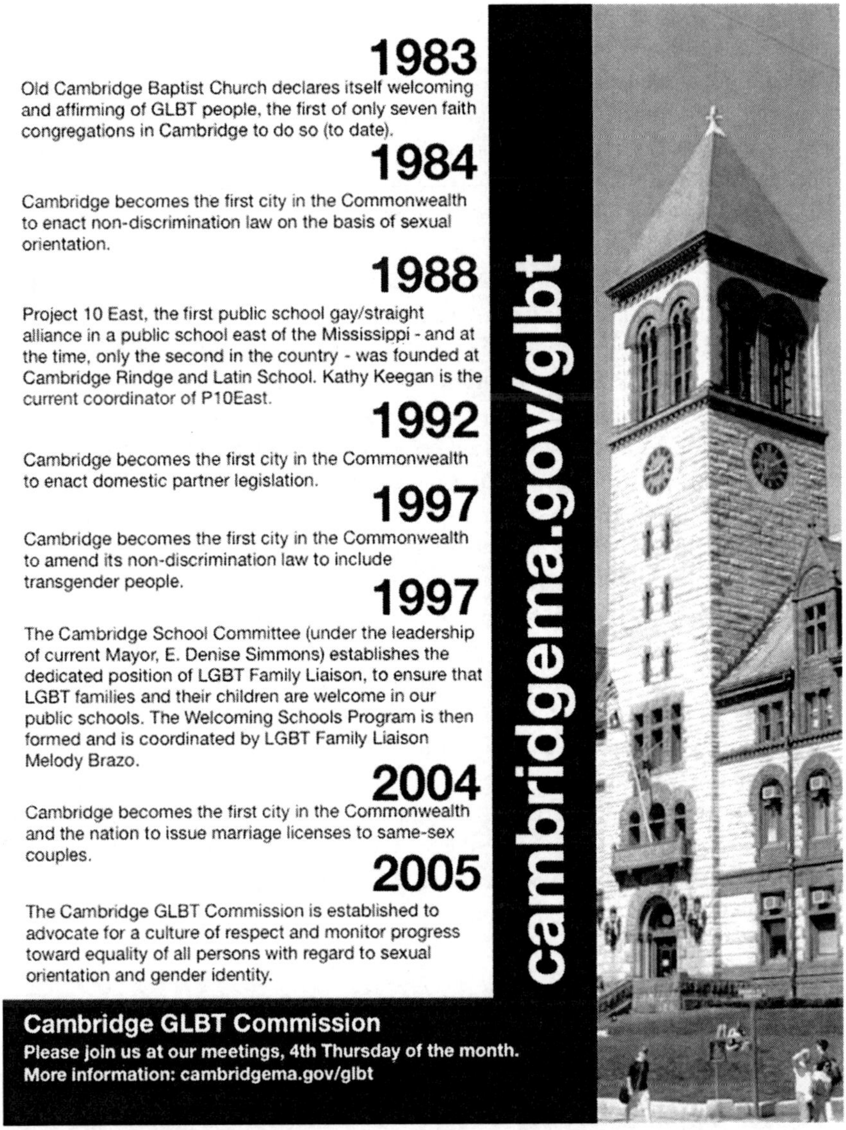

1983

Old Cambridge Baptist Church declares itself welcoming and affirming of GLBT people, the first of only seven faith congregations in Cambridge to do so (to date).

1984

Cambridge becomes the first city in the Commonwealth to enact non-discrimination law on the basis of sexual orientation.

1988

Project 10 East, the first public school gay/straight alliance in a public school east of the Mississippi - and at the time, only the second in the country - was founded at Cambridge Rindge and Latin School. Kathy Keegan is the current coordinator of P10East.

1992

Cambridge becomes the first city in the Commonwealth to enact domestic partner legislation.

1997

Cambridge becomes the first city in the Commonwealth to amend its non-discrimination law to include transgender people.

1997

The Cambridge School Committee (under the leadership of current Mayor, E. Denise Simmons) establishes the dedicated position of LGBT Family Liaison, to ensure that LGBT families and their children are welcome in our public schools. The Welcoming Schools Program is then formed and is coordinated by LGBT Family Liaison Melody Brazo.

2004

Cambridge becomes the first city in the Commonwealth and the nation to issue marriage licenses to same-sex couples.

2005

The Cambridge GLBT Commission is established to advocate for a culture of respect and monitor progress toward equality of all persons with regard to sexual orientation and gender identity.

Cambridge GLBT Commission
Please join us at our meetings, 4th Thursday of the month.
More information: cambridgema.gov/glbt

cambridgema.gov/glbt

FIGURE 6.1   Cambridge gay, lesbian, bisexual, and transgender (GLBT) history flyer

One way the GLBT Commission links to the queer community in Cambridge is through a number of Yahoo groups, including the Cambridge Men's Group, Rainbow Cambridge, Boston Masala, and the Queer Asian Pacific-Islander Alliance. The GLBT Commission co-chairs distributed our solicitation for interviews through these mechanisms (see Kitchin & Lysaght, 2003 for a similar solicitation strategy).[2] About a dozen individuals responded to this outreach. In addition, we reached out to potential participants through friendship networks, resulting in 13 interviews in total. While these strategies were a successful method of securing interviews in a limited amount of time, we acknowledge that a large proportion of the queer population is not part of these networks for any number of reasons. With more time, it would have been highly interesting to incorporate several additional methods, including both a venue- and a snowball-driven approach to connect with people who are not tapped into these networks, who do not use the Internet, or who wish to remain anonymous about their identities in public.

We developed a list of 17 questions focused on where in Cambridge interviewees felt the most and least comfortable being queer, as well as the physical and social characteristics of the spaces identified with a focus on nonresidential spaces. The initial question was "Where in Cambridge do you feel the most comfortable being gay/queer/lesbian/transgender/bisexual?" Most questions in the interview were open-ended, asking participants to reflect on their perceptions of the spaces that resonated most with them, including the specific point at which comfort levels change when approaching a space, the perceived relationship of each space to its surroundings, and emotions associated with particular elements of each space. All interviews were recorded and then transcribed.

Interviews were conducted with seven males, four females, and two genderqueers[3]; nine white persons and four persons of color; and three people in their 20s, five people in their 30s, two people in their 40s, two people in their 50s, and one person in his 60s. Interviews were conducted in person or over the phone, and each interview lasted between 30 minutes and an hour.

The interviewee-identified spaces were visited after the interviews to determine if and how physical and spatial relationships related to the Lynchian framework discussed above. Our goal was to use the framework to characterize the performance of a variety of urban spaces with which queers in Cambridge typically come into contact, as well as to see trends and differences based on age, gender, and race/ethnicity.

Results

Overall, each of the 13 interviewees in Cambridge felt comfortable as a queer person in Cambridge's public spaces. However, different interviewees expressed being out on the street in subtly different ways, ranging from being visibly out; to being comfortable with being perceived as out, even if behavior is not overt; to not having to constantly monitor one's surroundings and personal behavior in public spaces.

In regard to being visibly out, a bisexual non-Hispanic white woman in her 20s described it as "hold[ing] my partner's hand when I walk down the street." A gay, non-Hispanic white man in his 60s described it as "wearing rainbow paraphernalia anywhere in Cambridge." In regard to being comfortable with being perceived as out, a gay, non-Hispanic white man in his 30s mentioned that "there are implicit signs of intimacy […] like eating dinner together and walking around the city together and doing it all the time when we're outside of our home [...] and I feel comfortable doing that." In regard to not having to constantly monitor one's surroundings and personal behavior in public spaces, a gay, non-Hispanic white man in his 30s stated that "I feel comfortable in most places and not thinking twice," while a gay, non-Hispanic white man in his 40s stated that "I don't have to edit myself." These quotes help us to understand the many ways in which behavior is regulated in public space, even if only implicitly.

Many interviewees were conscious of symbols and signs in public spaces that made them feel more comfortable being queer. A bisexual non-Hispanic white woman in her 20s stated, "I've seen a lot of GLBT folk with identifiers [...] like putting the flag on their bag [...] I've seen a lot of that." A gay non-Hispanic white man in his 30s noticed "little stickers in windows for businesses [...] they're nothing new but they're showing up more and more." A gay, non-Hispanic white man in his 40s said, "You see a lot of equality stickers. People are very open about that."

Interestingly, one interviewee, a lesbian non-Hispanic white woman in her 50s, did not perceive symbolic signs to be present in the public realm, stating, "You certainly don't see rainbow flags hanging." This may point to a perceived difference in symbols that are generated by an individual or an individual business and those that are generated and affirmed by a collective body. For example, the stickers were closely associated with a specific individual or a specific business, whereas flags are more boldly situated in the public realm.

Besides reflecting on public spaces, the 13 interviewees identified 14 permanent queer and queering spaces in Cambridge (primarily around Inman Square) and in Somerville (an adjacent small city). Additionally, interviewees identified temporary queer spaces in Cambridge and Boston, typically in the form of a queer night at a bar that may be a one-off event or happen once a month. The interviewees also identified temporary queer spaces. Massachusetts Avenue in Cambridge had the greatest density and the greatest mix of permanent and temporary queer and queering spaces identified by interviewees (see also Browne, 2006; Kitchin & Lysaght, 2003; Pritchard et al., 2002).

"Particular features of buildings enhance and legitimate differences among individuals" (Edelman, 1995, p. 80). Often, queer space is not explicitly labeled as such, although many spaces use subtle symbols such as rainbow-colored lights or signage that suggests welcome. Queer spaces are often highly enclosed and characterized by the perceived high level of safety, acceptance, and human connection they provide. Sometimes queer spaces only provide these qualities for specific groups of queer people based on sexual preference, age, gender, and/or race and ethnicity. Queer spaces can be bars or church spaces, among others.

Queering spaces are often less enclosed than queer spaces, i.e., having more porous transitions between the sidewalk and the establishment such as outdoor seating or glass facades. Many queering spaces are coffee shops or districts that are physically differentiated in some manner, either by being semi-enclosed or by being architecturally distinct. Queering spaces typically utilize management practices, like hiring employees that are "alternative looking," and contain a diversity of users, increasing feelings of queer control.

Below we will discuss a few examples of queer space (Paradise, St. John's), followed by a few examples of queering space (Toscanini's, 1369 Coffee House, Darwin's, Harvard Square, One Kendall Square).

Examples of Queer Space: Paradise | Society of St. John the Evangelist

Paradise

Several interviewees recalled Paradise, a long-standing bar/sex club, but none had been there in years. They described Paradise as a formerly straight neighborhood bar that had found its current niche as queer space in the 1990s when other queer bars were dying out. Others described it as a sex club for a frequent clientele of older, working class men. Paradise has a flexible dance floor on the first floor, which is mostly used on weekends. Paradise also has an upstairs lounge, which is used each night. As a gay white man in his 60s stated, "They've got male dancers and male porn on TV sets above the bar."

In regard to fit, Paradise has free parking attached to the building so patrons can safely and quickly slip into and out of the bar. It also has a discrete entrance away from a busy thoroughfare (Massachusetts Avenue), allowing visitors to remain discrete about their visit. In regard to access, Paradise's interior is highly enclosed and removed from the public realm, but it is located on a major road, at the intersection with Albany Street, near the border of Cambridge and Boston, giving it a visible and accessible location.

In regard to control, the Paradise sign is painted in rainbow colors, implicitly advertising the bar as queer. Paradise's interior is highly enclosed and removed from the public realm through its tinted windows, preventing the public from looking in while allowing customers to monitor outdoor activity. Also, Paradise's lounge is upstairs, adding an additional layer of defense space from the street.

Society of St. John the Evangelist

Some interviewees pointed out the Society of St. John the Evangelist, an Episcopal monastery on Memorial Drive. One gay, black/African American woman in her 30s called it a "quietly queer" place. The monastery has a weekly worship space with a garden that is open to the public. The same interviewee responded, "I'll occasionally go there to sit and think."

In regard to fit, the monastery fronts Memorial Drive, a major thoroughfare along the Charles River that connects Boston and Cambridge. However, the entrance is set far back from the street. The monastery is a formal stone structure but not intimidating because of its modest scale and design. Inside, there are strict divisions among spaces. As the same interviewee noted, "so the internal space tends to feel intimate [...] and each one of those spaces feels a bit different."

In regard to access, although the monastery is on a major road, it sits at the edge of Cambridge, facing Boston. This location is both easily accessed and discrete. Just inside the entrance is a confined transitional space to collect oneself before entering the sanctuary. In that space, St. John's announces its welcoming monastic vision:

> A Monastery is a "liminal" place where visitors and guests cross a threshold, a thin place dividing earth and heaven. The silence and experience of safety that characterizes monastic hospitality enables them to listen deeply. A Monastery is counter-cultural.

In regard to control, monks play an important role in creating a safe place for contemplation as opposed to a place to work or be seen. As the same interviewee stated, "The monks work really hard to welcome young adults. They create a space for support. The monks see themselves as being called to hospitality."

Examples of Queering Space: Toscanini's | 1369 | Darwin's | Harvard Square | One Kendall Square

Toscanini's | 1369 Coffee House | Darwin's

Toscanini's is an ice-cream/coffee shop located on Main Street, about a five-minute walk from Massachusetts Institute of Technology (MIT). 1369 Coffee House has two locations in Cambridge, one in Central Square and one in Inman Square, both located at a ten-minute walk from Harvard and MIT, respectively. Darwin's coffee shop also has two locations, one on Mt. Auburn Street and one on Cambridge Street, each about a ten-minute walk from Harvard.

In regard to fit, coffee shops were mentioned as favorite spaces by nearly all respondents in their 20s and 30s, regardless of gender or race/ethnicity. However, one interviewee also described them as predominantly non-Hispanic white. Coffee shops serve a social and work function for interviewees. The spaces of the three analyzed coffee shops in this study are small and seating is often tightly packed. This lack of space creates intimacy but leaves little room for creating distinct spaces. To compensate, seating is either oriented near windows, granting visibility, or away from windows and the entrance door, offering some privacy.

In regard to access, all three analyzed coffee shops can be easily accessed from the sidewalks. Their facades achieve a high degree of transparency through the extensive use of glass, which enables double exposures, forming a strong connection between the indoors and the outdoors of these spaces, as can be seen in Figure 6.2 below.

Each of the analyzed coffee shops for this study had some sort of outdoor furniture to create transitional spaces, as illustrated in Figure 6.3 below.

FIGURE 6.2 Example of queering space in Cambridge with a high degree of transparency through extensive use of glass: Toscanini's

FIGURE 6.3 Example of queering space in Cambridge with transitional space through the use of outdoor furniture: 1369 Coffee House

In regard to control, the three analyzed coffee shops had employees who we think are strong contributors to the queering of coffee shop space. A bisexual non-Hispanic white woman in her 20s stated, "[…] [this coffee shop's] employees are nontraditional/nonconservative-looking people, and that also makes it more comfortable to be you." A gay black/African American woman in her 30s said, "It's more of an artists' culture […] and it seems like the owners intentionally hire artists and punk people […] it's a little more flexible in terms of how people look […] that's why I like it there." Of the three analyzed coffee shops, Darwin's is the one that most explicitly announced itself as a community place, as evidenced by the large area for flyers in its front window. Nevertheless, none of these queering places explicitly denoted themselves as queer or queer-friendly.

Harvard Square

Harvard Square is located close to Harvard Yard, the center and also the oldest part of Harvard University in Cambridge. Harvard Square's central point is the station of the Massachusetts Bay Transportation Authority, often referred to as the MBTA or the T, surrounded by a small plaza that brims with activity. This small plaza is home to a semipermanent periodical stand, street performers and exhibitors, and a variety of informal seating options around the station. Many of the buildings in Harvard Square are medium scale and constructed in brick, visually referencing the university. Whereas some street blocks end in intersections, others are interrupted by small alleys and pathways, as illustrated in Figure 6.4 below.

The Harvard Square neighborhood hosts a variety of restaurants, entertainment venues, and stores, for example Henrietta's Table (housed within Charles Hotel), Charlie's Kitchen, Cardullo's Gourmet Shoppe, and Harvard Book Store.

In regard to fit, Harvard Square was unanimously named as a highly favorable space by all interviewees, regardless of age, gender, or race and ethnicity. Many interviewees pointed out that this space has a lot of diversity and activity, along with many small and independent restaurants and shops. As a gay black/African American woman in her 30s stated, "It is a place for public art, […] vendors, musicians, dancers, […]. I think that's really important in terms of making a wide range of people feel comfortable." Several respondents described the perceived boundaries of Harvard Square radiating from the T station as the central point. As a gay, non-Hispanic white man in his 30s stated:

> Most specifically in the immediate vicinity of the T station […] so anywhere from the movie theater to Verdict's to where Crate and Barrel used to be to Harvard's restaurant to the Charles Hotel restaurant, to the burger place, Charlie's Kitchen, Wagamama's […] yeah it's almost like a complete radius […] and we even walk through Harvard Yard.

This sense of boundary helps to protect and define the space.

FIGURE 6.4 Example of queering space in Cambridge combining public spaces with more intimate paths: Harvard Square

In regard to access, Harvard Square is highly public and easily accessible by foot or through the MBTA. While the area around the T station is very exposed, one has the option to be in a more intimate or enclosed space by ducking into an alley or a set-back doorway (see Figure 6.4 above).

In regard to control, a genderqueer Asian American interviewee in his/her 20s commented on Harvard Square, comparing it with Cambridgeside Galleria, "Recognizing and serving an alternative audience makes me feel more comfortable [...], [in Harvard Square], there are mainstream and alternative stores but because they're all mixed together I feel better." A gay non-Hispanic white man in his 30s said:

> There are college students, homeless people, punks on the street, families of all different shapes and sizes and colors [...] that's one thing that I really like about it [...] it's quite vibrant, it's quite active [...] I think that's one reason why I feel comfortable there.

A gay, non-Hispanic white man in his 40s stated:

> There's a lot of activity, a lot of little shops that are geared towards the alternative life (coffee shops, health conscious, poetry places) [...] a lot of students [...] a lot of openly gay guys. I would definitely hold hands with a boyfriend in Harvard Square. Probably the campus, too, but I haven't tested it.

The same genderqueer Asian American interviewee added, "I always feel comfortable dressing the way I want to [...] presenting gender however I want."

Many interviewees also noticed queer stickers. One gay white man in his 30s said, "You see ten in one block and that starts to send a message."

One Kendall Square

One Kendall Square is about a 15-minute walk from Kendall Square, home of MIT and the Kendall/MIT station of the MBTA. One Kendall Square is a newly branded, 11-building campus, which is characterized by offices and laboratories along with some formal restaurants and entertainment venues. Nine of the eleven buildings were constructed before 1919, and several were part of the Boston Woven Hose Factory. It is owned and was redeveloped by two private-sector real estate firms.

In regard to fit, gay men were the most likely to recall One Kendall Square. Many interviewees perceived the space as a queering space because it is the home to Kendall Square Cinema, which has a history of showing edgy films since 1995. However, the cinema is on the fringe of the campus and not directly within it. Nevertheless, One Kendall Square's 1,500-space parking garage is connected to the cinema, making it very easy to park and directly enter the cinema safely.

In regard to access, One Kendall Square is also highly public and accessible by MBTA, although the T station is about a 15-minute walk from this area. In order to compensate for the corporate aesthetics of the laboratories nearby, human-scale passageways and gathering spaces that allow pedestrian movement throughout the campus were created by the developer. Perhaps because One Kendall Square is an office location at a distance from the T station, and because it has a more anonymous aesthetic and signage, it is less visible and thus particularly well suited for gay male gathering and cruising.

In regard to control, a gay, non-Hispanic white man in his 40s called One Kendall Square "the closest it gets to queer space in Cambridge." He added that there are:

> [A] lot of gay men [at One Kendall Square] [...] groups of gay people talking very openly [...] probably because it's an artsy place [...] the restaurants [it seems] have [...] just groups of gay people congregating there [...] I wouldn't say it is a gay area, but definitely a large percentage [so that] I feel *very* comfortable there.

In the vicinity, several movie posters signal the unconventional movies of this theater.

Conclusion

Doan (2011) states that "current planning practices have neglected the needs of the Lesbian, Gay, Bisexual, and Transgender (LGBT) community for safe urban spaces in which to live, work, and play" (p. 1). This statement contrasts the somewhat recent more theoretical discussions about diversity and inclusivity in the planning field in terms of gender, race, ethnicity, and nativity (Corber & Valocci, 2003; Fainstein & Servon, 2005; Fetner, 2008; Hendler & Harrison, 2000; Howe & Hammer, 2002; Miranne & Young, 2000; Ritzdorf, 2000; Spain, 2002), which has lagged behind in terms of the LGBT community (Doan, 2011).

In this chapter we discussed Cambridge's informal queer spaces, which are often public spaces where queer people have been known to gather to create community and safety, for example Harvard Square and One Kendall Square—although these could also be parks, waterfronts, monuments, etc. Interestingly, the use of these and other spaces by queer people has been ignored by planners.

Learning from the Cambridge experience, planners would do well to also remember Young's (2011) proposal to construct a normative ideal of city life:

> By 'city life' I mean a form of social relations which I define as the being together of strangers. In the city persons and groups interact within spaces and institutions they all experience themselves as belonging to, but without those interactions dissolving into unity or commonness. City life is composed of clusters of people with affinities – families, social group networks, voluntary associations, neighborhood networks, a vast array of small 'communities.' City dwellers frequently venture beyond such familiar enclaves, however, to the more open public of politics, commerce, and festival, where strangers meet and interact (cf. Lofland, 1973). (Young, 2011, p. 237)

At a more practical level, there are several strategies planners can pursue to increase ownership and/or control of queers when it comes to decisions around neighborhoods. First, planners should take advantage of the decennial U.S. Census, which contains the variable Unmarried Partner Households by Sex of Partners that can be utilized to see residential patterns (Anacker, 2011). Second, planners should take advantage of participatory planning approaches, for example, through inclusive citizen advisory councils to give citizens, including queers, voice (Gorman-Murray & Waitt, 2009). Third, planners should officially recognize LGBT historical sites "to ensure preservation and the designation of an area as an LGBT neighborhood in general or comprehensive plan" (Doan & Higgins, 2011, p. 21). Fourth, planners should recognize the existence of queer communities and "be aware of their needs for tolerant and safe spaces" (Doan & Higgins, 2011, p. 21), for example, by designating LGBT residents and communities as priority groups in a social plan, by employing a full-time LGBT project coordinator, by having a regular advisory committee to consult with LGBT residents, and/or by having liaison with LGBT and other organizations that focus on legal and social inclusion (Gorman-Murray & Waitt, 2009). Fifth, planners should recognize the central role of LGBT businesses and community organizations, as many "provide essential community gathering places and are important in establishing and maintaining a sense of neighborhood identity" (Doan & Higgins, 2011, p. 21). Finally, planners should boost queers' feelings of belonging through establishing dedications, murals, or other landmarks or markers (Gorman-Murray & Waitt, 2009).

Notes

1 In this chapter we will use the term "queer" interchangeably with "lesbian," "gay," "bisexual," "transgender," or "LGBT" (see also Doan & Higgins, 2011; Frisch, 2002).
2 We sought and received approval to conduct interviews from the Committee on the Use of Humans as Experimental Subjects (COUHES) at the Massachusetts Institute of Technology (MIT).
3 A person whose gender identity is neither man nor woman, is between or beyond genders, or is some combination of genders. This identity is usually related to or in reaction to the social construction of gender, gender stereotypes, and the gender binary system. Some genderqueer people identify under the transgender umbrella while others do not (UC Berkeley Gender Equity Resource Center, n.d., n.p.).

References

Anacker, K. (2011) Queering the Suburbs: Analyzing Property Values in Male and Female Same-Sex Suburbs in the United States, pp. 107–125 in Petra L. Doan (Ed.). *Queerying Planning: Challenging Heteronormative Assumptions and Reframing Planning Practice.* Farnham, U.K.: Ashgate.

Bell, D. (1991) Insignificant Others: Lesbian and Gay Geographies. *Area* 23, 323–329.

Bell, D. and Binnie, J. (2004) Authenticating Queer Space: Citizenship, Urbanism and Governance. *Urban Studies* 41, 1807–1820.

Black, D., Gates, G., Sanders, S. and Taylor, L. (2002) Why Do Gay Men Live in San Francisco? *Journal of Urban Economics* 51, 54–76.

Boyd, N.A. (2003) *Wide Open Town: A History of Queer San Francisco until 1965.* Berkeley, CA: University of California Press.

Brown, M. (2013) Gender and Sexuality II: There Goes the Gayborhood? *Progress in Human Geography* [in press].

Browne, K. (2006) Challenging Queer Geographies. *Antipode* 38.5, 885–893.

Browne, K. and Bakshi, L. (2011) We Are Here to Party? Lesbian, Gay, Bisexual and Trans Leisurescapes Beyond Commercial Gay Scenes. *Leisure Studies* 30.2, 179–196.

Castells, M. (1983) *The City and the Grassroots: A Cross-Cultural Theory of Urban Social Movements.* Berkeley, CA: University of California Press.

Chisholm, D. (2005) *Queer Constellations: Subcultural Space in the Wake of the City.* Minneapolis, MN: University of Minnesota Press.

City of Cambridge (n.d.) GLBT Commission: What is the GLBT Commission? Accessed 04/30/13. www.cambridgema.gov/glbt.aspx

Christensen, J. (2006) Welcome to the Gayborhood. *The Advocate (The National Gay & Lesbian Newsmagazine)* 965, np.

Collins, A. (2004) Sexual Dissidence, Enterprise, and Assimilation: Bedfellows in Urban Regeneration. *Urban Studies* 41, 1789–1806.

Corber, R. and Valocci, S. (2003) *Queer Studies: An Interdisciplinary Reader.* Oxford, U.K.: Blackwell Publishers.

Doan, P. (2011) Why Question Planning Assumptions and Practices about Queer Spaces, pp. 1–18 in Petra Doan (Ed.), *Queerying Planning: Challenging Heteronormative Assumptions and Reframing Planning Practice.* Farnham, U.K.: Ashgate.

Doan, P. and Higgins, H. (2011) The Demise of Queer Space? Resurgent Gentrification and the Assimilation of LGBT Neighborhoods. *Journal of Planning Education and Research* 31, 6–25.

Duncan, N. (1996) Renegotiating Gender and Sexuality in Public and Private Spaces, pp. 127–145 in N. Duncan (Ed.). *Body Space: Destabilizing Geographies of Gender and Sexuality*. London: Routledge.

Edelman, M. (1995) *From Art to Politics: How Artistic Creations Shape Political Conceptions*. Chicago, IL: The University of Chicago Press.

Fainstein, S. and Servon, L. (eds). (2005). *Gender and Planning: A Reader*. New Brunswick, NJ: Rutgers University Press.

Fetner, T. (2008) *How the Religious Right Shaped Lesbian and Gay Activism*. Minneapolis, MN: University of Minnesota Press.

Forsyth, A. (1997a) NoHo: Upscaling Main Street on the Metropolitan Edge. *Urban Geography* 18, 622–652.

Forsyth, A. (1997b) "Out" in the Valley. *International Journal of Urban and Regional Research* 21, 36–61.

Frisch, M. (2002) Planning as a Heterosexist Project. *Journal of Planning Education and Research* 21, 254–266.

Gorman–Murray, A. and Waitt, G. (2009) Queer–Friendly Neighborhoods: Interrogating Social Cohesion across Sexual Difference in Two Australian Neighborhoods. *Environment and Planning A*, 41: 2855–2873.

Hendler, S. with Harrison, H. (2000) Theorizing Canadian Planning History: Women, Gender, and Feminist Perspectives, pp. 139–156 in K. Miranne and A. H. Young (Eds.), *Gendering the City: Women, Boundaries, and Visions of Urban Life*. Lanham, MD: Rowman & Littlefield Publishing.

Hodge, S. (1995) "No Fags Out There": Gay Men, Identity and Suburbia. *Journal of Interdisciplinary Gender Studies* 1, 41–48.

Howe, D. and Hammer, J. (2002) EnGendering Change: Impacts of the Faculty Women's Interest Group on the Planning Academy. Paper presented at the Association of Collegiate Schools of Planning Annual Conference, Baltimore, Maryland.

Kidder, T. (1999) *Home Town*. New York, NY: Random House.

Kitchin, R. and Lysaght, K. (2003) Heterosexism and the Geographies of Everyday Life in Belfast, Northern Ireland. *Environment and Planning A* 35, 489–510.

Knopp, L. (1990) Exploiting the Rent Gap: The Theoretical Significance of Using Illegal Appraisal Schemes to Encourage Gentrification in New Orleans. *Urban Geography* 11, 48–64.

Knopp, L. (1992) Sexuality and the Spatial Dynamics of Capitalism. *Environment and Planning D* 10, 651–669.

Knopp, L. (1997) Gentrification and Gay Neighborhood Formation in New Orleans. Eds. A. Gluckman and B. Reed. *Homo Economicus*. London: Routledge.

Kuhr, F. (2004) There goes the Gayborhood. *The Advocate (The National Gay & Lesbian Newsmagazine)* 918, np.

Levine, M. (1979) Gay Ghetto. *Journal of Homosexuality* 4, 363–377.

Lewis, N.M. (2013) Ottawa's Le/The Village: Creating a Gaybourhood amidst the "Death of the Village." *Geoforum* 49, 233–242.

Lofland, L. (1973) *A World of Strangers*. New York: Basic Books.

Lynch, F. (1987) Non-Ghetto Gays: A Sociological Study of Suburban Homosexuals. *Journal of Homosexuality* 13, 13–42.

Lynch, F. (1992) Non-Ghetto Gays: An Ethnography of Suburban Homosexuals. Ed. G. Herdt. *Gay Culture in America: Essays from the Field*. Boston, MA: Beacon Press.

Lynch, K. (1984) *Good City Form*. Cambridge, MA: MIT Press.

Lyod, B. and Rowntree, L. (1978). Radical Feminists and Gay Men in San Francisco: Social Space in Dispersed Communities, pp. 78–88 in D. Langren and R. Palm (Eds.). *An Invitation to Geography*. New York, NY: McGraw-Hill Book Company.

Miller, V. (2005). Intertextuality, the Referential Illusion and the Production of a Gay Ghetto. *Social and Cultural Geography* 6, 61–79.

Miranne, K. and Young, A.H. (eds.). (2000). *Gendering the City: Women, Boundaries, and Visions of Urban Life*. Lanham, MD: Rowman & Littlefield Publishing.

Moss, M.L. (1997) Reinventing the Central City as a Place to Live and Work. *Housing Policy Debate* 8, 471–490.

Myslik, W.D. (1996) Renegotiating the Social/Sexual Identities of Place, pp. 156–69 in N. Duncan (Ed.). *Bodyscape: Destabilizing Geographies of Gender and Sexuality*. London: Routledge.

Nash, C. (2006) Toronto's Gay Village (1969–1982): Plotting the Politics of Gay Identity. *The Canadian Geographer* 50, 1–16.

Nusser, S.P. and Anacker, K.B. (2013) What Sexuality is This Place? Building a Framework for Evaluating Sexualized Space: The Case of Kansas City, Missouri. *Journal of Urban Affairs* 35, 173–193.

Podmore, J. (2001) Lesbians in the Crowd: Gender, Sexuality, and Visibility along Montreal's Boulevard St-Laurent. *Gender, Place, and Culture* 8, 333–355.

Podmore, J. (2006) Gone "Underground"? Lesbian Visibility and the Consolidation of Queer Space in Montreal. *Social and Cultural Geography* 7, 595–623.

Pritchard, A., Morgan, N., and Sedgley, D. (2002) In Search of Lesbian Space? The Experience of Manchester's Gay Village. *Leisure Studies* 21, 105–123.

Pritchard, A., Morgan, N. J., Sedgely, D., and Jenkins, A. (1998) Reaching Out to the Gay Tourist: Opportunities and Threats in an Emerging Market Segment. *Tourism Management* 19, 273–282.

Reed, C. (2003) We're from Oz: Making Ethnic and Sexual Identity in Chicago. *Environment and Planning D: Society and Space* 21, 425–440.

Reuter, D.F. (2008) *Greetings from the Gayborhood: A Nostalgic Look at Gay Neighborhoods*. New York, NY: Abram's Image.

Ritzdorf, M. (2000) Sex, Lies, and Urban Life: How Municipal Planning Marginalizes African American Women and their Families. Pp. 169–181 in K. Miranne and A. Young (Eds.), *Gendering the City: Women, Boundaries, and Visions of Urban Life*. Lanham, MD: Rowman & Littlefield Publishers.

Rothenberg, T. (1995) "And She Told Two Friends": Lesbians Creating Urban Social Space, pp. 165–81 in D. Bell and G. Valentine (Eds.). *Mapping Desire: Geographies of Sexualities*. London: Routledge.

Ruting, R. (2008) Economic Transformations of Gay Urban Spaces: Revisiting Collins' Evolutionary Gay District Model. *Australian Geographer* 39.3, 259–269.

Sibalis, M. (2004) Urban Space and Homosexuality: The Example of the Marais, Paris' "Gay Ghetto". *Urban Studies* 41, 1739–1758.

Spain, D. 2002. What Happened to Gender Relations on the Way from Chicago to Los Angeles? *City and Community* 1, 155–169.

UC Berkeley Gender Equity Resource Center (n.d.) Information Sheets. Berkeley, CA: UC Berkeley Gender Equity Resource Center. http://geneq.berkeley.edu/information_sheets

Valentine, G. (1993) (Hetero)sexing Space: Lesbian Perceptions and Experiences of Everyday Spaces. *Environment and Planning D* 11, 395–413.

Valentine, G. (1996) (Re)Negotiating the "Heterosexual Street": Lesbian Productions of Space, pp. 146–55 in N. Duncan (Ed.). *Bodyspace: Destabilizing Geographies of Gender and Sexuality*. London: Routledge.

Visser, G. (2003) Gay Men, Leisure Space, and South African Cities: The Case of Cape Town. *Geoforum* 34, 123–137.

Waitt, G. and Markwell, K. (2006) *Gay Tourism: Culture and Context.* New York, NY: The Haworth Hospitality Press.

Weightman, B. (1981) Commentary: Towards a Geography of the Gay Community. *Journal of Cultural Geography* 1, 106–112.

Winchester, H.P.M. and White, P.E. (1988) The Location of Marginalized Groups in the Inner City. *Environment and Planning D: Society and Space* 6, 37–54.

Winters, C. (1979) The Social Identity of Evolving Neighborhoods. *Landscape* 23, 14.

Young, I.M. (2011) *Justice and the Politics of Difference.* Princeton, NJ: Princeton University Press.

7

UNDERSTANDING LGBTQ-FRIENDLY NEIGHBORHOODS IN THE AMERICAN SOUTH

The Trade-off Between Visibility and Acceptance

Petra L. Doan

Introduction

Years of discrimination against non-normative genders and sexualities have created a deep-seated desire for safe spaces within urban areas among many lesbian, gay, bisexual, transgendered, and queer (LGBTQ) people, whether they live in large metropolitan areas, smaller cities, or rural communities. Although queer spaces in larger cities garner the most public attention, not everyone can afford the costs of relocation or afford the rents of such districts. Moreover, not all cities have sufficient numbers of LGBTQ people to create viable queer neighborhoods and retail/ entertainment districts. Given these challenges, what can smaller cities do to create safe and inclusive spaces for gender and sexual minorities? This study examines the habitation patterns and locational choices of LGBTQ people from a smaller metropolitan area in the southern United States—a region in which the climate for LGBTQ people is generally less than welcoming.

In particular, this chapter provides a closer examination of a single neighborhood, Indian Head Acres, in Tallahassee, a medium sized city in Florida, which has attracted an assortment of LGBTQ individuals. The analysis explores the ways that this space is subtly coded as an LGBTQ-friendly space. One interviewee in the study recognized the progressive nature of the area and characterized it as a "granola" neighborhood because granola is loaded with fruit and a lot of nuts (tongue in cheek reference to gays, lesbians, and other bohemians), and is most commonly sold in natural food stores and cooperatives. One such store is located just at the northern edge of the community examined in this study, making this term particularly apt.

Understanding the Diversity of LGBTQ Neighborhoods

Most discussions of North American LGBTQ neighborhoods focus on the iconic queer spaces of large cities, such as the Castro in San Francisco (Stryker and Van Buskirk, 1996), West Hollywood in Los Angeles (Forest, 1995), Boys' Town in Chicago (Reed, 2003), Greenwich Village and Park Slope in New York City (Rothenburg, 1995), the Gay Village in Toronto (Nash, 2005, 2006), and le Village Gai in Montreal (Podmore, 2006). These LGBTQ spaces are clearly enclaves as defined by Abrahamson (1996) with a large queer residential population as well as commercial establishments which cater to that community.

A narrow focus on the most visible queer spaces is not helpful in understanding the broader distribution of the LGBTQ community outside of large cities. In many cities lesbians are invisible (Wolfe, 1997), blending into multi-cultural neighborhoods where they do not stand out. For instance, Podmore (2001, 2006) has suggested that lesbians in Montreal were attracted to the Plateau district between the Boulevard St. Laurent and Rue St. Denis. Podmore describes this as "a diverse inner-city neighborhood where counter-cultural movements and 'marginal' forms of gentrification by a diversity of social groups thrived and expanded" (Podmore, 2006, p. 620). Elsewhere, Lo and Healey (2000) found that in Vancouver there are "female" landscapes in the working class and socio-politically active East End where lesbians have "used their bodies to write and mark their presence on the landscape, to identify and claim territory" (Lo and Healey, 2000, p, 41). Elwood (2000) suggested that in the Twin Cities area of Minnesota some lesbians used their homes to make clear their non-normative identity by visibly displaying "lesbian" artifacts. In some cases lesbian homes became gathering places that provided "a place for building connections between lesbians, fostering a community of women who share a common sexual identity" (Elwood, 2000, p. 21). These findings are reflected in some researchers' claims that queer space is created by bodies not buildings (Reed, 1996).

Although "rural areas may best be represented as settings for traditional (and not especially enlightened) moral (including sexual) standards" (Bell and Valentine, 1995), gay and lesbian people are nonetheless present nearly everywhere (Kramer, 1995; Forsyth, 1997b, Kirkey and Forsyth, 2001). For some lesbians the draw to create safe and queer spaces leads them outside the city to rural lands where they can separate themselves from the hetero-patriarchy of the cities and live with like-minded women (Cheney, 1985; Faderman, 1991; Lee, 1990). Some of these "land dyke" communities serve as a place of refuge for people who have been deeply wounded by patriarchal institutions and individuals (Rabin and Slater, 2005).

Less effort has been focused on LGBTQ populations in smaller cities and towns outside the largest metropolitan areas because they are more difficult to identify. Lynch (1987) found that gay and lesbian suburbanites tended to be more conservative and less "out" than LGBTQ people living in larger metropolitan environments. Forsyth's work (1997a) on Northampton, Massachusetts provided some insights into the challenges of creating visible queer space within a smaller community where there was insufficient income and density to support LGBTQ commercial establishments. Anacker (2011) used census data to argue that despite increasing numbers of same-sex couples living in suburban areas, the presence of these people is often over-looked. Gorman-Murray and Waitt (2009) suggest that the term "queer-friendly" neighborhoods may be a better descriptor of suburban areas that are welcoming to queer people and where there is significant cohesion between LGBTQ and heterosexual residents.

However, visible queerness may be self-regulated by LGBTQ people in smaller localities for fear of retaliation by the wider non-accepting populations. One survival strategy is to seek out progressive neighborhoods and areas with a sufficient diversity of residents where a gay or lesbian couple or individual might add a tasty bit of flavor to an otherwise intriguing mix (granola) of residents. This chapter will examine a particular granola neighborhood to explore the ways that non-normative identity is written on the bodies and on the landscapes in these kinds of diverse places.

Florida Context: Deep-Seated Resistance to Homosexuality

In the 1950s in the aftermath of the 1954 Brown vs. the Board of Education Supreme Court decision, the Florida Legislature established the Florida Legislative Investigation Committee (FLIC) led by state senator Charley Johns, also known as the Johns Committee, modelled on McCarthy's House Un-American Activities Committee in Washington, DC (Braukman, 2012). Though the initial mandate was based on national security, the Florida committee looked very carefully at radical groups such as the NAACP and homosexual groups that were threatening "the moral fabric" of the state. In 1961 the FLIC was given an extended legislative mandate to determine the "extent of infiltration into agencies supported by state funds of practicing homosexuals" (Schnur, 1997, p. 141). During this time the FLIC actively investigated students and faculty at the University of Florida, Florida State University, and the University of South Florida as well as other state agencies, using hearsay evidence to force many individuals to resign. While the public outcry against FLIC's heavy-handed tactics finally resulted in the shutdown of the committee in 1965, its final official act was to publish a report in 1964 entitled *Homosexuality and Citizenship in Florida*. This strongly-worded report argued that homosexuals were a "grave threat" to Florida's children as well as to its moral fabric.

Evidence of the persistent consequences of this damaging period can be seen in the historical record. The Anita Bryant crusade in 1977 to "Save Our Children" from homosexuals was built on this solid foundation of hatred and intolerance. Sears (1997) notes that there were lasting effects on teachers who were interrogated by FLIC and were still living in fear in the 1990s (quoted in Graves, 2009, p.10). While not all LGBTQ people in Florida remember the details of the Johns Committee and its vile work, many are aware of the hate-filled rhetoric of the Bryant crusade. The continuing influence of these arguments can be seen in the 2014 remarks by Florida Attorney General Pam Bondi who said that recognizing same-sex marriage would "impose significant public harm" (Stein, 2014).

Even though many cities in Florida have now passed anti-discrimination and human rights ordinances that are inclusive of LGBTQ individuals, the intensity of this ongoing social justice struggle can be seen in the fierceness of the language used. For instance, in 2010 when Leon County (in which the city of Tallahassee is located) passed an amendment to its Human Rights Ordinance that added sexuality and gender identity to the protected classes, some conservative pastors testified publicly that LGBTQ people were "abominations" and had no place in civil society. While the ordinance passed over the objections of these right wing commentators, their hateful testimony highlights the intolerance that remains very much alive in some parts of the state.

A direct result of this history of intolerance in Florida is that LGBTQ residents of smaller cities exhibit caution about openly displaying symbols of LGBTQ Pride. For example, one lesbian who declined to be interviewed formally wondered aloud why anyone would want to fly a rainbow flag on their house and thereby advertise their location. While some cities may have one or more gay and lesbian bars and possibly a progressive or feminist bookstore, these institutions may not be spatially connected to LGBTQ residential patterns. The lack of visibility does not mean that there are no LGBTQ areas; it simply means that planners must look more carefully at neighborhood patterns.

Data and Methods

This chapter uses two main sources of data to describe LGBTQ residential patterns. The first source is a sample survey of the LGBTQ population (first reported in Doan and Higgins, 2009) in Tallahassee, a medium sized metropolitan area in Florida. The survey was distributed using a snowball approach in which questionnaires were sent to individuals on the mailing list of the local LGBTQ community center, and others were distributed at the Metropolitan Community Church, an over 40 gay men's group, the Pride Student Union at the local university, and a transgender support group. In total 127 questionnaires were returned using this method. Respondents were largely from the city of Tallahassee, but a fair number were from outlying rural areas and nearby counties.

A set of follow-up interviews were then conducted by the author and various research assistants in one particular neighborhood, Indian Head Acres, chosen because both the 2000 Census and the survey data indicated a relatively high concentration of same-sex partners living there. The author made contact with the neighborhood association and was granted permission to circulate a brief description of the research via the association's email list. In total 19 persons agreed to participate in a face-to-face interview using a semi-structured instrument. Of the 19 respondents, 7 identified as LGBTQ and 12 identified as heterosexual. Additionally the group was composed of 6 men and 13 women.

The following sections will use these data to describe the situation for LGBTQ people in the Tallahassee metropolitan area. The first section uses cross-tabular analysis to examine patterns in the survey data that were different than anticipated based on expected preferences for residential location and concerns about personal safety. The next section describes the area with the highest concentration of LGBTQ people and then provides a range of insights about the neighborhood and its progressive nature gleaned from the interviews.

Neighborhood Preferences

One of the key questions posed by this chapter concerns the locational preferences for gays and lesbians outside the traditional LGBTQ neighborhood clusters found in large metropolitan areas. Are there patterns of residential choice for these populations in smaller cities? The results from the 2000 US Census indicate that gay and lesbian couples reside in virtually every census tract in the Tallahassee metropolitan area, and the author's survey of couples and individuals confirm that trend. The data also indicate that there is no clearly defined "gay enclave" in Tallahassee, although one tract does stand out with a higher concentration of same-sex partners. There are also clear differences in habitation patterns based on sex differences. Table 7.1 indicates that gay men are significantly more likely to describe their residential locations as in-town whereas lesbian women are more likely to describe their residential locations as at or beyond the urban fringe (Chi square statistic = 6.25 and significant at 0.04). The range of possible explanations for these differences between gays and lesbians include differential incomes, long term partnership patterns, and the likelihood of having children (Adler and Brenner, 1993). Earlier work on these factors confirms that there are indeed significant differences related to these variables in this sample (Doan and Higgins, 2009).

The survey results also indicate that for many respondents having one or more LGBTQ neighbors in close proximity makes them feel safer. These results do not vary by neighborhood type, suggesting that it is less important where LGBTQ people live than that they reside in areas where there are supportive neighbors. This residential level support system appears to be part of a "defensive" strategy for people who may feel quite marginalized by some social institutions. Table 7.2 uses a second cross-tabulation to examine perceptions of neighborhood safety with proximity to one's nearest LGBTQ neighbors. These data indicate that LGBTQ individuals who live in closer proximity to other LGBTQ people are significantly more likely to perceive that their neighborhood is a safe environment (Chi square statistic = 11.98 which is significant at 0.017). This finding suggests that a high concentration of LGBTQ people is not needed to ensure feelings of safety, but proximate and supportive neighbors are a key factor. This finding also suggests that in the absence of visible queer spaces, some LGBTQ individuals and couples make residential location decisions based on where others have found reasonably safe neighborhoods.

TABLE 7.1 Cross-tabulation Neighborhood Type by Sex of Respondents, Tallahassee, FL

			Sex of respondent		Total
			Male	*Female*	
Neighborhood type	in-town neighborhood	Count	28	27	55
		Expected Count	22.1	32.9	55.0
		% within sex	54.9%	35.5%	43.3%
	traditional suburban development	Count	16	26	42
		Expected Count	16.9	25.1	42.0
		% within sex	31.4%	34.2%	33.1%
	rural fringe	Count	7	23	30
		Expected Count	12.0	18.0	30.0
		% within sex	13.7%	30.3%	23.6%
Total		Count	51	76	127
		% of Total	40.2%	59.8%	100.0%
Chi square (*significance*)				6.254 (0.044)	

Source: survey by the author

TABLE 7.2 Proximity of LGBTQ Neighbors and Perceptions of Safety, Tallahassee, FL

		Proximity of nearest known LGBTQ neighbor		
		Next door/ nearby	*In the neighborhood*	*Not in my neighborhood*
Perceptions of Safety	Tolerable	8	3	13
	Fair	34	7	28
	Excellent	23	3	4
Chi square (*significance*)		11.9804 (.017)		

Source: survey by the author

Indian Head Acres as a Queer-Friendly Granola Neighborhood

The neighborhood of Indian Head Acres had the highest concentration of LGBTQ couples in the US Census as well as the most individuals in the previously described survey. The area was developed in the 1950s from a former plantation from which the name of the sub-division was drawn. The layout of the neighborhood was centered on a centrally located park and divided by two watercourses that cut through the property. The streets are laid out roughly in concentric circles around the park and along the creek beds, making navigation through the neighborhood somewhat challenging. In 1971 a neighborhood association was formed which has been actively involved in neighborhood preservation, blocking commercial development along adjacent arteries, protecting the canopy of live oak trees along adjacent streets, resisting city efforts to widen thoroughfares in the neighborhood, and working to preserve and enhance the neighborhood parks (adapted from the Indian Head Acres Neighborhood Association pamphlet). The neighborhood association also organizes monthly potluck suppers attended by many lesbians and holds an annual outdoor festival. There also appear to be relatively high levels of progressive energy and environmental activism in Indian Head Acres that is partly explained by the presence of a larger state office complex within easy walking distance of the area.

The results from the 2000 US Census indicate that this sub-division and one smaller adjacent community had 2,414 residents (1,062 men and 1,352 women). Approximately half the population was born in Florida with more than 40% originally from other US states, and just under 10% from other countries. The population in the census tract is quite stable with 57% reporting that they had lived in the same house for the past five years and another 37% reporting that they had been living elsewhere in Florida five years previously. Prior to undertaking the survey, the author spoke informally with several knowledgeable respondents who suggested a much higher percentage of lesbians lived in the neighborhood than the 19 lesbian couples indicated by the 2000 Census results. These numbers, of course, do not include single lesbians and gay men, nor do they include partnered gay men and lesbians who did not reveal their partnership status to the Census.

Most of the interviewees were attracted to this neighborhood because of its convenient location midway between employment in the central business district and a major office complex just to the east of the neighborhood. But the second most common response was linked to the community nature of the neighborhood, and this was true for all subject positions. Several respondents also reported liking the fact that they could walk to work. When respondents were asked for a general description of their neighborhood the single most common item was the beauty of natural surroundings and green spaces. The distinctive nature of the neighborhood is evident to the casual observer and is marked by the presence of mature live oak trees and tall pine trees that provide shade as well as its unique character.

Other repeated themes were the lush greenery in the several public parks, as well as the large and natural yards described by one respondent as "freedom lawns" (i.e. a lawn that does not need to be mowed every week because it is planted with native plants). The serpentine park bisecting the neighborhood provides a dense green center, and lots in the sub-division are well landscaped with trees, mature shrubs, and a fascinating assortment of yard art ranging from dancing girls to dragons. Other houses have raised-bed gardens in their front yards for growing vegetables or larval food plants used to attract butterflies to their gardens.

A number of the interviewee descriptions referred to the unique urban design features of the sub-division. Respondents used words including: "curvy streets," "design which is not thought out," "no drive through streets," "jumbled street intersections," and "interesting street layout." One respondent indicated that the streets were confusing to navigate. Several interviewees concurred and thought that the navigational challenges contributed to overall safety because strangers who wished to do harm might have difficulty finding their way around the neighborhood. Other individuals commented on the age of the building stock in the neighborhood. They suggested that Indian Head Acres is known for its "small houses on large lots," "1950s style older houses," "very little new construction," "houses that are offset from the street," and "affordable housing."

When respondents were asked to describe the social characteristic of their neighborhood, they used words that emphasized a progressive attitude of most residents including: "tolerant," "accepting," "diversity," "non-conformity," "artistic," "liberal," "granola," "eclecticism," "environmental activism," "bumper stickers," and "political yard signs." During election season the yards are typically festooned with political signs usually quite liberal in nature in keeping with the ethos of the neighborhood. Respondents also characterized their area with a variety of specifically LGBTQ related terms including: "lifestyle alternative", "queerness", "LGBT presence", and "rainbow flag." This latter comment is interesting because the neighborhood differs from LGBTQ residential areas in large metropolitan regions because on numerous visits to the area nowhere in the sub-division did the author see a visibly displayed rainbow flag. Evidently safety trumps visibility for residents of this neighborhood.

When respondents were asked how their neighborhood had changed, the most common response was that housing prices had risen markedly in the past five years.[1] Several others noted that the neighborhood was transitioning; as older residents moved out, increasing numbers of lesbians and gays had moved into the neighborhood. Three people remarked that many of the new residents were younger and had children, possibly attracted by the neighborhood amenities, including its centrally located park. One interesting marker of change in the neighborhood is the degree to which "sweat equity" has been invested in the housing stock. Several respondents described what they termed a "lesbian rite of passage" which was to turn the traditional carports of the houses built in the 1950s into usable interior living space. While not necessarily a reliable predictor of lesbian habitation, all of the lesbian houses visited did in fact have a carport that had been enclosed by the current residents. While gay men are often assumed to be skilled at home rehabilitation as part of gay gentrification, these results suggest that some lesbians can wield a hammer as well as any gay man.

When asked if the neighborhood was safe for LGBTQ people, all of the respondents (except one straight woman and one lesbian) indicated that it was "safe" to "very safe". In an open-ended question about why they felt this was the case, one male respondent indicated that "there are no anti-gay protests here." Another indicated that he had seen same-sex couples holding hands and feeling quite comfortable at neighborhood events. Another straight woman noted that she often sees children with their two mamas at the playground. Several women indicated that it was safe because there were "so many diverse people in the neighborhood, like mixed race couples, different family structures, so that everyone can fit in here."

Because the larger survey of the wider metropolitan area found a significant relationship between perceptions of safety and the proximity of other LGBTQ people (see Table 7.2), interviewees were asked how well they knew their neighbors and how many of their neighbors were LGBTQ. The responses indicated that the longer a person had lived in the neighborhood, the more people they knew. In addition, parents who regularly took their children to the local playground also knew many more people. However when respondents were asked how many LGBTQ individuals were among those that they knew well, the heterosexual respondents said that approximately one quarter of the people that they knew were LGBTQ, but the LGBTQ respondents indicated that close to 60% of their contacts were other LGBTQ neighbors. These results suggest a much closer set of connections and interactions based on identity and possibly mutual safety.

Findings

The data from the survey and the follow-up interviews provide some rich insights into LGBTQ residential choices. Specifically, the findings are that while LGBTQ people live in virtually every neighborhood in Tallahassee, most live quietly without revealing themselves to their neighbors. Safety for this population is more dependent upon proximity to other LGBTQ neighbors than a visibly queer gayborhood that might attract unwanted attention. Respondents from Indian Head Acres indicated that their neighborhood was an inclusive space that welcomed diversity and non-conformity, making the area feel safe for LGBTQ people.

There is a clear preference among gay men for residence in or near downtown Tallahassee compared to the stronger preference among lesbians for housing near the urban fringe. Although there is no obvious LGBTQ neighborhood, the gay and lesbian individuals who completed the survey indicated that they feel safer and prefer to live in proximity to other sexual minorities or other nearby residents that they know to be supportive. This finding from the survey is also reinforced by the interview data where LGBTQ people in Indian Head Acres were strongly connected to their LGBTQ neighbors, forming a kind of community within the wider community.

Other findings from the interviews of Indian Head Acres residents suggest that the physical design or layout of the neighborhood with curving (i.e. not straight) streets provide a measure of impenetrability to strangers, making the area feel safer for residents. In addition, the older housing stock in the area makes the neighborhood more affordable, as well as providing opportunities for residents to upgrade their homes by their own hard work (sweat equity). Furthermore, the progressive attitudes of many residents contribute to an overall atmosphere of inclusiveness. Although this tolerance does not encourage LGBTQ people to decorate their homes with rainbow flags, pink triangles, or other well-recognized markers of queer identity, LGBTQ couples do claim space with their bodies by holding hands at the annual outdoor festival (public displays of affection) or by taking their children to the park and playground as an obvious same-sex couple.

Conclusions

These findings are important for local governments who desire to make their communities more welcoming to LGBTQ individuals, couples, and families. While it may be difficult to "create" such queer-friendly spaces from scratch, it is useful to recognize when and where LGBTQ safe spaces are developing. Most urban neighborhoods change over time due to life cycle changes such as the aging of the existing population. The results from this study confirm that incremental change in neighborhoods can be positive. In the case of Indian Head Acres, as the older and possibly original residents of the sub-division moved into retirement housing or died, their properties became available. Word of mouth notified lesbians and gay men from elsewhere in the city to visit and make offers on the newly available property, allowing a concentration of LGBTQ identified people to form. The close connections between LGBTQ people living across the city enabled this process to occur gradually without noticeable displacement. Both a lesbian realtor and a gay realtor also helped to publicize this neighborhood to the wider LGBTQ community.

Neighborhood change can also be caused by wider social and economic factors that stimulate more abrupt shifts in residential patterns such as land use changes due to private development pressures or public investments such as road improvements or infrastructure. Unfortunately the negative consequences of such planned developments can often fall most heavily upon populations marginalized by their race or ethnicity (cf. Keating, 2001 in the case of Atlanta). Doan and Higgins (2011) suggest that planning can exacerbate the negative effects of rapid development on established LGBTQ neighborhoods by ignoring their unique social characteristics and supporting large redevelopment schemes. While Indian Head Acres is unlikely to experience significant urban redevelopment pressure, the proposed widening of an existing street that serves as a boundary for the neighborhood could result in land use changes that might alter its basic character. Planners seeking to support LGBTQ-friendly areas should support neighborhood preservation efforts by identifying and working closely with existing populations in the area.

Planners need to recognize that neighborhoods that provide safe and inclusive space for LGBTQ people do not always fly the rainbow flags associated widely with "queer space" in larger metropolitan areas. Having neighbors who are tolerant and welcoming to diversity is more important for LGBTQ location patterns than outward symbols. Efforts to strengthen neighborhoods through investments in public parks, playgrounds, and other shared facilities can be additional strategies for deepening cohesion among neighbors. Giving neighborhood associations greater input in local land use and development decision-making would also empower these local community members to take a more active role in preserving those aspects of their neighborhoods that they value. When LGBTQ people are a part of a neighborhood with an active association that values diversity and inclusion, they may feel more comfortable in adding their voices to public decision-making.

At the same time policy-makers should be careful about creating specific urban programs and policy that "fossilize life in the city" (Doderer, 2011) and privilege wealthy LGBTQ people (especially white gay men), thereby preventing other groups from creating their own space. Planners should be cognizant of the negative effects of intersecting forms of discrimination faced by LGBTQ people of color, especially women of color whose gender is non-normative. Doan (forthcoming) suggests that transgender women of color are frequently demonized and often categorized as sex workers by both straight and gay neighborhood residents who feel their non-normative presence threatens to undermine property values and the presumed attractiveness of the neighborhood. Planners should make every effort to ensure that measures to enhance diversity explicitly include sexual orientation and gender identity in any planned changes. Even highly regarded neighborhood safety programs, such as crime watch, can contribute to the marginalization of non-normative populations if diversity awareness is not included in the training for these programs.

Finally, urban planners and municipal officials may need to reframe their heteronormative assumptions and look for alternative ways to provide support (Doan, 2011). Cities that wish to strengthen the inclusivity of their neighborhoods should seek ways to deepen the connections between LGBTQ people through visible support for the LGBTQ community. Measures to achieve this would include: anti-discrimination ordinances, proclamations in support of annual Pride festivities (including permits for parades or other public celebrations), plus recognition and possible financial support for LGBTQ community centers which can create a nexus of connectivity for newly "out" or recently arrived LGBTQ individuals seeking to connect with other like-minded people. Allies at the neighborhood level as well as at city hall can make an enormous difference to otherwise marginalized groups who are seeking to create safe spaces in which to live and recreate.

Note

1   The survey was conducted in the summer of 2007, prior to the bursting of the housing bubble in 2008.

References

Abrahamson, M. (ed.) 1996. *Urban Enclaves: Identity and Place in America*. New York, NY: St. Martin's Press.

Adler, S., and Brenner, J. 1993. "Gender and Space: Lesbians and Gay Men in the City," *International Journal of Urban and Regional Research*, 16: 24–34.

Anacker, K.B. 2011. "Queering the Suburbs: Analyzing Property Values in Male and Female Same-Sex Suburbs in the United States," pp. 107–125 in Doan, P. (ed.),

Queerying Planning: Challenging Heteronormative Assumptions and Reframing Planning Practice. Farnham, UK: Ashgate.

Bell, D., and Valentine, G. 1995. "Queer Country: Rural Gay and Lesbian Lives," *Journal of Rural Studies*, 11, 2: 113–122.

Braukman, S. 2012. *Communists and Perverts under the Palms: The Johns Committee in Florida, 956–1965*. Gainesville, FL: University of Florida Press.

Cheney, J. (ed.) 1985. *Lesbian Land*, Minneapolis, MN: Word Weaver.

Doan, P. 2011. *Queerying Planning: Challenging Heteronormative Assumptions and Reframing Planning Practice*. Farnham, UK: Ashgate.

Doan, P. Forthcoming. "Planning for Sexual and Gender Minorities", in M. Burayidi (ed.) *Planning Cosmopolitan Cities: Concepts, Trends, and Strategies*. Toronto, Canada: University of Toronto Press.

Doan, P., and Higgins, H. 2009. "Cognitive Dimensions of Wayfinding: The Implications of Habitus, Safety, and Gender Dissonance among Gay and Lesbian Populations," *Environment and Planning A*. 41, 7: 1745–1762.

Doan, P., and Higgins, H. 2011. "The Demise of Queer Space? Resurgent Gentrification and LGBT Neighborhoods," *Journal of Planning Education and Research*. 31, 1: 6–25.

Doderer, Y. 2011. "LGBTQs in the City, Queering Urban Space" *International Journal of Urban and Regional Research*, 35, 2: 431–436.

Elwood, S. 2000. "Lesbian Living Spaces: Multiple Meanings of Home," in G. Valentine (ed.) *From Nowhere to Everywhere: Lesbian Geographies*. New York, NY: Haworth Press, pp. 11–28.

Faderman, L. 1991. *Odd Girls and Twilight Lovers: a History of Lesbian Life in Twentieth-Century America*. Harmondsworth, UK: Penguin.

Forest, B. 1995, "West Hollywood as Symbol: The Significance of Place in the Construction of a Gay Identity" *Environment and Planning D: Society and Space* 13, 2: 133–157.

Forsyth, A. 1997a. NoHo: "Upscaling Main Street on the Metropolitan Edge," *Urban Geography*. Vol. 18, 7: 622–652.

Forsyth, A. 1997b "Out in the Valley," *International Journal of Urban and Regional Research* 21: 38–62.

Forsyth, A. 2001, "Sexuality and Space: Nonconformist Populations and Planning Practice," *Journal of Planning Literature*, 15: 339–358.

Gorman-Murray, A. and Waitt, G. 2009. "Queer-friendly neighbourhoods: interrogating social cohesion across sexual difference in two Australian neighbourhoods," *Environment and Planning A*, 41: 2855–2873.

Graves, K. 2009. *And They Were Wonderful Teachers: Florida's Purge of Gay and Lesbian Teachers*. Urbana, IL: University of Illinois Press.

Keating, L. 2001. *Atlanta: Race, Class, and Urban Expansion*. Philadelphia, PA: Temple University Press.

Kirkey, K., and Forsyth, A. 2001 "Men in the Valley: Gay Male Life on the Suburban-Rural Fringe," *Journal of Rural Studies* 17: 421–441.

Kramer, J.L. 1995. "Bachelor Farmers and Spinsters: Lesbian and Gay Identity and Community in Rural North Dakota." In *Mapping Desire: Geographies of Sexualities*, Bell, D. and Valentine, G. (eds.) New York, NY: Routledge.

Lee, A. (1990) "For the Love of Separatism." in Allen, J. (ed.) *Lesbian Philosophies and Cultures*. New York, NY: State University of New York Press.

Lo, J. and Healey, T. 2000. "Flagrantly Flaunting It: Contesting Perceptions of Locational Identity Among Urban Vancouver Lesbians," in G. Valentine (ed.) *From Nowhere to Everywhere: Lesbian Geographies*. New York, NY: Haworth Press, pp. 29–44.

Lynch, F. (1987) Non-ghetto Gays: A Sociological Study of Suburban Homosexuals, *Journal of Homosexuality* 13: 13–42.

Nash, C.J. 2005 "Contesting Identity: Politics of gays and lesbians in Toronto in the 1970s," *Gender, Place and Culture* 12, 1: 113–135.

Nash, C.J. 2006. "Toronto's Gay Village (1969–1982): Plotting the Politics of Gay Identity," *The Canadian Geographer*, 50, 1: 1–16.

Podmore, J. 2001, "Lesbians in the Crowd: Gender, Sexuality, and Visibility along Montréal's Boulevard St-Laurent," *Gender, Place, and Culture* 8: 333–355.

Podmore, J. 2006. "Gone 'Underground'? Lesbian Visibility and the Consolidation of Queer Space in Montréal," *Social and Cultural Geography* 7, 4: 595–625.

Rabin, J.S., and Slater, B.R. 2005. "Lesbian Communities Across the United States: Pockets of Resistance and Resilience," *Journal of Lesbian Studies*, 9, 1–2: 169–182.

Reed, C. 1996. "Imminent Domain: Queer Space in the Built Environment," *Art Journal*, 55, 4: 64–70.

Reed, C. 2003, "We're from Oz: Making Ethnic and Sexual Identity in Chicago" *Environment and Planning D: Society and Space* 21: 425–440.

Rothenburg, T. 1995 "And She Told Two Friends, Lesbians Creating Urban Social Space" in D. Bell, and G. Valentine (eds.) *Mapping Desire*. London, UK: Routledge, pp. 16–181.

Schnur, J.A. 1997. "Closet Crusaders: The Johns Committee and Homophobia 1956–1965" in J. Howard (ed.) *Carryin' On in the Gay and Lesbian South*. New York, NY: New York University Press, pp. 132–166.

Sears, J. 1997. *Lonely Hunters: An Oral History of Lesbian and Gay Southern Life: 1948–1968*. Boulder, CO: Westview Press.

Stein, Letitia. 2014. "Florida Attorney General Defends Gay Marriage Ban as Cities Fight Back," *Chicago Tribune*. National Politics, June 25, 2014. Accessed July 3, 2014 at www.chicagotribune.com/news/politics/sns–rt–us–usa–florida–gaymarriage–2014 0625,0,1035974.story

Stryker, S., and Van Buskirk, J. 1996. *Gay by the Bay: A History of Queer Culture in the San Francisco Bay Area*. San Francisco, CA: Chronicle Books.

Wolfe, M. 1997. "Invisible Women in Invisible Places: The Production of Social Space in Lesbian Bars" in *Queers in Space: Communities, Public Places, and Sites of Resistance,* in (eds.) G. Ingram, A. Bouthillette, and Y. Ritter, Seattle, WA: Bay Press, pp. 301–323.

PART III

Expanding Planning Horizons

Recognizing LGBTQ Intersectionality

INTRODUCTION TO PART III

Petra L. Doan

The third section uses the concept of intersectionality to consider the ways in which women and people of color experience traditional gay villages and work to create alternate, more inclusive spaces that serve their needs. These populations frequently struggle with intersecting forms of discrimination, are all too often completely invisible to planning practitioners and, as a result, are neglected in most planning documents. When marginalized populations are ignored by mainstream planning efforts, there can be large negative consequences of this intended or unintended erasure. The relative invisibility of these communities allows planners to conveniently ignore the harmful social impacts of commercial redevelopment efforts.

The needs of LGBTQ people of color and non-normative women for urban spaces are less studied and not well understood by planners and municipal officials. The chapters in this section provide valuable insights into the ways that intersectionality colors what planners may or may not understand about marginalized minority populations. For example, in Chapter 8 Michael Frisch addresses the usefulness of intersectionality as a frame to understand planning issues. He reports on a survey of queer spaces in Kansas City, Missouri taken by a group of planning students, concluding that intersectional categories can illuminate different perceptions of urban safety and design features. He also reflects on his experience with a regional NGO working on sustainability to show that their neglect of marginalized identities skews planning impacts and privileges the heterosexual assumptions embedded in local plans. In Chapter 9 Joan Marshall Wesley explores how LGBTQ people of color in and around Jackson, Mississippi struggle with social equity, employment, and other quality of life concerns. While they report not always feeling safe in Jackson, they feel safer there than in other spaces in the surrounding rural parts of the state. In Chapter 10 Arianna Martinez examines the cosmopolitan nature of the Jackson Heights area of Queens, New York that mixes significant Latin and Asian populations with an LGBTQ community that has lived in that area for more than 60 years. She describes the aftermath of one particular hate crime that galvanized a diverse coalition of LGBTQ immigrants and other residents to elect more responsive city councilors, establish a network of activist social service organizations, and create a more tolerant and inclusive neighborhood. Finally, in Chapter 11 Catherine Jean Nash and Andrew Gorman-Murray analyze the ways that lesbians and queer women in Toronto, Canada and Sydney, Australia can be seen as a fluid and highly mobile population that are establishing new concentrations of women-oriented businesses and entertainment venues outside traditional LGBT neighborhoods. The chapter highlights planners' difficulty in recognizing the ways that urban spaces are being utilized in response to shifting gender and sexual subjectivities. They argue for the need to increase planners' sensitivity to the changing spatial imperatives of lesbians and queer women.

8

FINDING TRANSFORMATIVE PLANNING PRACTICE IN THE SPACES OF INTERSECTIONALITY

Michael Frisch

Introduction

Does the concept of intersectionality provide guidance for urban planners to deal with multicultural contexts in places? This chapter explores intersectionality and planning, illustrating how intersectionality might be applied in planning analysis of multiple "queer" communities.

Urban planning may be thought of as the profession of organizing cities for improvement (Fainstein and Fainstein 1996). Since the beginning of the 20th century, this organizing has included social, physical and design elements as well as a deepening emphasis on applying the tools of social science. Different types of urban planning lead to different outcomes. Classical urban planning performed within local government directs and facilitates land use and infrastructure decisions impacting development (Hoch et al. 2000). These decisions have social and cultural dimensions particular to the place being planned. Planning within this context responds to political forces and must struggle to maintain a sense of "public" purpose in order to put collective objectives before individual objectives (Meyerson and Banfield 1955). In the United States, these values are ascribed in our professional planning ethics codes.

This sense of public purpose of planning comes into question when we look at the results of planning. For whom are we really planning? Many critics have concluded that urban planning has a bias toward existing class relationships (Fogelsong 1986). Within any particular city in the US, members of the growth machine influence local government which in turn directs planning efforts toward favored development projects (Logan and Molotch 1986). Well-entrenched developmental interests promote their schemes with the reasoning that it will enhance the "public interest." Yiftachel (1998) points to the "dark side of planning" where planning as a tool of organizing cities is used to facilitate exclusion. Other work has documented planning's role in creating gendered and racialized spaces (Forsyth and Sandercock 1992, Thomas 2008). Frisch (2002) goes farther and describes how planning has facilitated the development and control of spaces to further heterosexuality over other sexual orientations.

The tension between planning for a unitary "public" interest versus planning for multiple public interests continues today (Sandercock 1997, 2000). The concept of "intersectionality" has been described by feminist writers as the point where an individual experiences membership in or exclusion from multiple identity categories. In a famous legal review article, Crenshaw (1991) descriptively explains how the experience of discrimination impacts white women differently than black women. In the last decade, analysts from other fields have begun using "intersectionality" as a term to describe and analyze forms of difference experienced within and across lines of identity (Valentine 2007, McCall 2005). How then might the concept of "intersectionality" be applied to urban planning? I hypothesize that attention to "moments" of intersectionality will reveal answers of how to develop a transformative planning practice that facilitates capabilities (Fainstein 2010). Yet, increasing capabilities is a necessary but not sufficient component of a transformational planning practice. I also hypothesize that these experiential "intersections" are the moments of opening to difference, and questioning pre-existing assumptions (Forrester 1999).

I will explore intersectionality in planning through a description of my own experiences as a LGBT planner and planning academic working on sustainability planning projects in Kansas City as well as the experience of teaching a class on "Queer in the City." I start by describing and defining intersectionality within the context of difference and the public interest in planning literature. Many of these questions about inclusion in planning are not new; planning theorists have explored these questions for the past 60 years. These theories revolve around conceptions of a "unitary public interest." I will briefly explore some of these conceptions of the public interest and then show how the field continues to exclude groups based on variations in definitions of diversity. While contemporary planning theorists have begun to incorporate theories of difference and multiculturalism within planning, planning practice still needs to build in inclusive language in regard to sexual orientation. Recognition is the first step to a transformational practice. I will also explore intersectionality as it is used by feminists following McCall's methodological piece (2005). Then I reflect upon how intersectionality might be operating in my own planning projects in Kansas City. I will note how different planning approaches might apply an "intersectional" analysis as a way to build transformative practice. I conclude by setting up possible research/practice paths that will provide more evidence of how attention to intersectionality might embody a transformative planning practice.

Inclusion and the Public Interest

The classic case study of the public interest in planning was Meyerson and Banfield's (1955) description of the development of public housing in the urban renewal era in Chicago. They found that through the localism of the Chicago machine, politicians were forced to address competing claims from numerous identity groups. The public interest then results from having to find a compromise between these competing claims. In contrast the staff of the public housing authority had their own code:

> At any rate the staff seemed to think that there was a "code" that was widely held, and that actions that ran counter to the code were not in the public interest. The code specified that racial amity and integration were very much to be desired, and that waste was to be avoided and that all citizens were to be treated with rigorous impartiality, and that the values of family, home and good citizenship should be furthered by public effort, and that public officials should subordinate neighborhood and private interests (particularly personal ones) to the public interest. (Meyerson and Banfield 1955, 301)

By the 1950s the idea of the progressive unitary public interest was well established among the workers (i.e. planners) in the urban renewal and housing authority. What is interesting is that the values that were implicit in the planners' actions in Meyerson and Banfield's case study in the 1950s are now explicitly stated in the APA's (American Planning Association) ethical principles for planning and the AICP's (American Institute of Certified Planners) Code of Ethics. Appeals to a unitary public interest then still resonate within contemporary planning practice.

The critique of the idea of a unitary "public interest" developed very quickly. Lindblom (1959) criticized the possibility of actually doing comprehensive planning based upon a common public interest. Instead he advocated a middle-range policy of "muddling through" whereby planning administrators limit the scope of processes to majority interests framed by conceptions of pragmatic possibility. Critics further addressed the inability to separate the politics of group inclusion from the practices of planning (Altshuler 1965). One answer to this failure is to develop a utilitarian market-based planning model built around the sum of individual interests.

In such a model of interests, how might inclusion work? The classic pluralism model of urban politics has interest groups bargaining and competing for power (Dahl 1961). Interest group success is built upon leadership in forming broad "inclusive enough" coalitions to attain power. Coalition building then is about figuring out areas of collective interest that eventually become part of the "public interest."

Pluralist models fail when vested interests manipulate the process to control the rules (Lindblom 1990). Davidoff's (1965) response was that planners should provide support for excluded groups in planning processes. Yet, true participation would require full inclusion, not just advocacy. Arnstein's (1969) analysis of the various rungs on the ladder of public participation notes that many planning processes fall into manipulation and/or tokenism categories. The type of inclusion matters. Since 1970, we have known about the failure of the theory of a single public interest, yet in practice planners persist in using it (Campbell & Marshall 2002).

Does the Public Interest Include Specific Diversities?

The planning profession has internalized these values inherent in the Code of Ethics. The thinking seems to be that if we work to expand opportunity to all, then our unitary expression of the public interest will become an inclusive collective vision. These professional values are presently encoded in the AICP Code of Ethics (2013):

> We shall seek social justice by working to expand choice and opportunity for all persons, recognizing a special responsibility to plan for the needs of the disadvantaged and to promote racial and economic integration. We shall urge the alteration of policies, institutions, and decisions that oppose such needs.

The APA's Ethical Principles for Planners (1992) states that planners should "[s]trive to expand choice and opportunity for all persons, recognizing a special responsibility to plan for the needs of disadvantaged groups and persons." Yet, these aspirational goals for inclusion have not led to a planning profession that is fully diverse and representative of minorities and disadvantaged groups.

In response to this lack of diversity there is now an effort to "take diversity seriously" in planning schools. While a step forward in terms of action, there have also been steps backward. The Planning Accreditation Board's (PAB) description of the obligation of planning schools to include diversity has stepped away from describing all of the various types of diversity. The 2006 standards described diversity as:

> **Diversity:** The program's goals shall reflect the program's intent to achieve and maintain diversity in its student body and faculty and to incorporate into its curriculum the knowledge and skills needed to serve a diverse society. Consideration shall be given to a broad definition of diversity including race, ethnicity, sex, origin or background, disability, sexual orientation, economic status, and other factors pertinent to the program's mission. The program shall describe how its diversity goals relate to its mission and to the mission of planning education in general. (PAB 2006 version of the accreditation document)

The latest standards describe student diversity as:

> The program shall adopt appropriate recruitment and retention strategies, including curricular strategies, to achieve its aspirations for a diverse student body, and shall document actual progress in implementing those strategies. The program shall foster a climate of inclusivity that appreciates and celebrates

cultural difference through its recruitment and retention of students. Students shall possess, in the aggregate, characteristics of diversity (e.g., racial and ethnic background) that reflect the practice settings where graduates work or where professional needs exist in the program's region of recruitment and placement. Notwithstanding, the demographic mix is not a static concept, and all planning programs should seek to be in the forefront of a diverse society. (PAB 2013)

The new standards describe faculty diversity in similar terms as representing the practice setting of where graduates work. Guidelines have been given to planning programs saying that "Full-time faculty members demonstrate diversity with respect to age, race, ethnicity, gender, and state or country of origin" (PAB 2013). Unfortunately, these latest requirements removed the words "sexual orientation" from the types of diversity planning programs should include. We now get acknowledgement that diversity is a dynamic and changing concept. The problem is that the field of planning in the US as reflected by these official statements has taken a step backward in inclusion by removing direct mention of sexual orientation. This type of change is not representative of being "in the forefront of a diverse society."

Inclusive Planning Intent Often Differs from Planning Actions

What is so important about this long listing of identity categories? Is the recognition that diversity is a dynamic concept not a step forward? Sexual orientation was not the only category removed from the changed criteria. Economic status was also removed from the list of diversities that academic planning programs must address. The problem here is that urban planning has a historic pattern of exclusion along the lines of sexual orientation (Frisch 2002). This exclusion was often done in a coded way with general appeals to "order" that were thought to be in the "public interest."

Research has documented exclusionary planning actions around categories other than sexual orientation. For example, planning and real estate development may be viewed as a technology of whiteness—aiming to reproduce structures organized around narrow conceptions of meritocracy, home, family and work life. Planners were often involved in actions such as urban renewal and highways, efforts that adversely impacted the black community by reinforcing segregation (Gotham 2002). These measures prevented access to the wealth building real estate markets and contributed to cycles of poverty still seen today. The tools of planning such as zoning are still used in greater Kansas City in an exclusionary way to prevent access to low-income residents (Frisch 2014).

Gender and sexual orientation have also been problematic for planning. The planning and zoning system in the US arose at the same time as the development of large scale suburban subdivisions in the 20th century. Gender norms, especially in the post-World War II era, connected women to home space and men to the work world. Today, some urban spaces such as bicycle transport, sport stadiums and playgrounds remain relatively gendered.

Planning continues to operate as a technology of heteronormality. Increasing acceptance of lesbians and gays has led to much wider recognition of same-sex marriages and increasingly raises the question of lesbian and gay conformity (Bell and Binnie 2004). Analysts who characterize research on lesbians and gays as research on non-conformists (Forsyth 2011) will miss how heteronormative space structures the individual action of lesbians and gays toward conformity. Recent research such as Anacker's "Queering the Suburbs" (2011) shows that same-sex partnered households are more likely to live in the suburbs than the central city. Ehrenfeucht (2013) in an analysis of policy responses to homelessness in public spaces in West Hollywood shows how class interests trump social solidarity around sexual orientation and/or queer identities. Finally, Doan (2011) calls on planning to recognize the "tyranny of dichotomous definitions of gender." Doan notes how planning continues to promote "family" space over inclusive space that would pay attention to the creation of safe spaces for all genders and orientations.

Analysis of the impact of planning along any one of these previously described categories of difference troubles the unitary conception of "public interest" accepted in planning. These components of difference are not equivalent, multiplicative, or more important than another (Young 1990, 1998). There is a tendency in planning to make these claims (Harvey 1993). These claims act as "gatekeeping" and express power in the sense that they define what is to be included or not included (Valentine 2007). On a recent global planning related listserve one professor wrote:

> Planning scholars are researching everything, from poverty, homelessness, climate change, ... to lesbian/gay, yet they still debate over what urban planning is or should be, falling in love with X theory or Y framework while missing urban planning's core, without which urban planning will not make true advances. (AICP listserve 2013)

Note that this writer posited that studies of sexual orientation in planning are outside of planning's "core." Maybe the exploration of the dimensions of difference within the lived experience of space will get to analyses that lead to true advances in urban planning's core. This exploration might be an important strategic step of an inclusive planning.

How then might planners deal with difference? Sandercock (2000) explores four possible strategies. First, planning might address difference by revising the legislative and regulatory structures of planning to be more inclusive. Legislative and regulatory change requires majority consent in democracies so Sandercock sees this change as one that will take time. At the time she was writing, she probably did not anticipate the generational shift in support of same-sex marriage in the US that will partly facilitate this change as marriage defines family and bestows on partners significant land use rights. Sandercock's second approach is that planning might address difference through aspects of the market. Planning policy could be used to facilitate the development of distinct spaces through signage and incentives. Yet the marketing of "gay" space creates class distinctions and has led to "homonormativity" (Bell and Binnie 2004). The third of Sandercock's planning approaches for addressing diversity is to create a dialogue (2000: 18). This approach falls distinctly within the communicative planning tradition of the last couple of decades. It is interesting because the communicative approach arose out of critiques of technocratic planning and conceptions of a "unitary" public interest (Innes 1995). Sandercock's fourth approach is related to the third: planners must be educated in such a way that they build the skills to facilitate such dialogues.

The intriguing part of Sandercock's approach to "managing cities of difference" is that she directly confronts the fear that we all may face in entering such a process (2000: 23). Careful attention must be paid then to power dynamics, making sure that disempowered people and groups are included. This inclusion comes about through a process of organizing where either a group demands to be included or planners reach out to include them. Sandercock calls this "transformative approach" therapeutic. Participants have to enter the dialogue with good listening skills and the freedom to express their "truth." The experience of the process has to have the potential to create personal growth. There is a strong parallel between this process laid out by Sandercock whereby empathy is created through a planning process and analysis that addresses intersectionality.

Intersectionality

The concept of intersectionality arose out of an attempt to describe the experience of living within multiple categories of identity. While this experience has been addressed by scholars before, Crenshaw (1991) identified the "intersectional" experience as the result of multiple types of intersectionality. Structural intersectionality is where discriminatory structures of racism, sexism, and class intersect. Political intersectionality refers to the politics of conflicting social movements responding to discriminatory structures. Crenshaw shows how anti-racist and feminist organizing may develop in contradictory ways in her discussion of the politics of anti-domestic violence organizing. Acknowledging the social construction of categories, Crenshaw goes on to recognize that exploring the:

> Identity politics taking place at the site where categories intersect thus seems more fruitful than challenging the possibility of talking about categories at all. Through an awareness of intersectionality, we can better acknowledge and ground the differences among us and negotiate the means by which these differences will find expression in constructing group politics. (Crenshaw 1991)

Operationalizing intersectionality then allows us to examine inequalities across multiple categories of identity (Verloo 2006, Cho et al. 2013). Any discussion of inequality and justice has to address the people who are subjected to unjust and indiscriminate uses of power. Rather than just framing people within a group as the objects of discrimination, intersectionality highlights the ways that individuals and collective organizations experience structures of power. It allows a post-structuralist critique of "categories" by examining how an individual chooses to be part of a group or not. It is concerned with how structures of power both capabilities, but also how individuals choose to engage with structures of power and movements of resistance (Crenshaw 1991, Valentine 2007).

Intersectionality, Sexual Orientation, Gender and Planning

I already contend that urban planning produces heteronormative spaces. Coming out into these spaces is a constant process given that the assumption in much urban and especially suburban space is that you are straight (Frisch 2002). The enforcement of heterosexuality in public space has become much less pronounced in recent years, although New York faced a series of public anti-gay hate crimes in public space in 2013. Queer space is often commercialized space—organized around bar culture, shopping, restaurants and entertainment. Commercialized space often reflects a commercialized culture. People who come out in such commercialized queer space can feel alienated when they realize that issues of race, looks, class, and status are often reified in these commercial queer spaces (Taylor 2010). These are situational moments that reveal intersecting axes of power that are directly experienced in people's lives (MacKinnon 2013).

Earlier in this chapter, I presented the modernist conception of planning. I contend that while theory may have taken a "communicative" turn, planning in practice still approaches the public interest in these older, classic modernization ways. We may debate the "unitary" public interest in academic sessions, but the planning profession's statements of ethics and the planning academy's statement of diversity objectives profess that a democratic effort in inclusion is what is needed. This inclusion would start by naming and recognizing that planning has a responsibility to address systematic inequities around issues of sexual orientation and gender identity. True recognition happens with explicit engagement. I wonder how planning would change with a true commitment to multiculturalism following Sandercock's vision (1997). Planning for multiple public interests would have to start by engaging the "situational accomplishment" of individuals negotiating categorical boundaries within urban space (Valentine 2007).

Intersectionality and Planning in Kansas City

Intersectionality may be found in every planning process and probably in most planning analyses. One category of identity always brought to this process is the self-defined community in which a person lives. The spaces and places we inhabit in everyday life as we go from home to work define us to some degree. These places frame our existence and define the possibilities of whom we might meet.

The geography of our everyday lives is intertwined with the institutions and individual relationships that reflect identity categories. These identities are both chosen by an individual and imposed upon an individual. Expression of these identities is a constant negotiation and it may differ as we move from a "safe" space to places of lesser safety (Valentine 2007). The work of urban planning is to improve the spaces and places we inhabit. Understanding patterns of everyday life in an area is a critical part of planning analysis. Thus inclusion and recognition of people and categories of people within these spaces may be a necessary ingredient of democratic practice.

What follows is a reflection of intersectionality in my own experiences as a planning academic and a practitioner in Kansas City. The academic experience presents the results of a survey of students taking a class entitled "Queer in the City." The second experience reflects my representation of my university in a regional sustainability planning process. Both experiences begin to illustrate aspects of how to apply intersectionality in planning.

Perceptions of Queering Space in Kansas City

A survey of students took place in a class at UMKC, an urban-serving campus of the University of Missouri. While there are residential dorms, the campus is primarily a commuter campus with students clustering in the neighborhoods nearest to the university as well as driving in from all parts of the Metropolitan Area. The class was co-taught by the Director of Women's Studies and myself. Students read classic works in gender and lesbian and gay studies. Then we began reading some works on sexuality and space including Frisch (2002). This work gave students a sense of how planning processes construct heteronormal space. We then read Doan's (2007) work on transgender perceptions of urban space. This reading raised questions about issues of safety connected to pressures to fit preconceived lines of gender conformity. Then we read recent work examining queer space in Kansas City. Through a limited set of interviews, Nusser and Anacker (2013) found a continuum of space from hostile space to spaces that they called queering. They started by identifying heteronormative space as the Power and Light District, a location where even I have witnessed someone asking two men to stop dancing. Nusser and Anacker then describe the locations of possible queering spaces—ones that go from tolerating queerness to acceptance of queerness. These spaces ranged from identification of tolerant districts and coffee shops to the accepting space of an MCC Church, a denomination started by a charismatic gay preacher. These readings set the stage for the development of the class exercise examining identity, safety and urban space in Kansas City.

The anonymous survey was a voluntary class exercise used to get students to think about the issues raised by the readings in their own lives. The survey repeated some of Doan's questions in terms of "safe" space and neighborhood definition. These questions included whether or not the student's neighborhood had lesbians and gays living there, was it safe for LGBT people to walk in the neighborhood holding hands, and was the neighborhood safe for transgender people? Questions also asked about how the students identify in terms of sex, gender, and sexual orientation, whether or not their neighborhood was urban, suburban, or rural, and whether or not they took part in LGBT Pride or events put on by the LGBTQIA Office on campus. What follows is an analysis of the survey results.

Table 8.1 shows the raw results of the survey. A total of 29 students took the survey. As an urban-serving university UMKC students tend to be working class, often living at home and working their way through college. The class also had a few older non-traditional students. In terms of gender, the majority of the class identified as women, with a significant group (24%) identifying in non-binary gender categories. In terms of sex, the group was more than two-thirds female with no one identifying as intersex. The class was very mixed in terms of orientation with more than 60% of students identifying as "not straight." This result is not surprising in a class entitled "Queer in the City." The majority of students lived in "inner city" Kansas City as opposed to the suburbs or the rural periphery. Already the survey results reveal the spectrum of possible categories negotiated by these individuals. These results all reflect self-selected categories.

Students' perceptions of space, while not necessarily representative of any group other than themselves, do reveal intersectional issues about planning and public space. In particular the questions about experiences and impressions about place, safety and identity produced interesting results. The majority of students answered "yes" in terms of having had to face a threat in the last year[1]. Responses about lesbian, gay, and transgender safety depend on how one views and codes the answer "maybe." The low rate of "yes" answers to both questions tells a lot about how far we have to go to make space safe for dimensions of difference and intersections of identity. Less than a majority in the survey were able to affirm that there were lesbians and gays living in their neighborhood. The many "maybe" answers to the questions about safety and lesbian and gay location may also be reflective of students' general youth. For many students this was their first urban planning/gender studies class and they may have little experience in critically observing their neighborhood. In these cases, a "maybe" response may reflect this lack of awareness.

The next step in the analysis was to see how one or another part of the respondent's identity correlated with various identities and perception of space. This analysis allows for examination of how category membership "intersects" with a response (McCall 2005). I performed a correlation analysis using Kendall's tau—a non-parametric measure for analyzing ranked and dichotomous data. This initial coding of all responses, as shown in Table 8.1, reflects these requirements.

The initial coding reflected the atmosphere of the discussions in class. We talked about how gender may be more fluid than commonly acknowledged and we talked about how there might be a variety of sexual orientations. The analysis of results about urban experience initially reflected only the "yes" answers and the strongest associations were between the types of urbanism, the knowledge of LGBT neighbors, and lesbian and gay safety. The association between sex and street hostility reflects sexism in public space and the negative association between

TABLE 8.1 Results from UMKC class survey on identity and perceptions of urban safety (n=29)

Question	Answer	Coding	Results	Percent
1. How would you categorize your gender?				
a.	Transgender	3		
b.	Male	1	6	20.7%
c.	Female	2	16	55.2%
d.	Other	3	7	24.1%
2. What is your sex?				
a.	Female	2	20	69.0%
b.	Male	1	9	31.0%
c.	Intersex	3	0	0.0%
d.	Other	3	0	0.0%
3. What is your orientation?				
a.	Gay	2	11	37.9%
b.	Bisexual	3	7	24.1%
c.	Straight	1	11	37.9%
d.	Other	3		
4. Where do you live?				
a.	Inner City Kansas City	1	17	58.6%
b.	Suburbs	2	9	31.0%
c.	Periphery	3	3	10.3%
5. Have you felt threatened by any of the following in your city in the last year?				
a.	Hostile Stares	1	15	51.7%
b.	Hostile Comments	1		
c.	Physical Harassment	1		
d.	None	0	14	48.3%
6. Do you think the place you live is safe for lesbians and gays who might hold hands in public?				
a.	Yes	1	10	34.5%
b.	No	0	5	17.2%
c.	Maybe	0	14	48.3%
7. Do you think the place you live is safe for transgender people?				
a.	Yes	1	6	20.7%
b.	No	0	11	37.9%
c.	Maybe	0	12	41.4%
8. Do many lesbian and gay people live in your neighborhood?				
a.	Yes	1	13	44.8%
b.	No	0	6	20.7%
c.	Maybe	0	10	34.5%
9. Do you go to LGBT events sponsored by the UMKC LGBTQIA office or Pride?				
a.	Yes	1	13	44.8%
b.	No	0	16	55.2%

Source: Survey given to prompt discussion in a 2012 class. Individual results coded to protect anonymity.

street hostility and lesbian/gay safety reflects that those who experience hostility think their neighborhood is not safe for lesbians and gays.

Exploring intersectionality in planning analysis means questioning assumptions about how power relations impact particular categories (McCall 2005). My exploratory recoding criteria capture one application of exploring where identity categories "intersect." I created "recoded" survey variables as shown in Table 8.2. These re-codes had multiple purposes. First, I wanted to explore the effects of ranking orientation. Kinsey created a continuum from straight to gay with various aspects of bisexuality in the middle (Kinsey et al. 1948). Yet, in today's world with finely defined gay and straight identities there are also those who would label bisexuality as the more transgressive and "non-conformist" of sexual orientations. I wanted to test to see if the different dimensions of gender and orientation reflecting intersectionality influenced responses about urban space and event participation. Second, when I originally coded the safety and lesbian/gay neighborhood variables, I created a dichotomous "yes" or "no" and mixed the "maybe" responses with the "no". Part of my initial coding of this variable is that as a target of anti-LGBT violence in the past, my bias is to rate most locations as unsafe. Recoding the "maybe" as an "in-between" response instead of a "not-yes"

TABLE 8.2 Recoded results from UMKC class survey on identity and perceptions of urban safety

Question	Answer	Coding	Results	Percent
3a. What is your orientation?				
a.	Gay	2	11	37.9%
b.	Bisexual	1	7	24.1%
c.	Straight	0	11	37.9%
4a. Where do you live?				
a.	Kansas City	1	17	58.6%
b.	Suburbs and Rural	2	12	41.4%
6a. Do you think the place you live is safe for lesbians and gays who might hold hands in public?				
a.	Yes	1	10	34.5%
b.	No	0	5	17.2%
c.	Maybe	0.5	14	48.3%
7a. Do you think the place you live is safe for transgender people?				
a.	Yes	1	6	20.7%
b.	No	0	11	37.9%
c.	Maybe	0.5	12	41.4%
8a. Do many lesbian and gay people live in your neighborhood?				
a.	Yes	1	13	44.8%
b.	No	0	6	20.7%
c.	Maybe	0.5	10	34.5%

Source: Recoded results from survey by the author.

response indicates a continuum of "safe" to "not safe" for space as well as a continuum for lesbians and gays in my neighborhood. This continuum of safety is analogous to Nusser and Anacker's spectrum of "queering space." Finally some recoding is necessary to take care of the degrees of freedom problem given such a small number of total responses.

The associations found after the recode, indicating a correlation between sexual orientation and knowledge of lesbian and gay neighbors, as well as between impressions of transgender safety and experiential urbanism, are shown in Figure 8.1. Different interpretations are possible depending on lines within the categories that then impact the relationships between categories (McCall 2005). As an exploratory analysis, the strength of the recoded "urban" category reveals how individual perceptions of density relate to understanding spatial characteristics of safety impressions by gender and sexual orientation. The direction of the recoded variables means that respondents who live in the less urban locations were more likely to think that their neighborhoods were safe for lesbians and gay men while at the same time they were also less likely to perceive having lesbian and gay neighbors. Why would lesbians and gays choose to live in a less safe place then? Urban brings with it a whole set of meanings in Kansas City (Schirmer 2002) around issues of safety and difference. Almost all of the "queering spaces" in Nusser and Anacker (2013) fall into the urban category.

This example shows how intersectionality might be applied to planning analysis. In some ways the categorization of the planning researcher mirrors society's application of categories to individuals. In order to operationalize this

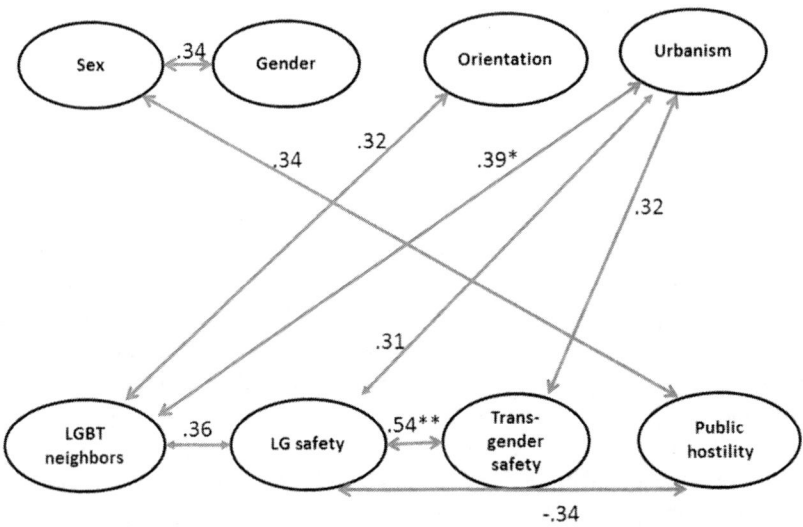

Post-recoding associations (Kendall's tau) results, significance levels of p<.10,
* p<.05, and ** p<.01 shown.

FIGURE 8.1 Relationships between identity and perception of safety after recoding

intersectionality-based analysis as a transformative planning practice following Sandercock (2000), I would need to go back to the survey respondents and ask them to discuss the results. Would new knowledge of each other's responses change an individual's view? An intersectional planning practice would entail listening to each other's stories of belonging and not belonging, and then reflecting how they might change one's individual view as well as the collective views of those participating in the process.

Regional Equity and LGBT Silence in Sustainability Planning

As part of the local Creating Sustainable Places project 2010–2013, the Mid America Regional Council (MARC), the metropolitan planning organization that prioritizes transportation capital projects among other work, put together a partnership of 60 organizations to facilitate implementation of regional sustainable development plans. With the support of the national intermediary Policy Link, MARC created a group called the "equity partners." The equity partners included the Hispanic Chamber of Commerce, More Squared (MORE²—the Metro Organization for Racial and Economic Equity), Communities Creating Opportunity (CCO), and a representative of a very successful neighborhood association from the mostly black East Side. Getting these organizations at the table within the context of the Metropolitan Planning Organization is a major step forward for the region.

While there has been much talk about inclusion and regional equity, there has been almost complete silence on LGBT inclusion in this process. Munro and Richardson studied intersectionality and sexuality in local governments in the UK doing equity work (2011). This absence reflects their finding that LGBT equality is often a "lower" priority even among people aware of intersectionality and doing equity work. The silence limits transformational dialogue.

Visions of sustainability in Kansas City tend to have a heteronormative framework surrounding ways to support stereotypical nuclear families and their future generations. Much discussion went into the idea of "nodes and corridors" (MARC 2013) but there was an avoidance of talking about the connections of density and difference, concepts that a recent quantitative work shows might be linked (Smart and Klein 2014). My limited exploratory survey brought out an association with living in denser areas with knowledge of lesbian and gay neighbors. When we do not address our fears, we will not get to the transformational space (Sandercock 2000).

In the context of a "policy silence" on LGBT issues in Kansas City, intersectional moments happen when the silence is broken. Using inclusive language that allows for lesbian and gay families, as well as a typical husband-wife family within the context of sustainable development, is one of those moments. Furthermore, the moment of talking about increased density and increasing housing options to create mixed-income neighborhoods may also mean creating the opportunity for more racial and ethnic interaction. I am afraid that the planners at the table may all be ascribing to some sort of professional code that recognizes the benefits of this interaction. This code may still be implicit just as it was 60 years ago when Meyerson and Banfield (1955) completed their case studies. Planners have to make these values explicit in the process and explain why or why not they might matter to individuals and groups. At this point (2015), the full implications of creating greater density in terms of gender and sexual orientation have still not been explored.

Conclusion

Doing intersectional planning work is hard. How do we move organizations, neighborhoods and city governments to address their fears (Sandercock 2000)? Creating a process where this can happen is risky and has to be well-facilitated. The starting place has to be a level of recognition of particular groups that need to be included. This recognition requires explicit welcoming statements. The field of planning in the US must address the backsliding that has happened in terms of the accreditation standards of the PAB. While an intersectional understanding requires a dynamic view of diversity, we are not at the point of abandoning the welcome of individuals and groups in categories.

This chapter starts a conversation around identity categories and how categories intersect in urban planning. I find that in practice, planning still uses a unitary "general public" approach when assessing community engagement. In regional planning exercises, LGBT organizations have too often not been included in the process. There is little perception that LGBT organizations might have an important place-based perspective that needs to be included. Choices of transportation, housing and environmental spending will certainly have an impact on LGBT communities and showing this impact is imperative as part of the work of planners concerned about queer spaces (Doan and Higgins 2011). I suggest that everyone has intersectional moments in their lives due to membership in multiple identity categories. All too often planning only addresses place and neighborhood attachment. In my trial survey instrument, I find differences in perceptions of safety of urban space that depend upon how one categorizes the respondent's orientation because the views of safety vary across different lines of identity. An intersectional planning approach might start by interviewing people about safety, inclusion, and their own neighborhood. This would be analogous to Valentine's (2007) approach.

Yet, a true intersectional analysis must also critically examine the categories and combinations. How does the city frame a category? What are the underlying assumptions and are there fundamental but unseen relationships? These assumptions influence the boundaries of identity categories and if one shifts the assumptions as modeled by the "recoding" exercise, one also shifts the results. The resulting change in results could be considered an "undoing" of identity. The doing and "undoing of identity" (Valentine 2007) can happen through this kind of careful examination. Planners should begin by including more possible identity categories in their analyses of place and space. Inclusion means expanding the invitation to groups that have previously been excluded in planning processes.

Finally, applying intersectionality improves Sandercock's (2000) proposals about how to manage cities of difference. It expresses the give and take in non-therapeutic terms that arises in a procedure where people listen and speak. As this practice develops the potential for change increases and the collective public interest may arise out of the whole. Planning has the potential to create new identities through a process informed by intersectional relationships that might also be a prerequisite for dealing with past unjust outcomes while still finding a way to move forward. Listening to intersectional claims and individual realities then might lead to Fainstein's (2010) non-reformist reforms.

Note

1   I recognize the exploratory nature of this study, and I await a chance to repeat this question with a more representative group of students to put this response in context.

References

Altshuler, A. 1965. "The Goals of Comprehensive Planning." *Journal of the American Institute of Planning*. 31, 3: 186–195.

American Institute of Certified Planners (AICP). 2013. Code of Ethics. Downloaded June 2013 from www.planning.org/aicp

American Planning Association (APA). 1992. Ethical Principles for Planners. Accessed June 2013 from www.planning.org/ethics/ethicalprinciples.htm

Anacker, K.B. 2011. "Queering the Suburbs: Analyzing Property Values in Male and Female Same-Sex Suburbs in the United States." Chapter 6 in P. Doan (ed.) *Queerying Planning: Challenging Heteronormative Assumptions and Reframing Planning Practice.* Burlington, VT: Ashgate.

Arnstein, S.R. 1969. "A Ladder of Public Participation." *Journal of the American Institute of Planners*. 35, 4: 216–224.

Bell, D. and Binnie, J. 2004. "Authenticating Queer Space: Citizenship, Urbanism, and Governance." *Urban Studies*. 41(9): 1807–20.

Campbell, H. and Marshall, R. 2002. "Utilitarianism's Bad Breath." *Planning Theory*. 1, 2: 163–187.

Cho, S., McCall, L. and Crenshaw, K. 2013. "Toward a Field of Intersectionality Studies: Theory, Applications, and Praxis." *Signs* 38, 4: 785–810.

Crenshaw, K. 1991. "Mapping the Margins, Intersectionality, Identity Politics and Violence Against Women of Color." *Stanford Law Review* 43, 6: 1241–1299.

Dahl, R. 1961. *Who Governs?* New Haven, CT: Yale University Press.

Davidoff, P. 1965. "Advocacy and Pluralism in Planning." *Journal of the American Institute of Planners*. 31, 4: 331–338.

Doan, P.L. 2007. "Queers in the American City: Transgendered perceptions of urban spaces." *Gender, Place and Culture*. 14(1): 57–74.

Doan, P.L. 2011. "Queerying Identity: Planning and the Tyranny of Gender." Chapter 5 in P.L. Doan (ed.) *Queerying Planning: Challenging Heteronormative Assumptions and Reframing Planning Practice*. Burlington, VT: Ashgate.

Doan, P.L. and Higgins, H. 2011. "The demise of queer space? Resurgent Gentrification and LGBT Neighborhoods." *Journal of Planning Education and Research*. 31, 1.

Ehrenfeucht, R. 2013. "Non-conformity and street design in West Hollywood, California." *Journal of Urban Design*. 59, 10: 59–77.

Fainstein, S.S. and Fainstein, N. 1996. "City Planning and Political Values: An Updated View." Chapter 12 in S. Campbell and S.S. Fainstein (eds.) *Readings in Planning Theory*. Malden, MA: Blackwell.

Fainstein, S.S. 2010. *The Just City*. Ithaca, NY: Cornell University Press.

Fogelsong, R. 1986. *Planning the Capitalist City*. Princeton, NJ: Princeton University Press.

Forrester, J. 1999. *The Deliberative Practitioner*. Cambridge, MA: MIT Press.

Forsyth, A. and Sandercock, L. 1992. "A Gender Agenda: New Directions for Planning Theory." *Journal of Planning Education and Research*. 58, 1: 49–59.

Forsyth, A. 2011. "Queerying Planning Practice: Understanding Non-Conformist Populations." Chapter 2 in P. Doan (ed.) *Queerying Planning: Challenging Heteronormative Assumptions and Reframing Planning Practice*. Burlington, VT: Ashgate.

Frisch, M. 2002. "Planning as a Heterosexist Project." *Journal of Planning Education and Research*. 21, 3: 88–108.

Frisch, M. 2014. "The Role of Environmental Justice in Regional Sustainable Planning." Unpublished manuscript.

Gotham, K.F. 2002. *Race, Estate and Uneven Development*. Albany, NY: SUNY Press.

Harvey, D. 1993. "Class Relations, Social Justice and the Politics of Difference," pp. 41–66 in S. Pile and M. Keith (eds.) *Place and the Politics of Identity*. London: Routledge.

Hoch, C., Dalton, L. and So, F. (eds.) 2000. *The Practice of Local Government Planning*, Third Edition. Washington, DC: International City/County Management Association.

IACP Listserve. 2013. International Association of China Planning. www.chinaplanning.org

Innes, Judith. 1995. "Planning Theory's Emerging Paradigm: Communicative Action and Interactive Practice." *Journal of Planning Education and Research* 14, 3: 183–189, April.

Kinsey, A.C., Pomeroy, W.B., and Martin, C.E. 1948. *Sexual Behavior in the Human Male*. Bloomington, IN: Indiana University Press.

Lindblom, C. 1959. "The Science of Muddling Through." *Public Administration Review*. 19, 2: 79–88.

Lindblom, C. 1990. *Inquiry and Change*. New Haven, CT: Yale University Press.

Logan, J. and Molotch, H. 1986. *Urban Fortunes*. Berkeley, CA: University of California Press.

MacKinnon, Catharine A. 2013. "Intersectionality as Method: A Note." *Signs*. 38, 4: 1019–1030.

McCall, L. 2005. "The Complexity of Intersectionality." *Signs*. 30, 3: 1771–1800.

Meyerson, M. and Banfield, E.C. 1955. *Politics, Planning and the Public Interest: The Case of Public Housing*. Glencoe, IL: The Free Press.

Mid America Regional Council (MARC). 2013. *Creating Sustainable Places*. Accessed June 2013 at www.marc.org/Regional-Planning/Creating-Sustainable-Places

Munro, S. and Richardson, D. 2011. "Intersexuality and Sexuality: The Case of UK Government Local Authorities." Chapter 5 in Y. Taylor, S. Hines and M.E. Casey (eds.) 2010 *Theorizing Intersectionality and Sexuality*. New York, NY: Palgrave Macmillan.

Nusser, S.P. and Anacker, K. 2013. "What Sexuality is this place? Building a Framework for Evaluating Sexualized Space: The Case of Kansas City MO." *Journal of Urban Affairs*. 35, 2: 173–193.

Planning Accreditation Board (PAB), 2013. *Accreditation Requirements* 2006 and 2013 downloaded from www.planningaccreditationboard.org

Sandercock, L. 1997. *Towards Cosmopolis*. New York, NY: Wiley.

Sandercock, L. 2000. "When Strangers Become Neighbors: Managing Cities of Difference." *Planning Theory and Practice*. 1, 1: 13–30.

Schirmer, S.L. 2002. *A City Divided: The Racial Landscapes of Kansas City 1900–1960*. Columbia, MO: University of Missouri Press.

Smart, Michael J. and Klein, Nicolas, J. 2014. "Neighborhoods of Affinity, Social Forces and Travel in Lesbian and Gay Neighborhoods." *Journal of the American Planning Association*.

Taylor, Y. 2010 "Complexities and Complications, Intersections of Class and Sexuality." Chapter 2, pp. 37–55 in Y. Taylor, S. Hines and M.E. Casey (eds.), 2010 *Theorizing Intersectionality and Sexuality*. New York, NY: Palgrave Macmillan.

Thomas, J.M. 2008. "The Minority Race Planner in the Quest for the Just City." *Planning Theory*. 7, 3: 227–247.

Valentine, G. 2007. "Theorizing and Research Intersectionality: A Challenge for Feminist Geography. *The Professional Geographer*. 59(1): 10–21.

Verloo, M. 2006. "Multiple Inequalities, Intersectionality and the European Union." *European Journal of Women's Studies* 2006 13: 211–223.

Yiftachel, O. 1998. "The Dark Side of Planning." *Journal of Planning Literature*. 12, 2: 395–408.

Young, I.M. 1990. *Justice and the Politics of Difference*. Princeton, NJ: Princeton University Press.

Young, I.M. 1998. "Harvey's Complaint with Race and Gender Struggles: A Critical Response." *Antipode*. 30: 36–42.

9

SOUTHERN DISCOMFORT

In Search of the LGBT-Friendly City[1]

Joan Marshall Wesley

Introduction

Historically, the South has taken a conservative posture toward sexual behavior perceived to be at variance with the dominant hetero–normative paradigm. The position eclipses needed considerations for equity surrounding the intersecting issues that contribute to a desirable quality of life: equal access to housing, freedom from employment discrimination, mistreatment and bullying, and acceptance to participate fully as citizens. Notwithstanding the obvious increased attention to this community in cosmopolitan and urban areas, lesbian, gay, bisexual and transgender (LGBT) persons remain an underserved and invisible community in many parts of the Deep South. Arguably, LGBT persons individually and as a community remain largely underappreciated for the diversity they offer, and unacknowledged for their contributions to the larger community. The chapter examines challenges faced by the LGBT community in Jackson, Mississippi. Drawing from data collected through surveys and interviews, the chapter examines core issues from a variety of perspectives: the LGBT community, law enforcement, city residents, and members of Jackson's Planning Department, as well as LGBT allies, friends and relatives.

Located in the Deep South, Jackson, Mississippi has a substantial LGBT community. Although enjoying a degree of visibility in some quarters, in 2014 LGBT individuals in Jackson continued to confront the same prejudices and biases faced by other groups considered outside of the dominant social order. The seeming contradiction of the invisibility alongside a very visible minority within the community lends itself to the ongoing enigma of the LGBT population in Jackson. The purpose of the study is to gain insight into the experiences of LGBT people in Jackson and to identify LGBT enclaves or areas that host significant numbers of LGBT residents. The work will give a louder voice and greater visibility to the Jackson LGBT community.

Overview: Mississippi and the LGBT Community

Mississippi, the Magnolia State, is widely known for socially conservative ideas steeped in Southern culture. InterExchange (n.d.) accurately captures the lasting legacy of the state: "The culture of the state is also closely tied to its history" (para.2). Internationally known for its contentious racial history, the Magnolia State appears to have transferred some of the lingering animus toward an increasingly vocal and visible group, the LGBT community. Inarguably, the disenfranchisement of LGBT persons lacks the full equivalency of the historical oppression of the state's black population. Still, the tactics used to deny full citizenship to LGBT people mirror in many ways the state's dark legacy in the treatment of some of its citizens, particularly efforts to codify discriminatory acts in open defiance of and resistance to federal mandates.

Legislatively, Mississippi has done more to hinder than advance equal rights for LGBT people. In 2004, the State Legislature approved and Mississippi voters passed the Defense of Marriage Act (Human Rights Campaign [HRC], 2012; National Conference of State Legislatures, 2013; see also "State Laws," Lambda Legal, 2013). The law reads in part (Holzer, 2012, p. 16):

> Marriage may take place and may be valid under the laws of this state only between a man and a woman. A marriage in another state or foreign jurisdiction between persons of the same gender, regardless of when the marriage took place, may not be recognized in this state and is void and unenforceable under the laws of this state.

Mississippi also prohibits same-sex couples the right to adopt and sexual orientation can be considered in "custody disputes" (Lambda Legal, n.d.). More recently, Mississippi became the last defiant holdout to comply with the federal mandate to process same-sex benefits for persons serving in the state's National Guard (HRC, 2013c; see also Margolin, 2013b).

The Magnolia State in 2014 offers few if any safeguards to LGBT people against discriminatory workplace practices based on real or perceived sexual orientation or gender identity. The state falls short in protections in the private workplace and state law does not expressly protect LGBT state and local government employees from discrimination on the basis of sexual orientation or sexual identity (Lambda Legal, n.d.). Further, Nave (2013) observes that Mississippi permits employers to punish openly gay persons. Notwithstanding opposition to LGBT workplace equality, the Employment Non-Discrimination Act passed the U.S. Senate in November 2013 with a final vote of 64 to 32 (Margolin, 2013a). The victory is a major advancement toward workplace equality.

While hardened attitudes and recalcitrant political operatives continue to embrace long-held opinions about LGBT equality, demands for equal rights for LGBT people continue to gain traction. Nave (2013) cites results from a Human Rights poll showing that 64 percent of Mississippians would support legislation to protect LGBT employees from workplace discrimination (as reported in HRC,

2013b). The same poll shows that 58 percent of the state's population under the age of 30 support LGBT marriage equality. Critics of the poll raise questions about the methods used, including Blaze (2011) who argues that the sample size of Christian respondents could have been larger and more diverse (less than a third of those polled self-identified as non-white Christians).

Supporters and allies work to move beyond the codification of LGBT discrimination. Examples include the Mississippi Chapter of the National Association for the Advancement of Colored People (NAACP). Chapter President, Derrick Johnson (n.d.), published an article in *The Jackson Advocate* that underscores the resolution on marriage equality passed by the NAACP Board of Directors. In part, the resolution reads (NAACP, 2012):

> The NAACP Constitution affirmatively states our objective to ensure the "political, educational, social and economic equality" of all people. Therefore, the NAACP has opposed and will continue to oppose any national, state, local policy or legislative initiative that seeks to codify discrimination or hatred into the law or to remove the Constitutional rights of LGBT citizens. We support marriage equality consistent with equal protection under the law provided under the Fourteenth Amendment of the United States Constitution. Further, we strongly affirm the religious freedoms of all people as protected by the First Amendment. (para. 5)

Johnson (n.d.) concludes, "we must not align ourselves with any effort to codify discrimination but instead to speak out on advancing equal treatment under the law." (para. 4)

Gender and sexual nonconformity in Mississippi is nothing new. In mid-twentieth century Mississippi, Howard (1999) asserts same-sex relationships in Mississippi were neither isolated nor invisible. Likewise, Sessums (2007) writes about being different in Mississippi alongside the intersection of racial animus and complex social and cultural norms. Similarly, Wise (2012) describes how journalists and others wrote about queer people in Mississippi: "they called attention to their gender nonconformity but stopped short of categorizing them" (p. 7). Indeed, like so much of the Deep South, Mississippi is a complex tapestry of intersecting contradictions of social and cultural values juxtaposed against a background of conflicting beliefs and realities.

Magnifying sexual nonconformity and advancing laws to restrict sexual and gender variations may be useful political wedges. The tactics may offer additional utility in keeping LGBT people in their places, silent and invisible where they do not cause discomfort to others. As Sutter (2013) points out, although census data show that not one same-sex couple lives in Franklin County, Mississippi, evidence of gayness clearly exists. Sometimes openly unacknowledged, the denial pushes LGBT people deeper into the "Southern Closet," a term used by a Franklin County resident in describing gays who remain in the closet with the door fully ajar (Sutter, 2013).

An article published in the *Jackson Free Press* by Straight Against Hate founder, Emory Williamson (2012), admonishes Mississippians to think about the consequences of non-action when witnessing the pain suffered by persons perceived to be at sexual variance with the hetero-normative orientation. Williamson asserts that by ignoring the mistreatment and derision of LGBT individuals, onlookers become a passive part of the problem.

The *Jackson Free Press* received a number of comments in response to Williamson's article. Some of the responses are quoted below:

> "I am new to Mississippi, so have been a bit cautious about being out. It gives me great hope to see articles like the column written by Emory Williamson... I know that I still run the risk of discrimination at work, where I live, and the places I frequent... Knowing there are allies in the community who have my back helps me to feel safer" (Dickey 2012).

> "Congratulations Emory. You've got amazing things ahead of you. I am really proud to know you and share a hometown and alma mater with you" (Mlindberger 2012).

> "As a Mississippian, this is inspiring to see, especially printed. It's great to know there are people like Emory in this country and state" (Batson, 2012).

In addition Kevin Sessums (author of *Mississippi Sissy* published in 2007 by St. Martin's Press) also wrote "Thank you, Emory Williamson, an example of what is good and progressive down in Mississippi" (Sessums 2012).

Eddie Outlaw, a frequent contributor to the *Jackson Free Press*, writes about a broad range of topics relevant to LGBT persons. Drawing from his personal daily experiences, Outlaw confronts the slights and unpleasant experiences faced by the LGBT community. One can glean much from the uncomfortable topics about which Outlaw writes: his childhood in the Mississippi Delta (Outlaw, 2012b, 2012c), the first time he registered to vote in 2008 (Outlaw, 2012d), and his first reaction to the Defense of Marriage Act (Outlaw, 2012a, 2013b).

Census Data and Mississippi Same-Sex Demographics

The Census Bureau published the first report of same-sex data from the 2010 decennial census (U.S. Census, 2013a). Analyzing the data, Gates (2010) finds that most same-sex couples with children settle in the most socially conservative geography, the South. Accordingly, Gates (2010) notes that 23.6 percent of same-sex couples in the East South Central Census Region (Alabama, Kentucky, Mississippi and Tennessee) parent children under the age of 18 years.

Gates & Ost (2004) report that Mississippi ranks number one among all states with the highest concentration of same-sex couples with children and number nine among all same-sex senior couples. Further, Gates & Ost (2004) find that Mississippi ranks number one in same-sex African American households, and number five among all Hispanic same-sex households. These data suggest a contradiction in the perceptions held about Mississippi and LGBT people.

Jackson: Mississippi's Capital City and the LGBT Community

The racial/ethnic composition of Jackson is 79.4 percent black/African American, 18 percent non-Hispanic white, 1.6 percent Hispanic/Latino, and a combined total of 0.5 percent other races, including two or more races (U.S. Census, 2013b). In addition, Jackson enjoys a colorful history punctuated by contested racialized space, civil rights battles, out-migration of majority and middle class groups, and overall city disinvestment. Jackson is a city of contradictions where Southern politeness often masks genuine feelings of disdain for and non-acceptance of LGBT people. Notwithstanding the dissonance between appearance, disingenuous behavior and deep-seated prejudices, the city hosts a significant LGBT population. Jackson ranks number 10 among metropolitan statistical areas with the highest concentration of African American same-sex couples, and a vocal, white and often visible LGBT community.

Jackson's Municipal Equality Index

The HRC publishes an Annual Scorecard for major cities and municipalities across the nation. Inaugurated in 2012, the Scorecard reflects how well cities and municipalities perform based on the Municipal Equality Index (MEI). The MEI evaluates six areas in which cities respond to and work proactively to advance equality for LGBT people: Nondiscrimination Laws; Relationship Recognition; Municipality as Employer; Municipal Services; Law Enforcement; Relationship with the LGBT Community. Scores can range from zero to a perfect 100 points. Cities may earn up to 20 bonus points for critical programs, protections or benefits not readily attainable (HRC, 2013a). Jackson earned 15 regular points – partial majority credit in services and programs, and partial minority credit in Relationship with the LGBT Community (p. 47). The city earned two bonus points, bringing Jackson's composite score to 17.

Southern Discomfort: Jackson and the LGBT Community

Data Collection and Methods

This research explores LGBT experiences in the City of Jackson, Mississippi. Data for the study were collected from primary and secondary sources. Primary sources included personal interviews with members of Jackson's LGBT community, discussions with persons from Jackson's Planning Department, a representative from law enforcement, and residents with knowledge about Jackson and the LGBT community.

In addition, a survey was conducted with persons self-identifying as LGBT. The survey consisted of 25 closed and open-ended questions segmented into four categories: Demographics; Place of Origin and Experiences in Jackson (city planning department and services, and LGBT antidiscrimination policies); Religious Affiliation/Faith Issues; and Other Issues (activism, role for post-secondary institutions with planning programs to address LGBT topics/concerns). With the exception of the section on demographics, a comment option followed each close-ended question to invite expanded discussion about each question posed. At the end of the survey, participants received a question about follow-up participation through group interviews with other LGBT people.

Through interviews and surveys participants:

• Discussed activities and social opportunities in which the LGBT community engages
• Identified LGBT neighborhoods, enclaves and communities in and contiguous to Jackson, including suburban and rural areas
• Identified areas of the city perceived to be LGBT-friendly
• Discussed the level of awareness about the city's Planning Department and the Office of Housing and Community Development within the Planning Department, including services sought and received
• Offered opinions about how the city and the Planning Department could become more responsive to LGBT needs
• Provided input about the role of academic planning programs in expanding the conversation about LGBT issues and equity, and promoting more inclusive and mixed communities comprised of heterosexuals, LGBT people and their families

Members from Jackson's LGBT community also discussed their experiences in the work environment, in social and civic settings, and their work as LGBT activists. They shared opinions about others' perceptions of them, and discussed their ideas regarding the need for the city planning department, and planning schools to advance awareness and promote social justice for the LGBT community.

Twelve persons participated in both the survey and interviews. Participants were recruited using snowball sampling. Limitations accompany this sampling method, and the study makes no claims about the definitive, broad applicability of responses to the whole of Jackson's LGBT population. Nonetheless, the openness of participants in discussing their experiences provides rich information about Jackson's LGBT community.

Through interviews and discussions, area residents, planners and other professionals contributed additional information. Their comments provided general information about Jackson's relationship with the LGBT community, outreach efforts, and specific information regarding services available and extended to that community. These persons did not complete the survey. Their comments enriched the stories surrounding the relationship between LGBT individuals and Jackson.

Terminology

One question emerged during interviews regarding differences in the LGBT community's preference for the words "queer" or "queerness" as opposed to the LGBT acronym. A small number of interviewees rejected the use of the word queer, viewing it as demeaning and derisive. Some expressed indifference about the word while others considered queer a more inclusive term that captured the historical evolution of gender nonconforming persons. Interviewees who objected to the use of the word indicated that prior negative and painful experiences influenced a dislike of the current use of queer. All interviewees indicated a comfort level with the LGBT acronym although queer and "gay" were the terms they used most frequently, even when referring to lesbians as gay females.

Findings

Each of the four sections of the survey captured significant information about Jackson's LGBT community. Survey questions provided specific information that opened dialog about the diverse experiences and opinions held by community members. The comments and stories shared by study participants provide insightful information about LGBT people in Jackson.

Demographics and Place of Origin

Consistent with Jackson's racial demographics, participants from Jackson's two dominant racial categories completed the survey: white (25%) and black/African American (75%). In the category of sexual orientation/gender identity: 50 percent self-identified as gay, 25 percent as lesbian, and 25 percent as transgender.

The participants reflected greater diversity in age, educational attainment, income and professional backgrounds. Participants identified their ages in ranges of five-year intervals beginning with 18–24 and continuing to 60 and older. The majority of participants fell in the age ranges of 25–29 and 45–49. No participant indicated an age exceeding 49 years.

Although some variations existed in educational attainment, participants appeared well educated. In terms of education levels: all but one participant had at least some college experience, 50 percent had a bachelor's degree, and 20 percent had a master's degree or higher. Only two participants indicated high school diploma as the highest level of education attainment, one of whom had two years of college. An equal number of participants indicated income ranges between $25,000 and $35,000 and between $35,001 and $45,000, and one indicated an income above $55,000. Only one participant indicated an income less than $25,000.

The wide range of professions and employment provide a snapshot of the work performed by the interviewees. Professions represented included law enforcement, higher education, hospitality, security, management, military (disabled veteran), skilled bakery workers, the trucking industry, and business proprietor.

A majority of survey participants (83%) indicated they were from Mississippi. The remaining 17 percent had relocated from larger cities in other states. Of the native Mississippians, 41.6 percent had relocated to Jackson from other parts of the state. When comparing the treatment of LGBT persons in Jackson with other places they had lived, responses varied. Participants who relocated from smaller Mississippi towns, cities, and rural communities indicated that Jackson is larger and people appear more open-minded about nonconforming sexual orientation and gender identity. One interviewee noted, "The Community here is more open and embracing." Another observed, "Major difference due to larger city."

Conversely, those who had lived in major cities such as New Orleans, Miami, Chicago, Dallas, and St. Louis considered Jackson less progressive and less open-minded. One respondent commented that he found that the LGBT community in "Jackson is more integrated into the larger culture but is less accepted." Like several other participants, he found the attitudes and behaviors of Mississippians toward LGBT people similar to the treatment of minorities during the Jim Crow era. People function and interact, but LGBT persons are not genuinely accepted.

Experiences in Jackson

There are a variety of opinions regarding experiences in Jackson compared to other places linked to prior experiences as well as the size and kind of environment in which they had lived prior to arriving in Jackson.

Is Jackson Friendly to the LGBT Community?

Half the respondents perceived Jackson to be unfriendly to LGBT people. The other 50 percent responded that Jackson was friendly to LGBT individuals with caveats to the positive responses. In the Southern tradition, one person cautioned that the affable demeanor remained nothing more than a "veneer of friendliness." He asserted that people in Jackson would not be "brash" in your face. Another cautioned that as a part of the LGBT community, one had "to be careful because there are those who are against us." Still, compared to surrounding suburban communities, Jackson is perceived to be friendlier. One can be "out" in the arts and creative community.

Comments from others suggest that in spite of the perception that Jackson is LGBT-friendly, much work remains. They underscore the frustration regarding the hypocrisy derived from the inconsistencies between rhetoric of acceptance and exhibited behavior of disdain and lack of genuine support. A constant concern surrounds discussion about Jackson's position as a Southern State in the Bible Belt, keeping entrenched attitudes and beliefs alive and unchanging. Community members lament that things have improved "over the years, but people remain close-minded." The problem of "not being fully accepted … is harder for lesbians." As observed by one LGBT community member, "Jackson has progressed some, but it is still a capital city within the Bible Belt."

Sexual Orientation and Gender Identity in the Workplace and Housing

At the time of this writing, more than a dozen states have laws that include sexual orientation/gender identity as a protected class to safeguard against discrimination (Hill, 2007). The American Civil Liberties Union (ACLU) places the number of states that include sexual orientation and gender identity as a protected class at 16 plus the District of Columbia; nine more states provide protections by Executive Order. Additionally, 143 cities and counties include sexual orientation and gender identity as a protected class (ACLU, 2013).

When queried about whether or not Jackson offers the same or similar protection to LGBT people, almost 42 percent did not know. More than half or 58 percent knew that the City of Jackson does not include nonconforming sexual orientation/gender identity as a protected class.

Fifty-eight percent never experienced treatment perceived to be unfair, harassing, or discriminatory on the basis of sexual orientation or gender identity. A small percentage stated that they know of friends who experienced harassment and discrimination in the workplace. One participant offered a personal story about the difficulty encountered at work as he began the transition from female to male:

> I had bad experiences because I changed my birth gender. When they found out at work, they didn't understand. They treated me better as a gay female. While transitioning, my supervisor told me I had to cut my dreads because of physical changes. Male and female guidelines are different. … others created serious issues, a lot of them…

> I had problems with the way I was being treated and went to EEOC [Equal Employment Opportunity Commission]. They told me I was not a protected class.

> Legally, I have no gender change. In Mississippi, when the change is complete I can change my name, but the birth certificate will show male-female, indicating my new sex and my birth sex. I have friends from other states who do not have to show both sexes on the birth certificate.

One participant commented that a friend was harassed and later denied access to an apartment on the basis of sexual orientation. Although the friend could not prove discrimination, she could offer no other explanation for the apartment manager's decision not to rent the apartment.

Harassment and discrimination do not remain confined to the workplace. They may occur outside the domain of the work environment. One participant complained about being treated unfairly at a straight club during Ladies' Night when females enter free of charge. Because she dressed in a way that was "boyish," the person on the door insisted that she pay. The incident may not be an isolated one. Outlaw (2013a) makes a similar observation when a group of teenage boys called him and his partner an anti-gay slur as they left one of Jackson's most gay-friendly Fondren restaurants.

Planning Department and Housing and Community Development

Jackson has an Office of Housing and Community Development located in the City Planning Department. The division offers a large complement of services ranging from funded programs such as Community Development Block Grants, Home Investment Partnership, Emergency Solution Grants, and Housing Opportunities for Persons with AIDS (HOPWA). Jackson residents can also take advantage of Neighborhood Services for emergency home repairs and obtain assistance with down payments for home purchases.

City officials, the Director of Planning and planners from the various units within the Planning Department, regularly discuss available services at City Council and community meetings. The city also publicizes information about these services on the City of Jackson's official website. Still, less than 2 percent of study participants indicated any knowledge about services offered through the Planning Department and the Office of Housing and Community Development. Less than 1 percent had ever tried to obtain services from the Planning Department. Only one participant indicated interaction with the Planning Department when applying for and receiving a permit to do renovation work.

The City of Jackson has room for improvement in the areas of housing, community and inclusiveness. Respondents commenting in this part of the survey think Jackson's planning department should be more inclusive, reaching out to the LGBT community for input and collaboration on issues. One expressed concern that the larger Jackson community views the LGBT community as a problem incited by "outside influence," which suggests ongoing denial of this community's humanity. There is a need to raise awareness and support the right of "people to know you can be yourself." In general, participants believe that more positive and accepting attitudes from the larger community would advance awareness, and that working in shared activities with LGBT people could help them develop a greater comfort level.

Amenities

A vast majority of study participants suggest overall satisfaction with amenities offered by Jackson, whether LGBT specific or amenities offered to the general public that the community accesses. Amenities identified include organizations that support LGBT causes such as the ACLU, and the HRC. Others discussed social and civic activities that provided enrichment and improved their sense of wellness and community: Mississippi HeARTS Against AIDS and Fondren activities (see Table 9.1). Some expressed appreciation for police protection during the Campaign for Equality March, which allowed LGBT marchers to assemble and walk free from harassment or physical harm. Several others identified the importance of city support for the arts and cultural activities. One participant expressed appreciation for Jackson's commitment to the Museum of Art and the Jackson Symphony through taxes used to support and maintain the arts (see Table 9.2).

LGBT After-Hours Entertainment Amenities

Many cities boast of after-hours places of entertainment that cater to LGBT persons, and survey participants identified a number of after-hour venues targeted specifically to LGBT persons. Each survey participant knew all of the establishments, although most did not frequent any of them for various reasons, including no desire to look for evening venues devoted to LGBT people. A small number of participants indicated regular attendance at the clubs. One participant identified a fifth venue that caters to LGBT individuals. This participant frequents two of the venues, as well as "straight" clubs. One local professional interviewed noted that

TABLE 9.1 LGBT related organizations and support services in Jackson, MS

Organizations	Purpose, activity, contributions to LGBT concerns
Unity Mississippi	Education, awareness, social and business networks for LGBT people.
National Association for the Advancement of Colored People	State Chapter President issued public statement in local newspaper reiterating support of LGBT equal rights, including marriage equality.
Young Democrats of America (MS)	Includes an LGBT Caucus.
MS Coalition Against Domestic Violence	Works with groups, including LGBT persons, to understand and combat domestic violence.
My Brother's Keeper	Focuses on education, training, and direct delivery of services in prevention and treatment of persons with HIV/AIDS. Comprehensive advocacy, research and capacity building.
HOPA (Housing for Older Persons)	Assists older persons with housing.
Human Rights Campaign	National organization with support for and from LGBT individuals and allies.
MS Center for Justice	Committed to equality and social justice.
Open Arms	LGBTI Health Center Developed under the auspices of My Brother's Keeper, Inc. in 2012.
Safe Harbor Family Church	Flowood, MS (Rankin County) Designated an Open and Affirming congregation, Safe Harbor Family Church provides a welcoming place for Jackson area LGBT people to worship and receive spiritual nurturing.
Southern Poverty Law Center	Advocacy for LGBT rights, civil rights, anti-hate litigation.

TABLE 9.2 LGBT activities and events in Jackson, MS

Activities and events	Purpose
Mississippi: I Am	Documentary examining struggles of young LGBT people to raise awareness about civil rights and reduce invisibility. Screening hosted by Northside Baptist Church in Jackson.
Pride Parade	Annual parade affirming LGBT pride.
MS HeARTS Against AIDS	Annual arts benefit to raise funds for and increase awareness about HIV and AIDS. The event is held annually at a popular and LGBT-friendly establishment in Jackson, Hal & Mal's.
LGBT Strategy meeting – sponsored by ACLU of MS	The objective is to assemble a reliable and knowledgeable network of LGBT advocates and allies.
Zippyty Doo Dah Parade Weekend	Benefit Parade. The event is part of the Sweet Potato Queens' Zippity Doo Dah annual parade and family fun activities weekend. LGBT participation increases visibility and raises awareness.

because some members of the community prefer to keep nonconforming sexual orientation or gender identity private, they attend more discreet, by invitation only clubs and social outlets.

After-hours venues that cater to LGBT persons are located in areas away from Jackson's adult entertainment corridor. Dispersed throughout the city, one club in the downtown area is located one block from Union Station, Jackson's Multimodal facility. Another is located well outside of the city along the Highway 80 West corridor approximately five miles or about 12 minutes from the CBD. Two other venues are located northeast of the city approximately four miles, or 10–15 minutes from the CBD. A fifth venue is located five miles or about 12 minutes from the CBD. Only two venues share the same zip code. Table 9.3 describes the demographics of persons who frequent the venues.

Enclaves and LGBT-Friendly Areas

When asked if participants knew of LGBT enclaves in Jackson or anywhere in the entire Jackson metropolitan area, 41.6 percent indicated they had no knowledge about LGBT enclaves and 16.6 percent did not respond. The remaining 41.6 percent indicated that enclaves are dispersed throughout Jackson and surrounding areas.

Study participants also provided input regarding where LGBT people live in substantial numbers. One respondent noted that younger blacks tend to gravitate to South Jackson, older white gays and lesbians tend to locate in North Jackson. Another respondent listed Metro Center Mall area in West Jackson as an area with a concentration of lesbian couples and Downtown Jackson as an emerging magnet

TABLE 9.3 LGBT clubs and race/ethnicity of primary patrons in Jackson, MS

Entertainment venues	Primary patrons
Sippi Citi Show Bar (Club)	Predominantly African American
Citi Lights (Club)	Predominantly African American. Occasionally female-male couples; little diversity but other racial groups welcomed. Downtown Jackson.
Club mR (Metro Reloaded)/Metro 2001	Mostly African American. Friday night is lesbian night. Located in West Jackson outside of central city.
JCs (Club)	Over 40s, white male bar. Periodically minorities "show up." Very few females. Located near thriving commercial area in northeast Jackson.
Bottoms Up (Club)	Younger (under 30) racially/ethnically diverse. Located near thriving commercial area in northeast Jackson.

TABLE 9.4 Perceived LGBT-friendly communities/emerging enclaves in Jackson, MS

Enclaves/LGBT-friendly communities	Description of LGBT population
Fondren	Considered LGBT-friendly; LGBT-owned businesses/community
Mid Town	Growing magnet for LGBT residents; creative, artistic area
Downtown Jackson	Increasingly a magnet for affluent gays
Metro Center Mall area	Mostly lesbian couples

for young affluent gays. Mid Town was cited as an area with a growing LGBT population (see Table 9.4).

All respondents indicating an awareness of LGBT areas with an existing and growing number of LGBT residents identified Fondren as an LGBT (gays) enclave and the most LGBT-friendly area (see Figure 9.1). LGBT enclaves, as described by study participants, may be comprised of a few households dispersed throughout an entire neighborhood, or two to three same-sex families living next door to each other. As one Fondren resident notes, "I'm not sure if I am in an enclave, but I'm on the corner and have one gay household on each side of me." This finding is consistent with the finding by Doan (Chapter 7, this volume) that LGBT people feel safer when they locate in proximity to other LGBT people.

Other Areas

The general perception among study participants is that LGBT people in Jackson tend to be more dispersed geographically compared to most other urban areas.

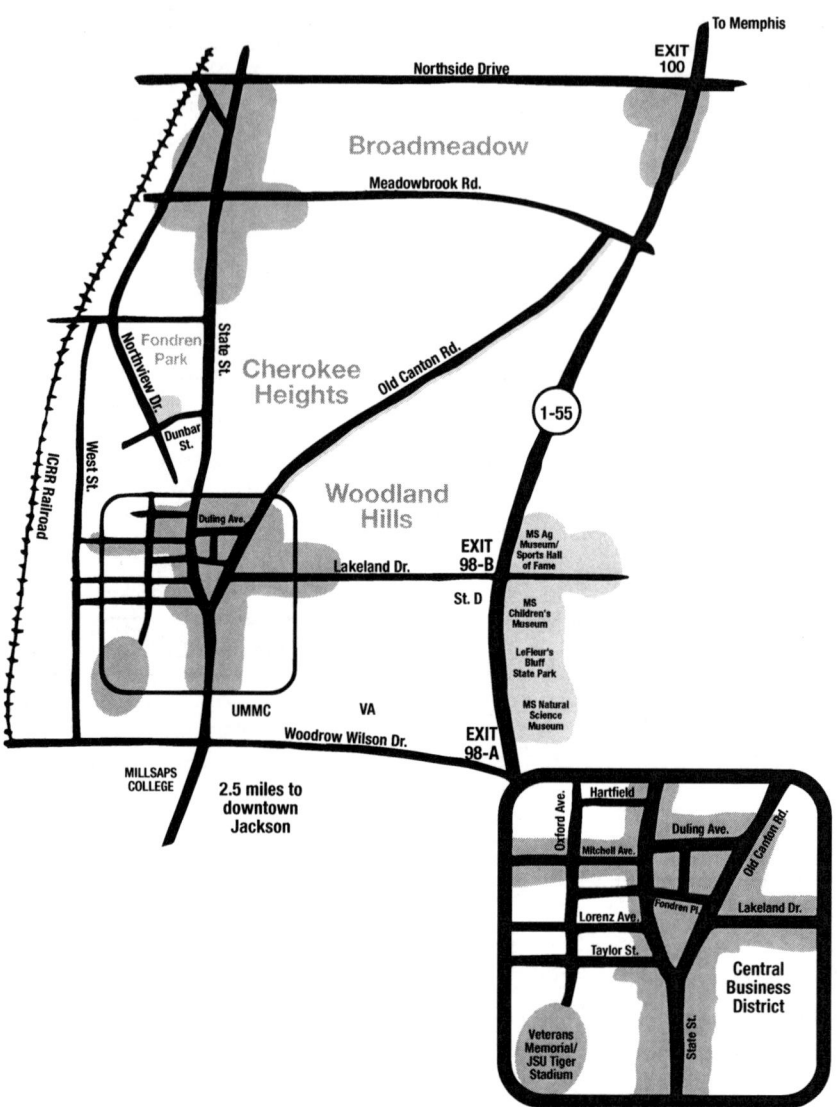

FIGURE 9.1 Fondren Business District, Jackson, MS

Although some Jackson communities host gays in larger numbers than others, concentrations of LGBT residents appear to not exist at the scale where they could be appropriately designated as "gayborhoods."

Participants also think lesbians gravitate to the suburbs. If correct, participants' ideas about the geographical locations of Jackson's gays and lesbians would be consistent with recent research regarding where gays and lesbians live. For example, Anacker (2011) finds that male same-sex households and female same-sex households exist in larger numbers in suburban neighborhoods than in urban.

Religious Affiliation and Faith Issues

Of the survey participants, 92 percent identified as Christian, and 8 percent indicated no religious affiliation. One commented that he is a "person of faith." While 33 percent attend infrequently, 67 percent attend church services regularly. Only one person indicated that church members do not know about their sexual orientation/gender identity. Accordingly, 83 percent of persons who attend church regularly or infrequently believe that members of their faith treat them well. One respondent commented that although members treat him well, that was not always the case as members had treated him poorly when he first "came out."

Most study participants point to Safe Harbor Family Church as the one church in the Jackson area that proactively reaches out to the LGBT community. Designated as an Open and Affirming Church, Safe Harbor Family Church (2013) posts a welcoming message on the website followed by an explanation of the designation:

> Safe Harbor Family Church of Christ is proud to be listed as an official Open and Affirming Church in the UCC! (para. 1)

> Open and Affirming (ONA) is the United Church of Christ's (UCC) designation for congregations, campus ministries, and other bodies in the UCC which make a public covenant of welcome into their full life and ministry to persons of all sexual orientations, gender identities, and gender expressions. (para. 2)

Almost all participants considered their religious affiliation an important aspect of their lives. They indicated a strong commitment to their faith, whether through church membership in mainstream denominations or as a non-denominational "person of faith."

Activism

The LGBT community in Jackson is not a collective group of passive observers. As indicated by responses provided by study participants, a majority (75%) engage in activities that illuminate LGBT causes and increase visibility. They participate in parades that reflect diversity of race/ethnicity, age, sexual orientation and gender identity, oftentimes engaging supporters and allies. They participate in the Annual Gay Rights March, and community outreach and education to inform the public about LGBT issues (cf. Table 9.2).

The self-assessment allowed respondents the opportunity to rate their involvement on a scale from zero to ten, with zero indicating completely inactive and ten indicating extremely active: 42 percent selected ten on the scale, 16.6 percent selected eight, 16.6 percent selected three, and 25 percent selected zero.

Respondents who indicated no involvement in LGBT causes provided no explanations for the lack of participation. Considering the unwelcoming environment in which some of Jackson's LGBT community live, work and play, it would not be unreasonable to raise the possibility that they may not feel comfortable engaging in such activities. However, none of the comments made to any of the survey questions suggested feelings of intimidation or fear of exposure. Rosenfeld (2003) rejects the idea that gay elders did not participate in liberationist activism because of fear about their sexual nonconformity during the 1960s and 1970s. Likewise, participants in the study who do not engage in current activist activities gave no indication of being ashamed of their sexual orientation or gender identity, nor did they indicate fear of reprisal because of it.

City Planners and Community Residents

Neither the City of Jackson nor the Planning Department has a liaison to the LGBT community. Neither provides community outreach nor does a public agenda currently exist that speaks about LGBT issues. Opportunities abound for the Planning Department to reach out to the LGBT community. Areas of the city where LGBT persons live in relatively significant numbers and those considered to be LGBT-friendly tend to be located in gentrifying areas. The Planning Department administers HOPWA funds. Both activities present open opportunities for developing stronger ties with the LGBT community through outreach and collaboration. The creative arts community in Mid Town, the growing interest in downtown living, and progressive Fondren – highlighted as a creative economy community – offer vast opportunities to engage LGBT people in planning initiatives. They are currently welcoming areas for LGBT individuals and can be exploited in a positive way.

Planning Schools and LGBT Awareness

Do planning schools have a responsibility to the LGBT community, especially in raising awareness and advancing ideas of equity and justice? LGBT persons participating in the study held very definite opinions about the role and responsibility of planning schools to the LGBT community: 92 percent indicated they think planning schools should incorporate LGBT issues in existing courses, although they consider it unnecessary to offer a separate course. They listed specific topics to cover: acceptance of sexual differences; history of nonconforming sexual behavior, and the LGBT movement, including activism. They also suggested including specific issues and topics so critical to the LGBT community, including legal, medical and other community concerns, especially equal opportunity.

Talbot & Viento (2005) insist that graduate curricula should include training and education relevant to LGBT issues. Despite the progress made in LGBT educational curricula, policies and scholarship, Sears (2005) asserts that interdisciplinary practice and collaboration remain lacking. Ball (2013) argues that higher education leaders should become more assertive in extending policies of inclusion to LGBT persons.

Other Findings

Overall, participants proved to be open and eager to respond to survey questions; 100 percent agreed to take part in follow-up group interviews and surveys. Two participants offered to assist with data collection in order to reach a wider audience for future research. All engaged in additional discussions and added comments about their experiences. The responses provided useful information for the Planning Department and planning schools, particularly at the local level.

The issue of race in Jackson as in the state and other parts of the country remains a challenge. Several members of the LGBT community believe that racial discrimination and unequal treatment persist in Jackson and among LGBT people as they do in the larger society. Disparate treatment and social slights manifest in various and sundry ways. Some are overt; others more nuanced. As one gay man observed when comparing the treatment of LGBT individuals to the Jim Crow era, the issue of race may eclipse other efforts to move LGBT issues forward.

Unstructured discussions and interviews with members of the gay community yielded additional information regarding LGBT community concerns: aging, depression, delayed response to earlier emotional trauma relative to growing up "different," bullying, and marginalization. The feedback is consistent with LGBT literature (Knauer, 2011; Sears, 2005; Witten & Eyler, 2012; Rosenfeld, 2003). Knauer (2011) believes that the interests of gays and lesbians remain inadequately represented and largely unaddressed; they may "bear scars from the days when sexual orientation was pathologized and criminalized ..." (p. 138).

Concluding Comments

Hendler and Backs (2011) propose the need for further examination to expand our understanding of how "the planning field reinforces or challenges heterosexism" (p. 87). Planning in Jackson appears to be all but oblivious to the LGBT community. It is not that planners have no awareness of this community, but they exhibit no overt interest in proactively responding to a growing community of people who are becoming a major force in the city and the state. The Office of Housing and Community Development has a particularly valuable role to play as the city continues to confront the growing need to provide affordable housing and build healthy, sustainable communities for all residents.

As the overall American population ages and lives longer, cities are forced to rethink ways of responding effectively to the social, economic and other needs that accompany longevity. Growing older requires making necessary adjustments to accommodate the aging process. The demands of growing older may be greater and more difficult for "gender minorities," especially transgendered people who may have the added consideration of medical challenges (Witten and Eyler, 2012). Jackson must begin to examine ways to respond to the full range of aging populations, including nonconforming sexual orientations and gender identities.

Mississippians do not collectively remain silently complacent about attempts to marginalize and dispossess LGBT persons. Organized efforts to mobilize LGBT supporters and allies continue to gain traction as heightened awareness invites Mississippians to coalesce around justice, to push for full protection under the law for all persons.

Planning professionals, both planning academics and practitioners, occupy strategic places for influencing decisions and helping formulate policy. Planning academics are purveyors of knowledge, ideas and critical thought. As major players in the marketplace of ideas, they have a responsibility to raise awareness, provoke thought and invite a commitment to equity and social justice. Planning practitioners touch every aspect of individuals' lives – where they live, work, play, go to school, and attend worship. They are often in positions of influence where they can frame an issue, advance equity, bring attention to social injustices in housing, community, urban and rural design, and promote inclusion.

As the voices of LGBT people grow louder and visibility more insistent, cities and communities must be prepared to respond equitably, justly and respectfully. Jackson is in a perfect place and time to plan progressively, step forward assertively, and take the lead proactively. Jackson's mayor should appoint a progressive, forward-thinking person to serve as a liaison between the city and the LGBT community. He could convene a committee to help identify creative and inclusive ways to engage LGBT citizens collaboratively in all areas of city business and planning activities. He could explore areas that have a city-wide effect on Jackson's economy through an aggressive public relations campaign connected to tourism and as an LGBT-friendly city. Currently, Fondren is the only well-known area to be LGBT-friendly in Jackson.

Political appointments representative of the LGBT community would go a long way in the message it sends about the city's commitment to LGBT inclusiveness. These ideas presented are practical, strategically sound, and just solutions for Jackson to begin the movement forward for a more inclusive and LGBT-friendly city.

Note

1　Americans, with our talent for nomenclature and labels, use various terms to describe the community of persons who consider themselves nonconforming to the heteronormative paradigm. In order to avoid confusion, I use the term LGBT throughout this chapter to refer to persons who self-identify as lesbian, gay, bisexual, transgender, intersexed, and questioning as well as individuals who may embrace the term "genderqueer" and other gender nonconformists. The LGBT designation covers the full range of persons whose sexual orientation and gender identity varies from the heteronormative construct.

References

American Civil Liberties Union. (2013, April 24). Know your rights – transgender people and the law. Retrieved from www.aclu.org/translaw

Anacker, K.B. (2011). Queering the suburbs: Analyzing property values in male and female same-sex suburbs in the United States. In P. Doan (Ed.) *Queerying Planning: Challenging Heteronormative Assumptions and Reframing Planning Practice*. Farnham, England and Burlington, VT: Ashgate, 105–125.

Ball, C. (2013, January 31). Institutions must ensure inclusion of LGBT community. *Diverse Issues in Higher Education 29* (26), 23.

Batson, B. (2012, October 3). Cheers to an ally. *Jackson Free Press* [Online]. Retrieved from www.jacksonfreepress.com/news/2012/oct/03/cheers-ally

Blaze, A. (2011, May 24). New poll finds 70% of people favor lgbt antidiscrimination laws. Retrieved from The Bilerico Project [Online] at www.bilerico.com/2011/05/new_poll_finds_70_of_people_favor_lgbt_antidiscrim.php

Dickey, L.M. (2012, October 3). Email. Cheers to an ally. *Jackson Free Press* [Online]. Retrieved from www.jacksonfreepress.com/news/2012/oct/03/cheers-ally

Gates, G. (2010, August). Same-sex couples in the census: Who gets counted and why. The Williams Institute, UCLA School of Law. Retrieved from http://williamsinstitute.law.ucla.edu/wp-content/uploads/Gates-Who-Gets-Counted-Aug-2010.pdf

Gates, G. & Ost, J. (2004). *The Gay and Lesbian Atlas*. Washington, DC: Urban Institute Press.

Hendler, S. & Backs, M. (2011). Querying planning (theory): Alphabet soup or paradox city, in *Queerying Planning: Challenging Heteronormative Assumptions and Reframing Planning Practice*, edited by P. Doan. Burlington, VT and Farnham, England: Ashgate, 71–79.

Hill, P. (2007). *LGBT Rights Law: A Career Guide*. Bernard Koteen Office of Public Interest Advising, Cambridge, MA: Harvard Law School.

Holzer, E.A. (2012, March 5). Defense of marriage acts: a fifty state survey. William Mitchell College of Law. Open Access. Retrieved from http://open.wmitchell.edu/cgi/viewcontent.cgi?article=1000&context=stusch

Howard, J. (1999). *Men Like That: The Southern Queer History*. Chicago, IL: University of Chicago Press.

Human Rights Campaign (2012) History of state constitutional marriage ban. Retrieved from www.hrc.org/resources/entry/state-constitutional-marriage-bans

Human Rights Campaign (HRC). (2013a). *Municipality Equality Index: A Nationwide Evaluation of Municipal Law*. Equality Federation Institute. Retrieved from http://s3.amazonaws.com/hrc-assets//files/assets/resources/MEI_2013_report.pdf

Human Rights Campaign (HRC). (2013b, July) New poll shows optimism for gay rights in Mississippi. Retrieved from www.hrc.org/press-releases/entry/new-poll-shows-optimism-for-lgbt-equality-in-mississippi

Human Rights Campaign (HRC). (2013c, December 13). State National Guards in all 50 states will process same-sex benefits. Human Rights Campaign Website [Online]. Retrieved from www.hrc.org/blog/entry/state-national-guards-in-all-50-states-will-process-same-sex-benefits

InterExchange. (n.d.) Mississippi – The Magnolia State. *Cultural Compass* [Online] at www.interexchange.org/american-culture/mississippi

Johnson, D. (n.d.) Why NAACP National Board of Directors voted to oppose codifying discrimination. *Jackson Advocate* [Online]. Retrieved from www.jacksonadvocateonline.com/?p=9157

Knauer, N. (2011). Gay and lesbian elders: History, law and identity politics in the United States. Burlington, VT; Farnham, England: Ashgate.

Lambda Legal (2013, June 3). State laws and constitutional amendments targeting same-sex relationships. Quick Facts. Retrieved from Lambda Legal [Online] www.lambdalegal.org/publications/state-laws-and-constitutional-amendments-targeting-same-sex-relationships

Lambda Legal (n.d.) Mississippi. Retrieved from Lambda Legal [Online] at www.lambdalegal.org/states-regions/mississippi

Margolin, E. (2013a, November 7). 'Let the bells of freedom ring' – Senate passes ENDA. Retrieved from www.msnbc.com/news-nation/let-the-bells-freedom-ring

Margolin, E. (2013b, December 14). National Guard ends holdout on same-sex marriage. MSNBC [Online]. Retrieved from www.msnbc.com/news-nation/national-guard-ends-holdout-lgbt-benefits

Mlindberger. (2012, October 3). Cheers to an ally. *Jackson Free Press* [Online]. Retrieved from www.jacksonfreepress.com/news/2012/oct/03/cheers-ally

NAACP. (2012, May 19). NAACP passes resolution in support of marriage equality. Retrieved from NAACP [Online] at www.naacp.org/news/entry/naacp-passes-resolution-in-support-of-marriage-equality

National Conference of State Legislatures. (2013, December 23). Defining marriage: State defense of marriage laws and same-sex marriage. Retrieved from National Conference of State Legislatures [Online] at www.ncsl.org/research/human-services/same-sex-marriage-overview.aspx

Nave, R.L. (2013, July 16). Same-sex rulings will test state laws. *Jackson Free Press* [Online]. Retrieved from www.jacksonfreepress.com/news/2013/jul/16/same-sex-rulings

Outlaw, E. (2012a, May 16). [Outlaw] Yes. We. Can. *Jackson Free Press*. Retrieved from www.jacksonfreepress.com/news/2012/may/16/outlaw-yes-we-can

Outlaw, E. (2012b, July 18). Tupelo's dirty little secret. *Jackson Free Press*. Retrieved from www.jacksonfreepress.com/news/2012/jul/18/tupelos-dirty-little-secret

Outlaw, E. (2012c, August 29). A pistol, and a plea. *Jackson Free Press*. Retrieved from www.jacksonfreepress.com/news/2012/aug/29/pistol-and-plea

Outlaw, E. (2012d, October 24). Behind the chair. *Jackson Free Press*. Retrieved from www.jacksonfreepress.com/news/2012/oct/24/shaping-my-political-views-behind-chair

Outlaw, E. (2013a, March 19). A purse, by any other name. Retrieved from http://eddieoutlaw.com/2013/03/19/a-purse-by-any-other-name

Outlaw, E. (2013b, August 14). I do. *Jackson Free Press*. Retrieved from www.jacksonfreepress.com/news/2013/aug/14/i-do

Rosenfeld, D. (2003). *The Changing of the Guard: Lesbian and Gay Elders, Identity, and Social Change*. Philadelphia, PA: Temple University Press.

Safe Harbor Family Church. (2013). Safe Harbor Family Church [Online]. Retrieved from www.safeharborfamilychurch.org

Sears, J. (2005). *Gay, Lesbian, and Transgender Issues in Education: Programs, Policies, and Practices*. Binghamton, NY: Harrington Park Press.

Sessums, K. (2007). *Mississippi Sissy*. New York, NY: Picador.

Sessums, K. (2012, October 3). Via Facebook. Cheers to an ally. *Jackson Free Press* [Online]. Retrieved from www.jacksonfreepress.com/news/2012/oct/03/cheers-ally

Sutter, J.D. (2013, March 24). Opinion: The county where no one's gay. Retrieved from www.cnn.com/2013/03/24/opinion/sutter-franklin-county-mississippi-lgbt

Talbot, D.M. & Viento, W.I.E. (2005, September 1). Incorporating LGBT issues into student affairs graduate education. *New Directions for Student Services*. Issue 111, pp. 75–80.

U.S. Census. (2013a, August). Frequently asked questions about same-sex couple households. Retrieved from www.census.gov/hhes/samesex/files/SScplfactsheet_final.pdf

U.S. Census. (2013b, December 17). State and county facts. Jackson (City), Mississippi. Census [Online] at quickfacts.census.gov/qfd/states/28/2836000.html

Williamson, E. (2012, September 26). Come out as an ally. *Jackson Free Press* [Online]. Retrieved from www.jacksonfreepress.com/news/2012/sep/26/come-out-as-ally

Wise, B. (2012). *William Alexander Percy: The Curious Life of a Mississippi Planter and Sexual Free Thinker*. Chapel Hill, NC: University of North Carolina Press.

Witten, T.M. & Eyler, A. (2012). *Gay, Lesbian, Bisexual, and Transgender Aging: Challenges in Research, Practice and Policies*. Baltimore, MD: Johns Hopkins University Press.

10

QUEER COSMOPOLIS

The Evolution of Jackson Heights

Arianna Martinez

Introduction

Like urban spaces in general, queer spaces have for the most part been defined by homogeneity and segregation. Today a typical "gayborhood" in New York City tends to be made up of upper-middle-class, white, gay men. Generally speaking these queer spaces are neither ethnically integrated, economically integrated, nor do they have a cross section of gender diversity. As Doan states in Chapter 1 of this book, most queer spaces have been "narrowly defined by class and race" (pp.3–4).

New York City has long been a destination for immigrants as well as a destination for LGBTQ people. Ethnic migration to New York City has been heavily researched and tends to focus on demographic changes, labor patterns, social capital, political, economic, and cultural integration, and the impact of racism and xenophobia. LGBTQ immigrants have been largely excluded from this history. Similarly, there is substantial scholarship about gay culture in the city, and how the "Great Gay Migration" and the emergence of the "gay ghetto" contributed to the creation and visibility of LGBTQ communities. The literature pays special attention to how the city looms large in the gay imagination, constructed as a space of anonymity, community, deviance, and desire.

With a few notable exceptions (Manalansan 2003, Decena 2011) immigrants have been largely left out of this literature. Jackson Heights is a site of queer, immigrant, and queer immigrant migrations generating an opportunity to bring together these two divergent literatures about immigrant and queer urban histories. Widely known as an immigrant enclave, Jackson Heights, Queens is defined by its ethnic, racial, and socio-economic diversity. Nearly two-thirds of Jackson Heights' residents are foreign born and speak over thirty languages between them. Census data for 2010 put the total population of the neighborhood at just over 66,000 residents. An additional 40,000 residents live north of Northern Boulevard, generally referred to as East Elmhurst, but sometimes considered part of Jackson Heights. For the purposes of this chapter Census data is for zip code 11372, which reflects the widely recognized and historical Jackson Heights. The majorities hail from South America (Ecuadorians, Colombians, Peruvians) and South Asia (Indians, Bangladeshis, Nepalese), although the Mexican and Chinese populations are growing.

Less well known is that Jackson Heights is also a queer space and has been since as early as the 1940s (Kasinitz, Bazzi and Doane 1998). Today the neighborhood is believed to be home to the second largest concentration of LGBTQ people in New York City and the largest community of LGBTQ immigrants. The LGBTQ community cuts across age, language, nationality, gender expression, and social class. Jackson Heights is the center of gay life in Queens, the most diverse county in the United States, and it is where the majority of Queen's LGBTQ population lives.

In Jackson Heights the amount of overlap between the LGBTQ and immigrant populations makes it difficult to even draw a distinction, which separates it from most other queer spaces and traditional "gayborhoods." The LGBTQ population is also much less affluent than the mostly upper-income white gay male population in the Manhattan neighborhoods of Chelsea and the West Village. In Jackson Heights income and social class ranges from low-income to middle-class, on a block-by-block, and building-by-building basis, from crowded, illegally subdivided, rental apartments to owner-occupied prewar co-ops with Historic Preservation status. Additionally, it is home to a diversity of genders including both sizable and growing lesbian and transgender populations. Despite many "gayborhoods" not having maintained their queer identity over time, Jackson Heights' LGBTQ community has existed and sustained a continuous queer presence for over 60 years, with many of the original LGBTQ residents remaining in the neighborhood to this day.

The title of this article "Queer Cosmopolis: The Evolution of Jackson Heights," should for urban planners and scholars invoke the famous work of Leonie Sandercock – *Towards Cosmopolis: Planning for Multicultural Cities* (Sandercock 1998), and *Cosmopolis: II Mongrel Cities of the 21st Century* (Sandercock and Lyssiotis 2003) who shifted the debate in urban planning theory and practice by highlighting the significance of postmodern planning with close attention to multiple publics, ethnicity, race, class, gender, and social justice. Sandercock's cosmopolis is defined by landscapes of difference, but it is an inclusive city, where "the project is intercultural co-existence" (Sandercock and Lyssiotis 2003). This chapter demonstrates how Jackson Heights, Queens developed into a cosmopolis, and even more remarkably into a queer cosmopolis. The chapter uses a variety of primary and secondary data including interviews, a documentary on Jackson Heights, and a review of the literature to explore the ways that immigrants and LGBTQ communities are often ignored in urban planning decisions. A neighborhood that incorporates both of these underrepresented communities and the intersection of the two is in need of special attention. This urban ethnography answers the questions: How did Jackson Heights evolve into a queer, immigrant, and queer immigrant space? How does a mixed income neighborhood that is home to a diversity of ethnicities, citizenship and immigration statuses, genders, and sexualities survive and thrive?

Jackson Heights' History: Ethnicity and Sexuality

Jackson Heights was established at the beginning of the twentieth century as the 7 train expansion was extending into Queens. The Queensboro Realty Company modeled Jackson Heights after Ebenezer Howard's "garden city" and planned it to be an elite neighborhood. Originally designed and built as "an exclusive suburban community for white, non-immigrant Protestants within a close commute of Midtown Manhattan" (Miyares 2004b), exclusionary covenants were used to *guarantee* that Jackson Heights be made up of middle- to upper-middle-class white Protestants, and to prevent immigrants, Jews, and African Americans from finding housing there (Miyares 2004b).

During this era while ethnic, religious, and racial minorities were being excluded from Jackson Heights, gay white men began unobtrusively moving to the neighborhood. It is widely acknowledged that the gay presence began as early as the 1930s and 1940s and that the main reason the neighborhood "attracted a colony of vaudevillians, many of whom were gay" was because the 7 train provided direct access to Times Square and the theater district (Maly 2005). By the 1950s there were already known gay bars in the neighborhood. The mere existence of a gay bar during this era is believed to be evidence of a significant gay population particularly outside of Manhattan. The documentary filmmaker Richard Shpuntoff[1], who has extensively researched Jackson Heights' queer history, speculates that since many of the exclusive co-op apartment buildings did not allow children, gay male residents – "as long as they were discreet," white, and childless – were ideal co-op members (Skype Interview with Richard Shpuntoff. July 17, 2013).

After the real estate crash of the 1930s and the post WWII suburbanization of white residents out of Queens to nearby Long Island there was considerable anxiety in Jackson Heights that in spite of its housing stock and transportation infrastructure that the neighborhood would fall into decay. However, after 1960 "while decline occurred, two very different yet simultaneous trends prevented residents' fears from being realized: post-1965 mass immigration to New York City, and the attraction of a movement toward historic preservation by middle-class whites during the 1980s and 1990s" (Maly 2005). It is also important to acknowledge that by the 1960s there was a sizeable gay community in Jackson Heights. These gay residents never left the neighborhood for the notoriously homogenous and heteronormative Long Island suburbs, mainly because they would not have been welcomed or comfortable there. Many of these early gay residents still remain in the community today, and are credited with creating stability and continuity during the periods of economic and cultural transition. It is for these reasons that Jackson Heights transformed "from its exclusive white Protestant origins to its current state of ethnic hyperdiversity" (Miyares 2004a) as well as gender and sexual diversity.

The Death of Julio Rivera to the Birth of Queer Visibility and Empowerment

For decades the queer geography of Jackson Heights included gay bars on Roosevelt Avenue and nearby cruising spots, most famously 37th Road or "vaseline alley." Tragically this area was also known for violence against gay men:

> Everybody knew about 37th Road and the pick up spots, even straight residents knew.... I remember 1979/80 somewhere in there, my mother telling me to be careful how I dressed and where I walked because gay men had been murdered on 37th Road. The thing I think that speaks to this the fact that a heterosexual housewife knew where the murders were, knew what those murders meant... there was some kind of awareness. (Skype Interview with Richard Shpuntoff. July 17, 2013)

While Jackson Heights was a queer space from the 1940s, the visibility of the LGBTQ community changed dramatically after the hate crime murder of Julio Rivera in 1990 (Kasinitz, Bazzi and Doane 1998, Maly 2005). Julio Rivera was twenty-nine years old, a New York born Puerto Rican, gay, and originally from the Bronx. He was living in Jackson Heights and working as a bartender. He was brutally murdered inside the P.S. 69 schoolyard by three, local, young white men[2].

When the New York Police Department (NYPD) would not classify Rivera's death as a bias attack and instead initially classified it as a drug related crime, the community responded with outrage, candlelight vigils, marches, and political organizing. As a result of these actions and the related media attention the city eventually re-classified it, and put a reward out for the arrest of the killers. The court case against the three assailants was the first time in New York State history that a person was put on trial and convicted of a hate crime. While Rivera was neither the first nor the last gay man to be murdered in Jackson Heights, the political, cultural, and historical moment was right for memorializing his death and bringing visibility to the plight of LGBTQ people living in the outer boroughs.

> You could not get even twenty people to come out and march in Jackson Heights, because either they were closeted, they feared for their lives because they knew bashings had happened, they did not want to be ostracized, and some of them were married men.... They outreached to Queer Nation.... People were amazed that the cause of Julio Rivera's death got picked up. People were marching for him. The death was recorded in the major newspapers.... This became a spark for change in Jackson Heights.... This community went from being a clandestine community to being a very

political movement, which lead to the possibility of being out in a much broader sense. (Skype Interview with Richard Shpuntoff. July 17, 2013)

Longtime gay community activist Daniel Dromm, who was elected to the New York City Council for Jackson Heights in 2009, co-founded the Queens Pride Parade in 1992 to raise visibility of the LGBTQ population in Queens and further memorialize Julio Rivera's death. The Queens Lesbian and Gay Pride Committee has organized the parade each year since. The parade takes place annually in early June and regularly attracts 25,000–40,000 people. It is the second largest Pride in New York City and the second largest parade in Jackson Heights after the Colombian Day Parade. The parade itself takes place along 37th Avenue which is closed to traffic, and covers ten city blocks. It ends at 75th Street where a full day street festival and party takes place. There are multiple stages for performances and hundreds of booths selling goods and promoting different non-profit health and community organizations. Unlike Manhattan Pride (the largest) it is far more diverse and not overrun with corporate sponsors. It has been called "Latino Pride" but in actuality it is host to many ethnic and racial groups. That the parade is held annually in Jackson Heights is one reason the neighborhood maintains its queer identity (see Figure 10.1).

The parade is the symbolic site of queer immigrant utopia and for many Queens residents an opportunity to perform and celebrate LGBTQ identities alongside ethnic, racial, and national identities. Imagine a transwoman in a "Miss Colombia"

FIGURE 10.1   Participants in Pride Parade from Safe Space, Jackson Heights, Queens, NY

pageant costume or a float of South Asians dancing to Bollywood music. It is also one site of integration with non-LGBT residents including heteronormative families setting up lawn chairs along the parade route, cheering in response to the previous two floats.

The founding of the Queens Pride Parade was one major LGBTQ political and community organizing success that came after Julio Rivera's murder, but it also marked the beginning of a focus on creating social service organizations and broadening the goals of the local movement.

> Twenty years before the parade was here there was a gay presence, but it was a very quiet presence.... We thought that in addition to visibility, having institutions was a sign of power in communities.... Those of us on the board had a commitment to start a new organization every year for the next few years. (City Councilmember Daniel Dromm. Interview by author. Personal Interview. Jackson Heights NY, July 29, 2013)

In a matter of a few years multiple organizations were founded to provide services to different LGBT communities. First a local chapter of PFLAG (Parents, Families, & Friends of Lesbians and Gays) was started. For many years Generation Q, an afterschool drop-in center, operated out of Jackson Heights and provided a safe space for LGBTQ youth. SAGE Queens, now called the Queens Center for Gay Seniors, is the only senior center in Queens serving LGBTQ residents. The Queens Center for Gay Seniors runs weekly educational and recreational activities for LGBTQ seniors including support groups, counseling services, health assessments, book clubs, movies, fieldtrips, exercise and meditation classes.

The Lesbian and Gay Democrats of Queens also originated during this time to increase political capital and mobilize support for local LGBTQ candidates. Since then Jackson Heights has been referred to as a "gay-influenced" district, "where gay interests would have to be taken into account" (Bailey 1999, p.237). The Jackson Heights' LGBTQ population is not a big enough voting block to dominate neighborhood politics, but when LGBT democrats aligned with newer immigrant communities in the late 1990s their influence widened and solidified. Bailey (1999) has documented how the gay community and the Latino and Asian American communities had similar goals, political agendas, and have voted as a progressive block in Jackson Heights. The effectiveness of this block can be seen in the subsequent election of the first openly gay city council member from Queens, former-public school teacher and longtime LGBTQ activist Daniel Dromm, who also chaired the City Council Immigration Affairs Committee.

The Queens Pride House, founded in 1997, is another important institution in the neighborhood. It runs numerous weekly support groups: a women's group called "Las Buenas Amigas," a transgender group, two men's groups (one in English, the other in Spanish), a youth group, and the newest group for LGBTQ parents. It also provides health fairs, counseling services, and Alcoholics Anonymous meetings. Queens Pride House's client base is over 40 percent Latino, 40 percent white, and the other 20 percent is Asian and African American, serving a large Spanish speaking population. The organization's board includes many people of color (50%) and most of the organization's small staff is bilingual. The longtime Director Dr. Pauline Park is a Korean American transwoman who has lived in Jackson Heights for over fifteen years. Recent special events like Know Your Rights Training for TransLatinas demonstrate the mission of the organization to serve the diverse community. In response to the Supreme Court ruling in United States v. Windsor (otherwise known as the DOMA case), Queens Pride House invited the non-profit Queens Legal Services to conduct a community workshop on the impact of the court ruling on LGBT immigrant and low-income families. Lawyers answered questions about the status of bi-national couples and how marriage-based federal benefits will be extended to same-sex couples. Director Pauline Park affirmed that, "Queens Pride House exemplifies Jackson Heights and Queens as a whole" (Personal interview with Pauline Park. Jackson Heights, NY, July 17, 2013).

The political organizing and coalition building that transpired in the years after Julio Rivera's death had an overwhelmingly positive impact on the neighborhood. A new culture of tolerance and respect for difference emerged from an exclusionary and closeted past. In 1998 scholars Kasinitz, Bazzi, and Doane concluded that "By and large Jackson Heights has become a community in which people of vastly different cultures and backgrounds live in very close physical proximity with little overt hostility" and that "local leaders almost universally point to Jackson Heights' diversity as one of the community's finest features and one of its proudest achievements" (Kasinitz, Bazzi and Doane 1998).

Fifteen years later their conclusions remain true. Local elected officials and leaders still point to the neighborhood's diversity as its crowning achievement, even as the diversity has *increased* (see Table 10.1). A closer look at the neighborhood demographics reveals the extent of the diversity. In 2000, 47,109 or 66 percent of the residents were foreign born. 40,211 residents, or 56.4 percent of the population was Latino: Colombian, Ecuadorian, Peruvian, Mexican, Puerto Rican, and Dominican (see Table 10.1). In 2010, 38,095 residents, or 57.2 percent of the population was Latino and, although the Latino population remains steady, the country of origin mix has shifted slightly. Simultaneously, in 2000, the Asian population was 11,935, with Indian, Bangladeshi, Chinese, Filipino, Korean, and Pakistani being the six largest groups. In 2010, the Asian population grew to 13,215. Indian, Bangladeshi, Chinese, Filipino, Korean, and Pakistani remain the largest groups, but the Korean population has dropped noticeably and there is a new and rapidly growing population of Nepalese immigrants (see Table 10.1). Between the same time period, 2000 to 2010, the white population shrank by approximately 5,000 residents.

The U.S. Census does not include questions about sexual orientation or gender identity, however, the data on "Unmarried-Partner Households by Sex of Partners" provides an incomplete window into the LGBTQ population. In 2010 out of 1,582 "Unmarried-Partner Households" in Jackson Heights, 369 (1.5%) were

TABLE 10.1 Growth in population by race and ethnicity in Jackson Heights, Queens, NY

Jackson Heights, NY (Zip Code 11372)	Census 2000	Census 2010
Total Population	71308	66636
White Alone	35617 (50%)	30546 (45.8%)
Hispanic or Latino	40211	38095
By Specific Origin		
Colombian	7705	7977
Ecuadorian	6169	8701
Peruvian	1285	1492
Mexican	5547	7282
Puerto Rican	2557	2046
Dominican	4242	4115
Asian Alone	11935	13215
With One Category		
Indian	3395	3132
Bangladeshi	941	2449
Chinese	3763	3358
Filipino	891	1017
Korean	1338	741
Pakistani	578	728
Nepalese	–	451

Source: US Census data compiled by the author.

"Same-Sex Partners," up from 266 in 2000. This is admittedly a poor measure of the number of LGBTQ residents because in addition to not counting single gays or lesbians it also does not reflect opposite-sexed queer families where one parent is transgender.

A better measure of the LGBTQ population is the extent of defined queer spaces. For example in Jackson Heights queer spaces include Queens Pride, the LGBTQ-focused social service organizations, and numerous gay bars. Over the decades bars and clubs have come and gone, but there have always been at least two or three open at a time. Currently, there are six LGBTQ bars and clubs and a few others that are "gay friendly." The bars are mainly located along Roosevelt Avenue, with a couple more located on the parallel 37th Avenue. Interestingly, unlike some cities where queer spaces are secluded, in Jackson Heights the LGBTQ spaces are dispersed throughout the neighborhood, next door to straight clubs, and pool halls. As stated by one local, "we have learned how to coexist with each other." According to local officials there has never been an attempt to get rid of the bars using local laws or zoning tactics. In fact, as far back as the 1970s the gay bars were viewed as an integral part of the larger community rather than an embarrassment or eyesore. At the moment the Jackson Heights Community Board considers the LGBTQ bars as the "model" bars in the neighborhood and generally speaking has fewer problems or complaints about them (Councilmember Daniel Dromm. Interview by author. Personal Interview. Jackson Heights, NY, July 29, 2013).

When asked about how Jackson Heights has changed since the 1990s, Pauline Park, Director of Queens Pride House, replied that "it has gotten more expensive, it has also gotten more diverse, more and more gay couples, even the LGBT community is becoming more diverse" (Personal interview with Pauline Park. Interview by author. Jackson Heights, NY, July 17, 2013). She added that when she moved to the neighborhood the LGBT population was overwhelmingly white; now the LGBT community reflects the community as a whole.[3] In her view there are many more people of color, more lesbians, and more transgender people, but that "diversity presents challenges."

Preserving Queer Immigrant Spaces

It is ironic that a neighborhood originally intended as a homogenous place that used planning interventions to exclude "the Other" is today diverse even by New York City standards, and a unique queer cosmopolis. Having maintained its queer identity over 60 years, it is now the site of the Queens Pride Parade, nightlife, and several organizations that assist this diverse LGBTQ population. However, in addition to the visibility and celebration of Jackson Heights' queer communities, it also remains the site of violence against LGBTQ people:

> On the one hand you are likely to find more acceptance here than in many other parts of Queens. That being said if you are a gay basher where are you going to go? So some of the recent hate crimes and violent attacks on LGBT people have been on people coming out of gay bars late at night.... Jackson Heights is more accepting for LGBT people, including people of color, however it is also a site of violence. (Personal interview with Pauline Park. Jackson Heights, NY, July 17, 2013)

In recent years when gay men or transwomen have been the targets of hate crimes or street harassment, the response from local LGBTQ leaders and organizations has been crucial, alerting the community to the harmful nature of these crimes and creating public discourse about why they are unacceptable. They have held press conferences and street protests, conducted informational campaigns, held self-defense classes, and put pressure on city politicians to direct attention and resources towards the safety of the queer community.

LGBTQ people of color in Jackson Heights have also been the victims of state-based violence, namely the NYPD's Stop and Frisk policy. For over a decade the Stop and Frisk policy disproportionately targeted people of color and immigrants with the stated purpose of preventing street crime. In 2012, Make the Road New York, arguably the largest and most politically powerful immigrant community organization in New York City (with its main office in Jackson Heights), together with the New York City Gay and Lesbian Anti-Violence Project, released a groundbreaking report entitled, *Transgressive Policing: Police Abuse of LGBTQ Communities of Color in Jackson Heights*. This report exposed the high rate at which all LGBTQ immigrants, and especially transgender people of color, were being "stopped and frisked" by the NYPD. Up until that point the chief accusation against Stop and Frisk had been racial profiling, but the report expanded the charges against the NYPD to include gender and sexuality profiling. Evidence suggested that the presumption of the NYPD was that all transgender people of color must be sex workers and criminalized as such. Make the Road was instrumental in forming coalitions across the city to oppose the policy and expanding the narrative about who is targeted to include immigrant and LGBT New Yorkers. Remarkably, after many years and court battles, these coalitions along with vocal city councilmembers garnered enough support to pass the Community Safety Act and forced an end to the use of Stop and Frisk. Jackson Heights' councilmember Daniel Dromm was a longtime supporter of the Community Safety Act and an early vocal opponent of Stop and Frisk. Over the last 20 years there has been a passionate activist and street protest response to both hate crimes and violence by the police, revealing the strength and political power of the LGBTQ organizations and communities in Jackson Heights.

Anthropologist Martin Manalansan has written about the ways in which neoliberalism has created the conditions for the exoticism and commodification of LGBTQ spaces, and the increased criminalization of immigrant sexualities (Manalansan 2005). Although the neighborhood continues to be a site of contested space, citizenship, sexuality, and social difference, it is also true that, unlike many other neighborhoods, in Jackson Heights the needs of LGBTQ residents are not ignored. Established local immigrant rights organizations and LGBT social service agencies, activists, and local elected officials work together not just to take LGBTQ needs into consideration but to make their needs a priority. They continue to fight for safety from discrimination and violence for LGBTQ individuals.

In the past, street harassment and violence against LGBTQ people in Jackson Heights from the police and others posed the most significant threat to the queer community, but in recent years the community has been successful in organizing against these. Today the question is whether these alliances will be strong enough to withstand a different kind of violence, the intense capitalist forces of the New York City housing and redevelopment market, often accompanied by the erasure of a community. Even though the LGBTQ population is currently growing not shrinking, there is still real concern among longtime residents about the rising cost of housing, and whether Jackson Heights will go the direction of notoriously gentrified Brooklyn, becoming unrecognizable and unaffordable, no longer an immigrant enclave nor a queer space.

During the Bloomberg administration large portions of New York City were rezoned and underwent large-scale redevelopment. Up until now Jackson Heights has not been targeted for rezoning or redevelopment, in part because a large portion of the neighborhood is landmarked and because Queens has been considered less desirable than Brooklyn or Manhattan.

Signs that city planning and real estate developers are focusing new attention on Queens and Jackson Heights include plans for the expansion of the neighborhood Business Improvement District (BID) and constructing a large mall on nearby parkland. There is a wide effort in Jackson Heights, spearheaded by the Roosevelt Avenue Community Alliance and supported by Make the Road, to raise awareness about the BID and to resist its proposed expansion. Many immigrant small business owners in the community see the BID expansion as a move to displace them from Roosevelt Avenue, replacing them with national chain stores, ultimately sanitizing and gentrifying the commercial district. Additionally, Flushing Meadows Corona Park, the nearest large park, is under threat of privatization. Residents and leaders in Jackson Heights have been very vocal in the community coalition, Save Flushing Meadows Corona Park, against this city effort that would put a mall on public space acreage in an area of Queens that has a dense population and little green space.

Urban policymakers and planners must intercede in the housing market before all middle-class and lower-income neighborhoods in New York City are destroyed. At this conjecture the most valuable planning intervention in Jackson Heights would be preserving the affordable housing that exists and creating more affordable housing to protect the most vulnerable LGBTQ populations, namely LGBT seniors and low-income immigrants. Jackson Heights' earliest gay residents are already senior citizens, but many immigrants that came post-1965 are aging, including LGBTQ immigrants, and there are serious issues because some from this population do not have Social Security, income, or medical coverage. Councilmember Daniel Dromm is interested in creating an assisted living facility and improved medical facilities in the neighborhood for the LGBTQ elders. Furthermore, many LGBT immigrants in response to the rising rents and unaffordability live in converted apartments, basement apartments, and deal with housing overcrowding. Councilmember Dromm has also been an active leader in the city council, fighting for more affordable housing, better rent regulation and protections for rent-controlled apartments.

The budding gentrification of Jackson Heights reveals a great deal about the multifaceted relationship of queer communities to gentrification. On the one hand gays and lesbians have been early gentrifiers to "marginal" neighborhoods. On the other hand many longtime gay enclaves have been erased by heteronormative gentrification. Jackson Heights further complicates the queer gentrification narrative because here many longtime white residents are LGBTQ and predate the Latino and South Asian residents. Meanwhile new multi-racial, multi-ethnic, higher income LGBTQ people have moved in, putting pressure on lower-income longer-term residents. This trend is reminiscent of intra-racial and cultural gentrification elsewhere in the city, such as affluent African Americans locating in Harlem because they are attracted to its black history, culture, and more affordable housing stock. LGBTQ people, both immigrant and non-immigrant, have moved to Jackson Heights for its queer history, culture, and affordable housing stock. In short, LGBTQ residents of Jackson Heights can be gentrifiers or the residents most vulnerable to displacement, and it is not always as simple as categories of race or foreign-born status who is who:[4]

> Because the nature of the LGBT community is so mixed, and immigrants are included in that, just the LGBT presence, I don't think leads to the gentrification necessarily…. If you look at the people who are moving into the community you see many mixed couples, and you see gay couples that are raising kids here. If you go to the 82nd Street afterschool program, there are lots of gay families, one father is an Asian immigrant, one father is white American, and the son is African American… it is not so easy to define or compartmentalize. (Interview with City Councilmember Daniel Dromm. Jackson Heights, NY, July 29, 2013)

Jackson Heights is a model queer space: because of its diversity, because a wide segment of the LGBTQ populations' needs are met by numerous accessible social service agencies, and because queer elected officials and leaders make a concerted effort to maintain the neighborhood as a place safe from discrimination and violence.

Despite the fact that there are constant issues with access to affordable housing in New York City and increasingly in Queens, local leaders agree that what makes Jackson Heights dynamic and desirable is its mixture of residents. They do not want to lose the diversity of people, businesses, or the affordability to middle-income and low-income residents. Councilmember Daniel Dromm, community organizations and coalitions and others in local politics are well aware of the very real threat of gentrification and hope that continuing to build the capacity of immigrant and LGBTQ organizations will hold back the tide of gentrification. Safeguarding a neighborhood against gentrification is no easy feat in 21st Century New York City, but efforts from numerous community leaders to organize against commercial displacement and for protecting affordable housing is ensuring some push back.

Jackson Heights has been discussed as the "new exotic gay mecca" and no longer a "space but a commodity to be consumed and literally eaten up by people who will spend a few hours being temporary gay tourists" (Manalansan 2005). However, this analysis considers it from the point of view of a consumer-outsider, but does not reflect on the demand for a diverse queer space by all different types of LGBTQ people, most of whom are local residents.

The current queer studies scholarship is preoccupied with debates over "the end of the gayborhood" and "the demise of queer space." Within these discussions there are two main threads; the first questions the impact of gentrification on the extinction of LGBTQ neighborhoods. The second questions the role of homonormativity and assimilation in the obsolescence of LGBTQ communities.

Though normativity and assimilation are arguably the mainstream LGBTQ cultural trend, Jackson Heights provides evidence that LGBTQ scholars may be ringing the death knell of queer neighborhoods too soon, bemoaning the death of queer communities in part because they are altogether missing the vibrancy of queer immigrant communities. Over the decades Jackson Heights has become a safe haven for LGBTQ people who are not easily assimilated: interracial queer families, LGBTQ people with non-normative gender expression, LGBTQ seniors, LGBTQ new immigrants and non-English speakers, to name a few.

Currently, gentrification is the most serious threat to Jackson Heights' queer cosmopolis. Protecting this diverse neighborhood for future decades is at the forefront of residents' minds. The progressive political alliance created in the 1990s between immigrant and LGBT residents must be advanced and then leveraged against real estate developers and large-scale neighborhood revitalization plans that have had little community input (Bailey 1999). LGBT residents should support the efforts that are underway to fight the BID and protect small business owners because pushing out small immigrant businesses would also mean pushing out small businesses like hair salons and bars owned and operated by LGBT immigrants. Furthermore, rising commercial rents could also mean the closing of the social service organizations like Queens Pride House and Make the Road that have been vital to protecting the rights of LGBT and immigrant New Yorkers. Continuing to advocate for the protection of small businesses and rent regulation, while fighting for increased affordable housing as well as oversight of policing that criminalizes immigrants and LGBT people are the best ways to ensure future continuity of queer spaces and queer visibility in Jackson Heights.

Notes

1   Filmmaker Richard Shpuntoff is the producer and director of the film "Julio of Jackson Heights" (www.juliofjacksonheights.com).
2   The corner of 37th Avenue and 78th Street was officially named Julio Rivera Corner by the city of New York at the twentieth anniversary of his murder.
3   For a window into the diversity, consider the LGBTQ residents on the block where I live. There are three gay male couples that I know of: a Korean man in his late 40s and his white partner in his 60s; a white man in his late 70s and his Latino partner in his 40s; two Latino immigrants who are both flight attendants and work out of nearby LaGuardia airport. There are at least three lesbian couples: white lesbians in their early 30s and their two Afro-Caribbean children; two white lesbians in their 50s; and a young Latina couple with the most all-American of jobs, firefighter and nurse. In addition, there are numerous other LGBTQ single people including a Korean American woman, a Guyanese American man, a young transwoman, a Thai man, and a white lesbian in her 70s. Recall that these are just the people I know on one block.
4   Of Colombian descent, queer, but new to the neighborhood, I embody this complexity. Regardless of my connection to Jackson Heights' immigrant history, being white and upwardly mobile does implicate me in the gentrification cycle.

References

Abraham, Julie. 2009. *Metropolitan Lovers: The Homosexuality of Cities*. Minneapolis, MN: University of Minnesota Press.
Aldrich, Robert. 2004. "Homosexuality and the city: an historical overview." *Urban Studies* 41, 9: 1719–1737.

Bailey, Robert W. 1999. *Gay Politics, Urban Politics: Identity and Economics in the Urban Setting*. New York, NY: Columbia University Press.

Bell, David, and Jon Binnie.2004. "Authenticating queer space: citizenship, urbanism and governance." *Urban Studies* 41, 9: 1807–1820.

Binnie, Jon, and Gill Valentine. 1999. "Geographies of sexuality – a review of progress." *Progress in Human Geography* 23, 2: 175–187.

Chauncey, George. 1994. *Gay New York: Gender, Urban Culture, and the Making of the Gay Male World, 1890–1940*. New York, NY: Basic Books.

Decena, Carlos Ulises. 2011. *Tacit Subjects: Belonging and Same-Sex Desire Among Dominican Immigrant Men*. Durham, NC: Duke University Press Books.

Doan, Petra L. 2007. "Queers in the American city: Transgendered perceptions of urban space." *Gender, Place and Culture* 14, 1: 57–74.

Doan, Petra L. (ed.) 2011. *Queerying Planning: Challenging Heteronormative Assumptions and Reframing Planning Practice*. Farnham, UK: Ashgate.

Doan, Petra L., and Harrison Higgins. 2011. "The demise of queer space? Resurgent gentrification and the assimilation of LGBT neighborhoods." *Journal of Planning Education and Research* 31, 1: 6–25.

Ghaziani, Amin. 2010. "There Goes the Gayborhood?" *Contexts* 9, 4: 64–66.

Guarnizo, Luis Eduardo, Arturo Ignacio Sánchez, and Elizabeth M. Roach. 1999. "Mistrust, fragmented solidarity, and transnational migration: Colombians in New York City and Los Angeles." *Ethnic and Racial Studies* 22, 2: 367–396.

Ingram, Gordon Brent, Anne-Marie Bouthillette, and Yolanda Retter (eds.). 1997. *Queers in Space: Communities, Public Places, Sites of Resistance*. Seattle, WA: Bay Press.

Kasinitz, Philip, Mohamad Bazzi, and Randal Doane. 1998. "Chapter 8: Jackson Heights, New York." *Cityscape* 4, 2: 161–177.

Levine, Martin P. 1979. "Gay ghetto." *Journal of Homosexuality* 4, 4: 363–377.

Lorch, D. 1991. "Jackson Heights' unlikely gay martyr." *The New York Times*, November 15. B1.

Make the Road New York. *Transgressive Policing: Police Abuse of LGBTQ Communities of Color in Jackson Heights*. October 2012. Retrieved from www.maketheroad.org/report.php?ID=2517

Maly, Michael T. 2005. *Beyond Segregation: Multiracial and Multiethnic Neighborhoods in the United States*. Philadelphia, PA: Temple University Press.

Manalansan I.V., & Martin, F. 2003. *Global Divas: Filipino Gay Men in the Diaspora*. Durham, NC: Duke University Press.

Manalansan I.V., & Martin, F. 2005. "Race, violence, and neoliberal spatial politics in the global city." *Social Text* 84/85: 141–155.

Marquez, Erika. 2007. "Transmigrant Sexualities." *Technofuturos: Critical Interventions in Latina/o Studies*: 213.

Miyares, Ines M. 2004a. "Changing Latinization of New York City," pp. 145–166 in D. Arreola (ed.). *Hispanic Spaces, Latino Places: A Geography of Regional and Cultural Diversity*, Austin, TX: University of Texas Press.

Miyares, Ines M. 2004b. "From Exclusionary Covenant to Ethnic Hyperdiversity in Jackson Heights, Queens." *Geographical Review* 94, 4: 462–483.

Sandercock, Leonie. 1998. *Towards Cosmopolis: Planning for Multicultural Cities*. London, UK: Wiley.

Sandercock, Leonie, and Peter Lyssiotis. 2003. *Cosmopolis II: Mongrel Cities of the 21st Century*. New York, NY: Continuum.

Shpuntoff, Richard. 2013. *Julio of Jackson Heights: The Story of a Hate Crime that Changed a World*. Unreleased version of a documentary film.

11

LESBIAN SPACES IN TRANSITION

Insights from Toronto and Sydney

Catherine J. Nash and Andrew Gorman-Murray

Introduction

In this chapter, we examine how lesbian urban geographies are currently being transformed through a comparative analysis of contemporary lesbian place-making activities in Sydney, Australia and Toronto, Canada. In doing so, we step away from more traditional scholarship on geographies of sexualities and queer geographies to argue that 'new mobilities' scholarship offers potential insights into the complex reorganizing of sexual and gendered inner-city landscapes. Through an exploration of the similarities and differences in sexual and gendered mobilities in Toronto and Sydney, we seek to delineate newly emergent and expressly 'lesbian'-identified urban locations that constitute entangled, fluid and networked geographies that reflect particular physical, representational and experiential interconnections and relations.[1]

The imagined and material heritage, the ongoing movement and the residual legacies of lesbian geographies are not easily understood or accommodated by planners and policy-makers, especially vis-à-vis the arguably more celebrated sexual and gendered landscapes of gay ghettos, gay bars and Pride parades. Therefore, one of our objectives in this critical discussion is to offer new insights that can be taken forward in planning practices and policies concerning urban space and public access for lesbians and queer women. We argue that putting 'knowledge' of lesbian geographies into practice is not simply about 'preserving' places that are historically or presently 'lesbian-identified,' although that might be important for some women (Lamont 2008). Rather, it is about understanding how urban spaces are (re)configured and (re)utilized in response to shifting gender and sexual subjectivities, and thus developing sensitivity about how to address the changing spatial imperatives of lesbians, queer women and their communities in planning.

We begin with a brief overview of contemporary scholarship on lesbian urban spaces with a focus on North American, British and Australian contexts before turning to review the most recent scholarship on traditional gay villages. This review will position the scholarship on lesbian urban geographies in relation to research on traditional or longstanding gay villages. Second, we discuss in some detail 'new mobilities' approaches with a particular focus on Cresswell's (2006, 2010) conceptualizations of mobilities, and Uteng and Cresswell's (2008) work on gendered mobilities. In our analysis, we explore how a mobilities-based perspective offers fruitful alternative conceptualizations of lesbian place-making, identities and practices. Through this discussion, we hope to contribute to (re)conceptualizations of the sexual and gendered dimensions of mobilities' reshaping of urban landscapes, which is often overlooked in new mobilities scholarship. As well, we want to consider how mobilities (and the possibilities of mobilities) are at play in the restructuring of urban landscapes more generally in the Global North.

Lesbians and Urban Place-Making

A rich body of scholarship from the 1960s onwards examines how sexual minorities carved out spaces for social interaction and political organizing in inner-city neighborhoods in urban centers in the Global North (Levine 1979; Castells 1983; Adler and Brenner 1992; Knopp 1992, 1995, 1998; Rothenberg 1995). In the 1980s, a now quite familiar scholarly debate broke out over why gay men seemed to have greater success in achieving political, economic and social territorial control as evidenced by the highly visible gay districts in places such as San Francisco and Toronto. Some posited that lesbians, as women, were less interested in spatial domination and more interested in developing broader political and social agendas (Castells 1983). Castells (1983), for example, posited that men were 'innately' more 'territorial,' while Lauria and Knopp (1985) suggested that gay men were more oppressed 'as men,' and therefore needed to create 'safe' places to congregate. Other scholarship was sharply critical of these perspectives, arguing, in part, that lesbians, as women, had less access to the economic resources necessary to control urban locations (Egerton 1990; Adler and Brenner 1992).[2] By the 1990s work by Rothenberg (1995) on the Park Slope neighborhood in Brooklyn, New York, demonstrated that in some instances, more visible lesbian residential and commercial neighborhoods could develop.

In what is now considered classic research on lesbian geographies, Gill Valentine (1993a, 1993b, 1993c, 1995) demonstrated how lesbians took up space using 'complex time-space' relations that cross-cut and interwove lesbian social networks and relations in and across public spaces. This work emphasized the centrality of gender in the mediation and constitution of lesbian social networks and gay male geographies. As Podmore (2001) notes, by the end of the 1990s, scholarship clearly demonstrated that "lesbians and gay men exhibited markedly different patterns of residence, neighborhood and visibility in urban public space," highlighting how gender and sexuality mediates engagements with urban landscapes (p. 333). While gay male interests came to dominate certain inner-city neighborhoods, lesbians, while utilizing spaces in these neighborhoods, also created networked, alternative spaces outside these areas.

Podmore's research (2001, 2006, 2013) on Montreal's lesbian community provides perhaps the clearest examination of the intertwined geographies of gay villages (understood as neighborhoods dominated by the interests of white, middle-class, gay men, e.g. Nast 2002; Southern 2004; Elder 2002) and lesbian commercial and residential life (cf. Bouthillette 1997). Podmore argues against privileging the idea of 'visibility' as central to what constitutes territorial control.[3] Lesbian place-making occurs, she argues, differently than that of gay men, in so-called 'spaces of difference' – those more marginal inner-city neighborhoods marked by demographic diversity and mixed land uses. Understanding lesbian geographies requires recognition of how "gender mediates geographies of sexualities in the urban landscape" (Podmore 2001: 335). Podmore documents how vibrant social networks operating through spaces of differences link lesbians and places in ways that are profoundly spatialized but largely 'invisible' in the more traditional sense. Lesbian communities, then, are arguably spatially constituted through these "fluid informal networks that linked a variety of public and private sites," giving these spaces a quasi-underground character (Podmore 2001: 596).

Podmore's (2006) later research expands these arguments through her fine-grained examination of the historical geographies of the highly visible and increasingly commodified Village Gai in downtown Montreal, on the one hand, and the decline in expressly lesbian community spaces in the nearby 'Plateau' neighborhood, on the other (2006, 2013). Podmore explores what she calls the 'gender asymmetries' that developed during the rise of "'queer politics' in the 1990s and the corresponding territorialization in gay commercial enclaves" (2006: 598). Podmore argues that, in part, shifts to more fluid 'queer' identifications (rather than essentialized, stable 'gay' and 'lesbian' identities) fostered a shift away from production of lesbian feminist, women-only spaces. Some women increasingly took on queer identifications (perhaps reflecting generational changes), resulting in the fragmentation of lesbian communities, identities and traditional spaces. Podmore links the loss of lesbian spaces in the Plateau with the growth of the increasing 'queer' identified Village Gai and the related development of queer politics.

Podmore develops this argument further in her most recent work examining the incorporation of Montreal's gay nightlife into what she calls 'queer village' (2013). Podmore argues that in the 1990s, with the rise of queer politics, queer identifications and practices, some lesbians experienced "a sense of dis-identification with [the] gay village" and an increasing difficulty "negotiating their presence in queer commercial spaces" (2013: 224). The Village Gai, with its queered spaces, politics, and identities was increasingly unfamiliar to and distant from lesbians' experiences. Although some lesbians may have experienced exclusion and marginalization in these newly queered locations, the Village simultaneously represented a place of LGBTQ diversity and queer culture. So while some may have felt included under the queer umbrella, many others did not identify with more specific forms of gay male consumer culture (Podmore 2013).

Podmore's research (2001, 2006, 2013) emphasizes the complex linkages between lesbian and gay villages locations, and turns our attention to the intersection of politics, place, identities and practices in the formulation and transformation of sexual and gendered landscapes. Other scholarship highlights the complex relationships amongst various members of the LGBTQ population and gay villages, including lesbians and queer women (Costello and Hodge 1999; Podmore 2013; Nash 2013a, 2013b; Nash and Bain 2007), transmen, transwomen and lesbian/queer women's spaces (Nash 2011; Taylor 1998) and a new generation of 'post-mos' for whom sexual orientation may not constitute a fixed and immutable identity (Nash 2013b). Given the multiplicity and complexity of the relationships emerging amongst and between variously gendered and sexualized landscapes, including traditional gay villages, we would like to suggest that new mobilities approaches offer a concrete way to examine these relationships and interconnectivities.

New Mobilities Approaches: Lesbian Place-Making Networks

There is considerable scholarship examining the seeming demise or 'decline' of traditional gay villages in the Global North. Many reasons are given for these changes, including the broader processes of neoliberalism and consumerism (Collins 2004; Ruting 2008; but see Visser 2013), changing generational choices within LGBT populations (Gorman-Murray and Waitt 2009; Reynolds 2009; Nash, 2013b), increasing internet use (Mowlabocus 2010; Usher and Morrison 2010), and complex reconceptualizations of political 'identity,' subjectivities and meanings associated with distinctive behaviors, practices and embodiments (Nash 2013a and b). Progressive social and legislative changes have enabled certain segments of sexual and gendered minority populations to be more freely visible across a variety of urban areas, creating new and alternative places (Brown 2004; Browne and Bakshi 2011; Gorman-Murray and Waitt 2009; Lewis 2013; Nash 2013b; Visser 2008, 2013). Frequently still, inner-city locations, although physically separate suburbs/neighborhoods from gay villages, often house some LGBT services, organizations and venues, but more importantly they have a LGBT residential congregation that is integrated with neighborhood life, with broadly conciliatory and convivial relations with the local 'mainstream' population. While certainly not outside neoliberal impulses, these neighborhoods are typically 'spaces of difference' (Podmore 2001) that are characterized by liberal politics and social relationships, and by the presence of counter-cultural communities (e.g. bohemians, Goths, hippies). Recent scholarly work suggests Newtown, in Sydney's inner western suburbs, as a key example of an alternative, 'queer-friendly' neighborhood (Gorman-Murray and Waitt 2009; Gorman-Murray and Nash in press; on Newtown's social and counter-cultural diversity, see Carroll and Connell 2000; Duruz 2005).

Much of the scholarship and public discourse considering these transformative processes tends to take a binary perspective, suggesting that gay villages are dissolving while these alternative inner-city neighborhoods are gaining political, social and economic importance for LGBT people (Gorman-Murray 2006; Nash 2013a). As Podmore (2006) argues, urban scholars tend to imagine the city as a collection of neighborhoods demarcated according to race, class and ethnicity – a conceptualization, she argues, masking their complicated and symbiotic interconnections, as well as the multiplicity of identities and practices in circulation within these networked spaces. In this section, we argue that new mobilities scholarship offers a way around this dilemma by developing a perspective that highlights movements, social networks and interconnections amongst and between locations – advancing alternative conceptualizations to the binary understanding of relations amongst and between 'sequestered' inner-city neighborhoods. A mobilities approach instead emphasizes that places (here, neighborhoods) are formed on specific intersections of relations that extend beyond any 'bounded' location. Moreover, places and their interrelations change because these external connections are always in flux. Rather than portraying gay villages as separate enclaves, then, we want to emphasize their place in a complex and stratified web of gendered and sexualized communities (Nash and Gorman-Murray 2014).

Within new mobilities approaches, scholarship argues against conceptualizations of place as fixed and definable and as a container where social, political and economic processes unfold. These approaches argue for a conceptualization of places as relational and networked, constituted and enabled through social lives that are lived 'on the move' (McCann and Ward 2011). We draw particularly on the work of Tim Cresswell, who argues "mobility is central to what it is to be modern. A modern citizen, among other things, is a mobile citizen" (2006: 20). This is a perspective that highlights the temporal and historical specificities of being 'mobile' as well as, we would argue, the geographic specificities of such mobilities.

Cresswell (2010: 18) argues that 'mobility' should be understood as a constellation of elements composed of "particular patterns of movement, representations of movement, and ways of practicing movement that makes sense together." This conceptualization directs attention to taking into account actual physical movement, narratives giving those movements meaning (representations), and the practices arising from actual movements. Here we examine each element in turn and briefly consider what this might mean for geographical research on lesbian urban geographies.

Cresswell takes a very broad perspective on what the physicality of mobilities might entail. He argues it could include the corporeal, embodied movement of people, together with the flows and networks of information, goods, services and knowledges, and the details of circulation systems, from the infrastructure of transportation systems to the diffusion of ideas (see also Hannam et al. 2006; Sheller and Urry 2006). Second, we need to be attuned to the representations, narratives or stories we tell about the nature, purpose and outcome of movement. As Cresswell (2010) argues, these narrative meanings about 'being on the move' are socially and culturally encoded; they are specific to the peoples and places embedded within movement and mobilities. The physical act of 'being mobile' is arguably insufficient to understanding the meanings attached to that act. The ability to be mobile can be understood as fundamental to citizenship; some movements may be represented as authentic or real, others as transgressive or resistive, and still others as a possibility for only a privileged few.

The third element in any set of mobilities is the embodied practices experienced by individuals or groups; a set of experiences that might not be captured "either in their objective dimensions or their social and cultural dimensions," and which might either confirm or contest representations or narratives of mobility (Cresswell 2010: 20). In any set of physical movements and practices, numerous narratives are in play and while one or two might become dominant, it is important to be attuned to alternative meanings and narratives. Methodologically then, researchers should explore these meanings through direct engagement with experiences of those who did the 'moving' to develop an understanding of the connections between the larger narratives and the embodied experiences.

Politics and power relations are pivotal ingredients in any discussion of mobilities. Cresswell (2010: 21) argues that politics can be understood as "the social relations that involve the production and distribution of power." The question of who has the ability to move and whether it is voluntary or involuntary is clearly a function of power relations. Kauffman's (2002) and Kauffman et al.'s (2004) notion of 'motility' helps to conceptualize the entwined relationship between mobilities and power relations. Kauffman (2002) defines 'motility' as the potential, the ability and the capacity for movement, and makes us consider what sorts of mobilities are possible for both individuals and groups (see also Jensen 2011). In turn, the capability or possibility of movement is dependent in part on having the resources to move (economic) and forms of knowledge and 'knowhow' that permit engagement with the complexity of mobility networks and systems (social and cultural capital) (Dufty-Jones 2012; Jensen 2011).

The next step in a mobilities framework is to consider the relationship between motility, individuals and the spatial, that is, how the possibilities, actions and practices of mobilities intersect with identities, subjectivities and the constitution of urban spaces. Jensen (2011) argues that Foucauldian notions of power relations and governmentality ensures we consider that 'power' is not a thing held by some but is a relational environment, which is constraining, enabling and productive, and that social relations are constituted within these power relations. Power relations constitute space as a 'dynamic and immanent dimension of the social,' rendering mobilities palpably spatialized and inherent in the production of social relations (see also Driver 1985).

Second, Foucault (2003) postulates 'governmentality' as a form of power relations constituting the regulation and control of populations. It is rendered operational through expert knowledges that ensure we come to understand ourselves as certain sorts of subjects within social relations through forms of self-discipline and surveillance. Sometimes this can even take the form of local government ordinances (Doan and Higgins 2011). Within historically and geographically particular social relations, subjects are also constituted through certain forms of mobile practices through which space is produced. Likewise, the motilities available to subjects are unevenly distributed, leading to the formation and re-inscription of expectations and placements of people in urban landscapes. Put more pragmatically, Jensen (2011: 259) argues that certain subjects, positioned within discourse, "behave, perform and shape their identities ... and are produced in historically particular ways that come to be taken for granted," but with a geographical specificity.

Lesbian Mobilities in Urban Space – Relational Geographies

Cresswell's (2010) concept of a constellation of mobilities (represented as entanglements of physical displacements, representations and practices), together with the notion of governmentalities (constituting modern subjects within particular mobilities embedded in urban spaces) allows us to rethink understandings of LGBT subjects and their spatialized practices through a mobilities framework. As Podmore's work (2006, 2013) makes clear, lesbians' engagement in urban place-making and their relationship to the Village Gai highlights how gender mediates relationships with urban places, including sexual minority landscapes. Within mobilities approaches, scholars work to understand the ways in which mobilities and genders intersect, which is a complicated process given both are "infused with meaning, power and contested understandings" (Uteng and Cresswell 2008: 3). Drawing on Uteng and Cresswell (2008), we would argue that the elements of mobilities (movement, meanings and practices), as well as motilities, have "histories and geographies of gendered differences" (p. 4), and that these motilities and mobilities are integral to the reproduction and contestation of gendered and sexualized selves.

We would argue then that the 'gendered asymmetries' explored by Podmore (2006, 2013) reflect the gendered differences in mobilities and that the possibilities for movement, the meanings attached to movement and the practices engaged in, facilitate the constitution and reproduction of gendered (and sexualized) experiences. In this section, we attempt to work through these ideas by considering how new forms of mobilities (and motilities), underpinned by particular narratives and practices, are both gendered and reproductive of specific forms of identity with spatialized consequences. We do this through a consideration of lesbian place-making in Toronto and Sydney.

Lesbian Mobilities in Toronto

Scholarship on lesbian place-making in Toronto is sparse. Elise Chenier (2004) has documented the connections between working-class lesbians and particular bars and restaurants in the downtown core in the 1950s and 1960s, while Becki Ross (1997) has explored connections between Street Haven, a community-based outreach center operating in the 1960s and the local lesbian populations. Ross' work (1995), examining lesbian feminist organizing in Toronto in the 1980s and early 1990s, delineates attempts to establish community venues and political and social organizations in the downtown area. There is some work exploring lesbian activism and engagement with the HIV/AIDS crisis in the 1980s and the 1990s as well as lesbian participation in gay political organizing into the 2000s (Kinsman 1996; Warner 2000, 2002).

More recently, work by Nash and Bain (2007) and Nash (2011, 2013a, 2013b) considers changing identities/subjectivities and practices and their implications for the formulations of new sorts of spaces, which range from (private) buildings to (public) neighborhoods. This includes an examination of the Toronto Women's Bathhouse events that sought to establish queer women's spaces for new forms of sexual expression (Bain and Nash 2007), the experiences of transmen in lesbian and queer women's spaces (Nash 2011), the establishment of alternative queer women's spaces in the Parkdale neighborhood west of the gay village (Nash 2013a), and the relationship of a new generation of men, identifying as 'post-mo,' to both gay village spaces and new alternative ones (Nash 2013b). All of this work utilizes an unproblematic, binary approach in conceptualizing the gay village as stable and potentially in decline while positing new or alternative spaces in juxtaposition to the gay village. What we want to do here is reconsider this work within a new mobilities framework.

Given that mobilities and motilities have a historical and geographical specificity, scholarship needs to consider the changing social, political and legislative contexts in which they are experienced. By 2006 Canadian gays and lesbians had full human rights protections and open inclusion in institutions such as the military and marriage. Currently, the battles are largely around conceptualization of religious 'freedom,' free speech and the school curriculum. In Toronto, the gay village continues to be central to gay political and social life, particularly around the delivery of social services, but there is growing concern about the gay village's 'decline' (Gee 2011; Nash 2013b) and recognition that sexual and gendered minorities are increasingly visible in other parts of the city.

Drawing on Cresswell's (2010) notion of mobility as a constellation of the physical, the representational and particular practices, it is instructive to reframe what is happening in Toronto as a result of new mobilities and motilities made possible by social and legislative changes. At this historical juncture, some gays and lesbians are enjoying a greater ability to visibly circulate within and through a larger number of downtown neighborhoods. What is interesting is an examination of the sorts of neighborhoods available through increased mobilities (e.g. Gorman-Murray and Waitt 2009; Nash 2013a, 2013b).

These new mobilities are embedded within particular narratives, which link these new spatial experiences to changing and newly constituted identities, subjectivities and practices. Within these new mobilities are narratives that rework understandings of the gay village as a location for a narrowly defined and constrained set of genders and practices associated with a historically specific era, which is now over (Nash 2013b). A new generation of individuals, cast as queer or 'post-mo' argue that they do not fit into the older and more restricted identities and practices associated with the Village and are now able to seek out (and be accepted in) a broader range of places (Nash 2013a, 2013b). New subjectivities are being constituted through and within new forms of mobilities. Clearly, though, these possibilities for movements and practices are tempered by gendered, classed and racialized identities.

This disassociation with Toronto's gay village is also driven by more practical concerns around housing prices and affordability and alternative locations such as Parkdale, Leslieville, Beaches or Junction offer greater choice while being open to a gay, lesbian or queer presence. Mobilities approaches ask us to consider how shifting, and in this case, gendered subjectivities and identities are being reshaped within new mobilities and are shaping the possibilities of mobilities themselves. Arguably what we are seeing in Toronto are new gendered mobilities, forged in part through legislative and social changes that regard the gay village as too narrow and limited for the new identities and subjectivities enabled through new motilities.

Another prominent narrative describes the perception that gay male interests and aesthetics, which are 'too commercial and commodified,' dominate the Village. And yet, while both queer and lesbian women echoed this critique, many also regarded the Village as a place to socialize on occasion, take in Gay Pride and other LGBTQ events, and as necessary for the continued health of LGBTQ politics, reflecting Podmore's (2013) findings about the paradoxical relationship between lesbian and queer women and Montreal's Village Gai. These narratives represent various locations in particular ways and illustrate the linkages and connections between the Gay Village and other locations in the downtown core. As well, there are considerable distinctions made between queer women's spaces and lesbian women's space. Queer women are often regarded as having greater spatial choice (and related mobilities) than do lesbian women (Nash 2013a).

Cresswell (2010) argues that in considering mobilities, we need to think through the interconnection between actual physical mobilities (including people, information and goods), narratives and practices. The various practices of distinctive LGBTQ groups might suggest that the Village remains a central node within increasingly complex networks stretched across bars, restaurants, neighborhoods, stores, and community centers. The historical narrative of the Village remains a strong one, characterizing the space as safe, welcoming and providing the services LGBTQ people need. There also remains the sense that the Village must continue as the major staging area for political dissent and economic strength.

So, we might argue the Village is in decline if we use the usual measures, including, for example, loss of gay-identified (and iconic) businesses and services, the increasing number of heterosexual people in the LGBTQ leisure spaces and the growing presence of heterosexual people in the surrounding residential neighborhood. However, in thinking about increased mobilities and motilities, we might argue that representationally, the Village remains part of the central spatial imagery for the local LGBTQ population. As well, it is now increasingly linked to a variety of other downtown locations, which might arguably be perceived as forging a more complex set of linkages (and political, social and economic strength) across urban space.

Sydney's Mobile Lesbian Geographies – Oxford Street, Leichhardt and Newtown

As with Toronto, a review of social sciences and humanities disciplines yields limited scholarship on Sydney's lesbian geographies. The literature includes Murphy and Watson's (1997) brief discussion of Leichhardt as lesbian space in *Surface City*, and Taylor's (1998) critique of the early-1990s Lesbian Space Project, which was an attempt to create a lesbian-only space – a lesbian-owned-and-run community center – in Newtown, Sydney. She examined disagreements about 'belonging' to the identities 'woman' and 'lesbian' between women-born-women and women-loving-transwomen, which revealed fractured lesbian communities and brought about the Project's failure. Jennings (2009) documented the history of lesbians in Sydney, focusing on the development of lesbian politics rather than geographies, but nevertheless pointed to the coalescence and movement of commercial and political spaces from the 1960s to the 1990s. Luzia (2008, 2010), meanwhile, studied the everyday geographies of lesbian parenting in suburban and inner-city Sydney. While not focusing on lesbian place-making, her work nevertheless showed where lesbian parents tend to live and frequent, and their comfort with their embodied mobility, as lesbian-mothers, through the public environments of certain places. This work, collectively, has implications for planning knowledge and practice. Extant scholarship shows the diversity and tensions cutting through Sydney's lesbian communities at the junctures of social intersections (i.e. gender, sexuality, motherhood, class, etc.), which means any form of planning must be sensitive to such differences and not assume a singular lesbian subjectivity. This work also demonstrates the importance of a range of spaces at various scales to individuals, families and groups, including residential, commercial and community spaces, from buildings to streetscapes.

Moreover, while all of the above work is vital for understanding Sydney's lesbian geographies, much more remains to be done. As with the previous case study, the aim here is to reconsider Sydney's lesbian geographies through the framework of 'new mobilities,' motilities, relational space, social power and identity politics. Reiterating Cresswell's positioning, mobilities are socially, geographically and historically contingent, as are the temporary outcomes of this mobility. In the case of Sydney's lesbian communities, we contend that shifts and dissensions in sexual identity politics since the 1950s, intersecting with the capacities of gender and class, have meant that lesbian place-making has been constantly 'on the move' in post-WWII Sydney – arguably more so than for gay male communities. There has been a collusion of women's marginalization in public space with women's inhibited economic means and proliferating tensions in lesbian identity politics, which has made Sydney's lesbian geographies both more marginal and more mobile than Sydney's gay male geographies (cf. Podmore 2001). The following presents a critical historical geography of mobile lesbian place-making in Sydney. We draw on existing scholarship and on oral histories and archival sources to understand the transitions of lesbian spaces.

In the immediate post-WWII era, Sydney's lesbian geographies comprised private or semi-public spaces rather than public or commercial spaces. Wotherspoon (1991) documents 'camp' bars in the city in the 1950s, frequented by homosexual men, but initially women were excluded from these spaces by law and, later, marginalized by social sanction, whereby the presence of women without men in public was frowned upon. Jennings (2009: 32) indicates that, instead, "lesbian socializing in the mid-twentieth century largely focused on private friendship networks and women entertained friends at private house parties on weekends and public holidays," while "many women did meet other lesbians at work or in social groups such as dance or sports clubs." Lesbian networks were 'hidden' in the everyday spaces of suburbia and work, through which women had to move with care to avoid unwelcome recognition as lesbian. It was not until the 1960s that networked movements through space began to coalesce into more public, albeit still 'underground,' spaces.

In the 1960s, opening hours of licensed venues were extended. This enabled a night-time commercial bar scene, which catered to a 'camp' clientele of both homosexual men and women, to develop in the inner eastern suburbs of King's Cross, Paddington and Darlinghurst (Jennings 2009; Pride History Group 2009) – around the area that would come to be called Oxford Street and be known as Sydney's 'gay ghetto.' The number of venues grew over the decade to the 1970s, and several were popular with lesbians, including Chez Ivy and Kandy's, Paddington, and Ruby Red's in the city, constituting Sydney's 'lesbian scene.' These were very much 'social' spaces and networks, which facilitated and supported new models of lesbian identity not as readily possible at home or work, such as butch/femme pairings (Jennings 2009; Pride History Group 2009). However, as the 1970s wore on, new identity politics and new lesbian spaces took shape.

During the 1960s and into the 1970s, gay men increasingly colonized Paddington, Darlinghurst and the other suburbs surrounding the 'camp' bar scene, beginning to transform the area into a gay residential as well as commercial concentration. Along with other newcomers, they prompted pioneer gentrification of the neighborhood. With less material means, lesbians and other women were gradually priced out of the housing market of the Oxford Street 'gay ghetto' due to rising values, purchase costs and rental rates for housing (in this inner-city area, comprising apartments and terraces).[4] This economic inequity intersected with new lesbian feminist identity politics to provoke a gender-based divide in the 'camp' community. Lesbian feminists also critiqued older forms of lesbian identity associated with the 'camp' bar scene, holding that "butch and femme lesbians were acting out heterosexual stereotypes of masculinity and femininity" (Pride History Group 2009: 31). Shifting landscapes of class and identity politics engendered the movement of lesbian communities from Oxford Street, and facilitated the development of a distinct 'lesbian ghetto' centered on the suburb of Leichhardt, in Sydney's inner west.

Little has been written on Leichhardt as lesbian space (although see Murphy and Watson 1997), but in the early 2000s the local municipal library developed the 'Dykehardt' Oral History Project, recording the oral histories of local lesbians and collecting archival material on networks, venues and institutions in Leichhardt and surrounding suburbs (Annandale, Lilyfield).[5] 'Dykehardt' is a nickname signifying general knowledge of the lesbian concentration in and around the suburb; and indeed, the interviews reveal that during the 1970s and 1980s, with lesbians leaving Oxford Street for political and economic reasons, lesbian organizations and communities took root in Leichhardt. Lesbian residents moved in partly because housing was cheaper than in gentrifying Paddington and Darlinghurst (Murphy and Watson 1997). They, and women coming from elsewhere, were also drawn by a range of community services and social venues that developed in the 1970s and 1980s. These included the Leichhardt Women's Community Health Centre, Lesbian Line Counselling, the Feminist Bookshop, Clover Businesswomen's Club, Elsie Women's Refuge, and regular lesbian nights at the Leichhardt Hotel. Lesbians also met in other spaces, such as the café Bar Italia.

Feminist politics and economic imperatives facilitated the development of a lesbian concentration in Leichhardt, but as the interviewees themselves noted, this space was beginning to dissipate by the end of the 1990s. This was again impelled by economic and political changes. Leichhardt was gentrifying in the 1990s, pushing up both housing costs and commercial rents, and again forcing out those women with limited material means (Murphy and Watson 1997). Simultaneously, lesbian feminism, with its emphasis on separatism, was giving way to a post-feminist generation that sought a new coalitional politics with gay male communities and other sexual and gender minorities (there were similar processes and effects for Oxford Street and the gay community (Reynolds 2009)). This has led to divisions in lesbian communities, for instance, about the inclusion of transwomen (Taylor 1998), but also new alignments in the current push for mainstream inclusion around such normative rights as marriage and parenting (Luzia 2008, 2010). This points to another change in identity politics with implications for lesbian geographies in Sydney: increasing claims of 'sameness' with (rather than difference or separatism from) the heterosexual majority and, consequently, for 'equal' rights.

Mobile place-making in light of this latest range of economic, social and political changes is complex and differentiated. The interviewees, and media reports (Gorman-Murray 2006), suggest that lesbians have increasingly moved to other areas in Sydney's inner west, notably Newtown and its surrounds. Fractions of the population have moved for different reasons, however. The Newtown area houses a diverse liberal identity politics that encompasses both homonormative sameness and radical/resistant queerness, both niche consumption and DIY anti-capitalism. Lesbian parents access lesbian-friendly day care, and lesbian and gay bars proliferate (Wednesday is lesbian night across a number of venues) (Gorman-Murray and Nash in press); meanwhile 'queer' political organizations openly question who is included in lesbian and gay mainstreaming, and 'queer' anti-capitalist rallies are held in local community halls. We make this case not to celebrate Newtown as 'utopian diversity,' but to indicate the 'knotty' lesbian geographies fomenting in this round of mobile place-making. Lesbian communities (and for that matter, gay and queer ones) are fractured along class and political lines, and as same-sex rights become more visible in Australian public debate, internal tensions also become more visible. We suggest these tensions are entwined in lesbian mobility and place-making in Sydney (and of other sexual and gender minorities), and the impossibility of 'pinning' a particular identity politics to Newtown is emblematic of this complexity.

Conclusions – and Implications for Planning

Geographical scholarship in lesbian urban geographies demonstrates how lesbians and gay men have utilized urban locations in the Global North in distinctly different ways. In particular, gay men have tended to form urban neighborhoods that provide social, political and economic strength. These traditional gay villages have simultaneously supported lesbians' and queer women's activities, while women have also established other locations as lesbian-only spaces and concentrations at scales from the building to the neighborhood. We argue that the relationships between these spaces – gay villages and lesbian urban spaces – are not an 'either/or' proposition but, in keeping with Podmore's research (2001, 2006, 2013), are part of an intertwined complex and relational set of geographies. Furthermore, we assert that these relational geographies are reflective of historically and geographically specific mobilities and motilities embedded in power relations engaged in the spatial reformulations of subjects, subjectivities and practices.

We want to conclude by reflecting on the implications that the shifting and relational geographies of lesbian and queer women have for planning practitioners and local governments. Addressing lesbians' and queer women's needs arguably falls under the remit of 'social planning,' which is concerned with understanding the aspirations of different social and cultural groups, and in equitably accommodating this diversity in planning policy and practice by both fostering respect for difference and protecting the interests of marginalized groups (Thompson 2007). Thompson (2007: 199–200) argues that "social planning … is at the core of all good contemporary planning, which should aim to integrate physical land use with socio-cultural factors in the question to build sustainable environments for us all". Access to physical space (public and residential) and material resources, and enabling social interaction and inclusion, are thus important considerations for planning. Indeed, extending Thompson's (2007) foregrounding of the social dimensions of planning, Fincher and Iveson (2008) argue that the principles of planning should recognize social and cultural diversity, encourage encounter between different groups, and redistribute wealth and services to alleviate social disadvantage and inequality.

In light of our critical discussion in this chapter, these principles and practices might take several complementary forms for lesbians, queer women and their communities. On the one hand, the mutable and mobile geographies of lesbian spaces might prompt some women to call for a remembrance, if not a 'fixing,' of lesbian legacies in certain sites (venues, neighborhoods) that have attained a lesbian 'identity'. Lamont (2008), for instance, reports on women's attempts to reclaim Leichhardt's lesbian heritage by lobbying the local council for the provision of services and facilities for women's groups, landscape symbolism that reflects the lesbian presence (women's symbols, rainbow flags), and a lesbian history collection in the local library. Consolidating the lesbian history of Leichhardt offers a means to acknowledge lesbians' contributions to the constitution of this place, and also embeds traces of lesbian heritage in the local landscape.

On the other hand, the shifting, mobile and relational lesbian geographies of Toronto and Sydney should also alert planners and policy-makers to the reality that lesbian lives and spaces are not immutable and cannot be 'fixed' in place. Arguably, part of the geographical heritage of lesbian communities is their mobility (even if this is the result of constraint and marginality due to gender, class or sexuality). This means that, to address the inclusive aims of social planning for diversity, planners and policy-makers must be aware of and accommodate at least two important realizations. First, lesbian communities are diverse, not singular, encompassing differences of ethnicity, generation, class, etc., all of which need to be attended to in planning and policy to meet the wide needs and aspirations of all women. Second, it is not only 'lesbian-identified' places that must accommodate sexual and gender diversity: all spaces need to be inclusive of broad differences, including lesbian lives and communities, in order to encourage people to encounter and respect difference.

We see these two dimensions of social planning for lesbians and queer women – acknowledging specific geographical heritage and building broad spatial inclusion – as complementary. Remembering (possibly reclaiming) significant lesbian urban spaces provides important moorings for lesbian communities in the context of mobile lesbian geographies. But it is equally important to be cognizant of how urban spaces are constantly reconfigured and utilized in different ways in response to shifting gender and sexual subjectivities. This behooves planners and policy-makers to develop sensitivity to the changing spatial imperatives of lesbians, queer women and their communities, and to accommodate these mobile lives in planning to ensure the ongoing strength, sustainability and mutual benefit of women's communities.

Notes

1   The definitional issues for gendered and sexualized individuals and their collective representations are becoming increasingly complicated. In this chapter, we use the term lesbian to refer to those individuals who understand themselves to be 'women' and who are interested in intimate relations (including sexual) with other individuals identified as women. The term 'queer' is used here by those subjects who refuse essentialist and fixed notions of gendered, sexualized and embodied subjectivities and identities.

2   There has also been notable work on lesbian place-making in non-metropolitan or rural spaces, discussing lesbian separatist movements, counter-urbanization and rural festivals.

While a review of this work is beyond the urban focus of this chapter, readers might be interested in the following scholarship: Forsyth 1997a, 1997b; Ion 1997; Valentine 1997; Browne 2008, 2009, 2011; Gorman-Murray 2013.

3   See also Costello and Hodge (1999) on visibility and lesbian and gay place-making in Melbourne and Sydney, Australia. In particular, their Melbourne-based case study critically discusses the 'assumed' lesbian territory of Brunswick Street, Fitzroy, in Melbourne's inner north, and deconstructs the visibility of the borders of this so-called lesbian space as well as lesbian bodies and performativity therein.

4   See Forsyth (1997a, 1997b) and Anacker (2011) on differences in property values for male and female same-sex households, and their comment on the lower values properties owned or rented by lesbians and queer women, in the US.

5   Andrew Gorman-Murray has copies of the archival material and interview transcripts; these are the basis of this discussion. Interviews were conducted by Michelle Holden, Leichhardt Municipal Library, October–December 2003, with Christine Rand, Margaret Jones, Teresa Savage, Adelaide and Laura Gregory, and Gail Hewison (co-owner of the Feminist Bookshop).

References

Adler, S. and J. Brenner. 1992. Gender and space: Lesbians and gay men in the city. *International Journal of Urban and Regional Research* 16, 24–34.

Anacker, K. 2011. Queering the suburbs: Analyzing property values in male and female same-sex suburbs in the United States. In P. Doan (ed.) *Queerying Planning: Challenging Heteronormative Assumptions and Reframing Planning Practice*. Farnham, UK: Ashgate.

Bain, A and Nash, C. 2007. The Toronto Women's Bathhouse raid: Querying queer identities in the courtroom. *Antipode*, 39, 1: 17–34.

Bouthillette, A.M. 1997. Queer and gendered housing: A tale of two neighborhoods in Vancouver. In G.B. Ingram, A.M. Bouthillette and Y. Retter (eds.) *Queers in Space: Communities, Public Places, Sites of Resistance*, Seattle, WA: Bay Press.

Brown, G. 2004. Cosmopolitan camouflage: (Post-) gay space in Spitalfields, East London. In J. Binnie, J. Holloway, S. Millington and C. Young (eds.), *Cosmopolitan urbanism*. New York, NY: Routledge.

Browne, K. 2008. Imagining cities: Living the other: Between the gay urban idyll and rural lesbian lives. *The Open Geography Journal* 1, 25–32.

Browne, K. 2009. Womyn's separatist spaces: Rethinking spaces of difference and exclusion. *Transactions of the Institute of British Geographers* 34, 541–556.

Browne, K. 2011. Beyond rural idylls: Imperfect lesbian utopias at Michigan Womyn's Music Festival. *Journal of Rural Studies* 27, 13–23.

Browne, K. and L. Bakshi. 2011. We are here to party? Lesbian, gay, bisexual and trans leisurescapes beyond commercial gay scenes. *Leisure Studies* 30, 179–196.

Carroll, J. and J. Connell. 2000. 'You gotta love this city': The Whitlams and inner Sydney. *Australian Geographer* 31, 141–154.

Castells, M. 1983. *The City and the Grassroots*. Berkeley, CA: University of California Press.

Chenier, E. 2004. Rethinking class in lesbian bar culture: living 'The Gay Life' in Toronto, 1955–1965, *Left History*, 9.2, 85–118. Reprinted in, M. Gleason and A. Perry (eds.) *Rethinking Canada: the promise of women's history* (5th edn.) Toronto, Canada: Oxford University Press.

Collins, A. 2004. Sexual dissidence, enterprise and assimilation: Bedfellows in urban regenderation. *Urban Studies* 41, 1789–1806.

Costello, L. and S. Hodge. 1999. Queer/clear/here: Destabilizing sexualities and space. In E. Stratford (ed.) *Australian Cultural Geographies*. South Melbourne, Australia: Oxford University Press.

Cresswell, T. 2006. *On the Move: Mobility in the Modern Western World*. New York, NY: Routledge.

Cresswell, T. 2010. Towards a politics of mobility. *Environment and Planning D: Society and Space* 28, 17–31.

Doan, P. and H. Higgins. 2011. The demise of queer space? Resurgent gentrification and LGBT neighborhoods. *Journal of Planning Education and Research*, 31, 6–25.

Driver, F. 1985. Power, space, and the body: A critical assessment of Foucault's *Discipline and Punish*. *Environment and Planning D: Society and Space*, 3, 425–446.

Dufty-Jones, R. 2012. Moving home: Theorizing housing within a politics of mobility. *Housing, Theory and Society* 29, 207–222.

Duruz, J. 2005. Eating at the borders: Culinary journeys. *Environment and Planning D: Society and Space* 23, 51–69.

Egerton, J. 1990. Out but not down: Lesbians' experience of housing. *Feminist Review* 36, 75–88.

Elder, G. 2002. Response to 'Queer patriarchies, queer racisms, international'. *Antipode* 34, 988–991.

Fincher, R. and K. Iveson. 2008 *Planning and Diversity in the City: Redistribution, Recognition and Encounter*. Basingstoke, UK: Palgrave MacMillan.

Forsyth, A. 1997a. 'Out' in the Valley. *International Journal of Urban and Regional Research* 21, 38–62.

Forsyth, A. 1997b. NoHo: Upscaling Main Street on the metropolitan edge. *Urban Geography* 18, 622–652.

Foucault, M. 2003. Governmentality. In P. Rabinow and N. Rose (eds.) *The Essential Foucault, Selections from Essential Works of Foucault, 1954–1984*. New York, NY: The New Press.

Gee, M. 2011. Thanks to gentrification my slum is now on the leading edge of cool. *Globe and Mail* (April 25), A16.

Gorman-Murray, A. 2006. Imagining King Street in the lesbian and gay media. M/C *Journal: A Journal of Media and Culture* 9, online at http://journal.media-culture.org.au/0607/04-gorman-murray.php

Gorman-Murray, A. 2013. Documenting lesbian and gay lives in rural Australia, pp. 95–109 in A. Gorman-Murray, B. Pini and L. Bryant (eds.) *Sexuality, Rurality, and Geography*. Lanham, MD: Lexington.

Gorman-Murray, A. and C.J. Nash. In press. Mobile places, relational spaces: conceptualizing change in Sydney's LGBTQ neighborhoods, *Environment and Planning D: Society and Space*.

Gorman-Murray, A. and G. Waitt. 2009. Queer-friendly neighborhoods: Interrogating social cohesion across sexual difference in two Australian neighborhoods. *Environment and Planning A: Society and Space* 41, 2855–2873.

Hannam, K., M. Sheller and J. Urry. 2006. Editorial: Mobilities, immobilities and moorings. *Mobilities* 1, 1–22.

Ion, J. 1997. Degrees of separation: lesbian separatist communities in northern New South Wales, 1974. In J. J. Matthews (ed.) *Sex in Public: Australian Sexual Cultures*. St. Leonards, NSW, Australia: Allen & Unwin.

Jennings, R. 2009. Lesbians in Sydney. *Sydney Journal* 2, 29–38.

Jensen, A. 2011. Mobility, space and place: On the multiplicities of seeing mobility. *Mobilities* 6, 255–271.

Kauffman, V. 2002. *Re-thinking Mobility*. Aldershot, UK: Ashgate.

Kauffman, V., M. M. Bergman and D. Joyce. 2004. Motility: Mobility as capital. *International Journal of Urban and Regional Research* 28, 745–746.

Kinsman, G. 1996. *The Regulation of Desire: Homo and Hetero Sexualities*. Montreal, Canada: Black Rose.

Knopp, L. 1992. Sexuality and the spatial dynamics of capital. *Environment and Planning D: Society and Space* 10, 651–669.

Knopp, L. 1995. Sexuality and urban space: A framework for reference. In D. Bell, and G. Valentine (eds.) *Mapping Desire: Geographies of Sexualities*. London, UK: Routledge.

Knopp, L. 1998. Sexuality and urban space: Gay male identity politics in the United States, the United Kingdom, and Australia. In R. Fincher and J.M. Jacobs (eds.) *Cities of Difference*. New York, NY: The Guilford Press.

Lauria, M. and L. Knopp. 1985. Toward an analysis of the role of gay communities in the urban renaissance. *Urban Geography* 6, 152–160.

Lamont, A. 2008. Lesbians look to reclaim Leichhardt. *Sydney Star Observer*, 1 October, online at www.starobserver.com.au/news/local-news/new-south-wales-news/lesbians-look-to-reclaim-leichhardt/1998

Levine, M. 1979. *Gay Man*. New York, NY: Harper & Row.

Lewis, N. 2013. Ottawa's Le/The Village: The creation of a 'gayborhood' amidst the death of the Village. *Geoforum* 49, 233–242.

Luzia, K. 2008. Day Care as Battleground: Using moral panic to locate the front lines. *Australian Geographer* 39, 315–326.

Luzia, K. 2010. Travelling in your backyard: The unfamiliar places of parenting. *Social and Cultural Geography* 11, 359–375.

Mowlabocus, S. 2010. Introductions: The personal, the political and the perverse, in *Gaydar Culture: Gay Men, Technology and Embodiment in the Digital Age*. Burlington, VT: Ashgate.

McCann, E. and Ward, K. (eds.). 2011. *Mobile Urbanisms: Cities and Policymaking in the Global Age*. Minneapolis, MN: University of Minnesota Press.

Murphy, P. and Watson, S. 1997. *Surface City: Sydney at the Millennium*. Annandale, Australia: Pluto Press.

Nash, C. J. 2011. Trans experiences in lesbian and queer space. *The Canadian Geographer/La Geographe canadien* 55, 192–207.

Nash, C. J. 2013a. Queering neighbourhoods: Politics and practice in Toronto. *ACME: An International E-Journal for Critical Geographies* 12, 193–219.

Nash, C. J. 2013b. The age of the 'post-mo'? Toronto's Gay Village and a new generation. *Geoforum* 49, 243–252.

Nash, C. J. and A. Bain, 2007. 'Reclaiming raunch'? Spatializing queer identities at Toronto women's bathhouse events. *Social and Cultural Geography* 8.1: 47–67.

Nash, C.J. and A. Gorman-Murray. 2014. LGBT neighborhoods and 'new mobilities': towards understanding transformations in sexual and gendered urban landscapes. *International Journal of Urban and Regional Research* 38, 756–772.

Nast, H. 2002. Queer patriarchies, queer racisms, international. *Antipode* 34: 874–909.

Podmore, J. 2001. Lesbians in the crowd: Gender, sexuality and visibility along Montréal's Boul. St-Laurent. *Gender, Place and Culture* 8: 333–355.

Podmore, J. 2006. Gone 'underground'? Lesbian visibility and the consolidation of queer space in Montréal, *Social and Cultural Geography* 7(4): 595–625.

Podmore, J. 2013. Lesbians as village 'queers': The transformation of Montréal's lesbian nightlife in the 1990s. *ACME: An International E-Journal for Critical Geographies* 12, 220–249.

Pride History Group. 2009. *Out and About: Sydney's Lesbian Social Scene 1960s–1980s*. Sydney, Australia: Pride History Group.

Reynolds, R. 2009. Endangered territory, endangered identity: Oxford Street and the dissipation of gay life. *Journal of Australian Studies* 33.1, 79–92.

Rothenberg, T. 1995. 'And she told two friends': Lesbians creating urban social space. In D. Bell and G. Valentine (eds.) *Mapping Desire: Geographies of Sexualities*, London, UK: Routledge.

Ross, B. 1995. *The House that Jill Built: A Lesbian Nation in Formation.* Toronto, Canada: University of Toronto Press.

Ross, B. 1997. Destaining the (tattooed) delinquent body: The practices of moral regulation at Toronto's Street Haven, 1965–1969. *Journal of the History of Sexuality* 7 (4): 561–595.

Ruting, B. 2008. Economic transformations of gay urban spaces: Revisiting Collins' evolution gay district model. *Australian Geographer* 39.3, 259–69.

Sheller, M. and J. Urry. 2006. The new mobilities paradigm. *Environment and Planning A: Space and Society* 38: 207–226.

Southern, M. 2004. (Un)queer patriarchies: Or "What we think when we fuck", *Antipode* 36.2: 183–190.

Taylor, A. 1998. Lesbian space: More than one imagined territory. In R. Ainley (ed.) *New Frontiers of Space, Bodies, and Gender.* London, UK: Routledge.

Thompson, S. 2007. Planning for diverse communities, pp. 199–223 in S. Thompson (ed.) *Planning Australia: An Overview of Urban and Regional Planning.* Port Melbourne, Australia: Cambridge University Press.

Usher, N. and E. Morrison. 2010. The demise of the gay enclave, communication infrastructure theory, and the transformation of gay public space, pp. 271–287 in Pullen, C. and Cooper, M. (eds.) *LGBT Identity and Online New Media.* New York, NY: Routledge.

Uteng, T. P. and T. Cresswell. 2008. *Gendered Mobilities.* Burlington, VT: Ashgate.

Valentine, G. 1993a. (Hetero)sexing space: Lesbians' perceptions and experiences of everyday spaces. *Environment and Planning D: Society and Space* 11: 395–413.

Valentine, G. 1993b. Negotiating and managing multiple sexual identities: Lesbian time-space strategies. *Transactions of the Institute of British Geographers*, NS 18: 237–248.

Valentine, G. 1993c. Desperately seeking Susan: A geography of lesbian friendships. *Area* 25: 109–116.

Valentine, G. 1995. Out and about: Geographies of lesbian landscapes. *International Journal of Urban and Regional Research* 19: 96–112.

Valentine, G. 1997. Making space: Lesbian separatist communities in the United States, pp. 107–117 in P. Cloke and J. Little (Eds.) *Contested Countryside Cultures: Otherness, Marginalization, and Rurality.* London: Routledge.

Visser, G. 2008. The homonormalization of white heterosexual leisure spaces in Bloemfontein, South Africa. *Geoforum* 39, 1344–1358.

Visser, G. 2013. Challenging the gay ghetto in South Africa: Time to move on? *Geoforum* 49, 268–274.

Warner, M. 2000. *The Trouble with Normal: Sex Politics, and the Ethics of Queer Life.* Cambridge, MA: Harvard University Press.

Warner, M. 2002. Publics and counterpublics. *Public Culture* 14, 1: 49–90.

Wotherspoon, G. 1991. *City of the Plain: History of a Gay Sub-culture.* Sydney, Australia: Hale and Iremonger.

Linking Planning and LGBTQ Activist Groups to Ensure Service Delivery

INTRODUCTION TO PART IV

Petra L. Doan

This section raises the critical issue of ensuring basic service delivery to LGBTQ populations that are often neglected by existing heteronormative social service agencies. The chapters in this section of the book highlight the role of LGBTQ activists in ensuring that the needs of their community are recognized and action is taken to resolve the most pressing problems. In the latter half of the 20th century activist groups began working to provide direct services to the LGBTQ population, especially in the area of health and safety, as well as pressure existing public and private service providers to expand the coverage of other services needed by LGBTQ people within the municipal arena. The authors argue that planners who understand the needs of this population and are able to forge strong links with local activists are better equipped to strengthen the LGBTQ community.

In Chapter 12 Gail Dubrow, Larry Knopp, and Michael Brown describe the role of LGBTQ community activists at the height of the AIDS crisis in Seattle. Activists both within and outside government agencies collaborated to provide both education about the disease and medical care to those most severely afflicted. They also draw parallels to the work of activists both inside and outside of government to preserve critical historic areas for the LGBTQ population in Seattle, Washington. In Chapter 13 Kian Goh explores the interaction of LGBTQ activists with FIERCE (Fabulous Independent Educated Radicals for Community Empowerment) in the West Village of New York City with planners and design professionals around the issue of queer youth access to the Christopher Street Pier. Goh also examines the efforts of young queers of color working through the Audre Lorde project to create safe spaces in two diverse neighborhoods in Brooklyn providing support and training to staff, employees, and owners of these spaces. Finally, in Chapter 14 John Paul Catungal examines the work of ethno-specific AIDS service organizations in Toronto, Canada, arguing that municipal politics has adversely affected how they work with ethnic sub-populations.

12

ACT UP VERSUS STRAIGHTEN UP

Public Policy and Queer Community-Based Activism[1]

Gail Dubrow, Larry Knopp and Michael Brown

Planners seeking to understand the process by which LGBTQ concerns become integrated into public policy and practice would do well to examine the relationship between grassroots, community-based organizations and activists strategically positioned in key agencies of the state. While the politics of queer activism classically has been depicted as almost always oppositional, a careful examination of several cases suggests progress in public policy and practice hinges on a more complex relationship between civil society and the state than previously was imagined. Indeed, progress in advancing an LGBTQ agenda on several fronts has hinged on a combination of pioneering services arising in civil society/the voluntary sector and queer professionals whose authority is recognized by the state. While oftentimes the relationships between actors in these two sectors have indeed been oppositional, they have at others been quite cooperative, if not always amicable. Moreover, even when the relationships have been tense or hostile, these have often turned out to be complementary in that they have resulted in outcomes both sets of actors desired.

By reconceptualizing the relationship between civil society and the state in advancing progressive reform, planners will be better prepared to develop strategies for advancing more equitable policies and practices relevant to LGBTQ communities. Toward this end, this chapter examines issues of historic preservation, public health, and anti-discrimination politics to illustrate how tensions, complementarities, and even cooperation between portions of LGBTQ communities, academic researchers, and professionals have advanced the integration of LGBTQ concerns into state policies and practices.

Queer Historic Preservation: Grassroots Activism, Queer Professionals, and State Authority

There was a time not long ago when places significant in the history of LGBTQ communities were not recognized by local, state, or federal historic preservation programs. Official recognition of sites and buildings related to the queer past was regarded as sanctioning homosexuality, which remained a contested issue with respect to public morality, and therefore policy. The few landmarks of queer heritage that made their way onto landmark registers did so for incidental reasons, such as their architectural significance. Like most social movements, the rise of LGBTQ activism was accompanied by a drive to recover a history that had been rendered invisible by the force of homophobia.

Portions of LGBTQ communities organized on a voluntary basis to carry out a variety of grassroots projects intended to document queer heritage, ranging from interviews with activists, archival and museum projects, and efforts to identify the sites and buildings associated with the LGBTQ past. Projects emerged in major cities with an organized movement, including Boston, New York City, Seattle, San Francisco, and Los Angeles – to name a few – that built foundational knowledge about histories yet to be integrated into the agenda of public entities such as archives, museums, cultural resource management programs, or the curriculum of educational institutions. Initiatives included, among other things, maps and walking tours that identified landmarks (e.g., Northwest Lesbian and Gay History Museum Project, 2002, 2004; Brown and Knopp, 2011). The mix of community activists and emerging professionals in these organizations is key to explaining the process by which these findings eventually became integrated into the policies and practices of state entities that previously had neglected the concerns of the LGBTQ community.

Community-based groups blazed the path for queer preservation in an era before public agencies recognized LGBTQ issues as an acceptable element in the state's cultural heritage agenda. They did so by conducting informal surveys of significant properties, raising public awareness of their significance, and serving as advocates for their preservation, public interpretation, and protection. Academic researchers and queer preservation professionals played a critical role in bridging the worlds of grassroots community activism, non-profit advocacy groups, and public agencies charged with responsibility for the protection of the nation's cultural heritage.

Progress on preserving LGBTQ landmarks in 1994 in New York City began when the Preservation and History Committee of the Organization of Lesbian and Gay Architects and Designers (OLGAD) prepared a map of the city's queer landmarks to honor the twenty-fifth anniversary of the Stonewall Rebellion (OLGAD, 1994). Though NYC's Landmarks Preservation Commission has been slow to formally designate places of significance in LGBT history, bridge figures who worked on the OLGAD map and served on the staff of the Landmarks Commission, such as Jay Shockley and Andrew Dolkart, kept up the pressure for change and helped to pave the way for the most significant NYC property, The Stonewall Inn, to gain National Historic Landmark status in 2000 (Dolkart et al., 1999). Widely recognized for his expertise on the preservation of NYC landmarks, in 2008 Dolkart was appointed director of Columbia University's Historic Preservation Program.

In San Francisco, a grassroots coalition known as Friends of 1800 that formed to preserve a historic building which served as a gay cultural and community center soon widened its mission to include a survey of places significant to LGBTQ heritage in the city. A key tactic in successfully soliciting public funding for the survey was establishing the professional expertise of the group and the legitimacy of queer history within the wider preservation agenda. Friends of 1800 produced the first historic context statement on LGBT heritage for any American city (Scott, 2004). Fortunately, two decades of gay political activism in San Francisco paved the way for a survey that brought recognition to sites already settled in the city's public memory, for example Harvey Milk's Castro District Camera Shop, as well as sites of more limited recognition, such as Compton's Cafeteria. Here gay architects, "out" staff at the Western Regional Office of the National Trust for Historic Preservation, and sympathetic voices in municipal government served as a network that advanced a queer preservation agenda. When in 2014 the San Francisco Planning Department ultimately committed to support a citywide historic context document, project directors Shayne Watson and Donna Graves, with combined professional expertise in preservation and LGBT history, in partnership with the GLBT Historical Society, proposed and were funded to carry out the work (San Francisco Planning Department, 2014).

The dynamics of progress on LGBTQ preservation issues, as with some of the other issues addressed in this chapter, point to the complex dynamics of expertise in early initiatives, where community activists often possess informal expertise (in this case about queer history) that gives them an essential role in public planning efforts. However, without sympathetic queer and allied professionals these activists lacked the credentials, technical expertise, and perceived authority needed to work within the procedural requirements of state agencies. As a result, projects such as these often are designed as complex partnerships that incorporate both expert advisors drawn from activist, academic, and professional circles, and extensive processes of community consultation.

Work on community-based projects to preserve LGBT history has often played a synergistic role in the advanced education and emerging professional careers of out preservationists who have become advocates for inclusive policies and practices. Participation in OLGAD's New York City mapping project, for example, seeded Ken Lustbader's Columbia University thesis on preserving gay and lesbian history in Greenwich Village (Lustbader, 1993). Similarly, Shayne Watson's University of Southern California thesis identified sites associated with lesbian history in San Francisco's North Beach neighborhood (Watson, 2009). In Seattle, meanwhile, Angie McCarrel's graduate work in planning at the University of Washington, which was focused on preserving the city's gay and lesbian sites, fed directly into the efforts of the Northwest Lesbian and Gay History Museum Project (NWLGHMP). She and other volunteers produced a sketch-map of sites that provided a foundation for the group's public walking tours of LGBT sites and, later, a glossy fold-out map of Seattle's lesbian and gay historical geography (NWLGHMP, 2004). She led tours of sites of significance to the LGBT community in Pioneer Square, later co-led by Michael Brown and Larry Knopp. Other NWLGHMP projects have focused on archival, oral history, and museum initiatives. In each case, community-based activists, university-based academics, and skilled professional practitioners have built alliances in the interest of making LGBT heritage visible in public places.

As LGBT preservation has advanced from the local to national stage, a similar combination of activist, academic and professional expertise necessarily has informed efforts to identify and interpret LGBT heritage. In May of 2014 the U.S. Department of the Interior announced that the National Park Service would launch a study of places and events associated with LGBT Americans for inclusion in the national parks system. Building on the 2000 approval of the Stonewall Inn as a National Historic Landmark, this project explicitly recognized the need to bring together:

> scholars, preservationists and community members to identify, research, and tell the stories of LGBT associated properties; encouraging national parks, national heritage areas, and other affiliated areas to interpret LGBT stories associated with them; identifying, documenting, and nominating LGBT-associated sites as national historic landmarks; and increasing the number of listings of LGBT-associated properties in the National Register of Historic Places. (U.S. Department of the Interior, 2014)

Two decades of local practice that brought together these overlapping groups to advance a LGBT preservation agenda became the official modus operandi for the first national effort to integrate queer history into federal preservation policy.

Rooted in multiple worlds, with relevant knowledge and legitimacy in each, bridge figures often have brought together the voluntary and state sectors to advance a queer preservation agenda. To the extent that the nation's surveys of historic places and registers of historic landmarks will include LGBTQ properties, progress is largely attributable to what until now has remained a poorly understood set of relationships between the grassroots community activists, queer professionals, academic researchers, and agencies of the state.

Queer Politics and the Politics of Public Health: Grassroots Activism, Institutional Authority, and Local Political Cultures in Vancouver and Seattle

Scholarly examinations of practices, policy, and planning around queer health issues have focused primarily on HIV/AIDS (Brown, 2000), though recent work by Brown (2000), Brown and Knopp (2014), and Batza (2002) has focused on queer health in the pre-HIV/AIDS era as well. This work, while not explicitly designed to make clear the intentional and unintentional synergies that are at the core of our argument here, does so fairly straightforwardly.

First, Brown's work on AIDS activism, radical democracy, and citizenship in Vancouver in the early 1990s (1994, 1997a, 1997b) considers various relevant implications of the blurring of boundaries between civil society and the state. He traces the emergence of a "shadow state" (Wolch, 1989, 1990) aimed at providing education and health services to gay/queer Vancouverites in the 1990s and demonstrates how a conservative provincial government came to surreptitiously rely on and fund this shadow state. In the process, he demonstrates how the actual delivery of health services to queer populations overlapped with both volunteerism and sexual identity politics, and how citizenship was reconfigured through this kind of work.

Brown describes the emergence of this shadow state in detail. While initially a collection of grassroots, community-based organizations that were enmeshed in a politics of gay and/or queer identity and defined self-consciously in opposition to the state, many of these organizations became quasi-professionalized (if not fully so) and worked closely, if often surreptitiously, with various state entities to deliver services and develop policy.

These groups' politics were varied and fluid but could probably be characterized overall as more pragmatic than ideological, though a local ACT UP organization was part of the mix. Indeed, there were deep, personal connections between this shadow state's infrastructure and all of these organizations, including ACT UP. The local ACT UP organization, for example, was first spearheaded by an activist gay lawyer and a former leader of the Vancouver Persons With AIDS Society (Brown, 1997b: 155). Brown quotes a former Executive Director of AIDS Vancouver as saying:

> I think it's important that there be that, sort of, radical-activist element out there to rabble-rouse. I mean, I think it's very important because it makes it easier for us (as a mainstream group) to then develop our programs because people are concerned. People are scared of ACT UP. It's quite ironic. I'm not scared by them. And I really understand why that organization needs to exist. And, I mean, we all know each other. It's not that big a group of people that you don't know each other. (Brown, 1997b: 159)

Similarly, an ACT UP member is quoted as follows:

> We already had groups like AIDS Vancouver [AV] and PWA [Persons with AIDS] Society. At that stage, PWA could not take drastic actions because of their funding. They would feel repercussions. Their aims are to meet the needs of the infected. And that's what they have been doing. I mean they've been working very hard. They can go to the proper agency or department

and request that needs be met, although they can't demand them. ACT UP can demand them. And it's obvious that if PWA isn't going to be listened to, the next stop will be an AIDS activist organization taking that responsibility on. That means that there is a position for ACT UP to take a more radical stand. I mean, most people you talk to individually at AV or PWA will agree that there's a place for us: when, you know, polite glad-handing doesn't work anymore then there is a need to take action. (Brown, 1997b: 159–160)

This kind of story is common in queer urban histories, whether in the context of HIV/AIDS politics, anti-discrimination politics, or representational politics more broadly. Indeed, Brown and Knopp's (2014) work on queer health politics in Seattle follows a similar trajectory. Utilizing a Foucauldian governmentality framework, they emphasize synergies between a relatively enlightened sexually transmitted disease (STD) research establishment at the University of Washington (UW), its collaboration with local public health authorities, and connections to a grassroots community healthcare movement in which many queer folks were involved.

For context, the post-WWII era in Seattle featured the decommissioning of service members from WWII, Korea, and Vietnam. Seattle has a local economy with strong ties to the military (especially the aerospace industry and its spinoffs), the presence of a major U.S. Public Health Service (USPHS) hospital (until the 1980s), a Veteran's administration hospital, and powerful representation in the U.S. congress (particularly the U.S. Senate). Culturally, the period was one of considerable social change nationally and internationally, including, notably, a revolution in sexual mores. Yet relatively little was known at the beginning of this era about sexual health and disease. In the decades following WWII this changed, as the UW became a leading site of research into infectious diseases, much of it funded by the federal government.

One leading international figure in infectious disease research at the University is quoted by Brown and Knopp (2014: 102) as saying that the UW already had the "best infectious disease" program in the country by the time he arrived in the 1970s. He then pioneered the field of sexually transmitted infection (STI) research and forged close relationships with the Seattle-King County Department of Public Health:

This was the era when STDs were seen as sort of a dead end career move because eventually they were all going to get cured anyway, you know, so why go into it? ... there was no teaching of any sort that was really going on for people in the health sciences: nursing, medicine, Public Health, and it was like it, it'd been isolated away from academia, because people didn't want to talk about it... and so the NIH [National Institutes of Health] and CDC [Centers for Disease Control] began to reach out looking for people who would work on this, and I was asked to be a reviewer of a grant proposal to the NIH for a program project that would be a multiple project program in STDs, and it was so clear that nobody knew anything – including the people proposing this.... So pretty soon... we got a training grant from the NIH to train junior faculty and about that time... some senior people in infectious diseases here began moving into more administrative positions, so like the second year I was here as a faculty member I had seven postdocs.... And so we started coming to the health department, and eventually I think they saw the opportunity to have me move to Harborview [the University's large teaching hospital] and to move a satellite clinic [of the health department] to Harborview.... I mean, people were very anxious to get every one of our fellows when they graduated to come and run their clinics in Atlanta or... Chicago or California.... So we had... the biggest training grant here in infectious diseases or for STD that there was in the country. (Brown and Knopp, 2014: 102)

Seattle's long and relatively rich queer history (Atkins, 2003) fed these developments as well. There thus emerged an interesting nexus of local public health officials, the USPHS, and eventually community clinics, including ones organized by and serving queer men and women. These individuals and groups did not always work in perfect harmony, but generally speaking there was much more cooperation than competition among them.

Collaborations between university-based researchers and public health practitioners led to an ethos of less judgment and stigma in treating people with STIs, including queer folks, than had been the case previously or was typical in most other places at the time. This relatively non-judgmental ethos did not, however, extend to the provision of free care at the UW. To the contrary, a gay physician who was instrumental in the founding of a community clinic focused on gay men's needs noted that prior to the closing of the USPHS hospital in the early 1980s "the University of Washington and Harborview refused to [provide in-patient care], they were pretty, pretty nasty... the university, for its own reasons, did not want, was unwilling to take basically free patients." The USPHS thus became what he called "the hero for the community clinic system" (Brown and Knopp, 2014: 105).

Referring to what came to be known as "the gay clinic," this same individual noted that:

a lot of people that came in, some of course were more closeted, were more embarrassed, they had been married... and wouldn't go to the Health Department, because the Health Department was sort of the public entity, and we were private.... I would say that substantial numbers of people who may have acquired an STD having sex with men would not be willing to go to a regular doctor or a Health Department clinic. (Brown and Knopp, 2014: 105–106)

By contrast, another gay physician, who treated patients "off the books" and for free through his private practice, notes that: "[practitioners in] the Public Health division… were properly trained, so that they did not really embarrass people. They made sure that they knew things were confidential so that they could line up the contacts" (Brown and Knopp, 2014: 106).

Evidence of cooperation between UW researchers, portions of the gay community, and the local public health establishment also emerges from recollections of the UW infectious disease specialist mentioned earlier:

> we made some sorties to some of the gay bathhouses where we tried to screen a sample of men… we offered to the people who ran the establishment to screen men free who were interested for STDs. So we set up a little clinic, screening clinic… the people who were doing the… contact tracing began [to be] interested in doing screening and promoting condom use in the bathhouses. (ibid)

> Interestingly, this individual also makes a connection between these developments and the political culture of Seattle more generally: "we are a liberal city, and have been for a long time, and I think we do not run into barriers, and that was a big part of what made things work effectively". (ibid)

Indeed, the nationwide community health movement was particularly vibrant in Seattle and drew on the long history and infrastructure of grassroots, radical activism that existed in the city, including in the area of health care. Group Health Cooperative, one of the first consumer-owned coops providing medical care in the country, was founded by a coalition of relatively radical union members, farmers, and members of other co-ops in 1947. Clinics serving women, African-Americans, and later LGBT folks, meanwhile, emerged across the city and region in the 1970s. Ironically, Ronald Reagan's closure of the USPHS hospital in the early 1980s actually made it easier for community clinics to hire physicians under the National Health Service Corps program: "As time went on, there was a way to hire physicians through the National Health Service Corp. And at one point I was the Regional Director of the city's cadre of docs in the National Service Corps" (ibid).

One founding physician at what became known as "the Seattle Gay Clinic" described the radical ethos of that clinic this way:

> perhaps there was a sense that they were not culturally appropriate, or maybe it was just [that] we were on Capitol Hill, and we were, you know, flaming radicals among other flaming things, and we had the – we had – we had the right way of doing things. (ibid)

Another long-time gay community activist, now a public health official working on HIV/AIDS issues, remembers the clinic this way:

> They had a politics that was openly supportive of gay men and lesbians. You could go there, you saw people who were like yourself… you would be

> treated well there. And you could be honest about who you are there…. It
> was a neighborhood institution… staff from [the clinic] were members of a
> number of other organizations. Almost everybody lived in the neighborhood.
> (ibid)

The Seattle Gay Clinic was not the only way that queer folks addressed their own
health needs. For many closeted people, people who did not identify as gay but had
gay sex, and others, there was still a gap. Their needs for health services were
addressed, in large part, by an informal network of providers who took it upon
themselves to provide care – particularly STI treatment – off the books and/or
outside of clinical settings (e.g., in patients' or providers' homes). This included
some gay physicians, nurses, and others who were themselves closeted (or semi-
closeted), and who negotiated this activity and their own identities very carefully.

One now-retired physician, gay but closeted to most of his straight colleagues
throughout his career, described his practice of treating venereal diseases in gay
people, prostitutes, married men, and others off the books, sometimes in his office,
sometimes in his or these patients' homes:

> Usually, they would arrange so that I could see them – not necessarily in my
> office, sometimes in this – in a home or social situation, and then I would
> have the slides. Because it's a very straightforward, easy thing to treat. (ibid)

This individual took pains to protect those he saw in his practice, too, and often
did not charge for these kinds of services:

> I had to code all of my contacts as to what kind of contact it was, you know,
> whether it was oral or anal or whatever. And when I had other doctors
> covering for me, they very often could not understand the codes until I told
> them why I had these codes…. I had my own charts on them, and I would
> just make a note in my chart that I made a house call. But – and sometimes
> there might be a charge, but many times I didn't make charges. (ibid)

This ethos and practice, which Brown and Knopp (2014) call "guerilla medicine,"
paid dividends for this particular closeted gay doctor in other ways: "There was a
lot of social activity as a result of my practice. People, you know, did nice things
for you. So it, it measured out in the long run" (ibid). Essentially, the network of
reciprocal care and concern he describes formed one foundation of gay community.

So arguably there was a fairly robust complex of health services for queer folks in
Seattle extending back to the 1970s that involved state and non-state actors,
researchers, community activists, and others. Tellingly, throughout this period both
the community health centers and the "guerilla medicine" practices operated with
minimal intervention on the part of local state actors. There was of course a certain
amount of bureaucratic oversight, in the sense of licensure and of non-credentialed
providers being overseen by MDs, but for the most part these entities were self-

policing in terms of "best practices," and "professionalism" was the norm (though this may have been more liberally defined than in other contexts). Moreover, neither the Seattle-King County Public Health department nor the city's political leadership ever chose to pursue closure of bathhouses or sex clubs, in contrast to very well-publicized decisions to do so in places like San Francisco (Shilts, 1987). To the contrary, the Seattle-King County Department of Public Health chose instead to work with bathhouse operators to do on site testing and education.

Thus the emergence of public health establishments at various scales, shadow state apparatuses comprised of and serving predominantly gay/queer populations, and local political cultures that value tensions and synergies between grassroots and institutional action, constitute one illustration of our thesis in this chapter. Another illustration, also drawn from Seattle in the 1970s, has to do with anti-discrimination politics.

Unexpected Complementarities: "Radical" versus "Liberal" Approaches to the Politics of Anti-Discrimination Protection in Seattle

The years 1977 and 1978 were critical in the history of anti-discrimination politics in the U.S. as it pertains to sexual minorities (Marcus, 1992). Several jurisdictions that had recently enacted non-discrimination ordinances covering gay, lesbian, and bisexual people (and some that had not) were targeted by a newly energized, religiously-based, movement that emphasized anti-gay politics. A precursor to Jerry Falwell's "Moral Majority" and James Dobson's "Focus on the Family" was Miami-based Christian singer and former Miss Oklahoma Anita Bryant's "Save Our Children" organization, which embarked on a series of campaigns to repeal such protections, and in some cases to codify explicitly anti-gay policies and practices (such as forbidding gay people to teach in public schools). Save our Children was a national leader in these Christian-populist campaigns and was initially quite effective, with a string of overwhelmingly successful ballot initiatives in Miami, Florida, St. Paul, Minnesota, Wichita, Kansas, and even the supposedly liberal Eugene, Oregon. By the summer of 1978 they had helped fund another initiative campaign to repeal protections in Seattle and supported a statewide initiative to require the firing of gay public school teachers in California.

The public face of the Seattle campaign was provided by two white, male police officers, one a conservative Mormon and the other a member of the John Birch Society. Their campaign was to pass a piece of proposed legislation known as Initiative 13. The initiative not only would have eliminated anti-discrimination protections in employment and housing based on sexual orientation, but also the City of Seattle's Office of Women's Rights, transferring its authority to investigate complaints of discrimination against women to the City's already overburdened Human Rights Department.

Almost immediately queer communities were divided in how to respond. Gary Atkins (2003: 242) describes the split as "downtown gays" versus "hill gays," by which he means a group with close ties to the downtown business community and political establishment as opposed to the more grassroots, movement-based groups with ties to radical politics and Seattle's Capitol Hill neighborhood. Divisions were personal as well as philosophical, and strategic as well as tactical.

Citizens to Retain Fair Employment (CRFE) was the campaign organization associated with the downtown group. It included large numbers of straight businesspeople, politicians, civic and religious leaders as well as "downtown gays." The organization emphasized threats to privacy as its central campaign message, and focused resources on radio and TV ads while also targeting key "swing" precincts in the city (Atkins, 2003: 255). A conscious decision was made not to focus on homosexuality, gay people, and non-discrimination, as CRFE's leaders saw these as hopelessly unpopular in the emotionally and religiously charged environment of the time. "Hill gays," by contrast, took the position that it was precisely *by* emphasizing these issues, and putting a personal face on both homosexuality and Initiative 13, that the string of overwhelming losses in other jurisdictions could be broken. In good radical fashion, hill gays created what were designed to be two non-hierarchical and collectively run organizations with committee structures rather than positional leaders. One was a feminist organization, Women Against Thirteen (WAT), that focused on the potential impact of Initiative 13 on women and women's issues and that respected the separatist ethos of many of the radical faction's women. The other was an organization comprised of both women and men called Seattle Committee Against Thirteen (SCAT). SCAT emphasized putting a human face on homosexuality and anti-gay discrimination, including encouraging gay people to come out as part of a campaign strategy.

SCAT and WAT, while overwhelmingly white organizations, also embraced theories and practices of solidarity against multiple forms of oppression, and made efforts to reach out to communities of color. In so doing they engaged, often collaboratively, in old-fashioned retail politics, including ringing doorbells in minority neighborhoods, coming out, and lobbying friends and family with personal appeals not to jeopardize their homes and jobs (SCAT in fact created "No on Discrimination, No on 13" yard signs and bus ads that read "Someone You Know is Gay. Don't Jeopardize Their Homes and Jobs").

The politics of race were never very far below the surface in the campaign, though it was not clear until relatively late in the campaign in which side's favor this might cut. The pro-Initiative 13 campaign, Save Our Moral Ethics (SOME), counted on socially conservative religious voters, including many non-white ones, to carry Initiative 13 to victory. Their leaders frequently invoked the notion of gays and lesbians not being a "legitimate minority" as part of this strategy. As indicated above, SCAT and WAT had histories of at least some outreach and collaboration with some factions of racial and ethnic minority communities in the city (Atkins, 2003: 247-250). CRFE, meanwhile, featured some key minority community leadership, including the heterosexual African-American bank executive and future mayor Norm Rice, as part of its public face.

It was, however, arguably issues of police power, police authority, and their impacts on minority communities that ultimately led to minority communities helping to defeat Initiative 13. Another initiative, I-15, had also qualified for the ballot in the same election. Initiative 15 was backed by the Seattle Police Guild and would have overturned a City rule restricting the circumstances in which officers could fire their guns. I-15 was strongly opposed by many in Seattle's minority communities, especially the black community, as empowering police to enforce structural racism with lethal force. Then, in mid-August, one of the two police officer-sponsors of I-13, Dennis Falk, fatally shot an unarmed 26-year-old black man who was fleeing the scene of a possible burglary. While a divided inquest panel cleared Falk in September, outrage at the killing, particularly in the African-American community, helped make opposition to I-15 an even hotter issue in Seattle's minority communities. The *Seattle Gay News* (whose ownership and editorial voice were more closely associated with SCAT and WAT than CRFE), as well as SCAT, and WAT themselves, then re-emphasized connections between both initiatives and bigotry, with SCAT producing a set of yard signs that read "No on 13, No on 15."

In the end, Seattle provided the first defeat in the nation of a campaign to repeal a municipal ordinance protecting people from discrimination based on sexual orientation. To the surprise of activists on both sides, the vote was not even close. I-13 lost by 63 to 37%, with its margin of victory coming from a broad coalition of medium-to-high-density, middle-to-upper-middle-class majority white areas, ethnic minority neighborhoods, and certain culturally liberal, high-income enclaves in the city. Only in traditionally conservative, low-density, predominantly white family-oriented neighborhoods relatively distant from the urban core was I-13 successful. I-15, meanwhile, was narrowly approved by City voters. Its margin of victory came from a cross-class coalition of majority white constituencies, many of which simultaneously voted against I-13. Thus the coalitional strategy of SCAT and WAT was successful as it pertains to I-13 but not I-15 (though in fairness, as their names suggest, SCAT and WAT were always organizations whose missions were first and foremost to defeat I-13).

Despite their failure to deliver enough white votes to defeat I-15, SCAT and WAT clearly mobilized blocs of citizens motivated by the issue of discrimination and social justice to vote against I-13. CRFE, meanwhile, made such a vote "respectable" by invoking the authority of a wide range of Seattle's civic leadership and by framing the issue as one of privacy, not a referendum on homosexuality or gay rights. Gary Atkins (2003: 255) characterizes the constructive tensions between the two anti-I-13 factions thusly:

> Suddenly the division in political strategy and organizing began to seem constructive. There could be – indeed, had to be – more than one political dance floor in town. CRFE could organize particular types of people with its appeals. It could raise thousands of dollars at low-key dinner parties. It could avoid using "gay" or "homosexual" in its ads. SCAT and WAT, on

the other hand, could hold highly public fund-raising events designed to raise the gay profile – a Halloween dance at the Seattle Aquarium, beer parties at taverns, roller-skating evenings. The money cleared might be minimal, but the excitement generated among potential volunteers was electric. Those volunteers then canvassed neighborhoods all over Seattle.

Conclusion: Moving Beyond "Act Up" versus "Straighten Up"

These examples indicate different ways in which LGBTQ activism based in civil society can and has interacted with more state-based entities to shape public policy that is sensitive to the needs of sexual minority populations, not just for effective services but for recognition. Sometimes this interaction is shrewdly cooperative and conciliatory, taking advantage of the professional authority of queer professionals "inside" the state bureaucracy (as in the historic preservation examples). In others it can represent more strategic and/or temporary coalitions of interests that otherwise represent vastly different cultures, agendas, and world-views. The Seattle Gay Clinic and related grassroots health care initiatives in Seattle, for example, grew out of a movement that was deeply distrustful of traditional public health programs and systems yet cooperated, more opportunistically than collegially, with key actors within those systems (some gay, some not). In the case of the ideologically fractured response to a threat to Seattle's gay rights ordinance in 1978, traditionally radical/oppositional and more liberal/accommodationist activists collaborated not at all – in fact deeply opposed each other's framings of and approaches to the campaign – yet their strategies ended up complementing each other rather than working at cross-purposes to beat back discrimination.

What lessons do these stories suggest for planners dedicated to advancing equity and social justice for LGBTQ communities? Providing public support to grassroots community organizations, and not just those that include skilled professionals with perceived authority, is important for advancing a queer planning agenda and bridging the gap between voluntary and state action. Similarly, there should be a recognition that tensions, distrust, and even occasional hostility among groups with shared interests but divergent strategies is to be expected and not feared. While navigating these tensions and conflicts may be uncomfortable and at times disheartening, the results need not always be negative. Indeed, they may turn out to be positive despite appearances to the contrary. Cultivating and strategically situating individuals with access to resources, to key non-queer players, and with perceived authority is clearly important. But so too is recognizing that "authority" cuts in multiple ways, with the grassroots' authority of experience constituting an asset potentially as important as professional expertise. That said, it is important to recognize that queer students and faculty in higher education and their allies, who are committed to redressing issues marginalized by a legacy of discrimination, play a critical role in subsidizing work that in a more just world would be considered part of the state's mandate. Such work need not entail "selling out" just because it is situated within the institutional bureaucracy of higher education or a broader political economy structured by hierarchy and inequality. Before our nation's cultural institutions took up the challenge of incorporating African-American history, women's history, and other marginalized pasts into museum exhibitions, archival collections, cultural resource management programs, and the like, the foundational work was carried out by a similar mix of grassroots activists and dedicated professionals operating in the interstitial space between community venues and the institutions where they held influence. A close examination of the dynamics of cultural change across all of these movements suggests that progressive planners might be well advised to advocate for directing public support for applied research and action projects to these sorts of groups as a vital mechanism for redressing injustice and preparing well-informed advocates to address LGBTQ issues, whether in the area of preservation or other neglected aspects of public culture, health, or policy.

Until genuinely affirmative policies and practices are fully implemented by the state, diverse forms of community activism, the space of (relatively) free inquiry in higher education, and publishing will remain key forces in growing a knowledge economy, and preparing dedicated professionals to address LGBTQ issues. Ultimately these professionals' capacity to bridge the worlds of academic research, community activism and state-sanctioned policies and practices will be critical in advancing equity and in making progress toward embedding queer concerns into the essential functions of the state. At the same time, there can be no doubt that various forms of protest and oppositional politics by social activists will continue to put pressure on the state to address a wide array of controversial issues. Our evidence here suggests that relationships among and between state-based and community-based activists that range from cooperative to opportunistic and even to oppositional – so long as there remain some common short-term goals or objectives – may play a more significant role in progressive social change than has been recognized in past accounts.

Note

1   Portions of this chapter are reprinted from *Health & Place*, Vol. 28, Michael Brown, Larry Knopp, "The Birth of the (Gay) Clinic," Pages 99–108, Copyright 2014, with permission from Elsevier.

References

Atkins, Gary L. (2003), *Gay Seattle: Stories of Exile and Belonging*. Seattle, WA: University of Washington Press.

Batza, Catherine (2002), *Before AIDS: Gay and Lesbian Community Health Activism in the 1970s*. PhD dissertation, Department of History, University of Illinois Chicago.

Brown, Michael (1994), "The Work of City Politics: Citizenship through Employment in the Local Response to AIDS," *Environment and Planning A* 26: 873–894.

Brown, Michael (1997a), *RePlacing Citizenship: AIDS Activism and Radical Democracy*. New York, NY: Guilford.

Brown, Michael (1997b), "Radical politics out of place: the curious case of ACT UP Vancouver, in S. Pile & M. Keith (eds). *Geographies of Resistance*, London: Routledge, pp. 152–167.

Brown, Michael (2000), *Closet Space: Geographies of Metaphor from the Body to the Globe*. London, UK & New York, NY: Routledge.

Brown, Michael and Larry Knopp (2011), "Queering the Map: The Productive Tensions of Colliding Epistemologies." In M. Dodge, R. Kitchin and C. Perkins (eds.), *The Map Reader: Theories of Mapping Practice and Cartographic Representation*, pp. 456–453. Oxford, UK: Wiley-Blackwell. (Edited and reprinted from *Annals of the Association of American Geographers* 98, 2008.)

Brown, Michael and Larry Knopp, 2014, "The Birth of the (Gay) Clinic," *Health & Place* 28: 99–108.

Dolkart, Andrew, David Carter, Andrew Scott, and Jay Shockley, 1999, "National Historic Landmark Nomination: Stonewall Inn." National Park Service.

Lustbader, Kenneth (1993), "Landscapes of Liberation: Preserving Gay and Lesbian History in Greenwich Village." Columbia University, Master's Thesis, Historic Preservation.

Marcus, Eric (1992), *Making History: The Struggle for Gay and Lesbian Equal Rights, 1945–1990: An Oral History*. New York: HarperCollins.

Northwest Lesbian and Gay History Museum Project (NWLGHMP) (2002), "Map of Historic Gay Seattle." Unpublished.

Northwest Lesbian and Gay History Museum Project (NWLGHMP) (2004), "Claiming Space: Seattle's Lesbian & Gay Historical Geography." Collaborative product consisting of glossy fold-out map with annotations and illustrations. Seattle, WA: Northwest Lesbian and Gay History Museum Project.

OLGAD (1994), "New York Lesbian and Gay Landmarks." Online at www.gvshp.org/LGBTguide.htm

San Francisco Planning Department (2014), "LGBT Historic Context Statement." Online at www.sf-planning.org/index.aspx?page=3673

Scott, Damon for Friends of 1800 (2004), "Sexing the City: The Development of Sexual Identity-Based Subcultures in San Francisco, 1933-1979." Online at www.friendsof1800.org/context_statement.pdf

Shilts, Randy, 1987, *And the Band Played On: Politics, People, and the AIDS Epidemic*. New York, NY: St. Martin's Press.

U.S. Department of the Interior, National Park Service (2014), "Lesbian, Bisexual, Gay and Transgender Heritage Initiative." Online at www.nps.gov/heritageinitiatives/LGBThistory

Watson, Shayne (2009), "Preserving the Tangible Remains of San Francisco's Lesbian Community in North Beach, 1933 to 1960." University of Southern California. Master's Thesis, Historic Preservation.

Wolch, Jennifer (1989), "The Shadow State: Transformations in the Voluntary Sector." In Jennifer Wolch and Michael Dear (eds.), *The Power of Geography: How Territory Shapes Social Life*. London, UK and Boston, MA: Unwin Hyman.

Wolch, Jennifer, (1990), *The Shadow State: Government and Voluntary Sector in Transition*, New York, NY: The Foundation Center.

13

PLACE/OUT

Planning for Radical Queer Activism

Kian Goh

With gay, lesbian, and even transgender visibility at a high point, and gay marriage gathering steam state by state, it might appear that the LGBT movement is riding a particularly long and resounding wave. In cities across the United States, gay enclaves like Chelsea, the West Village, the Castro, South End, and Dupont Circle are so "successful" that they threaten their own undoing, as these historic icons of the gay liberation movement have been increasingly subsumed by urban development. Some people might argue that the main struggles for LGBT-identified urbanites include fighting to protect the identity of their "gayborhood," and petitioning for their state to pass gay marriage, if it has not already. These issues are certainly important to LGBT people who find community and a sense of place in these enclaves, and those who subscribe to the institution of marriage. But other observers might counter that these concerns surely pale against the long-standing histories of oppression, shame, hate, violence, and invisibility that have dogged those with marginalized sexualities and gender identities.

Unfortunately, violence against LGBT people continues to be an alarming reality, with the recurring murders of transgender women of color particularly disturbing (NCAVP 2010). Homeless LGBT-identified youth are strikingly over-represented, estimated at 20% to 40%, within the broader homeless youth population (Durso & Gates 2012; Quintana et al. 2010; Ray 2006). In addition, socioeconomic disparities, including poverty, are reinforced in LGBT communities, particularly among women, people of color, the young and the old, and transgender people (Badgett et al. 2013; Sears & Badgett 2012). These facts and findings indicate that, while homosexuality is increasingly visible and accepted, overlapping identities and systems of oppression exacerbate the marginalization of LGBT-identified people. These "unjust geographies"[1] and ongoing queer[2] struggles play out distinctly in urban centers, themselves long-time hotspots of both gay agglomeration (Aldrich 2004; see also Bell & Binnie 2000) and class, racial, and gender oppressions (Warner 1972). They continue even in places that appear to epitomize the gay mecca, often shifting and accentuating the geography of marginalization across and within the LGBT spectrum. However, in urban places far from established gay centers, these queer struggles encounter a complex terrain of power, space, and identity.

Planning for LGBT Communities

Scholarship on planning for LGBT communities has focused on the assertion of LGBT issues within the field of planning – "queerying" planning, as it were (Doan 2011; Forsyth 2011). Whether focusing on development pressures, gentrification, preservation, municipal codes, or zoning, this research emphasizes the necessity and relevance of analysis through a LGBT-informed lens or framework. This "queering" of planning chips away, variously, at the dominant constructs of the institution, what Frisch (2002) called the "heterosexist project" of planning. A key debate that has emerged is centered on space, identity, and power – whether LGBT communities in cities contribute to neighborhood revitalization (and how), or whether they are complicit in market forces, contributing to gentrification. Scholarship around this issue builds on a number of influential texts, including Castells' (1983) study of gay men's collective political power in San Francisco, as well as Knopp's (1990, 347) elaboration of gay influence in land markets as an "alternative strategy of accumulation."

Indeed, planning's "structures of heterosexual domination" (Frisch 2002, 256) have meant that the formidable task of queering planning has often forced gay men and lesbians into a single category that also includes other sexual minorities. Key research like Adler and Brenner's (1992) on lesbian spatial concentration, a direct response to Castells' work, provides a welcome reframing of the inquiry from gender and sexual identity *per se* to patriarchal power structures. Nevertheless, such attempts to shift focus to lesbians and space has, in some ways, only reinforced the static nature of much planning research – ignoring the fluidity of gender and sexual identities within queer communities, as well as the often fraught politics of this fluidity[3]. Unfortunately, while often acknowledging the socioeconomic and cultural heterogeneity within the LGBT community, much planning scholarship has not been framed around inquiries into the complex spatial histories of identities and struggles within this community.[4]

The question of how heterosexist and heteronormative assumptions shape planning practice still matters, of course. Planning as a heterosexist institution remains. But should we also be asking how specific *homonormative* assumptions shape our inquiries now?[5] Planning studies, specifically, have to date rarely investigated the uneven distribution of queer marginalization in urban space, or the intersectionality between homophobia and other structures of oppression, including classism and racism.[6] This is important because such structural oppressions are often amplified within the LGBT population, and these oppressions are further sharpened in the context of the liberalizing of urban governance and urban development (Brenner & Theodore 2002; Brenner 2004; Jessop 2002).

Furthermore, there remains a lack of planning scholarship that links fine-grained, close-to-the-ground empirical research on the spatial, physical design of the urban built environment with the marginalization of LGBT communities (in the way that it has for racism, for example). Considering the ways that reclaiming and reformatting space on multiple scales have been and continue to be important parts of queer struggles, much more could be done in this regard (Betsky 1997; Goh 2011a, 2011b). The work in this chapter attempts to engage this issue by focusing, on one hand, on the intersection of gender, sexuality, and race through a critical spatial lens, and, on the other, the normative imperatives of planning theory and practice. How might planners engaged with LGBT-framed or oriented research work with and for communities at the intersection of marginalities or systems of oppression – particularly considering the institutional contexts in which many planners reside, and from which they practice? Can and should we expect planners to investigate and analyze beyond one framework of oppression, towards a broader and more radically inclusive view of planning? Finally, if this is a social *and* spatial problem, how might we conceptualize transformative sociospatial change?

Queer Space(s)

Interrogative studies on sexuality and space have been propelled by theoretical and empirical work at the intersection of critical geography and queer theory.[7] Stepping outside of debates on gay gentrification and displacement, Binnie and Skeggs (2004) probe the intersection of class and sexuality, uncovering the "essentializing of gayness" (51) and working class exclusion in the production, branding, and consumption of cosmopolitan "gay villages." G. Brown (2007) details the characteristics of what he calls "queer autonomous spaces" – places and actions that are as much opposed to homonormativity as they are to heteronormativity. This particular mode of radical queer activism conceives of queerness as a relational process in what is largely an anti-capitalist movement. Queer spaces open up a kind of "commons," or "counterpublic" space (2696). G. Brown (2006) as well notes the complexity and contradictions of spaces in the city where immigrants, people of color, and non-straight people coincide and interact, revealing and complicating the production of class and ethnicity within fluid queer spaces. Alongside and aligned, Knopp (2007, 27) associates queer geographies with a "radical sexual politics" that expands empirical terrain to embrace "messy realities, including fluidity, hybridity, incompleteness, moralities, desire and embodiment." These queer geographies help make the case that struggles of sexuality and gender identity are inextricably intertwined within multiple layers of structural oppressions that operate socially and spatially.

Radical Planning

Proponents of radical planning[8] acknowledge the institutional constraints of professional planning practices, broader sociopolitical and economic structures, as well as the situation of the planner within this context. While the specific recommendations often diverge, these scholars generally call for a broadening of the scope of planning beyond its technocratic, scientific basis, and for a more critical engagement with sociopolitical factors. Friedmann (1987; 1993) lays the groundwork for radical planning in a "transformative theory" that focuses on unearthing and overcoming structural oppressions in capitalist society. Planning, he asserts, should be explicitly normative and political. Radical planners propose to break the bureaucratic rules of planning, engage with the emotional terrain of on-the-ground contestations, and mobilize communities towards transformative social ends. Sandercock (2004), for example, appeals for planners to be "audacious," "creative," and "therapeutic" in practice. Yiftachel (2006) calls for a renewed attention to the conflictual contexts of contemporary societies, particularly focusing on sociocultural concepts such as ethnicity and homeland. In their "love songs to mongrel cities" (Sandercock 2006) and appeals to "insurgent citizenship" (Holston 1999), several scholars urge radical planners to deliberately and distinctly embrace the struggles of marginalized individuals and communities, and plan towards social change.

To tune a framework of queer geographies and radical planning to the complex, intersectional nature of queer struggles in urban space today would be to bear witness to power relationships that are often contradictory, multishaded, and situated within multiple modes of social and spatial oppression.

Radical/Queer

For this research I look at the organizing work of two New York City-based radical queer activist groups. In particular, I investigate the objectives and challenges of working to create access, cohesive communities, and safe spaces in urban neighborhoods both within and far beyond acknowledged and familiar "gay centers." My research focuses on two specific initiatives: 1) FIERCE's (Fabulous Independent Educated Radicals for Community Empowerment) campaign for safe spaces for youth in the West Village, and 2) the Audre Lorde Project's safe neighborhood campaign in the Bedford-Stuyvesant neighborhood of Brooklyn (see Figure 13.1).

Although I have worked directly with both these organizations,[9] the focus of this research is exploring the ways that these two groups have collaborated with other community groups to create progressive change in the very different locations in which they work. Both groups are allied organizations with frequent collaborations. They are both primarily community organizing groups, working for transformative social and political change – as opposed to community service providers. Furthermore, their work provides insights into the ways that similar spatial and sociopolitical objectives can be accomplished within two very different neighborhoods in the city. Most importantly, they are part of a network of progressive LGBT organizations in New York City[10] and nationally who have taken critical, and radical, positions on LGBT issues in reference to the mainstream

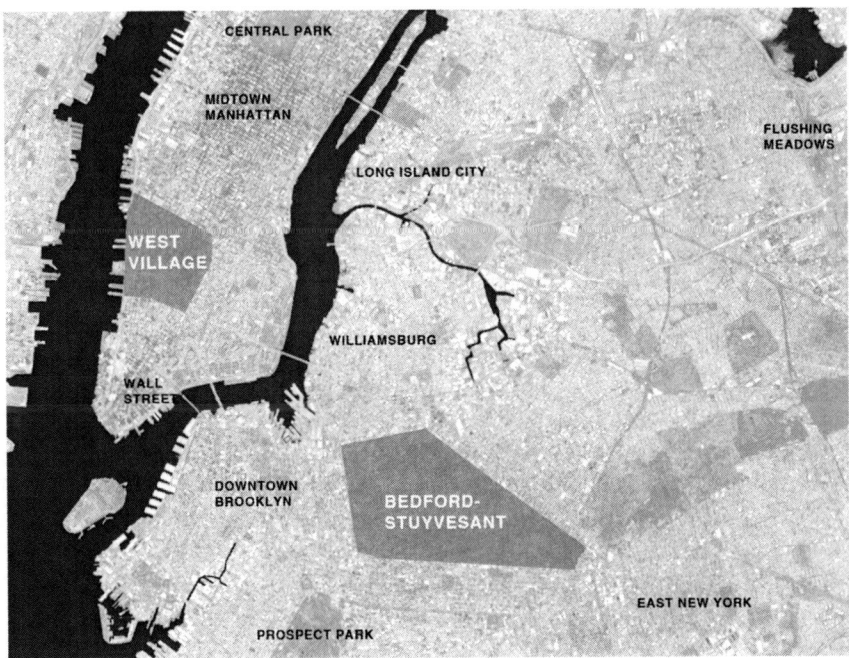

FIGURE 13.1   Map of West Village and Bedford-Stuyvesant in New York City

LGBT movement. I propose that the specificity of this political analysis, and the clarity of its difference from mainstream conceptualization, provides an avenue to research queer urban space beyond the strictures of both heteronormativity and homonormativity that tend to propel much LGBT planning research.[11] Key points of this critical analysis are worth pointing out:

- These groups have taken a stand against the broader movement's prioritizing of gay marriage, arguing that such single focus misallocates resources and attention towards an inherently conservative institution that leaves much of the LGBT community out.[12]
- They also question the focus on gays in the military, the other key mainstream LGBT issue, arguing that this kind of inclusion cannot be separated from the larger issue of U.S. military imperialism. Instead, this coalition of groups embraces a broader framework of social and economic justice.
- One noteworthy platform is their shared stance against hate crimes legislation. They assert that expanding the massive and unequally punitive criminal justice system further harms already marginalized people, particularly communities of color.[13] Instead, they promote an alternative framework of community accountability and "transformative justice" (Mogul et al. 2011; Whitlock 2012).

The issues at the forefront of their work – for safety, access, affordability, and shelter – are prominently issues of urban space and planning. Through an analysis of the motivations, political analyses, and spatial implications of such activist work, I hope to delineate the ways that urban designers and planners can understand and work with queer-identified community organizers on the ground who are fighting for social change, particularly outside of and in spite of dominant and institutional economic and sociopolitical structures. How might we conceive of a radical planning for radical queer activism?

FIERCE and the West Village: The Queer-Exclusionary Gayborhood

The West Village in New York City is often held up as the epicenter of the LGBT rights movement in the United States. During the Stonewall Rebellion, in June 1969, queers fought back *en masse* after yet another police raid on a bar. The Christopher Street Liberation Day, the precursor to the annual Pride Parade, took place a year later in 1970. It was named after the street that cuts through the Village, in front of the Stonewall Inn and leading to the Hudson River at Manhattan's western edge. Predating the removal of the elevated West Side Highway in the late 1970s and early 80s, LGBT and queer youth living on the margins found a home and a manner of belonging among the increasingly dilapidated piers at the end of Christopher Street, memorialized in Jennie Livingston's 1990 documentary *Paris Is Burning*.

A massive waterfront redevelopment project began in 1998 under the landmark Hudson River Park Act (New York State Legislature 1998).[14] The revamped (and newly christened) Hudson River Park now showcases rejuvenated piers and jogging and biking paths, watched over by gleaming condos and offices by architects such as Richard Meier, Frank Gehry, and Jean Nouvel (see Figure 13.2). The following years saw increased policing in the area, initiatives that had begun with the Giuliani Administration's "quality of life" policies in the mid-1990s. Queer youth – largely youth of color, many homeless – were confronted in the streets and commercial establishments in the area not only by NYPD officers, but also by resident street patrols (Mananzala 2011). "Gay youth gone wild," proclaimed the headline of an opinion piece in the local newspaper *The Villager* in 2005, written by members of a resident street patrol and a merchants association (Poster & Goldman, 2005).

FIERCE,[15] a community organizing group led by and for LGBTQ youth, largely youth of color, has been working for more than a decade to keep the West Village and Christopher Street Pier area in Manhattan safe and accessible for queer youth.[16] In 2000, the year of its founding, it produced *Fenced Out*, a documentary film detailing the gentrification in the Village, the imminent closure of the Christopher Street Pier and the redevelopment of both pier and the adjacent waterfront, the subsequent increased policing of the area, and their fight to keep access to safe spaces for youth. In *Fenced Out*, personal accounts from youth who

FIGURE 13.2   Christopher Street Pier, 2011

rely on the piers as a space of community are juxtaposed against the misaligned priorities of the city – $330M for park redevelopment versus an almost total lack of support, including shelters and services, for homeless LGBT youth. FIERCE has been successful in holding to a radical and transformative political analysis (Goh 2011a), even while working with those in more traditional institutional structures. They developed and maintained tenuous but working relationships with administrators in the Hudson River Park Trust (HRPT), the organization charged with operating the Hudson River Park, and with Community Board 2, which represents the West Village. With their youth constituents, FIERCE promotes peaceful shows of community strength at community board meetings, and constant dialogue with the neighborhoods.[17]

John Blasco, currently lead organizer of FIERCE, recalls his early days as a member of the organization, learning "what the mainstream LGBT community doesn't tell you about our community" (Interview with the author, January 2014). Blasco's association with the organization exemplifies the model of community and leadership building that FIERCE promotes. He was brought in as a youth member – as a constituent and a key part of the community – and was supported and encouraged into roles of increasing responsibility, finally emerging in a leadership position. In this way FIERCE is able to establish a meaningful and durable presence in the lives of their constituents, and succeed in developing effective long-term relationships with allies and neighborhood institutions.

Blasco describes, in 2003, West Village residents "not even wanting to look at LGBTQ youth if they walked into those [community board] meetings." Now, in 2014, the chairpersons of Community Board 2 specifically reach out to FIERCE to talk about issues affecting LGBT youth. He stresses that many members now recognize the importance of understanding the impact on youth, and that they rely on their relationship with FIERCE organizers to help educate other residents on the issues. "It was important for us to be there," Blasco says of the earlier days of relationship building, work that later resulted in various victories: later curfew hours along the park, Porta-Potties, summer programs, and the now annual Mini-Ball. "Because of the way FIERCE has done the work, this has become a reality now.... It's not enough, but it's a lot."

FIERCE initiated the Our S.P.O.T. campaign in 2007. Building on their previous work to maintain and promote safe spaces for youth on the pier and along the park, the campaign's objective was to create a 24-hour drop-in center for queer youth (2008). Organizers targeted the planned redevelopment of nearby Pier 40 as a site for the youth center. Pier 40, previously a terminal for the Holland America cruise line, was in the early 2000s (and still is) a neglected space used for recreation and parking, badly in need of repairs. Responding to proposals that called for large-scale private development (including, in one eye-opening instance, a theater for Cirque du Soleil), FIERCE decided to back a plan that prioritized community uses at the pier. Tensions were high around what was inevitably a contested site. At a memorable meeting, HRPT board member (and former NYC Parks commissioner) Henry Stern called suggestions for the city or state to help fund repairs to the pier "socialist" (Rogers 2007).

In early 2008, with the earlier redevelopment proposals stalled, FIERCE kicked up the intensity of the initiative with characteristic twin-prong organizing: a protest rally at Pier 40, with placards decrying large-scale privatized development, and a written and illustrated proposal for the youth center directed at the HRPT, complete with urban and architectural design concepts, and zoning and funding analyses. The proposal (aided by a community needs assessment survey of almost 300 LGBT youth) emphasized maintaining public space on the pier, encouraging physical activity and opportunities for emotional outlets, space for personal and professional development, and space for access to healthcare. FIERCE emphasized that directly and boldly addressing the needs of LGBT youth would simply be part of ensuring a "healthy and vibrant West Village community," and that such a project was entirely in line with the Hudson River Park's own mission to be inclusive and available for all New Yorkers (FIERCE 2008).

Among community-led organizations, particularly those whose constituents are largely marginalized and disempowered in mainstream cultural and political spaces, FIERCE has shown itself to be extremely capable in harnessing the power of collaboration, including with members of the design and planning fields. An example of this is the way FIERCE developed the Our S.P.O.T. campaign for a proposed youth center. I worked with FIERCE as a supporter and pro-bono architect, helping with the campaign conceptualization and producing urban and architectural designs (see Figure 13.3). In addition to my own collaboration with them, the organization has worked with the Center for Urban Pedagogy (CUP) and the Hester Street Collaborative, both highly admired community design and education organizations in the city.

In November 2013, the Hudson River Park Act was amended (New York State Legislature 2013). Controversially, the amended act allows the sale of air

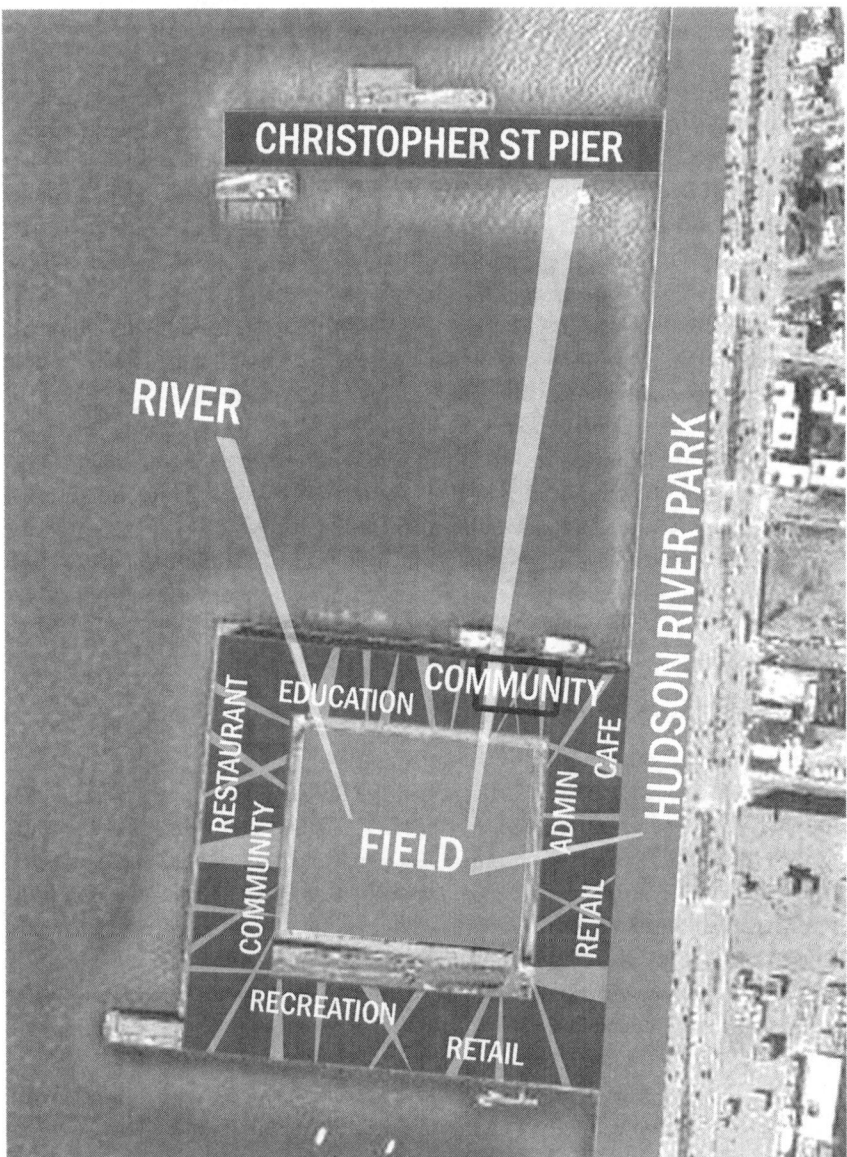

FIGURE 13.3 Site plan of FIERCE's Pier 40 proposal, with youth drop-in center indicated at north–east corner of Pier 40

rights above its piers, including Pier 40, for development – not just adjacent to the pier, but one block east of the park, likely setting up a precedent where the transfer of air rights "jumps" a street. With this new legislation, the Hudson River Park follows the example of "elite parks" like the High Line and Brooklyn Bridge Park to find "innovative" means of financing, usually involving a manner of privatizing so-called public amenities or selling development rights. Later that year in December, FIERCE called an end to the Our S.P.O.T. campaign. It cited a shift to a broader vision, asserting that a drop-in center in the neighborhood could not be realized without ensuring that the West Village remained a safe and accessible space for community members.[18] Instead, FIERCE would shift their organizing to focus on police harassment and discrimination of queer youth. This move followed organizing victories of a broader coalition of groups against the NYPD's stop-and-frisk policies.

In many ways, the ending of the campaign for a physical presence in the neighborhood is a strong indication of the challenges that continue to confront truly transformative organizing agendas. Even having built up a significant institutional presence and support in the West Village, real estate development pressures combined with ongoing on-the-ground distrust and fear of queer youth rendered it impossible to stake out a physical, permanent space. FIERCE's work in the last decade and the new direction offers two sides to the importance of place. The organization maintains its strong historical and emotional connection to the West Village and Christopher Street Pier, and continues to savor and build on its victories (2013 saw the sixth iteration of the annual Mini-Ball on Pier 46). But FIERCE now looks beyond, broader and somewhat more diffused, in shifting focus to the objective of city and nationwide change in the key issue of policing.

Safe OUTside the System in Bed-Stuy: Striving for Community-Based Anti-Violence

Formed in 1994, the Audre Lorde Project (ALP)[19] is a New York City-based community organizing center for lesbian, gay, bisexual, two-spirit, transgender, and gender nonconforming people of color.[20] Named after the black, feminist, lesbian poet Audre Lorde, ALP's organizing work focuses on social and economic justice, in particular access to services and safety for its most marginalized community members. ALP's current work includes a long-running campaign to pressure the New York City Human Resources Administration (HRA) to change its practices of discrimination and harassment against transgender and gender nonconforming welfare recipients, and an initiative, called 3rd Space, to build a community support network outside of institutional systems.

The S.O.S. (Safe OUTside the System) Collective, started as a working group within ALP, initiated the Safe Neighborhood Campaign in Bedford-Stuyvesant in 2007. Bed-Stuy (as it is nicknamed), lying east of downtown Brooklyn, has historically been a working and middle class black residential neighborhood, more recently experiencing its share of post-2008 Financial Crisis housing struggles and foreclosures (Botein 2013). Cemented in popular imagination by Spike Lee films like *Do the Right Thing*, it now exemplifies the urban issues of the outer boroughs of the late-Bloomberg mayoral term, in particular the tension between lower-income communities of color and rapid gentrification.[21] Bed-Stuy, home to many ALP constituents, has also witnessed both violence against LGBT people, and violence at the hands of police officers.[22]

Working from the premise that young LGBT people of color, especially young black men, are often targeted not just by anti-LGBT violence, but by police violence and an unjust criminal justice system, the S.O.S. Collective attempts to create community accountability without relying on law enforcement. For this campaign, activists challenged neighborhood institutions, including commercial establishments, schools, churches, and other businesses and community centers, to create "safe spaces" – visibly identifiable places that serve as refuges from physical violence and anti-LGBT hate speech. This was new territory. Activist Ejeris Dixon, previously program coordinator of the S.O.S. Collective of ALP and currently deputy director at the Anti-Violence Project, stated that there were not many examples to use as a model. Many of the existing community accountability frameworks that did not involve the criminal justice system, concerned domestic violence and, generally, incidents between people who knew each other (Ejeris Dixon interview, January 2014).

The collective embarked on a three-phase plan. The first phase involved building relationships and garnering agreements from "friendly" institutions, as well as providing support and training to staff, employees, and owners of these initial safe spaces. The second phase would then expand the initiative to include all (or many more) institutions in the neighborhood (ideally encouraged by the initial set of institutions), with the ideal objective of eventually saturating the neighborhood with these safe spaces. The third and final phase would involve "restoring the harm," or in other words not simply addressing the violence, but making things better – something Dixon admits was difficult to conceptualize.

Explaining S.O.S.'s strategy, Dixon indicated that, in a more "traditional" systemic policy-based organizing campaign there would be a clear target to focus on. In this case, the target would have been the New York City police department. But ALP organizers had determined, in early discussions, not to proceed along that route. The target, therefore, became "violence as it runs through the neighborhood," stated Dixon, such that every new safe space would constitute a win for the campaign (Interview, January 2014). Designated safe spaces would be tagged with an S.O.S. Collective sticker, and their location made known through community meetings and written materials including brochures and the organization's web presence.

By 2011, the collective had a network of ten such "safe spaces" throughout Bed-Stuy, including local retail establishments and community spaces (see Figure 13.4). The subsequent years have made clear the difficulties of maintaining such safe spaces, particularly in neighborhoods facing rapid socioeconomic transition. The initiative "lost a lot of safe spaces due to gentrification," says Dixon (Interview,

January 2014). In 2010, the community rallied, unsuccessfully, to save one of the spaces, the much-loved Starlite Lounge in adjacent Crown Heights, a victim of raised rents. Other spaces like coffee shops and restaurants fall victim to the whims of Brooklyn tastes. While the combination of commercial establishments and community centers ensures that safe spaces are available throughout the hours of the day and evening, questions remain about the density and location of safe spaces. How do you count on safe spaces to be where you need them to be, when you need them?

Dixon acknowledged the difficulties that a rapidly changing neighborhood poses for creating and maintaining such a network, particularly for a relatively small, volunteer-led initiative. Besides the pressures of gentrification, S.O.S. organizers were forced to deal with numerous other challenges. One was the hierarchical nature of decision-making. Smaller institutions and establishments were easier to convince than larger ones, but were less stable or able to resist development pressures and neighborhood change. Another issue was the nature of the problem itself, and the necessity for a level of political education. None of the proprietors/owners with whom the organizers spoke at that time were LGBT-identified. Organizers had to build up an understanding of the intersection of violence and LGBT issues, including, for example, homophobic language. Shopkeepers were apprehensive about potentially having to deal with incidences of violence in their premises. Organizers, in turn, were reluctant to dictate other people's safety strategies. In addition there were concerns about the ever-present problem of keeping employees aware and trained about S.O.S. When I visited one of the safe spaces in late 2013, I found it featuring the S.O.S. sticker on its window and inside the establishment there was a S.O.S. Collective flyer in the restroom. The person working there, however, did not know about the initiative when asked about it. He said he had been working there for three years. Another space,

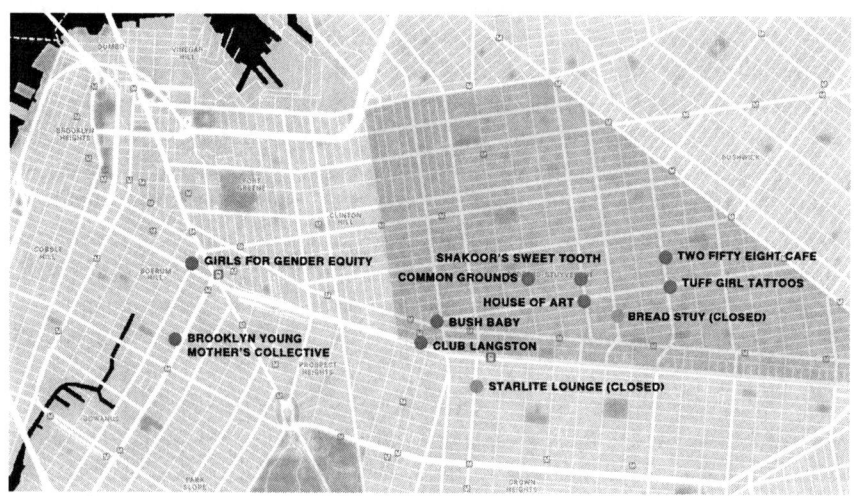

FIGURE 13.4   Map of S.O.S. Collective's "Safe Spaces"

an art gallery, had evidently gone through a renovation, and the new space did not display the sticker, making it difficult, if not impossible, to perceive it as one of the safe spaces.

Dixon brings up another particularly daunting problem of this work: what to do when people do get attacked. Victims of violence often came to S.O.S. for help, and the organizers, capacity already stretched thin, found themselves offering support on individual cases. In these cases the campaign itself would suffer, and sometimes grind to a halt.

The spatial nature of this initiative is immediately evident on an urban level and a "street" level. For a network of urban safe spaces to be really successful, they have to be located spatially where they might be needed, both dense enough and distributed enough. Dixon noted that the only specific strategy in terms of the locations of the spaces on an urban scale was a loose correlation with locations with previous incidences of violence. On the street level, she explained that the organizers' prioritized storefronts – visible locations with access right off the street. These aspects of the multiple scales of safety – the scale of the neighborhood, of the street, as well as of the building – deserve more research and elaboration. Serious literature on the design of safe spaces is clearly lacking, though there has been some discussion of the design of spaces for learning and some work on the relationship between design of built environment and crime prevention. This is particularly apparent when one probes into the more complex realms of safety and accountability beyond "traditional" institutional crime prevention.

The work of the S.O.S. Collective provides an important context and lesson for urban designers and planners since it engages basic, accepted notions of safety, overturns the conventional responses, and challenges our dependency on institutional frameworks that may not be working for the most marginalized urban residents. At the same time, the campaign also exposes the serious difficulties encountered by grassroots community organizers working on initiatives that target structural conditions and envision transformative change. That reality, too, has implications for urban designers and planners who have to make critical decisions about how to develop community partnerships and alliances. These include choices about how to engage with organizers from larger, more established institutions, when to participate directly with community organizing movements, and how to incorporate scholars and students from academic research institutions.

Lessons for Planning

Beseeching planners to break from a stable, centrist practice, Friedmann (1993, 482) urges them instead to engage the "*real time* of everyday events" (emphasis in original). Following this advice, planners should strip bare the veneer of a monolithic, uncomplicated gayness in spatial politics to understand that queer urban struggles continue, heightened by sociopolitical and economic pressures, including race and class, and state violence.

Dixon of ALP's safe neighborhoods campaign proposed that activists and planners engage and learn from each other. Planners, she suggested, know how to "culture shift" through space. Activists and planners could develop shared political analyses about safety and space. Dixon also suggests that planners could contribute to the organizing initiatives using their professional skills, including mapping areas of violence and safety, and collecting data for analytical purposes.

There appear to be two levels of possible engagement. The first is simple, that urban designers and planners can do what they do best, focusing their knowledge and skills on the spaces and issues that are clear problems. The second level is more challenging. Planners and activists could build shared political awareness and analyses that enable strategies and implementation towards social and spatial change. This is not a straightforward task. Planners can train their GIS tools to expose the geographies of oppression, but will they be able to fine-tune an analysis of power to tease out the relevant factors behind these? For example, when asked whether they needed to build up a shared political analysis with a collaborator like the Hester Street Collaborative, Blasco of FIERCE stated that they did not. The analysis was already there. An effective collaboration *began* with a shared understanding.

Ultimately, the struggles in the campaigns discussed here make clear that spatial and physical interventions in urban space are at stake, and are essential elements of transformative change. In addition to marshaling CAD cursor, 3D print head or whatever one's preferred means of elaboration to produce elegant designs, urban designers and planners concerned with the built environment need to consider what they have learned from their work with marginalized queer communities and especially how to do things differently. It is critical to train urban designers and planners not simply in how to address inequality, but also in how they might confront and attempt to dismantle power structures. Friedmann, of course, would recognize this call. I suggest that designers and planners also need to go one step further – beyond empowerment and social learning, beyond simply "non-Euclidean," as it were – to be not just explicitly political and normative, but explicitly spatial and physical. For queer urban struggles, social and spatial change are wrought together.

Notes

1 See Soja (2010, 31).
2 The question of *identities* is, of course, of critical importance in discussions around LGBT histories and sociopolitical issues. In this chapter I use "LGBT" to denote lesbian, gay, bisexual, and transgender communities more generally, and "queer" when specifically referencing queer sexualities and politics deliberately positioned outside of and/or in opposition to mainstream concepts and awareness of gender and sexuality (see, for elaboration, K. Browne, 2006; H. Davis 2005; Halberstam 2005).
3 See, for example, debates on gender identity in Halberstam (1998) and E.C. Davis (2008).
4 Notable exceptions by Doan (2007, 2010) expose the "tyranny" of gendered spaces.
5 See Bell and Binnie (2004) and Duggan (2002) for discussion about the "new homonormativity," the assimilation of gay rights agendas within neoliberal modes of

economic growth and mainstream political debates. Duggan writes, "There is no vision of a collective, democratic public culture or of an ongoing engagement with contentious, cantankerous queer politics. Instead we have been administered a kind of political sedative – we get marriage and the military then we go home and cook dinner, forever" (189).

6 See Crenshaw (1991) for a foundational discussion on the concept of intersectionality.
7 Binnie (1997) outlines the epistemological and methodological challenges of queer geography, taking on, among other issues, the "heterosexism of positivism" (234).
8 By "radical planning" I refer to planning thought that may or may not use that term, but generally extends and builds on Friedmann's (1987, 409) notion of "transformative theory."
9 I worked with FIERCE to plan and produce urban and architectural designs for their Our S.P.O.T. campaign in 2007. I also served on the board of directors of the Audre Lorde Project from 2007 to 2010, and contributed pro bono architectural designs for the organization's headquarters.
10 This network includes the Sylvia Rivera Law Project (SRLP) and the recently closed Queers for Economic Justice (QEJ).
11 For extended discussions on this alternative analysis, see J. DeFilippis et al. (2011).
12 See www.beyondmarriage.org
13 See, for more elaboration, "A Compilation of Critiques of Hate Crimes Legislation" by Black and Pink, an organization of LGBT prisoners and allies for the abolition of the prison industrial complex, at www.blackandpink.org/revolt/a-compilation-of-critiques-on-hate-crimes-legislation, and a statement by the Sylvia Rivera Law Project, at http://srlp.org/our-strategy/policy-advocacy/hate-crimes
14 See www.hudsonriverpark.org/about-us/hrpt/hrp-act
15 www.fiercenyc.org. See also Mananzala (2011).
16 FIERCE defines a "safe space" as space in which gender identities, performance, and diverse experiences are respected, with no threat of physical, emotional, or institutional violence (FIERCE 2008).
17 I attended a town hall meeting that FIERCE organized in 2006, and was immediately impressed by then-executive director Rickke Mananzala's ability to connect with youth members about issues of power and justice.
18 FIERCE, e-mail message to supporters, Nov 25, 2013.
19 www.alp.org
20 This specific collection of identities, generally abbreviated to LGBTSTGNC by the organization, was formulated to be deliberately inclusive of all of ALP's constituents.
21 News stories and commentaries in the *New York Times* (Priluck 2000; Roberts 2011), *Brooklyn Daily Eagle* (headlined "Bed-Stuy – Buy or Die" (Nixon 2014)), *City Journal* (Hymowitz 2013), and *New York* magazine (Coplon 2005) detail some of this tension. See also the Envisioning Development toolkit by community design and advocacy group Center for Urban Pedagogy (CUP) for a graphic illustration of Bed-Stuy for a visualization of income and affordability metrics, at http://envisioningdevelopment.net/map
22 See the work of the Anti-Violence Project (AVP) for news accounts of specific incidences and ongoing work around anti-LGBT violence, including an alleged incidence of anti-LGBT police violence in June 2013, www.avp.org

References

Adler, Sy, and Johanna Brenner. 1992. "Gender and Space: Lesbians and Gay Men in the City." *International Journal of Urban and Regional Research* 16 (1): 24–34.
Aldrich, Robert. 2004. "Homosexuality and the City: An Historical Overview." *Urban Studies* 41 (9): 1719–37.

Badgett, M.V. Lee, Laura E. Durso, and Alyssa Schneebaum. 2013. "New Patterns of Poverty in the Lesbian, Gay, and Bisexual Community". Los Angeles, CA: The Williams Institute.

Bell, David, and Jon Binnie. 2000. *The Sexual Citizen: Queer Politics and Beyond*. Cambridge, UK; Malden, MA: Polity; Blackwell Publishers.

Bell, David, and Jon Binnie. 2004. "Authenticating Queer Space: Citizenship, Urbanism and Governance." *Urban Studies* 41 (9): 1807–20.

Betsky, Aaron. 1997. *Queer Space: Architecture and Same-Sex Desire*. New York, NY: William Morrow.

Binnie, Jon. 1997. "Coming out of Geography: Towards a Queer Epistemology?" *Environment and Planning D* 15: 223–38.

Binnie, Jon, and Beverley Skeggs. 2004. "Cosmopolitan Knowledge and the Production and Consumption of Sexualized Space: Manchester's Gay Village." *The Sociological Review* 52 (1): 39–61.

Brenner, Neil. 2004. *New State Spaces: Urban Governance and the Rescaling of Statehood*. Oxford, UK: Oxford University Press.

Brenner, Neil, and Nik Theodore. 2002. "Cities and the Geographies of 'Actually Existing Neoliberalism.'" *Antipode* 34 (3): 349–79.

Botein, Hilary. 2013. "From Redlining to Subprime Lending: How Neighborhood Narratives Mask Financial Distress in Bedford-Stuyvesant, Brooklyn." *Housing Policy Debate* 23 (4): 714–37.

Brown, Gavin. 2006. "Cosmopolitan Camouflage: (Post-)Gay Space in Spitalfields, East London." In *Cosmopolitan Urbanism*, edited by Jon Binnie, 130–45. London, UK; New York, NY: Routledge.

Brown, Gavin. 2007. "Mutinous Eruptions: Autonomous Spaces of Radical Queer Activism." *Environment and Planning A* 39 (11): 2685–98.

Browne, Kath. 2006. "Challenging Queer Geographies." *Antipode* 38 (5): 885–93.

Castells, Manuel. 1983. *The City and the Grassroots: A Cross-Cultural Theory of Urban Social Movements*. London, UK: E. Arnold.

Coplon, Jeff. 2005. "The Tipping of Jefferson Ave: How Gentrification Is Effecting One Block in Bedford-Stuyvesant." *New York*, April 15. http://nymag.com/nymetro/realestate/neighborhoods/features/11775

Crenshaw, Kimberle. 1991. "Mapping the Margins: Intersectionality, Identity Politics, and Violence against Women of Color." *Stanford Law Review*, 1241–99.

Davis, Erin Calhoun. 2008. "Situating 'Fluidity': (Trans) Gender Identification and the Regulation of Gender Diversity." *GLQ: A Journal of Lesbian and Gay Studies* 15 (1): 97–130.

Davis, Heather. 2005. "The Difference of Queer." *Canadian Woman Studies* 24 (2).

DeFilippis, Joseph N., Lisa Duggan, Kenyon Farrow, and Richard Kim, (ed.) 2011. *A New Queer Agenda* [Special Issue]. Scholar & Feminist Online 10 (1-2). http://sfonline.barnard.edu/a-new-queer-agenda

Doan, Petra L. 2007. "Queers in the American City: Transgendered Perceptions of Urban Space." *Gender, Place and Culture* 14 (1): 57–74.

Doan, Petra L. 2010. "The Tyranny of Gendered Spaces: Reflections from beyond the Gender Dichotomy." *Gender, Place and Culture* 17 (5): 635–54.

Doan, Petra L. 2011. "Why Question Planning Assumptions and Practices about Queer Spaces?" In *Queerying Planning: Challenging Heteronormative Assumptions and Reframing Planning Practice,* edited by Petra L. Doan, 1–18. Farnham, Surrey, UK; Burlington, VT: Ashgate.

Duggan, Lisa. 2002. "The New Homonormativity: The Sexual Politics of Neoliberalism." In *Materializing Democracy: Toward a Revitalized Cultural Politics,* edited by Russ Castronovo and Dana D. Nelson, 175–94. Durham, NC: Duke University Press.

Durso, Laura E., and Gary J. Gates. 2012. "Serving Our Youth: Findings from a National Survey of Services Providers Working with Lesbian, Gay, Bisexual, and Transgender Youth Who Are Homeless or at Risk of Becoming Homeless". Los Angeles, CA: The Williams Institute with True Colors Fund and The Palette Fund.

FIERCE. 2008. "LGBT Youth Center. Pier 40 Recommendation". New York, NY.

Forsyth, Ann. 2011. "Queerying Planning Practice: Understanding Non-Conformist Populations." In *Queerying Planning: Challenging Heteronormative Assumptions and Reframing Planning Practice,* edited by Petra L. Doan, 21–51. Farnham, Surrey, UK; Burlington, VT: Ashgate.

Friedmann, John. 1987. *Planning in the Public Domain: From Knowledge to Action.* Princeton, NJ: Princeton University Press.

Friedmann, John. 1993. "Toward a Non-Euclidian Mode of Planning." *Journal of the American Planning Association* 59 (4): 482–85.

Frisch, Michael. 2002. "Planning as a Heterosexist Project." *Journal of Planning Education and Research* 21 (3): 254–66.

Goh, Kian. 2011a. "From and Toward a Queer Urbanism." *Progressive Planning,* no. 187 (Spring): 4–7.

Goh, Kian. 2011b. "Queer Beacon: LGBT Spaces in New York City." *Places: Design Observer.* June 23. http://places.designobserver.com/feature/queer-beacon/28048

Halberstam, Judith. 1998. "Transgender Butch: Butch/FTM Border Wars and the Masculine Continuum." *GLQ: A Journal of Lesbian and Gay Studies* 4 (2): 287–310.

Halberstam, Judith. 2005. "Queer Temporality and Postmodern Geographies." In *In a Queer Time and Place: Transgender Bodies, Subcultural Lives,* 1–21. Sexual Cultures. New York, NY: New York University Press.

Holston, James. 1999. "Spaces of Insurgent Citizenship." In *Cities and Citizenship,* edited by James Holston, 155–74. Durham, NC: Duke University Press.

Hymowitz, Kay S. 2013. "Bed-Stuy's (Unfinished) Revival by Kay S. Hymowitz, City Journal Summer 2013." *City Journal,* Summer. www.city-journal.org/2013/23_3_bed-stuy.html

Jessop, Bob. 2002. "Liberalism, Neoliberalism, and Urban Governance: A State–theoretical Perspective." *Antipode* 34 (3): 452–72.

Knopp, Lawrence. 1990. "Some Theoretical Implications of Gay Involvement in an Urban Land Market." *Political Geography Quarterly* 9 (4): 337–52.

Knopp, Lawrence. 2007. "From Lesbian and Gay to Queer Geographies: Pasts, Prospects and Possibilities." In *Geographies of Sexualities: Theory, Practices, and Politics,* edited by Kath Browne, Jason Lim, and Gavin Brown, 21–28. Aldershot, Hampshire, UK; Burlington, VT: Ashgate.

Mananzala, Rickke. 2011. "The FIERCE Fight for Power and the Preservation of Public Space in the West Village." *Scholar & Feminist Online* 10 (1–2). http://sfonline.barnard.edu/a-new-queer-agenda

Mogul, Joey L., Andrea J. Ritchie, and Kay Whitlock. 2011. *Queer (In)Justice: The Criminalization of LGBT People in the United States.* Boston, MA: Beacon Press.

National Coalition of Anti-Violence Programs (NCAVP). 2010. "Hate Violence against Lesbian, Gay, Bisexual, Transgender and Queer Communities in the United States in 2009". New York, NY: New York City Anti-Violence Project.

New York State Legislature 592. 1998. The Hudson River Park Act. Ch. 592, S. 7845.

New York State Legislature. 2013. Amendment to the Hudson River Park Act.

Nixon, Melody. 2014. "Bed-Stuy – Buy or Die?" *Brooklyn Daily Eagle,* January 23. www.brooklyneagle.com/articles/bed-stuy-%E2%80%93-buy-or-die-2014-01-23-204500

Poster, Dave, and Elaine Goldman. 2005. "Gay Youth Gone Wild: Something Has Got to Change." *The Villager,* September 21, 76(18). http://thevillager.com/villager_125/gayyouthgonewild.html

Priluck, Jill. 2000. "Neighborhood Report: Bedford-Stuyvesant; Even in a Long-Troubled Section, Gentrification is on the Horizon." *New York Times,* December 10. www.nytimes.com/2000/12/10/nyregion/neighborhood-report-bedford-stuyvesant-even-long-troubled-section-gentrification.html

Roberts, Sam. 2011. "Striking Change in Bedford-Stuyvesant as the White Population Soars." *New York Times,* August 4. www.nytimes.com/2011/08/05/nyregion/in-bedford-stuyvesant-a-black-stronghold-a-growing-pool-of-whites.html?pagewanted=all&_r=0

Rogers, Josh. 2007. "Hudson Park HUAC: Pier Plan Foes All 'Socialists.'" *The Villager,* August 8, 77(10). http://thevillager.com/villager_223/hudsonparkhuac.html

Quintana, Nico Sifra, Josh Rosenthal, and Jeff Krehely. 2010. "On the Streets: The Federal Response to Gay and Transgender Homeless Youth". Washington, DC: Center for American Progress.

Ray, Nicholas. 2006. "Lesbian, Gay, Bisexual and Transgender Youth: An Epidemic of Homelessness". New York, NY: National Gay and Lesbian Task Force Policy Institute and the National Coalition for the Homeless.

Sandercock, Leonie. 2004. "Towards a Planning Imagination for the 21st Century." *Journal of the American Planning Association* 70 (2): 133–41.

Sandercock, Leonie. 2006. "Cosmopolitan Urbanism: A Love Song to Our Mongrel Cities." In *Cosmopolitan Urbanism,* edited by Jon Binnie, 37–52. London, UK; New York, NY: Routledge.

Sears, Brad, and Lee Badgett. 2012. "Beyond Stereotypes: Poverty in the LGBT Community". TIDES | Momentum. http://williamsinstitute.law.ucla.edu/headlines/beyond-stereotypes-poverty-in-the-lgbt-community/#sthash.Cj80G7e1.dpbs

Soja, Edward W. 2010. *Seeking Spatial Justice.* Minneapolis, MN: University of Minnesota Press.

Warner, Sam Bass. 1972. *The Urban Wilderness: a History of the American City.* New York, NY: Harper & Row.

Whitlock, Kay. 2012. "Reconsidering Hate: Policy and Politics at the Intersection". Somerville, MA: Political Research Associates. www.politicalresearch.org/wp-content/uploads/downloads/2012/11/HateFrames.pdf

Yiftachel, Oren. 2006. "Re-Engaging Planning Theory? Towards 'South-Eastern' Perspectives." *Planning Theory* 5 (3): 211–22.

14

THE RACIAL POLITICS OF PRECARITY

Understanding Ethno-Specific AIDS Service Organizations in Neoliberal Times

John Paul Catungal

Timely Research?

I begin this chapter with a quote from Dina*, a worker in Toronto's AIDS sector and a participant in my doctoral research on the emergence and evolution of ethno-specific AIDS service organizations (e-ASOs) in Toronto. Her quote happens literally at the beginning of the interview, as soon as the voice recorder was turned on. It was her response to my thanking her for participating. It reads: "Thank you for undertaking this type of research. I think it is a very important topic, and like I said, it's timely" (Dina).

Asked what about the research she thinks is timely, Dina replies in an extended – and revealing – reflection on the political economy of ethno-specificity in Toronto's AIDS sector:

> I think there is a lot of mainstreaming of HIV programs and services in health care settings, which is also a good thing, right? It's good that the mainstream is questioning its own stigmas and judgments ... So there is this question of larger organizations having HIV services and offering those. If you have that, what is it that makes us [e-ASOs] unique?
>
> ... If you're gonna fund a broad-based health organization that did reproductive health and mental health and HIV and cancer care and a number of other things ... would you [also] fund something that only does one specialized area of care?
>
> ... We also have the question of why not just have a person who speaks [another language] housed in a larger ASO. Do we really need whole other organizations for Asian communities, for South Asian communities, Caribbean? There are these questions that we get faced, so for that reason it is timely. It is a good way and a good time to concentrate on what are those

differences, what are the needs, and what makes our organizations unique, where the benefits are.

It is important to note, at this juncture, that my interview with Dina occurred in the highly politicized context of local debates about municipal austerity, popularized in public discourse by Toronto's Mayor Rob Ford's statement about the supposed need to cut 'the gravy train.' Social programs funded and/or offered by the municipal government were especially prone to attack during this recent bout of funding reviews and proposed cuts. Thus, the precariousness that Dina references could be understood as emerging from neoliberal attacks on public funding for social programs, state-delivered or community-based. However, such a view only captures part of the story. I contend that e-ASOs, as community-based sexual health organizations that are run by and serve ethno-racial communities, are especially precarious given their explicit mandate to offer services to ethno-racialized communities. I argue, in other words, that austerity agendas have racialized effects, and that therefore, we need to attend to how the racial politics of the AIDS sector contributes to e-ASO workers' experiences and understandings of precarity. This task is all the more important given the centrality of community-based social service delivery mechanisms like e-ASOs in achieving key social planning and public health goals in cities.

After a brief introduction to the history and politics of Toronto's e-ASOs, I use the concept of 'neoliberal governmentality' to shed light on the ways that neoliberal projects affect, on the ground and in practice, the conduct of sexual health promotion in the City of Toronto. Arguing that neoliberal governmentality needs to take stock of difference, the chapter then considers the threat of funding cuts in specific relation to the racial politics of *ethno-specific* AIDS service organizations. This section illustrates that funding cuts are part of a broader set of attacks on e-ASOs and that the constant call for e-ASOs to justify their value is experienced by e-ASO workers not only as the devaluation of e-ASOs' histories and contributions, but also as indicative of more widespread ignorance of the multiplication of issues that people of color face in relation to sexual health. The paper ends with a short reflection on why ethno-specific AIDS service organizations continue to matter today and also in the near future.

Planning 'For Us, By Us' Spaces: Ethno-Specific AIDS Service Organizations in Toronto

This chapter draws on dissertation research that examined the emergence and evolution of three e-ASOs in the City of Toronto: Asian Community AIDS Services (ACAS), the Alliance for South Asian AIDS Prevention (ASAAP) and the Black Coalition for AIDS Prevention (Black CAP) (see Catungal, 2014). These e-ASOs were founded between the late 1980s and the mid-1990s by local leaders in the Asian, South Asian and black communities who were concerned with the inability of existing local AIDS organizations to deal with the culturally and linguistically specific needs of people of color with HIV/AIDS. In previous work (Catungal, 2013, 2014), I argued that the neglect of people of color and their concerns in early (1980s) community responses to HIV/AIDS in Toronto was made possible through their adoption of color-blind approaches to organizing and social service provision. Through such color-blind approaches, concerns about race, ethnicity, culture and language were sidelined and often painted by mainstream sector workers as either distracting from or unrelated to the main concern, which was HIV/AIDS. Local mainstream AIDS organizations who utilized such approaches were thus, by design, inappropriate and ineffective spaces for people of color with HIV/AIDS to seek support.

Concerned leaders from racialized communities, particularly those who were already involved in community organizations for gays and lesbians of color (e.g., Gay Asians of Toronto, Khush and Zami) in the early 1980s, sought to fill the void created by mainstream organizations. Using already established networks and the energies of these gays and lesbians of color organizations, these leaders created programs of support and services that utilized an alternative 'for us, by us' approach to social service provision in the late 1980s. Eventually, these programs evolved into stand alone e-ASOs, energized partly by the creation of municipal funding for community-based responses to HIV/AIDS that was introduced by the City of Toronto's public health arm in 1987.

At present, a significant portion of e-ASO funding comes from the City of Toronto through the Toronto Urban Health Fund (TUHF), which was created in September 2013 through the amalgamation of two municipal funding streams for community-based programming, the AIDS Prevention Community Investment Program and the Drug Prevention Community Investment Program. TUHF allocates one- and three-year grant funding based on project proposals submitted by community organizations like e-ASOs. Other sources of funding may include provincial grant funding sources such as the AIDS Bureau of the Ontario Ministry of Health and Long-Term Care or private donations or grants from philanthropic organizations or individuals. Not unlike other parts of the social service sector, e-ASOs have also heavily invested in developing mechanisms for fundraising (e.g., through galas and silent auctions), a task made necessary by the precarious, short-term, and program-based funding that may be available from the state.

Organizations like ACAS, ASAAP and Black CAP employ ethno-specificity as an approach to sexual health promotion, centering people of color and their culturally and linguistically inflected understandings of sexuality, health and sexual health in the provision of support, education services, and outreach. The ethno-specifying strategies used by e-ASOs in their sexual health work are diverse, but generally include the translation of sexual health promotion materials in multiple languages, the use of culturally situated ways of talking about sexual identities and behaviors in materials and programming, the representation of racialized bodies and cultural markers in social service spaces, and the development of partnerships with cognate ethno-specific organizations whose mandate may not necessarily be sexual health.

Precarity by Design: E-ASOs and Governmentalities of the Neoliberal City

Given that e-ASOs rely on an assemblage of funding sources that are generally competitive, short-term and project-based, it is not surprising that the issue of funding and the precarity of e-ASOs loom large in most of my interviews, with many participants mentioning these without much prompting. That the issue of funding was a 'hot topic' during interviews was likely also because interviews were conducted at a time when the City of Toronto was undergoing a Core Services Review, a context in which the availability of funding for HIV/AIDS organizations was an immediate concern and indeed a very publicly discussed issue among social service organizations throughout the city.

During the Core Services Review, the discourse of 'gravy' was employed by Mayor Rob Ford and his supporters to characterize city spending that they deemed to be unnecessary and frivolous 'fat' that needs to be cut in order to keep the city government 'lean.' Mah and Thang (2013) note that this discourse was constitutive of Ford's very rise to mayoral power given his "memorable promise," during the campaign period and after, "to 'stop the gravy train' in the public sector" (106–107). The exorbitant use of discourses of 'fatness' and 'leanness' by local state officials such as Ford rehearses corporeal and spatial metaphors that treat the city politic as a body politic (c.f., Rasmussen and Brown, 2005). In this case, so-called fiscal fatness comes to signify the ill health of the city politic. This discourse also relies on the collapsing of lean bodies and good citizenship, and of lean governments and good governments, both of which are perfect neoliberal subjects because they are said to have self-discipline and rationality. Such a discourse calls to mind points made by critical scholars of obesity, who argue against public health interventions that treat obese people as lazy, suboptimal subjects and lacking discipline (see, for example, Guthman and DuPuis, 2006).

In the Core Services Review, the Community Partnership and Investment Program (CPIP) was identified as an area for potential cuts. The CPIP is an umbrella funding program that "supports Council's social, cultural, housing, health, employment, recreation, economic and neighborhood improvement goals by supporting a city-wide network of community agencies" (City of Toronto, n.d. b, 1). It enables the provision of a "mixed delivery system of City services," whereby certain key services are delivered directly by local government while others are outsourced or contracted out to community organizations (ibid). The CPIP is important to the AIDS sector given that it is through this funding stream that the AIDS Prevention Community Investment Program (APCIP) supported AIDS organizations, including and especially e-ASO programs.

The threats to APCIP funding and other important city services engendered by the City Core Services Review produced amazing and unprecedented performances of citizenship in the form of deputations to City Council and its committees. In one all-nighter meeting alone, over 300 people spoke back to their local government, making eloquent, impassioned and often highly creative deputations to City Council, addressing proposed cuts to community services and organizations, including funding for sexual health. During these deputations, it was not uncommon for conservative city councilors to question deputations made by workers in community organizations, arguing that they are deputing merely to maintain their paychecks. A tremendous show of reductive thinking, such an argument understands work in and with community-based organizations to be motivated merely by financial or market considerations.

In addition, when councilors questioned e-ASO employee motivations for working in the sector, their actions conveniently erased e-ASO workers' embodied and experiential expertise, acquired through frontline work. This line of questioning relied on the assumption that e-ASO workers were merely careerist subjects whose main link with HIV work was a market relationship symbolized by the paycheck. However, in the context of e-ASOs, the lines between worker, volunteer and client get extremely blurry, as clients often also volunteer or acquire paid work in the organizations from which they access services. The reductive thinking of ill-informed councilors was negated by the empirical reality of the complexity of laboring in the AIDS sector, particularly in ethno-specific ASOs. A different reading would be one following Brown's (1997) work on radical citizenship and AIDS activism, that regards frontline work – paid or otherwise – in AIDS service organizations to be important performances of citizenship because 'being there' for people marginalized for sexual health reasons, and in the case of e-ASOs for reasons related to race, is, in many ways, a radical act in itself.

Indeed, during interviews e-ASO workers suggested that the 'paycheck' does not necessarily explain fully why they do their work. Tanya★, for example, explains that she does work above and beyond what she gets paid for:

> like, personally I've found like I'm passionate about that and I want to do it so you don't care about hours at some point. Like, on the weekend, like yeah I'll go do a workshop even though that's not my working day.

Irena★ adds, referring to a memo from a funder that lists required deliverables, that:

> a lot of workers … go above and beyond what is on this piece of paper. We do cover the minimum but we always go over what's required. Such noble discourses, while admirable, could have the effect of naturalizing neoliberal rollback by reducing the work of e-ASOs into practices of personal passion, a point that parallels arguments by feminist theorists that 'labor of love' discourses have been used to devalue the work of homemakers and caregivers in the domestic sphere. (Khan, 2009; England, 2010)

Interviewees made very clear that the issue of funding is, in no way, purely about the recent changes and challenges posed by Mayor Ford's municipal austerity agenda. Indeed, many suggested that the over-worked and under-resourced sector had been battling with the City of Toronto over the shifting contours of funding for quite some time, certainly since the introduction of municipal funding for community-based and project-based responses to HIV/AIDS in the late 1980s.

However, the increase in short-term, project-based approaches to sexual health promotion in Toronto – a desire and result of neoliberal agendas – has certainly exacerbated this issue, to the extent that community coalitions such as the Stop the Cuts Network have dubbed these cuts a set of orchestrated attacks against city funded community services (see Byrnes, 2011).

This political economic context provides an opportunity to trace how ethno-specificity – and the racial politics that are key to its presence in the sector – matters in positioning e-ASOs as particularly precarious in the neoliberal context. Using the experiences and perspectives – or vernacular knowledges – of e-ASO workers as a starting point, this analysis could usefully illuminate how neoliberalism interacts with racial politics in such a way as to reproduce racialized patterns of exclusions that were evident during the emergence of the AIDS sector in the 1980s.

Much has been written about neoliberalism and the societal shifts associated with it (see Peck, 2011; Harvey, 2007). Peck and Tickell (2002) understand neoliberalism as:

> a commitment to the extension of markets and logics of competitiveness with a profound antipathy to all kinds of Keynesian and/or collectivist strategies. The constitution and extension of competitive forces is married with aggressive forms of state downsizing, austerity financing, and public service 'reform'. (p. 381)

In more active terms, *neoliberalization* entails a series of shifts in state-society relations that can be characterized by the rollback of the state through deregulation and downloading (especially in education, health care and other forms of collective consumption) and the concomitant or subsequent "purposeful" rollout of new social and political arrangements, including the extension of market logics into other realms of everyday life (ibid). Moreover, Brenner and Theodore (2002) argue that neoliberalization should also be conceptualized as path-dependent and tied to "the legacies of inherited institutional frameworks, policy regimes, regulatory practices, and political struggles" (ibid: 349), including and especially racial formations.

Complementing, extending and at times contesting these political economic approaches to neoliberalization, post-structuralist approaches have also pointed out that these rollback and rollout shifts engender new political arrangements and modalities of rule. Scholars have called this set of political shifts 'neoliberal governmentality,' a term that draws on Foucault's theorizations of power beyond the sovereign. Lemke (2001: 203) notes that:

> the theoretical strength of the concept of governmentality consists of the fact that it construes neo-liberalism not just as ideological rhetoric or as a political-economic reality, but above all as a political project that endeavors to create a social reality that it suggests already exists.

Such an approach therefore requires attention to '*how*' questions: that is, how the political project that appears to be 'common sense' achieves such an illusion, and how – i.e., through what strategies – it reconfigures social relations.

Neoliberal governmentality refers to those strategies of rule that understand political subjects to be, first and foremost, "entrepreneurial, enterprising and innovative" (Larner, 2000: 13). It encourages individuals and organizations to govern themselves through rules of the market, while also specifying that new agencies for social welfare (e.g., social service organizations) are most effective when they are "governed, not directly from above, but through technologies such as budget disciplines, accountancy and audit" (ibid). A neoliberal governmentalities approach therefore adjoins political economic emphases on the shifting responsibilities of the state and the rollout of new forms of government, and post-structuralist emphases on the organization and 'messy actualities' of power, including the production or reformulation of new subjectivities.

In the specific context of e-ASOs, neoliberalism is most obviously associated with the issue of state funding for social service organizations. For example, much of the non-government AIDS service sector in Toronto, particularly ethno-specific AIDS service organizations, relies heavily on *short-term* and *project-based* state funding, largely but not exclusively from the municipal government. These include funding through the APCIP, which emerged in 1987 as a state funding mechanism for local community responses to HIV/AIDS (Shepherd, 2013). In 2013, APCIP was combined with the Drug Prevention Community Investment Program to create the TUHF.

The design of these funding models – short-term and project-based – means that a focus on funding applications and the performance of fundability is increasingly central to the conduct of sexual health promotion. Moreover, the specification of deliverables and the required task of report writing serve to govern the conduct of sexual health promotion by making accounting a key component of the responsibilities of sexual health promotion workers. Thus, for e-ASO workers, the need to perform 'fundability' requires them to be constantly proving that the work falls within the specific guidelines of the funding body.

In order to be ideal, fundable, accountable subjects, e-ASO workers ensure that they are compliant subjects, 'legible' and 'legitimate' to the funding body by doing work only within prescribed municipal boundaries, and by tapping into socio-spatial tropes that are embedded in the funding body's construction of 'priority groups.' Many interviewees mention, for example, that they have been involved in work within Gay Village spaces, particularly bathhouses and night clubs, spaces that are easily marked as 'gay' and therefore legible to funders as acceptable and ideal spaces for sexual health promotion. The focus on Gay Village spaces, especially in outreach to MSM (men who have sex with men) populations, is interesting because several interviewees themselves mention that these are not necessarily the same or the only places that men of color who have sex with men might frequent. Nevertheless, e-ASO workers do a lot of work in these spaces partly because of the requirements of funding bodies.

One task that ensures fundability is reporting and this activity is actually a constitutive part of the work that e-ASO workers perform. For example, an interviewee discussed how APCIP required e-ASO workers to document various aspects of their work:

> After each of these outreach sessions, I document how many condoms I gave out, how many brochures I gave out, how many contacts I made. All of that goes back to the reporting. All the things they tell me to do have to go back to the reporting. (Irena*)

It is clear from this quote that specific 'deliverables,' embedded in funding agreements, can serve to govern the types of sexual health promotion work offered by e-ASO workers. Thus, in this context, reporting can be understood as a technology of neoliberal governmentality in so far as it makes use of accounting frameworks to specify the tasks that e-ASO workers must do. As Rose (1991) argued almost twenty-five years ago, one way that accounting logics are tied to governmental practices is that they produce metric truths through which subjects can be evaluated and thereby governed. This is captured nicely when interviewees note that proper and accurate reporting of deliverables, whether or not they met deliverable requirements, are part of how e-ASO programs are evaluated by funders.

Another decidedly political effect of the tyranny of fundability is the disciplining of social service workers. The need to please – or at the very least, not anger – funders in order to maintain or even improve future funding prospects serves as a mechanism for governing the conduct of sexual health promotion workers. Some interviewees, for example, were reluctant to discuss funding specifically because they did not want to jeopardize their future chances to acquire funding for programs. Similarly, and more importantly, some interviewees discussed the fact that municipal funding can serve to deflect the possibility of agonistic politics, especially ones that have the state as their focus. Connor* passionately argued, for example, that:

> Anywhere upwards of 90% of [e-ASO] funding is from the city of Toronto. And they're afraid to do, to complain to the city or, like, to do research and stuff like that would critique the city. But I think it's important to do that because they're the organizations that know this the most. They're the ones that work on it day in and day out … [on] the frontlines of dealing with racialized minorities and HIV/AIDS prevention and STI/STD prevention in the city. And that simply because they get all their funding from the city of Toronto should not preclude them from being able to critique the city of Toronto.

Such an arrangement can therefore serve to condition organizations and workers into being compliant and docile subjects, as opposed to creating a space for an agonistic but nevertheless potentially productive and transformative relationship between the sector and its funders.

The Racial Politics of Neoliberal Governmentality

It is within this political, economic, and governmental context that the notion of timeliness with which I began this chapter emerges. To Dina, the research was "timely" because of the attacks faced recently by e-ASOs as a result of the threat of funding cuts by the Ford government. However, the threats faced by e-ASOs in recent times were not merely financial. They were also tied to broader political struggles, about race for example, whose histories are, arguably, as old as – or even older than – e-ASOs.

Recall that Dina expressed worries that e-ASOs are seen to be duplicating work that is already being done by others. This comment critically reads the trend of mainstreaming cultural sensitivity as a challenge to the necessary and specific work that e-ASOs do. The discourse of duplication that this mainstreaming enables conveniently forgets that – through the use of ethno-specificity and the centering of people of color as subjects of sexual health promotion – e-ASOs conduct sexual health promotion work quite differently from mainstream organizations. During interviews, e-ASO workers resisted the questioning of their work by pointing out that their 'for us, by us' approach is:

> recognition that … we can represent our issues better than anybody else, and create our own organizations, create our own programs and services, and really lead the response. Not only be a part of this response, but lead the response to HIV. (Adrian*)

Combined with Dina's point, Adrian's argument underscores the irreplaceability of e-ASOs for people of color, since the 'for us, by us' approach cannot be achieved in mainstreamed forms of cultural sensitivity.

Arguably, the undue questioning of the need for e-ASOs rests on the assumption that the issues that e-ASOs themselves deal with on a daily basis do not exist or are not important anymore. These issues include the persistence of racialization and its impact on the delivery of social services, the continued need for culturally and linguistically appropriate sexual health services, and the necessity for supportive spaces in which people of color can gather in community. Rather than framing these as new issues, several interviewees suggested that they are very similar to the challenges faced by people during the early days of e-ASOs. They argued that while medical therapies for and public literacy on HIV/AIDS and STIs might in broad terms be better, racialization and cultural barriers in the AIDS sector as well as homophobia and AIDS phobia in ethno-cultural communities, are still at play and continue to affect the ability of people of color to access culturally appropriate sexual health information and services. In a powerful reiteration of the persistence of these issues, an interviewee, speaking from their perspective as someone involved with ASAAP, made the following point in terms of the persistence of inaccurate conceptualizations of HIV/AIDS within the South Asian community and why this continues to matter for the work that ASAAP does as an e-ASO:

> Because HIV is, you know from the 1980s, has always had that 'this is a gay person's disease,' 'this is a white person's disease' – that notion is still present in a lot of South Asian communities. When we do our workshops, we try to address those issues, talk about people's fears, ask them what they are scared about.

Indeed, for some interviewees, the continued veracity of these issues means that e-ASOs remain some of the only safe spaces available for them. Referring to issues related to his sexuality and sexual health, Connor noted that the e-ASO that he is involved in is "probably still the only place where [I] still talk about that stuff predominantly."

Moreover, interviewees suggested that issues faced by people of color relating to sexual health are actually not decreasing, but instead multiplying. For example, an interviewee who works for Black CAP identified shifting legal frameworks relating to immigration and criminalization as emergent issues that have recently affected the organization's sexual health promotion work:

> we're dealing with a refugee claims system that is increasingly unfriendly to a certain kind of refugee, and we're seeing that our clients are being less successful in their refugee claims, but that's about clients living with HIV, our PHA clients, and also LGBT clients who are fleeing environments that are, you know, highly homophobic … Criminalization [of non-disclosure of positive serostatus] is also a huge issue for us. Upwards of 40% of those who are charged are black men. Really, it's too many. Black straight men represent not even close to that number of those people that are living with HIV. Not only is it a challenge in terms of the legal system but also in terms of the media – it's often a black man's face that's put in the media around these issues.

This quote highlights the ways that immigrants, refugees and people of color, especially those racialized as black, continue to be framed as threats to the purity and health of the body politic. In the context of neoliberal funding cuts, the continued presence and multiplication of issues that e-ASO workers face on a daily basis are either elided or irrelevant. This form of forgetting – especially of persistent racialization – serves to enable the 'cut-ability' of e-ASOs in the neoliberal city.

A final point that bears making is that the questioning of the continued necessity for e-ASOs is linked to the devaluation of e-ASOs and their contributions as actors involved in AIDS organizing and social service provision in Toronto. Pointing to a tendency to ignore the important and innovative work of e-ASOs to the broader sector, an interviewee offers this example:

You know, ACAS is actually one of the first groups who pioneered a lot of the innovative work on the [inter]net. But it wasn't supported. It wasn't recognized as innovative. Now … years later, everybody else is doing the same kind of thing, and nobody remembers that ACAS started doing that before anybody else. That's another incidence of how your contribution is undervalued, and how you're marginalized, because when you do certain things, people think that it's only good for your own community. People didn't think that you can contribute and lead mainstream thinking.

Such erasure of e-ASOs' contributions is tragic, not least because, in the context of neoliberal cuts, innovativeness in social service provision is an important metric of worth. These erasures are, of course, more-than-market, that is, more than about austerity in strictly financial terms. They exceed neoliberalism if we understand neoliberalism to be, simply, about the infiltration of market logics into everyday life, a definition that scholars have recently noted does not capture the inability of neoliberal agendas to colonize all aspects of the social (Hall, Massey and Rustin, 2013). Hence, though e-ASO workers experienced the questioning of their work most immediately in terms of threats to their funding, racialized valuations of sexual health promotion work also figured in making them prone to erasures engendered by neoliberal agendas. In other words, judgments about the value of e-ASOs are not merely econometric in logic but rather are mediated by important racial discourses that have been entrenched in the sector for much longer.

Refusing Erasure: A Short Conclusion

Given the difference that e-ASO workers make to the global-multicultural city and especially to its racialized populations, it is important for planning practitioners and urban scholars to acknowledge the role of such organizations in providing not only safe places for services and care, but also alternative spaces for citizenship, belonging and community. This is especially so given the deeply entwined histories of the fields of planning and public health (Corburn, 2004). Moreover, given recent attention within planning to urban issues affecting multicultural and sexual minority populations (Murayidi, 2000; Sandercock, 2003; Forsyth, 2001; Doan, 2011), e-ASOs offer an important window into the complex relationship between municipal governments and community-based responses to the needs of marginalized populations. One important lesson that e-ASOs offer for planning practitioners and urban scholars is that marginalized people have the capacity to assert their unmet or ignored needs and to create alternative organizing mechanisms through which to meet these needs.

Notwithstanding such agentive capacities, the challenges posed by a resurgence in austerity politics in many North American cities necessitates a commitment from planning practitioners and urban scholars to highlight the inequalities that emerge from neoliberal projects of program and funding rollback. Accordingly, this chapter has sought to examine the ways that e-ASOs are rendered vulnerable to such neoliberal projects, partly due to the racialized political context within which funding cutbacks are embedded. In response to their precarity, e-ASO workers assert the continued necessity of ethno-specific forms of sexual health services and the important contributions e-ASOs have made not only to the lives of people of color in Toronto, but also to the AIDS sector more broadly. The narratives and perspectives of e-ASO workers that are contained in this chapter refuse the erasure engendered both by more recent local austerity politics and by a more embedded politics of racialization in the AIDS sector. It is in a similar spirit that this chapter also refuses the undue questioning of e-ASOs' work some twenty years after their official founding and over twenty-five years since the founding of their precursor queer-of-color organizations.

In light of the constant specter of erasure, it is important to return to and affirm the question posed by Dina at the beginning of the chapter: "Do we really need whole other organizations for Asian communities, for South Asian communities, Caribbean?" First, Toronto's status as a global-multicultural city will continue to increase, with Toronto's population expected to become predominantly non-European in origin by 2017 (Black, 2013). Given these demographic trends, the need for culturally and linguistically appropriate services, including in the realm of sexual health, will only likely increase. Organizations like Black CAP, ACAS, and ASAAP remain crucial.

More importantly, however, e-ASOs produce spaces of belonging, trust and community among people of color, including and especially LGBTQ people of color living with and affected by HIV. This role is crucial given the classed and racialized inequalities that scholars like Hulchanski (2007, 2010) have documented in Toronto. Moreover, as social service spaces, e-ASOs affirm people of color not only as recipients, but also as providers of care, support and education. In other words, in e-ASO spaces people of color are not an afterthought. They occupy positions of leadership, participate in decision-making, and design sexual health promotion strategies drawing on their embodied experiences and positions to provide services and programs specific to the sexual health lives of other people of color. E-ASOs' 'for us, by us' approach centers the capacity and agency of people of color not only to identify the issues that are most relevant to them, but also to produce strategies for action and support in response to these issues. In summary, e-ASOs are important especially to people of color because they literally provide them not only with spaces to respond to their specific needs, but also, inevitably, to shape the city's social services and public health landscape. Given all of this, e-ASOs remind us, by their presence and politics, that race continues to shape the social geographies of North American cities and that marginalized people's practices and spaces of care are powerful responses to the neglect they face in mainstream sites of community, social services and health.

Note

* Names have been changed to protect the identity of those interviewed.

References

Black, D. (2013). Immigrant underclass in GTA fuels simmering frustrations. *Globe and Mail.* Available online www.thestar.com/news/immigration/2013/05/08/immigrant_ underclass_in_gta_fuels_simmering_frustrations.html. Last accessed: August 21, 2013.

Brenner, N. and Theodore, N. (2002). Cities and the geographies of "actually existing neoliberalism." *Antipode*, 34(3), 349–379.

Brown, M. (1997). *Re-placing citizenship: AIDS activism and radical democracy.* New York, NY: Guilford.

Byrnes, E. (2011). Community groups protest KPMG over budget-trimming recommendations. *National Post.* Available online: http://news.nationalpost. com/2011/07/21/community-groups-protest-kpmg-over-budget-trimming-recommendations. Last accessed: July 14, 2013.

Catungal, J.P. (2013). Ethno-specific safe houses in the liberal contact zone: Race politics, place-making and the genealogies of the AIDS sector in global-multicultural Toronto. *ACME: An International E-Journal for Critical Geographies*, 12(2): 250–278.

Catungal, J.P. (2014). *For us, by us: Political geographies of race, sexuality and health in the work of ethno-specific AIDS service organizations in global-multicultural Toronto* (Unpublished doctoral dissertation). University of Toronto, Toronto, Ontario, Canada.

City of Toronto. (n.d.). *Council briefing: Community Partnership and Investment Program (CPIP).* Toronto, Canada: City of Toronto.

Corburn, J. (2004). Confronting the challenges in reconnecting urban planning and public health. *American Journal of Public Health*, 94(4): 541–546.

Doan, P. (ed.). (2011). *Queerying planning: Challenging heteronormative assumptions and reframing planning practice.* Burlington, VT: Ashgate.

England, K. (2010). Home, work and the shifting geographies of care. *Ethics, Place and Environment*, 13(2): 131–150.

Forsyth, A. (2001). Nonconformist populations and planning sexuality and space: Nonconformist populations and planning practice. *Journal of Planning Literature*, 15(3): 339–358.

Guthman, J. and DuPuis, M. (2006). Embodying neoliberalism: Economy, culture, and the politics of fat. *Environment and Planning D*, 24(3): 427–448.

Hall, S., Massey, D. and Rustin, M. (2013). After neoliberalism? The Kilburn manifesto. *Soundings.* Available online www.lwbooks.co.uk/journals/soundings/pdfs/manifesto framingstatement.pdf

Harvey, D. (2007). Neoliberalism as creative destruction. *Annals of the American Academy of Political and Social Science*, 610(1): 21–44.

Hulchanski, D. (2007). *The three cities within Toronto: Income polarization among Toronto's neighborhoods, 1970–2000.* Center for Urban and Community Studies. Research Bulletin 41.

Hulchanski, D. (2010). *The three cities within Toronto: Income polarization among Toronto's neighborhoods, 1970–2005.* Toronto, Canada: Cities Center.

Khan, S.A. (2009). From labor of love to decent work: Protecting the human rights of migrant caregivers in Canada. *Canadian Journal of Law and Society*, 24(1): 23–45.

Larner, W. (2000). Neo-liberalism: policy, ideology, governmentality. *Studies in Political Economy*, 63: 5–25.

Lemke, T. (2001). The birth of biopolitics: Michel Foucault's lecture at the College de France on neoliberal governmentality. *Economy and Society*, 30(2): 190–207.

Mah, C.L. and Thang, H. (2013). Cultivating food connections: The Toronto Food Strategy and municipal deliberation on food. *International Planning Studies*, 18(1): 96–110.

Murayidi, M.A. (ed.). (2000). *Urban planning in a multicultural society*. Westport, CT: Praeger Publishers.

Peck, J. (2011). *Constructions of neoliberal reason*. Oxford, UK: Oxford University Press.

Peck, J. and Tickell, A. (2002). Neoliberalizing space. *Antipode*, 34(3): 380–404.

Rasmussen, C. and Brown, M. (2005). The body politic as spatial metaphor. *Citizenship Studies*, 9(5): 469-484.

Rose, N. (1991). Governing by numbers: Figuring out democracy. *Accounting, Organizations and Society*, 16(7): 673–692.

Sandercock, L. (2003). *Cosmopolis II: Mongrel cities in the 21st century*. London, UK: Continuum.

Shepherd, S. (2013). *2013 AIDS Prevention Community Investment Program Staff Recommendations*. Toronto, Canada: City of Toronto.

PART V

Conclusions

15

BEYOND QUEER SPACE

Planning for Diverse and Dispersed LGBTQ Populations

Petra L. Doan

On the Supposed Decline of the Gay Village

Although it has taken considerable struggle on the part of LGBTQ rights activists, over the past 20 years a number of large metropolitan areas have recognized the presence of residential clusters of gay men and businesses located in and around "gay villages" in their midst. Some of these cities have shown their appreciation in various forms including: rainbow flags, gay-themed pylons, historic markers, and street signs denoting the boundaries of the gay village. Several cities advertise their gay villages as a gayborhood (Philadelphia) or pink village (Manchester) in hopes of attracting LGBTQ tourist dollars. Pride parades in these largest cities are colorful, diverse, and attract hundreds of thousands of spectators, and in a few cases more than a million. One might argue that this kind of acceptance and celebration shows the coming of age or perhaps more accurately the coming out of the closet of visible LGBTQ residential and commercial areas in the broader urban public consciousness.

At the same time there is increasing evidence that gay villages in many cities are changing as a result of gentrification that raises housing prices, making these neighborhoods less affordable for some LGBTQ people. In the "post-gay era" traditional gayborhoods like Capitol Hill in Seattle and the Castro in San Francisco are becoming significantly less gay, a process that some have called de-gaying (Ghaziani 2010). Ghaziani (2014) suggests that the popular press has begun to trumpet the end of white gay male neighborhoods using phrases that suggest the gay village is "passé" or having an "identity crisis," proclaiming "there goes the gayborhood" (Collard 1998; Buchanan 2007; Leff 2007; Sullivan 2007; Brown 2007). As partial confirmation of these eye-catching headlines, Spring (2013) reports that the number of lesbian and gay partners living in segregated census tracts has declined between 2000 and 2010, indicating that LGBTQ neighborhoods may indeed be declining. Her analysis is based on the 2000 and 2010 US Census question that asked householders whether they were living with a same-sex partner.

While clearly gentrification is having a substantial effect in many communities, sounding the death knell for gay villages is certainly premature. Of course these data from the US Census are problematic for planning purposes because they do not count gay and lesbian-identified individuals who are single or who prefer not to be categorized as gay or lesbian in official government records. Furthermore, they do not capture any bisexuals or transgendered individuals unless they happen to be in a same-sex partnership, although the whole notion of same-sex partnership is complicated by these more fluid sexual and gender identities. In addition, some men do not identify as gay but simply as men who have sex with men (MSM), an identity category that is a more common identity among ethnic and minority communities. Finally the boundaries of census tracts often do not reflect the exact areas of municipally-identified neighborhoods, much less the extent of gay villages which are less well defined. Without more precise evidence from current and former residents about where they live now, where they have lived previously, why they might have moved, and whether they continue to identity with the gay village, it is difficult to assess whether these neighborhoods are indeed at such risk.

Yet another explanation of the decline of the gayborhood comes from researchers examining the consequences of the HIV/AIDS epidemic. Several scholars have argued that the change in gay villages may be due to the high death rates in the gay community after the scourge of HIV/AIDS. The number of HIV/AIDS related deaths peaked in the mid-1990s and continued at a reduced rate over the next decade (Rosenfeld et al. 2012; Rosser et al. 2008). The higher survival rates are largely a result of the cocktail of anti-retroviral medications, but this drug regimen is also quite expensive. Many of the surviving partners may not have re-partnered and therefore may not have been counted in the census data. Partners of those who have died may have found their resources so exhausted by caring for their loved ones that they were no longer able to afford the increase in rents due to gentrification or may have simply decided to "cash out" of their homes to re-coup some of the cost burden from fighting this disease.

Rather than assume the decline of the gay residential neighborhoods that flourished in the 1980s and 1990s, chapters in this volume have argued that it is essential for planners to expand their understanding of the white gay male village into a more inclusive LGBTQ or queer space. The presumed demise of the gay village presents an opportunity to enlarge the planning horizon beyond the well-established queer spaces to explore the interactions between planners and LGBTQ residents in a broader array of locations, and with a more diverse spectrum of the LGBTQ population. With strong planning and municipal support it may even be possible to seize the opportunity to revision these once exclusive gayborhoods into more dynamic and inclusive spaces for the broader LGBTQ population because the need for inclusive queer space remains strong. To achieve these objectives, planners must recognize that while significant proportions of the LGBTQ community have found residential locations outside the gay village, this does not mean that the concentrated gay village is irrelevant, but simply that its character is changing and needs more careful examination (Brown 2013). Given these findings, there are a number of ways that planners can help to create a wider array of spaces that are more broadly inclusive of LGBTQ individuals and families.

Planning for Inclusive Queer Spaces as Focal Points for a Dispersed and Diverse Community

Several chapters in this book provide useful insights into how residents perceive the functions of existing queer spaces. Although gentrification in Washington, DC has certainly contributed to a shifting of the population of gay men away from the traditional gay area of Dupont Circle to other neighborhoods further east and north, Dupont Circle continues to be a touchstone for the gay community throughout the metro area (Lewis Chapter 4). Similarly in Toronto many queer women do not feel particularly well served by the traditional gay village at Church and Wellesley Streets and have moved to other neighborhoods which are less expensive and more diverse. Yet the Church and Wellesley Village remains part of the "central spatial imaginary" for lesbians, as well as the entire LGBTQ population as a whole (Nash and Gorman-Murray Chapter 11). The importance of having queer focal points in the LGBTQ imagination is echoed by Greene (2014) who suggests that vicarious citizens maintain vital identification with traditional gay villages even if they live some distance away. This result suggests that in spite of any changes to residential patterns, it is still imperative to preserve and protect the core of the gayborhood for LGBTQ individuals and families.

While it may be partly correct to proclaim that many historical gay villages have been "degayed," this turn of phrase represents a misnomer that marginalizes large segments of the LGBTQ population who do not identify as gay. For instance in New York City the rise in property values associated with gentrification in Greenwich Village continues to encourage LGBTQ people to look for alternative residential areas. This is especially true for LGBTQ people of color who have found that the vibrant cosmopolitan identity of the Jackson Heights neighborhood in Queens is very attractive and has seen an increase in same-sex partners from 2000 to 2010 (Martinez Chapter 10). It is unlikely that a single gay village will meet all the diverse needs of this population, and yet it is still quite valuable to have a central location in which services are provided and LGBTQ organizing can happen around a range of social and political issues.

The question of how planners should continue to support the idea of a gay village is more complex. In most places planning still lags far behind more recent neighborhood trends. In Chicago planners had a role in creating a rainbow-themed streetscape, but Winkle (Chapter 2) illustrates that the gentrification of this area along with the fluidity of the gay population raises concerns about the longevity of this queer space. Municipal investments in overtly queer-themed spaces is a step forward in one sense, but these efforts to make LGBTQ spaces more widely visible is also about "branding" such spaces as a means of commodifying those neighborhoods to facilitate the urban redevelopment process. A more useful intervention would be to provide municipal recognition and possible financial support for broadly inclusive LGBTQ community centers which can create a nexus of connectivity for newly "out" or recently arrived LGBTQ individuals seeking to connect with other like-minded people (Doan Chapter 7). Such centers also can strengthen the ability to provide basic services to marginalized and dispersed populations, as described below.

Too often redevelopment efforts result in rapidly rising rents and the closure of the iconic LGBTQ institutions (bars, bookstores, and other community gathering spaces) that helped to create the original gay village ethos. While these changes may be part of a natural "evolution" for some gay villages (Doan Chapter 1), other scholars argue that too much attention has been paid to gay villages and the concept is not really useful in large parts of the Global South (Visser Chapter 5). At the same time a significant proportion of the LGBTQ population cannot afford to live anywhere near the gay villages in question and yet they may depend on LGBTQ social services to survive. In a period of increasing change in LGBTQ residential patterns, Winkle (Chapter 2) suggests that planners must recognize the fluid and at times fragile nature of LGBTQ spaces. Nash and Gorman-Murray (Chapter 11) concur that a key element of the geographical heritage of lesbian communities is their very mobility. It is critical for planners to recognize these spaces and not exacerbate their demise through inadvertent re-shaping of LGBTQ spaces as a result of efforts to stimulate neighborhood redevelopment, or to make neighborhoods "safe for families" (Doan and Higgins 2011). Whittemore (Chapter 3) suggests that instead of municipal promotion of large scale development in these neighborhoods, planners should seek to raise awareness of the importance of existing or new affordable housing for LGBTQ individuals, couples, and families. Several other authors (Wesley Chapter 9; Martinez Chapter 10; Goh Chapter 13) highlight the same problem and call for community leaders to resist commercial development and protect affordable housing.

It is also very important to note that negative factors can shape the spread of LGBTQ spaces. Winkle (Chapter 2) suggests that threats from both the Chicago police and mobs of angry heterosexuals reinforced the decentering of gay and lesbian commercial establishments. Martinez (Chapter 10) indicates that a strong reaction from the community after a brutal hate crime solidified the developing queer consciousness of Jackson Heights, but that continued police harassment (Stop and Frisk) of immigrants and LGBTQ people of color threatens to undermine the neighborhood's safe feeling. Both Winkle (Chapter 2) and Doan (Chapter 7) argue that the passage of municipal non-discrimination ordinances can be critical steps in enabling more openly queer communities.

Planning Measures to Recognize Existing Queer and Queering Spaces

Given the fluid nature of gay commercial and residential districts, it is essential to commemorate queer spaces because of the vital historical roles they have played (Dubrow, Knopp, and Brown Chapter 12) as well as their continuing function as a focus and locus for a more dispersed LGBTQ community (Winkle Chapter 2). Other less well known LGBTQ neighborhoods that have served a more diverse population also need to be celebrated. Nash and Gorman-Murray (Chapter 11) suggest that embedding visible elements of lesbian heritage in the local landscape is a concrete means of acknowledging lesbian contributions to the city. Rather than investing in physical markers of gay neighborhood borders with rainbow flags or pylons, city officials should recognize LGBTQ historical sites with placards, dedications, or murals (Nusser and Anacker Chapter 6). Creating physical landmarks in an urban setting both visibly records the history of LGBTQ people in a particular place, and also can help establish an atmosphere of tolerance and acceptance that signals a welcome to queer people.

Other planning measures should be explored to ensure access to physical spaces that encourage social interactions among diverse LGBTQ groups (Nash and Gorman-Murray Chapter 11). Nusser and Anacker (Chapter 6) provide a range of specific urban design suggestions to enable "queering spaces" including: public spaces with outdoor seating, gathering spaces, easy transit accessibility, and smaller alleyways for more intimate encounters. Nusser and Anacker also recommend that commercial enterprises such as coffee shops and artsy stores can make their welcome known by hiring non-traditional, gender non-conforming wait staff, placing LGBTQ stickers in their windows, and designing store fronts to maximize transparency through the use of large windows and sliding glass doors. Goh (Chapter 13) echoes the importance of safe spaces that can be provided outside traditional safe spaces if business owners are willing to advertise their visible commitment to non-discrimination. In addition, municipal support for annual Pride festivities (including permits for parades or other public celebrations) can provide the occasional public space that may help to solidify marginalized groups (Doan Chapter 7).

Planning as a Tool to Strengthen Inclusive LGBTQ Communities

It is essential for planners to recognize that the LGBTQ population is very diverse, reflecting a rich mixture of age, race, ethnicity, and immigration status, with intersecting identities based on sexuality and gender identity. One of the important contributions of this book has been an explicit emphasis on analyzing the whole spectrum of the LGBTQ community, inclusive of a range of sexualities and gender presentations, and more representative of a wide array of ethnicities. In Chapter 8 Frisch illustrates the silencing effect of trying to encapsulate the LGBTQ community in too few identity categories, or in failing to recognize that LGBTQ organizations exist with a stake in discussions of sustainability. Wesley (Chapter 9) argues that within the "Deep South" in Jackson, Mississippi there is a diverse and dispersed LGBTQ community that has been largely ignored by city officials, including planners. Martinez (Chapter 10) argues that in Queens, New York the neighborhood of Jackson Heights functions as a "Queer Cosmopolis" that creates an atmosphere of inclusion for immigrants and queers of color that could be emulated elsewhere. Other chapters (Goh Chapter 13 and Catungal Chapter 14) explicitly consider the importance of recognizing queer communities of color, especially queer youth, arguing that planners must reach out to these marginalized communities by valuing and recognizing their contributions.

Specific steps are needed to ensure that queer communities are defined broadly so that they can have a voice in planning those spaces that may be critical to their survival. Planners should be much more aware of the concerns of community activists, especially the queer youth of color described by Goh (Chapter 13) whose needs for access to safe spaces are too often neglected. When city agencies and task forces are assembling community representatives to examine specific city or regional issues, it is vital to use inclusive language that names the list of LGBTQ identities and recognizes the reality of intersecting discriminations (Frisch Chapter 8). Diverse LGBTQ individuals and groups should be represented on citizen advisory councils to enable LGBTQ people to express their views (Nusser and Anacker Chapter 6). City governments should also consider the appointment of a liaison between the city and the LGBT community (Wesley Chapter 9). Many cities have done this for the Police Department, but why not a liaison for the Planning Department?

Locating LGBTQ people who do not live in a concentrated gayborhood may be more challenging since they can and do live in just about every type of urban and suburban neighborhood. However, planning officials should begin to recognize that clustering does occur because LGBTQ people feel safer if they know that other queer folks live nearby (Doan Chapter 7). These concentrations may not be as visible as traditional LGBTQ neighborhoods with rainbow flags and overt displays of queerness, but progressive neighborhoods that attract "artsy" or "hip" residents that Nash and Gorman-Murray (Chapter 11) label "post-mo" are likely gathering places. Planners would do well to examine such areas in their own cities and learn how these "edgy" neighborhoods have created an inclusive atmosphere that is accommodating of sexual and gender diversity, and have enabled residents to encounter and treat each other with respect (Nash and Gorman-Murray Chapter 11).

Planning to Create and Maintain Strong Community Linkages

The long history of marginalization and oppression experienced by LGBTQ people has created a unique set of needs for social services (counseling, health services, information exchanges, and support groups). Some of these needs can be met through the LGBT businesses and community organizations that are often located close to the heart of the gay village and serve as the foundation upon which community for LGBTQ families and individuals is built (Nusser and Anacker Chapter 6). The loss of gathering places such as bookstores, coffee shops, and bars can have ripple effects on the LGBTQ community, creating perceptions of decline that exceed the economic impacts of business closures due to a redevelopment scheme.

Planners seeking more equitable policies and practices for the LGBTQ community should recognize the critical relationship between civil society actors and the state in advancing progressive reform. In particular, during the HIV/AIDS epidemic, the struggle to obtain basic health care and other support services both enraged and inspired a generation of activists. In this period a loose grouping of community-based organizations eventually became quasi-professional and worked closely with various state agencies to provide services and help to shape policy (Dubrow, Knopp and Brown Chapter 12). The ability to forge strong linkages between activists and like-minded individuals working inside local government was critical in establishing health programs that did not stigmatize persons with sexually transmitted diseases, including people living with HIV/AIDS, setting up gay and lesbian health clinics, and providing health education programs. Efforts to reach more ethnically diverse LGBTQ communities are likely to require ethno-specific AIDS service organizations (Catungal Chapter 14). One of the difficult impacts of gentrification is that rising rents may make it harder for these vital community organizations to remain in a central location where visibility and ease of access are maximized.

Beyond Queer Space

Planners and academics must shift away from static conceptions of queer space that are tightly linked to the gay villages developed in the 1980s and 1990s in North America, Western Europe, and Australia. By the second decade of the 21st century the traditional gayborhood model is no longer sufficient for providing services and community-building activities for today's diverse LGBTQ population, nor does it explain the urban habitation and recreation needs of LGBTQ people in the Global South. It is past time to retire the simplistic conception of queer space tied to gay male spaces, and embrace a more fully inclusive and dynamic understanding.

It is critical for planning professionals and urban researchers to examine more closely the actual patterns of the highly mobile and fluid LGBTQ populations. Tracking the presence of partnered same-sex couples is only a partial picture and is wholly inadequate to understand the needs of the most marginalized LGBTQ people, including: queer youth of color, persons living with HIV/AIDS, LGBTQ seniors, LGBTQ immigrants, and the transgendered population as a whole. It is important to acknowledge that change is occurring and will continue to occur in the urban environments in which these people live, work, and play. The old model of queer space as a white gay male village is in decline, but is far from moribund. However, this very decline presents opportunities for a reconstruction and revisioning of what truly queer kinds of space might be: loci that welcome a more diverse LGBTQ population and provide opportunities for networking, recreation, and support services.

As this book has demonstrated, there is a clear need for organizing and socializing spaces for LGBTQ people, many of whom are diverse and live outside the traditional boundaries of gay neighborhoods. Ghaziani (2014) describes the massive turn out of queer youth of color from across the City of Chicago who came to protest proposals to redevelop Boystown. Doan's research (forthcoming) indicates that gentrifying gay neighborhoods often struggle with the continued presence of transgendered sex workers, many of whom are minorities. Specifically, some gay male property owners in and around existing gayborhoods see these non-white, gender non-conforming individuals as undesirable because they assume that a visible trans presence might lower property values. These tensions reflect differences of opinion within the LGBTQ community about the wisdom of "assimilation" versus the value of remaining visibly queer and different.

Perhaps the most critical role for planning around the issue of queer space is to enable and empower diverse LGBTQ interests to work together and plan for the future of the whole community. A collective vision for queer urban space needs to include a range of spaces where the community can gather and organize, including young queers of color and gender-queers. An inclusive queer space need not exclude heterosexual people, and yet people who wish to live in a queer-identified urban space should be willing to live next door to or share a street with a diverse array of queer people. LGBTQ bars and clubs are an important part of queer socializing, and if living in proximity to visibly queer patrons entering and leaving these establishments makes potential home-buyers uncomfortable, they should explore alternative locations. If prospective parents are upset by having their children see a drag queen on her way to work or a gender non-conforming young person who has just arrived in the city, they should not expect to "clean up the neighborhood." Given the demonstrated needs for inclusive queer spaces, planners can and indeed must support new ways of understanding the LGBTQ community and their aspirations for urban environments that are welcoming and affordable.

References

Brown, M. 2013. "Gender and Sexuality II: There Goes the Gayborhood?" *Progress in Human Geography*. 1–9. DOI: 10.1177/0309132513484215

Brown, P.L. 2007. "Gay Enclaves face Prospect of Being Passé," *New York Times*, October 30, A1.

Buchanan, W. 2007. "SF's Castro District Faces an Identity Crisis," *San Francisco Chronicle*. February 25, A1.

Collard, J. 1998. "Leaving the Gay Ghetto," Newsweek. August 17, p. 53.

Doan, P. Forthcoming. "Planning for Sexual and Gender Minorities," Chapter 6 in M. Burayidi (ed.) *Planning Cosmopolitan Cities: Concepts, Trends, and Strategies*. Toronto, Canada: University of Toronto Press.

Doan, P. and Higgins, H. 2011. The Demise of Queer Space? Resurgent Gentrification and LGBT Neighborhoods. *Journal of Planning Education and Research*, 31, 6–25.

Ghaziani, A. 2010. "There Goes the Gayborhood?" *Contexts*, Vol. 9, No. 4, pp. 64–66.

Ghaziani, A. 2014. *There Goes the Gayborhood?* Princeton, NJ: Princeton University Press.

Greene, T. 2014. "Gay Neighborhoods and the Rights of the Vicarious Citizen," *City and Community*, 13, 2: 99–118.

Leff, L. 2007. "In San Francisco's Castro District, a Cry of 'There Goes the Gayborhood'," *Washington Post*, March 18, D01.

Rosenfeld, D., Bartlam, B., and Smith, R.D. 2012. "Out of the Closet and into the Trenches: Gay Male Baby Boomers, Aging and HIV/AIDS," *The Gerontologist*, 52, 2: 255–264.

Rosser, B.R., West, W. and Weinmeyer, R. 2008. "Are Gay Communities Dying or Just in Transition? Results from an International Consultation Examining Possible Structural Change in Gay Communities." *AIDS Care: Psychological and Socio-medical Aspects of HIV/ AIDS*, 20, 5: 588–595.

Spring, A. 2013. "Declining Segregation of Same-Sex Partners: Evidence from Census 2000 and 2010," *Population Research and Policy Review*, 32: 687–716.

Sullivan, R.D. 2007. "Last Call: Why the Gay Bars in Boston are Disappearing," *Boston Globe*. December 2, E1.

INDEX

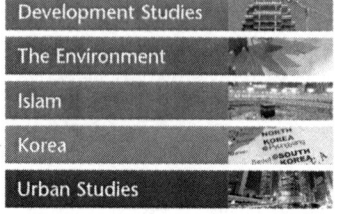